THE COMPLETE BOOK OF
CORVETTE
EVERY MODEL SINCE 1953

First published in 2006 by Motorbooks, an imprint of MBI Publishing Company, 400 First Avenue North, Suite 300, Minneapolis, MN 55401 USA

Motorbooks titles are also available at discounts in bulk quantity for industrial or sales-promotional use. For details write to Special Sales Manager at MBI Publishing Company, 400 First Avenue North, Suite 300, Minneapolis, MN 55401 USA

ISBN-13: 978-0-7603-4140-7

Editor: Lindsay Hitch
Designer: LeAnn Kuhlmann

Printed in China

The Library of Congress has cataloged the hardcover edition as follows:

Mueller, Mike, 1959-
  The complete book of Corvette: every model since 1953 / Mike Mueller.
     p. cm.
  Includes index.
  ISBN-13: 978-0-7603-2673-2 (hardbound w/ jacket)
  ISBN-10: 0-7603-2673-8 (hardbound w/ jacket)
  1. Corvette automobile—History.
  2. Automobiles—United States. I. Title.
  TL215.C6M839725 2006
  629.222'2—dc22

Credits: Unless otherwise specified, all images courtesy of General Motors.

Appendix data courtesy Mike Antonick, from Corvette Black Book 1953–2011, by Mike Antonick.

CORVETTE

motorbooks

Contents

01 ···> The Solid-Axle Years 16

02 ···> Enter the Sting Ray 84

50 Years and Counting

Thoroughly Modern

There is no better source for Corvette numbers than Antonick's *Black Book*, which has been around now for more than 25 years.

Acknowledgments

No doubt about it, I can't begin thanking all the fabulous folks who helped make this epic possible without first mentioning my gracious editor, Lindsay Hitch, who now has put up with me through three projects at MBI Publishing—and still lives to tell the tale. Lindsay may only be half my age, but another job like this one and her hair might just end up the same color as much of mine. That is, if she hasn't pulled it all out by now.

Much the same goes for her boss and mine, Zack Miller, who for some strange reason continues to turn to me with assignments after more than a dozen years of dealing with the Mueller way. As Zack knows well, I've never met a deadline I couldn't miss.

The only person I know more forgiving than Mr. Miller is Mrs. Mueller, as in Nancy, my mom up in Champaign, Illinois. Don't worry, ma, you'll get your five copies. And tell pa (Jim Mueller, Sr.) I said hi. Thanks for supporting me through all these years.

Let's not forget two of my brothers, Jim Jr. and Dave, both also of Champaign, Illinois. Now that we're all single again, the three of us have seemingly spent more time together in recent years than we did growing up, and that only means that I now have more free labor at my disposal than ever before. Jimbo and Dave have been of able assistance on countless photo shoots and are on constant lookout at car shows throughout the Midwest for future photo candidates. All I have to do is show up with a camera and a cooler for the beverages, which

they presently supply. No worries, mates, I'll start picking up the tab some day. I'd also like to thank my other sibling, little brother Kenny—I'd like to but can't due to the fact that he's never lifted a finger to help. Nor has he ever paid for a round.

Fortunately, other family members have stepped up. My sister, Kathy Young, and her husband, Frank, have always been more than willing to subsidize my many photographic junkets. Their lovely abode in Savoy, Illinois, has been my home away from home for many years now while I've worked on this book and others,

and Frank has grown especially adept at standing around watching while I shoot cars, including their beloved 1989 coupe, which appears later on within these pages. I promise, Kathy, I won't skip out on one of your spaghetti dinners ever again.

Brother Jim Mueller's three Corvettes also make appearances here, as do many dozens of others that I've had the pleasure of photographing over the years. The list of car owners I've dealt with during my 20-year career is a long one, a bit too long to fit here. So I hope you all will forgive me if I simply offer one blanket thank you.

Additional big thanks go to Larry Kinsel at GM Media Archives in Detroit. Larry allowed me to spend a day glancing through more than 12,000 Corvette photos, then repeatedly jumped through hoops to make sure my picks were delivered to the proper places at MBI. How he kept smiling throughout this ordeal is beyond me. GM people Matt Curran and Bob Tate also were of great help during the early stages of my photo research.

Last, but certainly not least, I must mention fellow author Mike Antonick, who allowed material from his annual *Corvette Black Book* to be included at the back of this book. There is no better source for Corvette numbers than Antonick's *Black Book*, which has been around now for more than 25 years. Readers interested in the latest update of this handy reference booklet can check out www.corvetteblackbook.com.

Look up "biggest bang for the buck" in the dictionary and you'll surely find a picture of the latest, greatest Corvette.

Introduction
Forever Young

In 2003, Chevrolet®'s Corvette® celebrated its 50th birthday by barely slowing down to blow out the candles. Why dilly-dally when even better times lay ahead? Two years later, Chief Engineer David Hill's team took what was already one of America's supreme performance machines and transformed it into arguably the planet's greatest. Standard performance now qualified as downright surreal: 0–60 in 4.2 seconds and a top end of 186 miles per hour.

Explaining "why this could be the best sports car in the world," *AutoWeek*'s Wes Raynal had nothing but raves for the reenergized 2005 Corvette and its newfound 400 horses. "Acceleration is right now, and the engine pulls and howls beautifully up to the 6,500-rpm redline. And there are just gobs of torque—you could probably get away with a two-speed manual instead of the six-speed: one gear to get off the line, another to take you to 186 mph." Refusing to rest on their laurels, Hill and crew then came back in 2006 with the most awesome 'Vette yet, the 505-horsepower Z06™, a race-inspired road rocket that *AutoWeek* called "the best supercar buy of all time."

"When you compare the Z06 performance stats to other supercars, you see numerous examples where you're getting better performance for one-third the sticker price of some of the competition," added Chevrolet General Manager Ed Peper. According to company tests, the 2006 Z06 can scorch the 0–60 run in 3.7 seconds, roast the quarter-mile in 11.7 ticks at 125 miles per hour, and reach a ridiculous top end of 198 miles per hour. Sure, there are stronger, faster performance machines running around the world, but none are as comparatively easy on the wallet as the Z06. Right here in America, Dodge's V-10 Viper is presently making 510 horsepower—at a base price of $86,995. We don't even need to consider Ford's six-figure (not to mention cramped-quartered) GT and its 500+ horses. Now quicker (as well as more comfortable and convenient) than the Viper, the new Z06 is priced at a relatively tidy $66,000. Look up "biggest bang

Chevrolet celebrated 50 years of Corvette history with a special anniversary model (left) in 2003.
Only 300 1953 Corvettes (right) were built on a makeshift assembly line in Flint, Michigan.

for the buck" in the dictionary and you'll surely find a picture of the latest, greatest Corvette.

What a long, strange trip it's been. Nearly cancelled a few years after its birth, rumored near death or dilution more than one time since, Chevy's fantastic, plastic two-seater is rolling on more confidently than ever, this after six distinct generations of development. Code names for those generations came into vogue during the radically redesigned 1997 Corvette's long haul to market after Chevrolet people let it be known that this all-new platform was identified in-house by the simple "C5™" designation. It was only logical to retroactively label previous generations accordingly: Original solid-axle models built from 1953 to 1962 made up the C1™ group; the C2™ family consisted of the classic Sting Rays of 1963 to 1967; the C3™ era spanned from 1968 to 1982; and the C4™ ran from 1984 to 1996. (Chevrolet skipped the 1983 model year as

fourth-generation development work ran a little long past its deadline.)

Originally considered in 1988, the fifth-generation Corvette was initially targeted for introduction in August 1992, just in time to help commemorate the Corvette's 40th anniversary. But various pitfalls pushed that debut back repeatedly, first for the 1994 model year, then 1995. When all was said and done, the long-awaited C5 officially appeared in January 1997.

Sure, there are stronger, faster performance machines running around the world, but none are as comparatively easy on the wallet as the Z06.

The latest rendition, the expectedly tabbed C6™, followed eight years later to take the Corvette legacy to all-new heights.

That legacy originated on an auto show stage in New York in January 1953, and among the wowed witnesses then was a Belgian-born Russian engineer named Zora Arkus-Duntov. During a 1967 interview with *Hot Rod* magazine's Jim McFarland, Duntov recalled his initial impressions of the intriguing two-seater that ended up being his baby. "Now there's potential," he began. "I thought it wasn't a good car yet, but if you're going to do something, this looks good."

At the time, Duntov was a talented engineer in search of a new job with a U.S. automaker after resigning from a position with British race car builder Sydney Allard in 1952. Before leaving Great Britain for America, he had written to Chevrolet Chief Engineer Ed Cole hoping for an interview, but he received only a lukewarm response. Re-inspired after encountering the first Corvette, Duntov queried Cole a second time with better results: he went to work at Chevrolet Engineering in May 1953. "Not for [the] Corvette or for anything of that sort," he told McFarland in

Above
Dave McLellan became the Corvette's second chief engineer after Duntov retired in 1975. Behind him is the heart of the ZR-1 Corvette, the 32-valve DOHC LT5 V-8. *Mike Mueller*

Below
David Hill stepped in as chief engineer following McLellan's retirement in 1992, just in time to oversee C5 development. *Mike Mueller*

Here's to another 50 years.

1967, "but for research and development and future stuff." Once on Chevy's payroll, Duntov wrote Cole yet again, this time to detail his passionate feelings about the Corvette's future. Soon afterward, he was assigned to the Corvette's engineering team, where he would stay until his retirement in 1975.

Duntov was the first of four Corvette chief engineers. Dave McLellan picked up where Zora left off and stayed on until 1992. Cadillac® man David Hill took over from there and retired in January 2006. Filling Hill's shoes now is Tom Wallace, formerly the lead engineer for General Motors' small and midsize trucks.

As for the car's true father, that honor goes to long-time GM exec and styling guru Harley Earl, who first envisioned the regular production of a two-seat sports car late in 1951. Able to throw some serious weight around, it was his powerful support that allowed Ed Cole the opportunity to put wheels to his dream. Going from initial sketches to Cole's auto show prototype required a scant 18 months.

Production then began on a makeshift assembly line in Flint, Michigan, in June 1953 before being transferred to Missouri in December. Chevrolet's old St. Louis plant remained the Corvette's home until 1981, when it was relocated to Bowling Green, Kentucky. In September 1994, the National Corvette Museum opened up across the street from the Bowling Green facility to honor the four-wheeled flight of fancy that has somehow survived a half century, losing nary a step in the process.

Here's to another 50 years.

Above
Although Zora Duntov is commonly described as the father of the Corvette, he wasn't even around at the time of the car's conception. The real main man behind the creation of America's Sports Car was GM design chief Harley Earl.

Right
The National Corvette Museum opened in September 1994 across the street from the Corvette assembly plant in Bowling Green, Kentucky. *Mike Mueller*

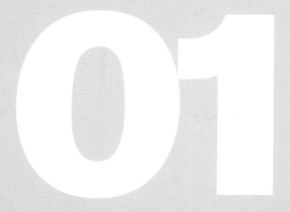

Above
All critics agreed that the new 1956 shape came off far more pleasing than the original Corvette design. The cove panels in the fenders allowed for optional two-tone paint schemes.

Middle
The top-dog fuelie Corvette in 1957 featured a solid-lifter V-8 that produced 283 horsepower. A four-speed was the only transmission offered behind the 283/283. Two 283-horse injection options were listed: RPOs 579B and 579E. The latter was the race-ready air box package. Shown here is one of the 43 air box Corvette models built for 1957. *Mike Mueller*

Right
The bright gas cap protruding through the fuel filler door on this 1961 Corvette identifies it as a rare big-tank model.
An optional oversized gas tank forced the filler neck to conflict with the filler door, thus the compromising modification. *Mike Mueller*

The Solid-Axle Years

C1
1953–1962

- → All solid-axle Corvettes were convertibles
- → Only automatic-backed six-cylinder engines offered in 1953 and 1954
- → V-8 power option introduced (1955)
- → Standard V-8 power (1956)
- → Three-speed manual transmission introduced (1955)
- → Removable hardtop option introduced (1956)
- → Optional two-tone paint introduced (1956)
- → Ed Cole becomes Chevrolet general manager (1956)
- → Optional fuel injection introduced (1957)
- → Optional four-speed manual transmission introduced (1957)
- → William Mitchell becomes General Motors design chief (1958)
- → Annual production finally surpasses 10,000 (1960)
- → Last Corvette enclosed trunk (1962) until 1998

Chevrolet officials sure had high hopes when they ordered the renovation of a section of their aging St. Louis assembly plant in order to relocate Corvette production there for 1954. After building a mere 300 1953 models in Flint, the Bowtie boys planned to move as many as 10,000 Corvettes a year out of their Missouri facility. Silly them—nearly a third of the 3,640 '54 Corvettes they managed to build that first year in St. Louis sat unsold outside the plant in January 1955, leaving more than one General Motors exec poised to pull the plug right then and there.

Apparently America wasn't ready for its own sports car. Making matters even worse was Ford's September 1954 introduction of its sporty, upscale two-seat Thunderbird, which outsold its Chevy counterpart by a whopping 23–1 margin (16,155 to 700) in 1955. Such sad numbers would speak for themselves today. But Detroit was a far different place 50 years ago. Bean counters had yet to take control, and the gallant hearts of a few strong-willed movers and shakers could actually outweigh the conservative, cost-conscious minds of the executive brain trust. Harley Earl alone wielded enough power atop GM's ivory tower to prevent anyone from tossing his baby out with the bathwater no matter how badly sales sagged. And rapidly rising Chief Engineer Ed Cole wasn't about to see his crew's

hard work go to waste, at least not without a fight. It was left to Zora Duntov to help convince adventurous Yankees that they indeed wanted their own brand of sports car. Replacing the Corvette's original Stovebolt six-cylinder with Chevy's hot new V-8 in 1955 instantly helped turn the tide; reshaping the entire package into a timeless work of art the following year sealed the deal. A half-century later, we can only wonder why anyone at GM ever had a worry at all.

Major doubts in 1953 hinged on various factors, not the least of which was the untested market then awaiting Earl's innovative idea. While some American servicemen had brought the sports car bug back from World War II duty in Europe, their enthusiasm didn't exactly infect the

Opposite
Only 300 Corvettes were built for 1953, all with Polo White paint, red interiors, and Powerglide automatic transmissions.

Above
The Corvette carried over essentially unchanged into 1957, while production nearly doubled. The final count for 1957 was 6,339.

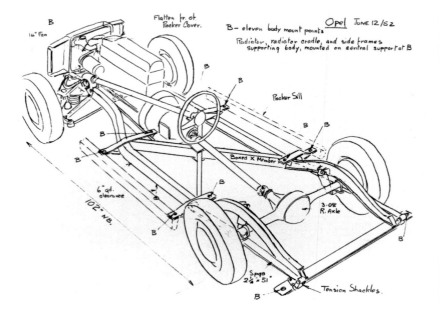

Left
This sketch of the Corvette chassis, dated June 12, 1952, refers to the car's original code name: "Opel."

Below
The original wooden buck for the 1953 Corvette body was a work of art itself. Yes, that is mahogany.

masses. Small, sporty two-seaters were still few and far between when the first Corvette came to be. Of the 4.16 million automobiles registered in the United States in 1952, a mere one-quarter of 1 percent of that mix consisted of sports cars, most of them cute little MG TDs from jolly old England. But fortunately, there were those in Detroit who didn't believe that numbers told the whole story. Among them was Duntov.

"Considering the statistics, the American public does not want a sports car at all," began Zora's address before the Society of Automotive Engineers (SAE) in 1953. "But do the statistics give a true picture? As far as the American market is concerned, it is still an unknown quantity, since [sic] an American sports car catering to American tastes, roads, ways of living, and national character has not yet been on the market."

Duntov wasn't the first to present a case for the production of a certified red-white-and-blue sports car. Legendary automotive journalist Ken Purdy had, four years before, foretold a second coming of sorts. In his 1949 *True* magazine feature entitled "The Two-Seater Comes Back," he wrote that all things that go around eventually make an encore:

"Before the Kaiser War, when Americans were serious about their motoring, the fast, high-performance two-seater automobile was as common as the 5-cent schooner of beer, and a lot more fun. But time passed, and inevitably the U.S. automobile began to change from an instrument of sport, like a pair of skies, into a device for economical mass transportation, and the two-seater was lost in the shuffle. Comes now a cloud on the horizon bigger than a man's hand which may portend a revival on this side of the water of the sports car—an automobile built for the sole purpose of going like a bat out of hell and never mind whether the girlfriend likes it or not."

"There is no reason why America should not be able to produce a good sports car," added *Argosy's* Ralph Stein in 1950. "We have engineers and designers with enough on the ball to create a crackerjack car, but, from observations, it looks very much as if they don't know what it takes. With

Construction began on the prototype Corvette, designated EX-122, late in 1952; the goal was to show it off during General Motors' traveling Motorama show, which opened in New York in January 1953.

EX-122's engine was dressed up with extra chrome for its Motorama debut. Note the special air cleaners, automatic chokes, and hydraulic hood-operating cylinders. The latter items automatically opened and closed the hood during the car's time on the Motorama stage.

a fast-growing band of sports car fans, however, the demand will gradually make itself felt."

That demand, however, was slow in coming after World War II, as most Americans concerned themselves with resuming, or starting, their family lives. Two-seat transportation was definitely out of the question once kids entered the picture. And with so few car buyers clamoring for fun machines as the 1950s dawned, Detroit wasn't in any particular hurry to start offering them. Then.

Fortunately, sports car fans did start banding together during the early 1950s, thanks in part to U.S. Air Force General Curtis LeMay, who hoped to boost military morale by arranging sports car races at various strategic air command bases. Reportedly, LeMay also put a bug in good friend Harley Earl's ear concerning the prospects of GM

building a true sports car. Furthering the cause was the emergence of the Sports Car Club of America (SCCA), which, during its first years immediately following the end of the war, showcased only foreign machines because domestic counterparts essentially were nowhere to be found.

Early American two-seat pioneers included Crosley's tiny Hot Shot and race car builder Frank Kurtis' Kurtis Kraft, both introduced in 1949 and both built in equally tiny numbers. An American–British hybrid, the Nash-Healey, followed in 1951 and remained in production until August 1954, with the total run barely surpassing 500. Also offered that latter year (again, in a highly limited fashion) was the all-American Kaiser Darrin, with its intriguing sliding doors that

disappeared into the front fenders. Also of note, the Kaiser Darrin's sleek body was molded from glass-reinforced plastic (GRP).

Discounting various experiments in the 1930s, GRP construction first came into vogue during World War II as a cheap, lightweight replacement for metals then in short supply. Making this stuff was simple enough: mix together hardening polyester resins with a woven mat made of fine glass fibers. The result was fiberglass, not to be confused with the trade name "Fiberglas" that Owens Corning has long used for its glass-fiber insulation.

It was only a matter of time before automakers discovered this high-tech material (later renamed "FRP," for fiberglass-reinforced plastic) after the war. Fiberglass body kits began

"There is no reason why America should not be able to produce a good sports car," said *Argosy*'s Ralph Stein in 1950.

Chief Engineer Ed Cole (left) and Chevrolet General Manager Thomas Keating admire the Corvette prototype on the Motorama stage at New York's Waldorf-Astoria in January 1953. Notice the unique fender trim and push-button door handle—neither of these items made it into regular production.

appearing by the end of 1951, followed by America's first fiberglass-bodied regular-production car, the Woodill Wildfire, in 1952. In February that year, *Life* magazine published an article entitled "Plastic Bodies for Autos," attracting even more attention, most prominently from Henry Kaiser, who then contracted fiberglass boat builder Glasspar to produce the body for his Kaiser Darrin.

Chevrolet people were attracted at the same time, and by the end of 1952, GM was exploring the feasibility of GRP body construction. According to research and developmental head Maurice Olley, whom Ed Cole had hired away from Rolls-Royce after he became Chevy chief engineer in April 1952, fiberglass produced "a very usable body of light weight which will not rust [and] will take a paint finish. A fiberglass panel of body quality three times as thick as steel will weigh half as much and will have approximately equal stiffness."

Harley Earl, too, took note of GRP possibilities. He had begun considering a sporty two-seater late in 1951, then started actual design work after an experimental fiberglass-bodied car was brought to GM Styling in March 1952.

The New York Motorama incorporated a rotating display, and as the car turned, its hood and trunk opened and closed hydraulically.

Earl assigned designer Robert McLean the task of establishing parameters for his dream machine. McLean's initial drawings depicted a low two-seater with a wide stance and a short 102-inch wheelbase. Earl's direct contributions to the design included his trendy wraparound windshield and clear headlight covers that fared the recessed headlamps into rounded fenders.

A full-size clay mockup of the design was prepared in April 1952, followed by a plaster model, which was shown to Ed Cole. Cole loved what he saw, and he joined Chevrolet General

Above
Unlike a standard 1953 Chevrolet passenger car, which relied on an archaic torque tube to transmit power to the rear axle, the new Corvette incorporated a modern driveshaft with U-joints.

Right
It may have looked like nothing seen before on the outside, but beneath its skin the 1953 Corvette featured many familiar, mundane Chevy components, including braking and steering systems.

Manager Thomas Keating to present the model to GM President Harlow Curtice, with the goal to build an experimental prototype for the upcoming Motorama auto show, scheduled for New York's Waldorf-Astoria in January 1953. Curtice gave the project two thumbs way up, opening the door for Maurice Olley's team to create a suitable chassis. In June 1952, Olley drew up an initial design, code-named "Opel." Chevrolet officials, however, preferred the name "Corvette," taken from a lightly armored, certainly fast warship built during World War II.

Olley's foundation featured a rigid X-member frame. While the front suspension consisted of many stock passenger-car parts, the rear layout incorporated special leaf springs to help locate a modified live axle, because a modern Hotchkiss drive was used instead of the archaic torque tube found beneath regular Chevrolet vehicles. Braking and steering systems too came right off the standard parts shelf.

And with Chevy's all-new V-8 still two years away, Cole was forced to rely on the division's existing Blue Flame six-cylinder, which made 115 horsepower from 235 cubic inches in typical trim.

Various tweaks helped boost output to 150 horses for the Corvette application. Behind the boosted Blue Flame six went Chevrolet's two-speed Powerglide automatic transmission, a not-so-popular choice that represented the easiest, least-expensive way to complete the driveline on such short notice.

Topping it all off was a hand-laid fiberglass shell made from plaster molds pulled directly from McLean's original clay model. But while plastic body construction would, of course, carry over from the show car into regular production, it wasn't the first choice. As Body Engineer Jim Premo later told the assembled SAE, "The body on the show model was made of reinforced plastic purely as an expedient to get the job built quickly. At the time of the Waldorf show, we were actually concentrating on a steel body utilizing kirksite tooling." Though kirksite dies were cheaper and could be fabricated more quickly than typical steel counterparts, they had much shorter working lives. Such considerations, however, were rendered moot once Premo's team proved they could work successfully in fiberglass. Besides, the auto show crowd loved the stuff.

"People seemed to be captivated by the idea of the fiberglass plastic body," continued Premo. "Furthermore, information being given to us by the reinforced plastic industry seemed to indicate the practicability of fabricating plastic body parts for automobiles on a large scale."

With the decision made to transform the Motorama prototype into a production reality, GM officials immediately began accepting bids for Corvette body construction following the car's debut in January 1953. The Molded Fiber Glass Company in Ashtabula, Ohio, won the contract, and then had to hustle to open a special plant dedicated to the process. Opened in April, the facility wasn't fully up and running until July 1954, leaving the MFG body people no choice but to subcontract some of the work to make up for slack in the meantime.

Once fabricated in Ohio, the various body parts were shipped to Michigan, where they were glued together and finished by hand. Completed bodies were then mated to their chassis on the Flint assembly line, which began rolling in June 1953. The rest is automotive history.

1953

1953

Specifications	1953

Model availability	convertible
Wheelbase	102 inches
Length	167.25 inches
Width	72.2 inches
Height	51.5 inches
Shipping weight	2,705 pounds
Tread (front/rear, in inches)	57/58.8
Tires	6.70x15 inches
Brakes	11-inch drums
Wheels	15x5 inches
Fuel tank	18 gallons
Front suspension	independent short and long wishbones, coil springs, and stabilizer bar
Rear suspension	solid axle with longitudinal leaf springs; tubular shock absorbers
Steering	worm and sector, 16:1 ratio
Engine	150-horsepower 235-ci OHV inline six-cylinder with three Carter one-barrel carburetors
Transmission	Powerglide automatic with floor shifter
Axle ratio	3.55:1

For the most part the show car simply rolled right off its stage onto Main Street USA.

Left
Chevrolet contracted the Molded Fiber Glass Company of Ashtabula, Ohio, to fashion the first Corvette's body. Here, a test fender takes shape at a GM fabrication shop.

Below
The various body parts were bonded together at the Flint facility for final assembly.

1953

Variety certainly wasn't the spice of life as far as Corvette buyers were concerned early on. All 300 Flint-built 1953 models were identically equipped with the Powerglide-backed Blue Flame six, and all were painted Polo White with contrasting red interiors. Although a heater and signal-seeking radio were listed as options, they were included in all 300 deals whether customers wanted them or not. Various minor trim differences set the production versions apart from their Motorama forerunner, but for

Left
General Motors set up a makeshift assembly line in Flint, Michigan, to build the first 300 Corvettes.

Far left
The Corvette's fiberglass floorpan was comparatively light, but this stunt shot doesn't exactly tell the real story. This molding weighed 210 pounds.

Below
The first Corvette rolled off the Flint line on June 30, 1953.

Left
A 1953 Corvette is treated to its Polo White finish in the Flint paint booth.

Right
What a difference 40 years can make. Chevrolet concentrated solely on affordable transportation when the Royal Mail roadster (at left) was built 1913. In 1953, the truly new Corvette proved that a Chevy could be fun and exciting too.

Below
Early 1953 models were fitted with Bel Air wheel covers because the planned knock-off style units weren't ready in time.

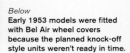

According to *Motor Life*'s Hank Gamble, "The Corvette is a beauty—and it *goes!*"

the most part the show car simply rolled right off its stage onto Main Street USA.

Supplying the standard 150 horses was a nicely warmed-over version of Chevrolet's overhead-valve inline six-cylinder. Modifications included more compression (8:1 instead of the stock 7.5:1 squeeze), a more aggressive solid-lifter cam, a beefed-up valvetrain, and a special

induction setup, featuring three side-draft Carter one-barrel carburetors mounted on an aluminum intake manifold. Handling spent gases was a split exhaust manifold that dumped into dual pipes and mufflers.

The sum of these parts equaled a top end of nearly 110 miles per hour, a sensational achievement for the day. Equally impressive at the

time, the 1953 Corvette was able to run from rest to 60 miles per hour in only 11 seconds. According to *Motor Life*'s Hank Gamble, "The Corvette is a beauty—and it *goes!*"

Road & Track staffers felt that straight-line speed was the car's most "outstanding characteristic," but they didn't stop praising there. "The second most outstanding characteristic is its

Fed by three side-draft carburetors, the 1953 Corvette's Blue Flame six-cylinder produced 150 horsepower. Notice the small, bullet-type air intakes attached to each carburetor. *Mike Mueller*

really good combination of riding and handling qualities. The Corvette corners flat like a genuine sports car."

Yet could a sports car be a sports car without a clutch and stick? Though it featured a sporty floor shifter, the original Corvette's Powerglide auto box left purists scoffing—and Chevy people defensive.

"The use of an automatic transmission has been criticized by those who believe that sports car enthusiasts want nothing but a four-speed crash shift," explained Maurice Olley. "The answer is that the typical sports car enthusiast, like the 'average man,' or the square root of minus one, is an imaginary quantity. Also, as the sports car appeals to a wider and wider section of the public, the center of gravity of this theoretical individual is shifting from the austerity of the pioneer toward the luxury of modern ideas. There is no need to

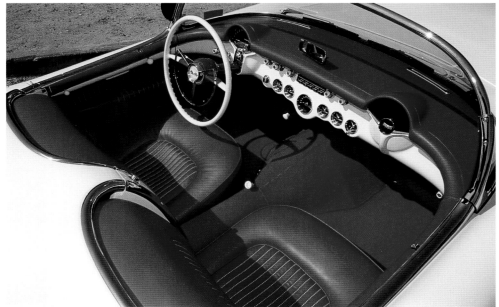

Along with red upholstery, all 1953 Corvettes were equipped with heaters and signal-seek radios, items listed as options in official paperwork that year. *Mike Mueller*

Tachometer location drew early complaints. A lead-footed driver had to look down and to the right to find the rev counter at a time when keeping both eyes on the road was preferred. *Mike Mueller*

Above
Sports car purists especially pooh-poohed the first Corvette because of its automatic transmission; the two-speed Powerglide unit at least featured a sporty floor shifter. *Mike Mueller*

Opposite
Owners in 1953 noted a problem with body panel staining in back due to the original Corvette's short exhaust tips. These tips were lengthened early during the 1954 run to cure the malady. *Mike Mueller*

apologize for the performance of this car with its automatic transmission."

Others outside Chevrolet confines weren't so sure: "That statement should get a rise from 100,000 *Road & Track* readers!" wrote *R&T*'s John Bond.

As it was, whether they bought Bond's magazine or not, few Americans got the chance to make their own conclusions concerning Chevrolet's first Corvette. Hoping to promote an exclusive image for their innovative two-seater, company officials initially limited availability of the first production run to VIP customers only. Most of the eager show-goers who saw the Motorama Corvette in January 1953 never even sniffed an opportunity to touch a regular-production counterpart.

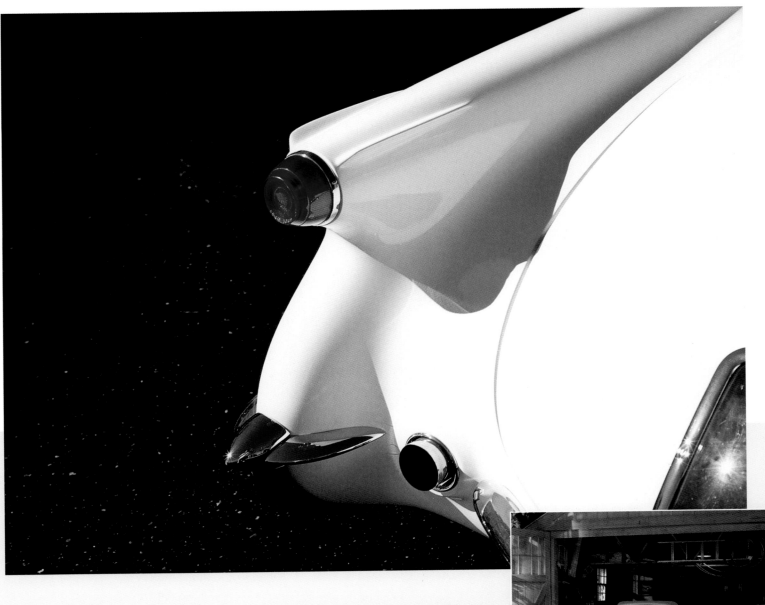

"If you've got an itch to get behind the wheel of a Chevrolet Corvette, you might as well scratch it," wrote *Motor Trend*'s Floyd Lawrence in the late summer of 1953. "Better are your chances of winning the Mille Miglia on a kiddie car." After explaining that the very few cars then available were going to GM executives, Lawrence also quipped, "If [the] present distribution pattern continues, the hoped-for output of 300 units this year will scarcely take care of the top GM brass."

By the end of the year, only about 180 of the 300 1953 Corvettes built had found homes, as Chevrolet couldn't drum up enough very important people willing to come to its invitation-only party. Much momentum had already been lost by the time the VIP qualification was dropped in the summer of 1954. As Don MacDonald explained in *Motor Trend*, "The long gap between initial publicity and availability has cooled the desires of many buyers."

Limiting the 1953 Corvette's scope were the more foreign aspects of its sports car appeal. There were no exterior door handles, there were side curtains instead of roll-up glass, and a leaky, crude soft top only marginally kept the weather at bay.

1954

1954

Specifications	1954
Model availability	convertible
Wheelbase	102 inches
Length	167 inches
Width	72.2 inches
Height	51.5 inches
Shipping weight	2,705 pounds
Tread (front/rear, in inches)	57/59
Tires	6.70x15 inches
Brakes	11-inch drums
Wheels	15x5 inches
Fuel tank	18 gallons
Front suspension	independent short and long wishbones, coil springs, and stabilizer bar
Rear suspension	solid axle with longitudinal leaf springs; tubular shock absorbers
Steering	worm and sector, 16:1 ratio
Engine	150-horsepower 235-ci OHV inline six-cylinder (early); 155-horsepower 235-ci OHV inline six-cylinder (midyear change), both with three Carter one-barrel carburetors
Transmission	Powerglide automatic with floor shifter
Axle ratio	3.55:1

Not even the addition of optional paint choices could turn the heads of potential customers, who stayed away in droves.

Exterior color choices were introduced for the 1954 Corvette; Pennant Blue is shown here. In back are two later models, a 1978 Indy pace car replica and a 1984 Corvette. *Mike Mueller*

1954

St. Louis assembly plant manager William Mosher was told in March 1953 that Corvette production eventually would move to his facility, and it was there that the first 1954 model was completed late in December. Reportedly as many as 15 Corvettes were built that month in Missouri before the St. Louis line really started cooking in January. The plant was soon rolling out 50 two-seaters a day as Chevrolet geared up for its highly optimistic 10,000-cars-a-year production minimum. But the

process soon stalled as demand remained lukewarm. In June, Chevy officials cut back production in St. Louis and halted fiberglass body panel construction entirely in Ohio.

Not even the addition of optional paint choices could turn the heads of potential customers, who stayed away in droves. While nearly 85 percent of the 1954 models were again painted Polo White, about 300 received Pennant Blue finishes, roughly 100 were sprayed Sportsman Red, and less than 10 rolled out in

Corvette construction moved southwest to St. Louis, Missouri, late in 1953. Here, a 1954 Corvette body finds a home in the Show Me State.

Telling a 1954 Corvette apart from its 1953 forerunner is no easy task at a glance. Lengthened exhaust tips in back represent the quickest clues, but some early 1954 models were released with the shorter 1953 tips.

Save for the new colors offered for 1954, there was virtually no way to differentiate a new model from a 1953 from a frontal perspective. Here, a collection of 1954 Corvettes parade on the way to the Rose Bowl in Pasadena, California.

black. The rubberized canvas convertible-top color changed for 1954, from black to beige. A beige interior also was introduced.

Additional updates were barely noticeable. Distinguishing between those 300 1953 Corvettes and the following 1954 models wasn't easy at a glance, with the most prominent clue coming in back, where the latter cars were treated to longer exhaust extensions to cure an exhaust staining problem that plagued the Flint-built cars. Some early 1954 Corvettes received the short extensions before this change was made.

Another running change involved the installation of a different cam early in 1954, a move that upped the Blue Flame six's output to 155 horsepower. At some point that year, engineers also traded the triple carburetors' three bullet-shaped air inlets for a more functional arrangement of two round air cleaners perched in conventional, upright fashion. Most 1954

Above
A trio of intriguing concept cars made the rounds during GM's 1954 Motorama tour. In front is a standard 1954 Corvette. Behind is a hardtop Corvette with roll-up windows, the fastback Corvair coupe, and the passenger-car-based Nomad wagon.

Upper left
Press critics loved the way the 1953 and 1954 Corvettes performed, but initial customer responses fell flat. Officials early on hoped to build 10,000 two-seaters at St. Louis in 1954; actual production amounted to about a third of that projection.

Left
Midyear changes for 1954 included trading the Blue Flame six's bullet-style air inlets for two round air cleaners. A cam change early in the year also boosted output from 150 to 155 horsepower. *Mike Mueller*

Corvettes featured a hood latch mechanism controlled by only one interior release, while some early 1954 cars and all 1953 models used two releases, one for each latch.

Various baubles were added to the 1954 options list, although all 3,640 Corvettes built that year apparently were again equipped with every available feature. The Powerglide automatic was designated an option even though it was once more the only transmission choice, to the continued dismay of sports car purists and performance-seeking playboys.

Above
European influences led to the creation of the Corvair, a sleek machine based on a 1954 Corvette.

Left
The 1954 Motorama coupe's removable hardtop would appear as a Corvette option two years later.

1955

1955

Specifications	1955

Model availability	convertible
Wheelbase	102 inches
Length	167 inches
Width	72.24 inches
Height	48.5 inches
Shipping weight	2,695 pounds (six-cylinder), 2,665 pounds (V-8)
Tread (front/rear, in inches)	56.7/58.8
Tires	6.70x15 inches
Brakes	11-inch drums
Wheels	15x5 inches
Fuel tank	18 gallons
Front suspension	independent short and long wishbones, coil springs, and stabilizer bar
Rear suspension	solid axle with longitudinal leaf springs; tubular shock absorbers
Steering	worm and sector, 16:1 ratio
Engine (early)	155-horsepower OHV inline six-cylinder with three Carter one-barrel carburetors
Engine (midyear addition)	195-horsepower 265-ci V-8 with single four-barrel carburetor
Transmission (early)	Powerglide automatic
Transmission (late)	three-speed manual
Axle ratio	3.55:1

Five colors were offered for the 1955 Corvette: the traditional Polo White, Pennant Blue, Corvette Copper, Gypsy Red, and Harvest Gold.

The really big news for 1955 involved a switch from the Blue Flame Six to Chevrolet's new overhead-valve V-8.

The 1955 Corvette was the last model to wear these Eurostyle stone shields on its headlights. *Mike Mueller*

The big news for 1955 involved the introduction of Chevrolet's hot new overhead-valve V-8, which replaced the Blue Flame six-cylinder beneath fiberglass hoods early in the year. Announcing the 265-ci V-8's presence was a large gold V added to the Chevrolet fender script. *Mike Mueller*

1955

Notable upgrades for 1955 again began with expanded color choices, although some mystery still exists concerning the actual palette offered that year. Polo White was once more the popular choice on the outside, with about half of the 700 Corvettes built for 1955 receiving this familiar finish. Gypsy Red and the newly offered Harvest Gold adorned the bulk of the remaining orders. Pennant Blue briefly carried over from 1954, but reportedly was dropped in April 1955. Some sources say that Pennant Blue was then replaced by Corvette Copper, while others list Coppertone Bronze. By either name, this latter shade was all but unknown in 1955.

Interior colors included red, dark beige, light beige, green, and yellow, with the latter two appropriately reserved for the yellowish Harvest Gold exterior paint. Convertible-top shades were also expanded, as white and dark green (again for the Harvest Gold cars) joined beige.

All these artistic touches, however, simply represented icing on the cake. The really big news

for 1955 involved a switch from the Blue Flame six to Chevrolet's new overhead-valve V-8, the fire-breathing small block that overnight transformed the old, reliable Chevy into the "Hot One." This modern, high-winding powerplant displaced 265 cubic inches and made 180 horsepower in "Power Pack" trim beneath a 1955 Bel Air's hood. Its potential between fiberglass flanks was obvious.

A prototype V-8 Corvette was undergoing testing as early as May 1954 under the direction of performance consultant and three-time Indy 500 winner Mauri Rose. Cole hired Rose in August 1952 to oversee the division's performance parts development projects, and his earliest challenges included developing the somewhat tricky triple-carb setup for the Blue Flame six. Dropping the new V-8 into the Stovebolt's place was comparatively simple, with only one minor frame modification required to allow clearance for the 265's fuel pump. "Installation of the compact V-8 in the Corvette is

very neat," wrote *Motor Life*'s Ken Fermoyle. "The engine fits so nicely, in fact, that one suspects that the possibility of using a V-8 was considered when the Corvette was designed."

With a lumpier cam and a Carter four-barrel carburetor topped by a low-restriction chrome air cleaner, the Corvette's 265 V-8 was rated at 195 hefty horsepower. Compression remained 8:1. On the outside, this born-again hot rod was identified by the large gold "V" added to the "Corvette" script on each fender.

While some (as few as seven, perhaps) very early 1955 Corvettes were equipped with the 155-horse Blue Flame six, the majority featured the 265 V-8. Enhancing the attraction further was a new three-speed manual transmission, offered exclusively behind the V-8. Estimates put three-speed Corvette production that year at about 75. As in previous years, all remaining listed options were included on all 1955 models.

As for more important numbers, according to *Road & Track*, the muscled-up V-8 Corvette

An early Corvette prototype was later modified as a V-8 prototype. This car goes airborne during chassis tests at GM's Milford Proving Grounds in May 1954.

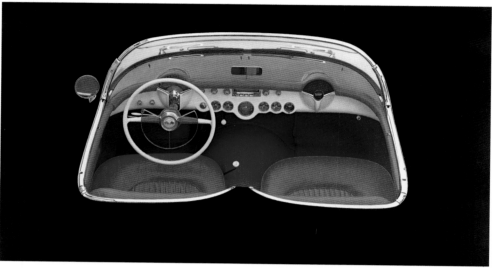

The Corvette interior rolled over essentially unchanged for 1955. Tachometers differed depending on engine choice: the rare six-cylinder models got 5,000-rpm tachs; V-8 cars got 6,000-rpm units.

Three-time Indy 500 winner Mauri Rose (at right) was the man who oversaw early Corvette performance developments. He shows off the new V-8 Corvette in 1955.

A warmly welcomed manual transmission, a three-speed, also appeared midyear in 1955. Estimates claim stick installations numbered about 75 that year.

could go from 0–60 in a reasonably scant 8.7 seconds. Quarter-mile performance was listed at 16.5 seconds, and the top end was about 120 miles per hour. "Loaded for bear," was *R&T*'s description of the 195-horse Corvette. "The V-8 engine makes this a far more interesting automobile and has upped performance to a point at least as good as

anything in its price class," added Ken Fermoyle.

Such accolades aside, many witnesses remained hesitant to predict a brightened future for Chevrolet's struggling two-seater. "Whether addition of the V-8 engine will hypo Corvette sales remains to be seen," continued Fermoyle. "The blazing performance the Corvette now offers should attract more buyers." Meanwhile,

Road & Track's Euro-conscious critics continued to complain about the car's yeoman chassis, which, while good by American standards, couldn't quite compete with what lay beneath the world's best sporting machines.

Fortunately, Zora Duntov and crew weren't through tinkering. Not by a long shot.

1956

Boosting power was key to the Corvette's turnaround after 1955, but so too was Chevrolet's "Americanization" of the sports car ideal. Not only was America not quite ready for the original Corvette, the original Corvette wasn't quite ready for its country's countrymen. Like sports car purists, American sensibilities were at first offended by Chevrolet's unique open-air machine, which originally featured more downsides—from a Yankee perspective, that is—than its initial Powerglide-only restriction.

While surely intrigued by this new breed, many early customers simply couldn't get past the car's comparatively crude nature. Unlike Ford's first T-bird, which, along with standard V-8 power, featured conventional roll-up windows and a classy, convenient removable hardtop, Chevy's original Corvette protected its occupants from the weather only with a clumsy, hand-folded rag top and pesky side curtains. In reference to the situation, *Motor Trend*'s Don MacDonald explained that apparently Chevrolet's "conception of the Corvette market is that no owner will be caught in the rain without a spare Cadillac." Americans also were not thrilled about a feature familiar to many European sports car fanatics—opening the doors required a reach inside to fumble around for the interior door knob. Exterior door handles were not present.

So it was that both form and function were radically redone for 1956. Love at first glance was guaranteed by a restyled, modern-looking body that represented a marked improvement on what came before, as well as a faithfully updated rendition of the original image. While the toothy grille up front helped remind onlookers that the 1956 model was indeed a Corvette, the conventionally located headlights and recessed taillights more easily inspired thoughts of forward motion. Overall, the new look was sleek, clean, and truly American—no more Eurostyle headlamp stone shields here.

Specifications	1956
Model availability	convertible, with optional removable hardtop
Wheelbase	102 inches
Length	168 inches
Width	70.46 inches
Height	51.9 inches (top up), 50.98 inches (with hardtop)
Shipping weight	2,825 pounds (with Powerglide), 2,730 pounds (with three-speed manual)
Tread (front/rear, in inches)	57/59
Tires	6.70x15 inches
Brakes	11-inch drums
Wheels	15x5 inches
Fuel tank	16.4 gallons
Front suspension	independent short and long wishbones, coil springs, and stabilizer bar
Rear suspension	solid axle with longitudinal leaf springs; tubular shock absorbers
Steering	recirculating ball, 16:1 ratio
Standard drivetrain	210-horsepower 265-ci V-8 with single four-barrel carburetor, three-speed manual transmission, 3.70:1 axle ratio
Optional engine	225-horsepower 265-ci V-8 with dual four-barrel carburetors
Optional engine	240-horsepower 265-ci V-8 with dual four-barrel carburetors and special high-lift camshaft (three-speed manual transmission only)
Optional transmission	Powerglide automatic (with 3.55:1 axle ratio)
Optional gear ratios	3.27:1, 4.11:1

This early 1956 clay mockup wore 1955 wheel covers. Also notice the missing scoops atop each fender—items that were added when the restyled Corvette went into production.

A beautiful new body, roll-up windows, and conventional door handles helped transform the Corvette into a real winner in 1956.

fighting each other"—this because considerable oversteer was designed in up front and almost as much roll understeer was inherent in back. Duntov changed this situation in 1956. As he wrote in *Auto Age*, "The target was to attain such handling characteristics that the driver of some ability could get really high performance safely."

This goal was met by adjusting geometry. Caster angle was increased in front by adding shims where the suspension-locating crossmember attached to the frame. Roll oversteer was minimized by changing the steering's main idler arm angle, again by shimming. In back, roll understeer was reduced by revamping the leaf spring hangers to decrease the slope of the springs.

More power also appeared in 1956, as the Corvette V-8 received a compression boost from 8:1 to 9.25:1. A second Carter four-barrel carburetor was added to help produce 225 healthy horses in top-performance trim. Standard power came from a single-carb 265, rated at 210

Equally American were newfound comfort and convenience qualities: fiberglass firsts for 1956 included exterior door handles, an adjustable seat for the passenger, and real side windows that actually rolled up and down. Even more newfangled features appeared on the options list. Power steering was introduced, as was hydraulic operation for the folding convertible top and a removable roof that made the latest, greatest Corvette nearly 100 percent weatherproof. About two out of three customers chose this $215 option in 1956.

Beneath all that beauty was a mildly revamped chassis, courtesy of Zora Duntov. In his mind, the first Corvette was a car with "two ends

More performance and added class and comfort saved the Corvette from an early grave after demand had fallen off precipitously in 1955. Production for 1956 increased by nearly five times. The final tally read 3,467.

Left
Improvements beneath the 1956 Corvette's restyled skin included various suspension tweaks and even more muscle, the latter supplied by a dual-carb 265-ci V-8 rated at 225 horsepower.

Below
While some early 1956 Corvettes featured painted headlight bezels, most cars were fitted with chrome trim rings up front.

horsepower. The standard transmission in 1956 was the three-speed manual, with the two-speed Powerglide automatic now an option.

According to *Road & Track*, a three-speed 225-horse model could click off the quarter-mile in 15.8 seconds and run 0–60 in 7.3 ticks, numbers that inspired *Sports Car Illustrated*'s

Roger Huntington to call the dual-carb 265 "one of the hottest production engines in the world." But there was more to come.

Duntov was confident he could squeeze 150 miles per hour out of the new '56 Corvette, and to that end he developed the legendary "Duntov cam," a potent solid-lifter bump stick

Love at first glance was guaranteed by a restyled, modern-looking body that represented a marked improvement on what came before.

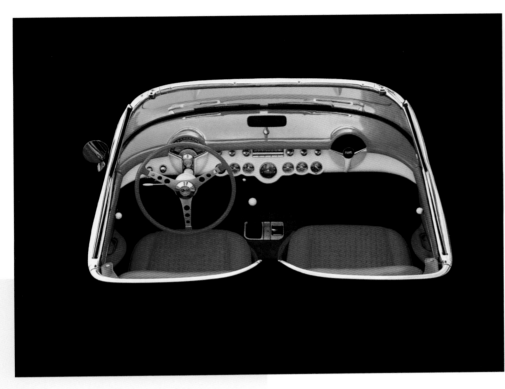

The rarely seen three-speed stick officially became a standard Corvette fixture in 1956. The Powerglide automatic was a $188.50 option.

that really brought the little 265 to life. Output for the Duntov-cam V-8, although not officially listed in 1956, was commonly put at 240 horsepower. Chevrolet paperwork recommended that this engine be used "for racing purposes only."

Duntov did just that in February 1956 during Daytona Beach's fabled Speed Week trials. On the Florida sands, he managed a two-way average speed of 150.533 miles per hour in the new Corvette, while comrade John Fitch set a two-way record of 145.543 miles per hour. A third Corvette driver, champion aerobatic pilot and stunning spokesmodel Betty Skelton, managed a 137.773-mile-per-hour two-way clocking.

John Fitch then led a four-car team south to Sebring the following month for the 12-hour endurance race there. While Chevrolet officials publicly tried to distance themselves early on from this all-out racing effort, the team obviously was fully factory backed. Chevy-subsidized engineering advancements beneath those blue-striped white-fiberglass skins were plenty, including special heavy-duty springs and shocks, and brakes that featured finned drums with wider shoes wearing sintered "cerametallix" linings.

The latter components represented real keys to survival on a course that could literally melt both car and driver. Two of the Sebring Corvette racers failed to survive the day in March 1956, as did 35 rivals. But Fitch's machine, co-driven by Walt Hansgen, finished ninth overall and tops in its

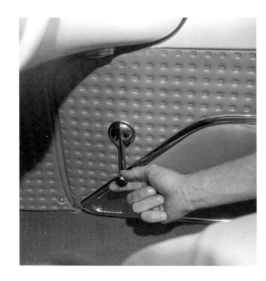

Left
Zora Duntov clocked 150.533 miles per hour in his Corvette during the 1956 Speed Week trials in Florida. John Fitch managed 145.543 miles per hour, while Betty Skelton ran 137.773.

Far left
Along with conventional exterior door handles, Corvette buyers in 1956 were treated to another new feature: real glass side windows that cranked up.

Below
GM sent three Corvette racers to Daytona Beach in February 1956 to kick up a little sand and set a few speed records. The cars were driven by Zora Duntov, John Fitch, and Betty Skelton.

Brainy, beautiful, and tough, Betty Skelton was already an experienced, well-known pilot and test driver when GM put her to work in 1956. She also served as corporate spokesperson during the many Motorama auto show tours to follow.

class, an achievement that was worth a fortune in publicity for Chevrolet.

The now-famous "Real McCoy" advertisement appeared immediately after the race. The ad described the '56 Corvette as "a tough, road-gripping, torpedo on wheels with the stamina to last through the brutal 12 hours of Sebring." But Campbell-Ewald's copywriters also touted the two-seater's more civilized side, claiming it was "the most remarkable car made in America today." Why? "Because it is two cars wrapped up in one sleek skin. One is a luxury car with glove-soft upholstery, wind-up windows, a removable hardtop, ample luggage space, a velvety ride, and all the power assists you could want. The other is a sports car."

Critics who earlier questioned that latter aspect overnight began changing their minds. "Without qualification, General Motors is now building a sports car," wrote Karl Ludvigsen in *Sports Car Illustrated*.

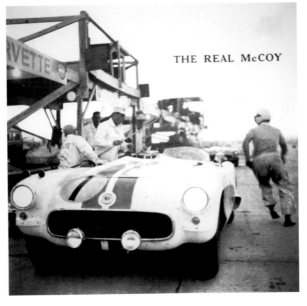

THE REAL McCOY

Above
In March 1956, John Fitch led a four-car Corvette racing team to Sebring, Florida, where Fitch's machine finished first in class and ninth overall.

Left
Campbell-Ewald, Chevy's ad agency and Betty Skelton's employer, wasted little time promoting the Corvette's racing exploits early in 1956. Indeed, this little two-seater was "the real McCoy."

According to *Road & Track*, a three-speed 225-horse model could clock off the quarter-mile in 158 seconds and run 0–60 in 7.3 ticks.

It was also building a successful one. Corvette sales shot up by 400 percent in 1956, with the bulk of these fitted with the 225-horse 265. In one year's time, Chevrolet had taken what would soon become known as America's only sports car and transformed it into the world's only *American* sports car.

1956 SR-2

If prospective buyers still weren't sure just how hot Chevrolet's two-seater had become by 1956, they only needed to watch Zora Duntov, John Fitch, and Betty Skelton during their high-flying record runs down Daytona Beach that February. After Fitch's trip to Sebring the following month, it was time, as ads proclaimed, to "bring on the hay bales." The Corvette now truly was an honest-to-goodness racing machine.

Nonetheless, Jerry Earl remained unconvinced. So what if his dad worked for General Motors? Earl liked to race sports cars, and when it came time to hit the track in 1956, he initially chose a Ferrari to do all the hitting. Father, however, knew best, and there was no way GM Vice President Harley Earl was going to let any son of his drive an Italian exotic when he could be behind the wheel of Detroit iron—or Detroit fiberglass.

The elder Earl convinced his hot-blooded offspring to dump his Ferrari for a specially prepared Corvette racer featuring a custom fiberglass shell on a muscled-up chassis. Included in the deal were all the heavy-duty suspension tricks veteran driver John Fitch had put to the test at Sebring in March 1956. Inside Chevy Engineering, the beefed production parts supplied for Fitch's four-car Sebring team had become known by an "SR" designation, which may or may not have originally stood for either "sports racing" or "Sebring racer." In any case, the Fitch team's four Corvette racers were the first competition SRs, meaning that any variation to follow would've naturally become the second. Thus, the Corvette Harley Earl ordered for his son ended up wearing the moniker "SR-2."

Above
Three great racing Corvette models: a 1956 SR-2, Bill Mitchell's Stingray, and a 1963 Grand Sport.

Below
Three SR-2 Corvette racers were built in 1956—two competition machines and one show car. This SR-2 racer was built for Bill Mitchell. *Mike Mueller*

A collection of GM Styling staff members' customized Corvettes surround two of the SR-2 cars. In the center is the blue, street-going SR-2 built for GM President Harlow Curtice.

Demonstrating just how nice it is to have friends in high places, Jerry Earl's custom racer—listed under shop order number 90090—took no more than four weeks to complete, leading some to believe that the first SR-2's body was simply dropped right onto an existing track-ready chassis from one of Fitch's Sebring racers. The body featured metallic blue paint, an extended snout, and bright aluminum bodyside cove panels. Both

the louvers on the hood and the vents on each door were functional, the latter delivering all-important cooling air to the rear brakes. Up front, twin short screens replaced the windshield, while a small tailfin was added down the center of the deck lid in back.

Twin cutout exhausts, an oversized fuel tank, and a set of Halibrand mag wheels were also included. Inside, Earl's SR-2 initially looked more

like a show car and less like a racer, a situation that wasn't entirely far from the truth. All that extra flash translated into extra weight, which in turn translated into a disappointing racing debut at Wisconsin's Road America in June 1956.

A return to the drawing board transformed a lightened SR-2 into a more competitive machine, but true success didn't come until Earl sold his custom Corvette late in 1957 to Jim Jeffords, who

Top and above
SR-2 modifications included special brake-cooling duct work. Airflow entered a scoop on each door and flowed rearward into this vent in the rear quarter panel, which sent the breeze to the rear brake drums. *Mike Mueller*

Bill Mitchell's SR-2 finished 16th at Sebring in March 1957. The other SR-2 racer, originally built for Harley Earl's son Jerry, was later an SCCA champion after it was sold to Nickey Chevrolet's Jim Jeffords.

campaigned it for Chicago dealer Nickey Chevrolet. Wearing Nickey's distinctive "Purple People Eater" paint scheme, Jeffords' SR-2 sped off with an SCCA B/Production Championship in 1958.

By that time, Chevrolet's first SR-2 Corvette was sporting a reshaped, enlarged tailfin set off to the driver's side in order to incorporate both a headrest and an integral roll bar. Earl requested the "high fin" after seeing it on Chevrolet's second SR-2, built for GM Styling mogul Bill Mitchell.

Varying slightly here and there compared to its forerunner, Mitchell's red-and-white SR-2 made its high-profile public debut in February 1957 at Daytona, where Buck Baker drove it through the Flying Mile at 152.866 miles per hour, a figure topped only by a D-type Jaguar. SR-2 number two finished 16th at Sebring a month later and was eventually relegated to a GM storage basement in 1958.

Following Mitchell's lead, GM President Harlow Curtice requested a third SR-2 in 1956, only his was constructed entirely for show. Virtually a stock '56 Corvette underneath, Curtice's "low fin" SR-2 also featured metallic blue paint but rolled on Dayton wire wheels and

Above
Jerry Earl's original racing SR-2 was built with a small tailfin, but this design was later exchanged for a tall, asymmetrical fin after the second SR-2 showed up wearing one.

Right
After a short racing career, Bill Mitchell's SR-2 went into storage at GM in 1958. It was then bought by racer Don Yenko, who resold it in 1965. Collector Bill Tower acquired the car in 1979 and still owns it today.

was fitted with a removable stainless-steel hardtop. Curtice drove his SR-2 briefly and then sold it to a neighbor.

All three SR-2 Corvette racers have gone through various owners over the years, and each has experienced a modification or two. Originally powered by dual-carb small blocks, the trio today rely on fuel injection, with the two race cars now equipped with bored and stroked V-8s. Four-speeds are found in the SR-2s as well, even though, like the fuelie setup, this transmission type didn't appear on the Corvette options list until 1957.

1957

Specifications

Specifications	1957

Model availability	convertible, with optional removable hardtop
Wheelbase	102 inches
Length	168 inches
Width	70.46 inches
Height	51.9 inches (top up), 50.98 inches (with hardtop)
Shipping weight	2,796 pounds (with Powerglide), 2,704 pounds (with three-speed manual)
Tread (front/rear, in inches)	57/59
Tires	6.70x15 inches
Brakes	11-inch drums
Wheels	15x5 inches
Fuel tank	16.4 gallons
Front suspension	independent short and long wishbones, coil springs, and stabilizer bar
Rear suspension	solid axle with longitudinal leaf springs; tubular shock absorbers
Steering	recirculating ball, 16:1 ratio
Standard drivetrain	220-horsepower 283-ci V-8 with single four-barrel carburetor, three-speed manual transmission, 3.70:1 axle ratio
Optional engine	245-horsepower 283-ci V-8 with dual four-barrel carburetors, hydraulic lifters
Optional engine	250-horsepower 283-ci V-8 with fuel injection, hydraulic lifters
Optional engine	270-horsepower 283-ci V-8 with dual four-barrel carburetors, solid lifters (optional Powerglide transmission not available)
Optional engine	283-horsepower 283-ci V-8 with fuel injection, solid lifters (optional Powerglide transmission not available)
Optional transmission	Powerglide automatic (with 3.55:1 axle ratio)
Optional transmission	four-speed manual
Optional gear ratios	3.70:1, 4.11:1, 4.56:1, all with Posi-Traction

The Corvette carried over essentially unchanged into 1957, while production nearly doubled. The final count for 1957 was 6,339.

1957

Big news for 1957 began with a bigger engine as Chevrolet's 265 small-block V-8 was bored out to 283 cubic inches. Maximum output predictably increased, with the top-shelf dual-carb option now producing a whopping 270 horsepower.

To better handle those ponies, engineers on April 9, 1957, released the Corvette's first optional four-speed, the Borg-Warner T-10. According to a Chevy press release, "The four forward speeds of the new transmission are synchronized to provide a swift and smooth

Above
New for 1957 was an optional four-speed manual transmission, priced at $188.30. A three-speed manual remained the standard gearbox. *Mike Mueller*

Left
The ever-present Betty Skelton complemented many equally attractive Corvette models in 1956 and 1957, both in press photos and during public appearances.

Above
Chevrolet's small-block V-8 was boosted to 283 cubic inches in 1957, and a four-barrel-fed 283, rated at 220 horsepower, was standard for the Corvette. Two optional dual-carb V-8s were offered: a hydraulic-cam 245-horsepower version and its solid-lifter 270-horse counterpart. *Mike Mueller*

Below
Optional Ramjet fuel injection (RPO 579) debuted for 1957, kicking off a high-powered legacy that lasted up through 1965. *Mike Mueller*

response." Walt Woron of *Motor Trend* felt those words represented an understatement: "When you can whip the stick around from one gear to any other the way you'd stir a can of paint, that's a gearbox that's synchronized."

Yet as much as the four-speed represented just what the doctor ordered to help maximize Corvette performance, an even hotter new option also debuted for 1957—Ramjet fuel injection (FI). Initially the work of engineer John Dolza, Ramjet injection was perfected with the help of Duntov, whom Cole assigned to the project in early 1955. Fuel injection was nothing new on the world stage, but it was a real sensation on the American market.

In *Road & Track's* words, "The fuel injection engine is an absolute jewel, quiet and remarkably docile when driven gently around town, yet instantly transformable into a roaring brute when pushed hard." Built by Rochester Products, Ramjet injection delivered fuel more evenly in a much more efficient manner than those dual four-barrels, and it did so instantly. The FI equipment also eliminated flooding and fuel starvation common to the carburetors of the day whenever hard turns sent the gas supply in the bowl centrifuging off sideways away from the pickup. That latter problem in particular had worked against the dual-carb Corvette racers at Sebring in 1956.

On the downside, fuelie Corvette models earned an early reputation for hard starts and finicky operation. Keeping everything in proper tune was a must, although that was difficult considering that so few local mechanics were qualified to tinker with a fuel-injected Corvette in 1957.

Teething problems aside, the fuel-injected 283 V-8 helped put Corvette performance at the cutting edge in 1957. *Road & Track* testers managed a 0–60 run in a stunning 5.7 seconds. Quarter-mile times, at 14.3 seconds, were equally alarming.

Various fuel-injected 283s were offered that first year, all listed under RPO 579. RPOs 579A and 579C both featured a hydraulic-cam FI V-8 rated at 250 horsepower. The letters "A" and "C" referred to the transmission choice: 579A was the four-speed manual, 579C the Powerglide

Above
The top-dog fuelie Corvette in 1957 featured a solid-lifter V-8 that produced 283 horsepower. A four-speed was the only transmission offered behind the 283/283. Two 283-horse injection options were listed: RPOs 579B and 579E. The latter was the race-ready air box package. Shown here is one of the 43 air box Corvettes built for 1957. *Mike Mueller*

Left
Four different fuel injection packages were offered in 1957. RPOs 579A and 579C featured a hydraulic-cam fuelie V-8 rated at 250 horsepower, with the A option featuring a four-speed manual, the C an automatic. The latter appears here. *Mike Mueller*

automatic. RPO 579B was the designation assigned to the fabled 283-horsepower 283 fuelie, a certified screamer with 10.5:1 compression and the solid-lifter Duntov cam. The four-speed manual was the only transmission available behind the 283/283, which Chevrolet promo people have long loved to claim was Detroit's first engine to reach the 1-horse-per-cubic-inch plateau. Sorry, guys, Chrysler beat you to it the previous year with the 300B's optional 355-horse 354 hemi V-8.

A fourth version of the 283 fuelie Corvette was also offered in 1957, this one clearly built with competition in mind. One of the lessons learned during the high-speed runs at Daytona and Sebring in 1956 was the value of allowing the engine to breathe in cooler, denser outside air instead of the hot under-hood atmosphere. Experimentation with cool-air induction setups led to the creation of the "air box" Corvette.

The idea was simple. A plenum box was fabricated and mounted on the fender well panel on the driver's side. At the front, this box mated to an opening in the support bulkhead beside the radiator. Inside the box was an air filter. At the rear was a rubberized duct that ran from that filter to the Ramjet injection unit. Cooler outside air entered through the bulkhead opening into the box, then through the filter into the FI system. The result was the release of a few extra ponies on top end as the air box Corvette's injected 283 sucked in its denser supply of precious oxygen.

Additional air box modifications included moving the tachometer from its less-than-desirable stock spot in the center of the dash to atop the steering column where it could do its job like it should. A round plate then covered the

"When you can whip the stick around from one gear to any other the way you'd stir a can of paint, that's a gearbox that's synchronized," said *Motor Trend*'s Walt Woron.

Above
Widened 15x5.5 wheels (RPO 276) also appeared for 1957. Small dog-dish hubcaps were included with these rims. *Mike Mueller*

Top left
A heavy-duty racing suspension package, RPO 684, was introduced early in 1957. Included in this deal were metallic brakes with special cooling apparatus. Duct work ran the length of the car through the rocker panels to deliver cooling breezes to the finned drums in back—notice the air intake mounted on the backing plate just above the leaf spring. *Mike Mueller*

opening at the standard location. Additionally, the radio and heater—items rarely needed at a racetrack—were both deleted. And with a radio not present, ignition shielding wasn't required. This meant plug wires could be run more directly from the distributor to the spark plugs over the valve covers as far away from the hot exhaust manifolds as possible. Plug wires on all other 1957 Corvettes were routed the long way, down along the cylinder heads below the manifolds, because this was the easiest place to mount the static-suppressive shielding.

Other racing-inspired pieces debuted along with the air box equipment in 1957, beginning with a Posi-Traction differential and wide 15x5.5 wheels. The steel wheels, RPO 276, were 1/2-inch wider than stock rims and came crowned with small, plain hubcaps in place of the standard, ornate knock-off wheel covers.

A heavy-duty suspension option, RPO 581, entered the fray early on. Included were beefed springs front and rear; larger, stiffer shocks; a thicker front stabilizer bar; and a quick-steering adapter. Early in the 1957 model run, this option was repackaged under RPO 684, after a heavy-duty brake package was added into the mix along with the race-ready suspension components.

Sounding very much like the equipment found on the four Sebring Corvette racers of 1956, the RPO 684 brakes featured cerametallix linings, finned drums, and vented backing plates with scoops to catch cooling air. Helping deliver this air to the rear wheel scoops was a somewhat odd ductwork arrangement that began at each side of the radiator, ran back through the engine compartment and down around each front wheelwell, and then made its way inside the lower rocker panels. At the trailing end of each rocker was a short, fiberglass deflector duct that directed the airflow inboard toward the scoops on each vented backing plate.

The Posi rear was mandatory with RPO 684, which itself was only available with the 270- and 283-horse engines. Only 51 Corvettes were fitted with this Sebring-inspired performance package in 1957.

1957 SS™ racer
In Zora Duntov's mind, beating the world's best sports cars at their own game represented the quickest way toward a long and prosperous

Specifications	1957 SS

Construction	magnesium roadster body on tubular space frame
Wheelbase	92 inches
Length	168 inches
Height	48.7 inches
Weight	1,850 pounds
Tread	51.5 inches, front and rear
Tires	6.50x15 inches front, 7.60x15 inches rear, Firestone Super Sports
Brakes	12-inch Chrysler center-plane drums, finned for cooling (rears mounted inboard on Halibrand differential housing)
Wheels	15x5 inches, Halibrand cast-magnesium knock-offs
Front suspension	independent short and long wishbones, coil-over shock absorbers, and stabilizer bar
Rear suspension	de Dion axle with coil-over shock absorbers
Steering	Saginaw recirculating ball, 12:1 ratio
Engine	310-horsepower 283-ci V-8 with fuel injection, tubular headers, and sidepipes
Transmission	aluminum-case synchromesh four-speed manual (with 1.87:1 low)
Differential	Halibrand quick-change with aluminum housing (ratios ranged from 2.63:1 to 4.80:1)

Above
Zora Duntov's beautiful blue SS was hastily constructed during the winter of 1956–1957 to (it was hoped) put the Corvette on the international racing map. It ran once, at Sebring in March 1957, before the Automotive Manufacturers Association's ban on factory racing cut its career short. *Mike Mueller*

Bottom left
The SS cockpit was both purposeful and pretty, and on race day it gave all new meaning to the term hot seat. *Mike Mueller*

Bottom right
An aluminum-head injected 283 powered the SS. Among other weight-saving features was a magnesium oil pan. *Mike Mueller*

Right
A tubular space frame served as the SS Corvette's foundation. Notice the sintered metallic brakes already installed up front.

Below
The SS shell was fashioned from magnesium, which proved to hold in the heat both beneath the hood and behind the wheel. The design team also fabricated a transparent top, per prototype racing mandates.

future for the Corvette. "All commercially successful sports cars were promoted by participation in racing with specialized or modified cars," he explained in his 1953 address to the SAE. Plain and simple, Duntov wanted to take the Corvette to the track, both to prove its merits up against rivals from around the planet and to promote sales at home.

Chevrolet's first big shot at the world's racing elite—John Fitch's assault at Sebring in March 1956—may have supplied the firm with ample advertising fodder. But Fitch's modified production Corvette racers actually did little to convince Jaguar, Ferrari, Porsche, and the rest that America's only sports car had risen to world-class status. Everyone from Ed Cole on down recognized that they either needed to invest full force in an all-out competition Corvette, or stay home.

Enter Harley Earl. A few months after the dust settled at Sebring, Mr. Earl "borrowed" the

12-hour race's third-place finisher, a D-type Jaguar. Earl's Jag went into a GM Styling studio in June 1956 with the plan to fit it with a Chevy V-8 and take it racing as an experimental Corvette. Duntov, of course, would have nothing of such shenanigans. He immediately began work on a proposal for a purpose-built, all-American racing Corvette. Soon afterward, Cole rose from chief engineer to Chevrolet general manager, perhaps in part explaining how Duntov's project, labeled XP-64, was quickly approved in August.

So what about Earl's Jaguar? It was returned to its owner equally as quickly, which may have been part of the far-fetched plan all along. Perhaps the idea was to bluff Duntov and Cole into action. If so, the ploy worked.

Initial paperwork called for "a competition racing car with special frame, suspension, engine, drivetrain, and body." The plan involved building four such machines, one nonrunning mockup for

show duty and three functional racers intended for a March 1957 debut at Sebring, then on to Le Mans. But that schedule allowed barely six months to design, build, and test the XP-64 Corvette. Such heavy deadline pressure quickly convinced all involved that four cars were out of the question. Final approval of the project involved only one race car, dubbed the "Corvette SS."

The SS was a Corvette in name alone, save for its familiar toothy grille—wearing two more teeth than its stock counterpart—and contrasting bodyside cove panels. Beneath its slippery, hand-formed magnesium skin was a low-slung tubular space frame, featuring 1-inch chrome-moly tubing. Total weight for the SS frame was only 180 pounds.

Chevrolet people tried in vain to cure the SS racer's various maladies on race day at Sebring. One of these fixes included cutting body panel portions away to help cool things down inside.

Along with the magnesium SS, a fiberglass-bodied mule was built in 1957. This car's chassis later became the foundation for Bill Mitchell's Stingray.

Additional pounds were shed thanks to the liberal use of aluminum throughout, including the four-speed gearbox, bell housing, water pump, radiator, and cylinder heads. The engine's special oil pan and the five Halibrand knock-off wheels (a spare was included per international racing rules) were made of magnesium, yet another weight-saving consideration. All told, the Corvette SS tipped the scales at 1,850 pounds, about 100 less than the dominating D-type Jaguars.

Suspension was by coil-over shocks at all four corners. A typical short-arm/long-arm (SLA) design went up front, and a not-so-typical de Dion axle was added in back. Located by four trailing links, the curved de Dion axle wound its way from wheel hub carrier to wheel hub carrier behind a frame-mounted Halibrand quick-change differential housing.

Sending torque to that differential was a modified 283 fuelie V-8. Compression inside this race-ready small block was kept at 9:1 to ensure the powerplant would hang in there for 12 hours at Sebring. The lightweight aluminum heads were treated to some port reworking, and tuned headers were installed to speed spent gases on their way. Output estimates ran from 300 to 310 horsepower.

SS brakes were big, burly 12-inch drums (with cerametallix linings) at all four wheels. Rear drums were mounted inboard on the Halibrand quick-change housing to reduce unsprung weight. Completing the package was an innovative vacuum-controlled booster system that kept the rear brakes from locking up during hard deceleration.

The Corvette SS truly was a state-of-the-art racer, at least in American terms. But with only six months between its birth and its Sebring debut in March 1957, there was little chance to iron out bugs. Fortunately, Duntov did manage to also cobble together an SS "mule," a crude fiberglass-bodied running mate to his blue magnesium baby. Despite weighing about 150 pounds more (thanks to that fiberglass shell) than the SS, and armed with a few less horses, the white mule nonetheless impressed

Although crude compared to its blue running mate, the plastic-bodied mule didn't cook its driver. And it impressed many witnesses with its power and speed during Sebring practices sessions. Here, the mule undergoes testing in wintry Michigan.

witnesses at Sebring with its performance during early test sessions.

But the star of the show simply was not ready for the race. It literally didn't arrive in Florida until the last minute and by then didn't have a driver. Juan Fangio was the original choice, with Stirling Moss considered as a co-driver. But Moss was already taken and Fangio was released from his Chevrolet commitment once it became clear the SS wouldn't arrive in time for proper testing.

The job was then given to John Fitch, who in turn suggested that Chevrolet call veteran Italian driver Piero Taruffi to serve as co-driver. What both Taruffi and Fitch discovered during their all-too-short practice time was that the SS was an entirely different animal compared to the mule. First off, the mule's fiberglass body helped insulate the driver from heat, while the magnesium SS shell served as a heat conductor. It didn't take long on the track for the SS to cook its rider. Rising cockpit temperatures, coupled with failing brakes and a loose rear suspension, brought the Corvette

SS's debut at Sebring to a quick end after only about 20 laps.

Though it looked like a disaster, Duntov and the rest saw this as just a beginning—a hastily concocted one at that. Plans existed for additional testing and reworking, leading up to a resounding return to the track at Le Mans later that summer. But such hopes were dashed after the Automobile Manufacturers Association (AMA) issued its factory racing "ban" in June. We can only wonder about true potential, especially after the SS hit 183 miles per hour at GM's Phoenix test track in December 1958.

The SS never did experience the racing glory Duntov originally envisioned. In 1967, he donated the blue racer to the Indianapolis Motor Speedway Hall of Fame museum, where it was refurbished in 1987. In August 1994, the SS temporarily left its home for Kentucky to help mark the National Corvette Museum's opening. While in Bowling Green, it took its honored place up front in the museum's lobby, representing the first in a long line of Corvette factory racers.

1958

Revised styling made headlines in 1958, at least up front. In keeping with a corporate-wide design trend, the 1958 Corvette sported new quad headlights, and these were joined by enlarged bumpers at each front corner and backed by large aircraft-style air intakes. Purely ornamental in standard form, those openings were put to work sucking in cooling breezes whenever the race-ready heavy-duty brake/suspension equipment (RPO 685) was ordered. Eagle eyes also might have noticed a less-toothy grille with 9 vertical chrome pieces in place of the 13 seen in 1957.

Additional artistic updates for 1958 included 18 simulated louvers on the hood, two parallel chrome bands on the trunk lid, long chrome trim atop each front fender, and nonfunctional vents added to the leading sections of each bodyside cove panel. All these additions overnight transformed the beautiful, understated body of 1956–1957 into a package that *Road & Track* critics called "too fussy." "That supposedly hard-to-sell commodity, elegant simplicity, is gone," added the *R&T* guys concerning the 1958 makeover.

Apparently, Chevrolet stylists too concluded that the 1958 Corvette was a bit overdressed.

Quad headlights burst onto the GM Styling scene across the board in 1958. And along with an extra pair of headlights, the 1958 Corvette was adorned with simulated hood louvers. Also notice the new grille, with 9 teeth instead of the 13 seen in 1956 and 1957. *Mike Mueller*

1958

Specifications	1958
Model availability	convertible with optional removable hardtop
Wheelbase	102 inches
Length	177.2 inches
Width	72.8 inches
Height	51.09 inches (top up); 51 inches (with removable hardtop)
Shipping weight	2,781 pounds
Tread (front/rear, in inches)	57/59
Tires	6.70x15 four-ply
Brakes	11-inch drums
Wheels	5Kx15
Fuel tank	16.4 gallons
Front suspension	independent short and long wishbones, coil springs, and stabilizer bar
Rear suspension	solid axle with longitudinal leaf springs; tubular shock absorbers
Steering	Saginaw recirculating ball (16.0:1 ratio; 16.3:1 adapter available option)
Standard drivetrain	230-horsepower 283-ci V-8, three-speed manual transmission, 3.70:1 axle ratio (3.55:1 ratio standard behind optional Powerglide automatic)
Optional engine	245-horsepower 283-ci V-8, dual four-barrel carburetors, hydraulic lifters
Optional engine	250-horsepower 283-ci V-8, fuel injection, hydraulic lifters
Optional engine	270-horsepower 283-ci V-8, dual four-barrel carburetors, solid lifters
Optional engine	290-horsepower 283-ci V-8, fuel injection, solid lifters
Optional transmission	Powerglide automatic (not available behind solid-lifter V-8s)
Optional transmission	four-speed manual
Optional gear ratios	4.11:1, 4.56:1, both with Posi-Traction (Posi differential also available for 3.70:1 axle)

Corvette production jumped again in 1958, this time to 9,168. Base price was $3,591.

Although the chrome fender trim and fake cove vents stuck around to the solid-axle era's end, the hood louvers and deck lid chrome were quickly deleted, after appearing for one year only.

Cockpit impressions were new for 1958, as the basic dashboard used since 1953 was finally updated, this after critics had annually complained of the original Corvette's poor instrument layout. All instruments were now located directly in front of the driver in a modern-looking pod layout. An enlarged speedometer (calibrated up from 140 miles per hour to 160) was added, as was a 6,000-rpm tachometer in place of 1957's 7,000-rpm unit. An 8,000-rpm tach replaced the standard piece whenever the optional solid-lifter engine was ordered, and reading either rev-counter was made easier by moving it from down low in the center of the dash to atop the steering column.

Two chrome bands were added to the deck lid in 1958 and then were quickly deleted the following year.

Above
Standard output went up to 230 horsepower in 1958. Painted valve covers were used on the base 283 V-8. *Mike Mueller*

Top left
A 1958 Corvette body drops onto its frame on the St. Louis assembly line. The restyled nose added about 9 inches to the car's overall length.

Left
A totally new dashboard appeared for 1958, and that time around the tachometer was located where it belonged—directly in front of the driver. Factory-installed seatbelts were another first; they had been dealer-installed features previously. *Mike Mueller*

Left
Two optional dual-carb V-8s were again offered in 1958 at 245 and 270 horsepower (shown here). Notice the new single air cleaner in place of the two small units previously used. *Mike Mueller*

Bottom Left
William L. Mitchell took over at GM Styling in December 1958 after Harley Earl's retirement. Mitchell's babies would include the 1963 Sting Ray and Buick's Riviera.

Bottom right
The fake louvers on the 1958 Corvette's hood were deleted in 1959. Production leveled off that year at 9,670.

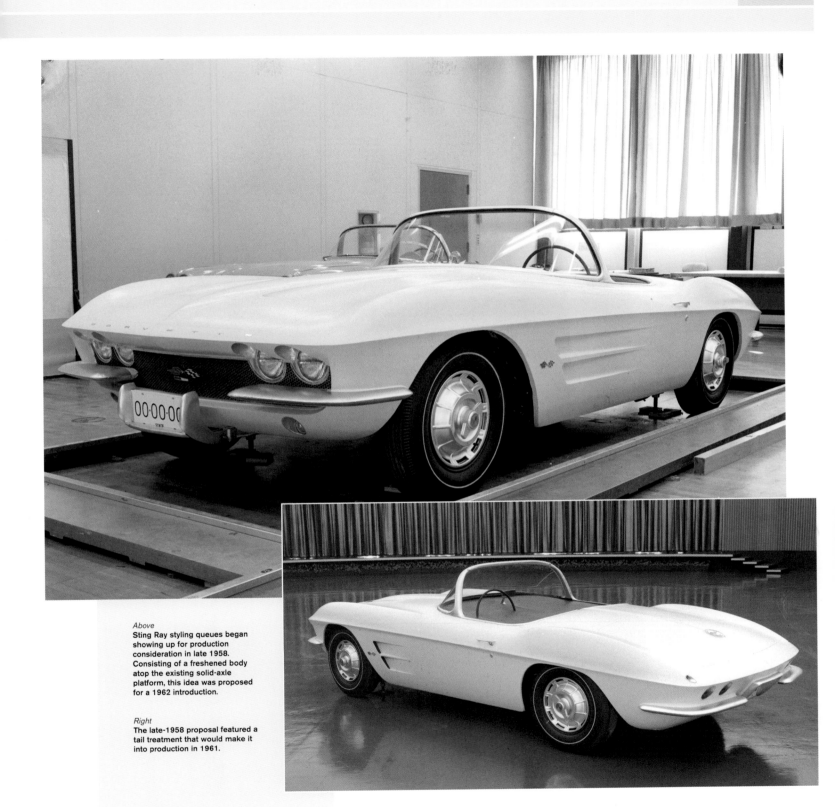

Above
Sting Ray styling queues began showing up for production consideration in late 1958. Consisting of a freshened body atop the existing solid-axle platform, this idea was proposed for a 1962 introduction.

Right
The late-1958 proposal featured a tail treatment that would make it into production in 1961.

Standard output for 1958 rose to 230 horsepower, up 10 ponies from 1957. Top optional power increased as the hottest Ramjet-injected 283 V-8 was now rated at 290 horses. Another change beneath the hood involved relocating the generator from the driver's side to the passenger's to help increase the fan belt's grip on the water pump pulley.

Corvette production rose dramatically after 1955: 3,467 in 1956, 6,339 in 1957, and 9,168 in 1958.

Above
Wheel covers continued unchanged from 1956 to 1962 save for one aspect: 10 brake-cooling slots were added in 1959.
Mike Mueller

Right
Men work in St. Louis' paint booth in 1958.

1959

1959

Specifications	1959
Model availability	convertible with optional removable hardtop
Wheelbase	102 inches
Length	177.2 inches
Width	72.8 inches
Height	51.09 inches (top up); 51 inches (with removable hardtop)
Shipping weight	2,729 pounds (standard drivetrain)
Tread (front/rear, in inches)	57/59
Tires	6.70x15 four-ply
Brakes	11-inch drums
Wheels	5Kx15
Fuel tank	16.4 gallons
Front suspension	independent short and long wishbones, coil springs, and stabilizer bar
Rear suspension	solid axle with longitudinal leaf springs; tubular shock absorbers
Steering	Saginaw recirculating ball (16.0:1 ratio; 16.3:1 adapter available option)
Standard drivetrain	230-horsepower 283-ci V-8, three-speed manual transmission, 3.70:1 axle ratio (3.55:1 ratio standard behind optional Powerglide automatic)
Optional engine	245-horsepower 283-ci V-8, dual four-barrel carburetors, hydraulic lifters
Optional engine	250-horsepower 283-ci V-8, fuel injection, hydraulic lifters
Optional engine	270-horsepower 283-ci V-8, dual four-barrel carburetors, solid lifters
Optional engine	290-horsepower 283-ci V-8, fuel injection, solid lifters
Optional transmission	Powerglide automatic (not available behind solid-lifter V-8s)
Optional transmission	four-speed manual
Optional gear ratios	4.11:1, 4.56:1, both with Posi-Traction (Posi differential also available for 3.70:1 axle)

Above
Revised seats for the 1959 Corvette featured side-to-side pleats. Pleats ran nose to tail in 1958 and again in 1960.
Mike Mueller

Left
A reasonably roomy trunk was a solid-axle feature up through 1962. A deck lid didn't return to the Corvette lineup until 1998.

1959

Corvette production rose dramatically after 1955: 3,467 in 1956, 6,339 in 1957, and 9,168 in 1958. Though slowing slightly, that upward trend continued the following year as 9,670 cars left the St. Louis line. The original annual production goal mentioned late in 1953 was finally reached in 1960, when Chevrolet rolled out 10,261 'glass-bodied two-seaters.

Only minor changes were made inside and out for 1959, with the deletion of 1958's hood louvers and chrome deck lid bands representing the most notable change. Ten slots were added to

No one said Chevy people couldn't keep competition-conscious parts coming for supposedly independent racers who took their own Corvettes to the track.

the wheel covers (the same simulated knock-off pieces used from 1956 to 1962) to cool the brakes, and interior updates included reshaped, reupholstered seats, rearranged door panels, and revised instrument lenses (for improved legibility). A convenient storage bin was added to the dash beneath the passenger-side grab bar introduced in 1958, and a new T-handle shifter appeared for the optional four-speed. New as well with 1959's four-speed box was a safety-conscious reverse lockout mechanism.

Mechanical changes involved adding two radius rods in back to attach the live axle

more confidently. Shock absorber mounting points also were relocated to improve their damping effect.

New on the 1959 options list were high-speed 6.70x15 tires and a second heavy-duty brake package that simply added special sintered-metallic linings supplied by GM's Delco Moraine division. The metallic shoes didn't torture the drums' inner surfaces as severely as their ceramic-based counterparts, nor did they work as poorly when cold. From the beginning, the cerametallix brakes included in RPO 684 didn't become effective until warmed up.

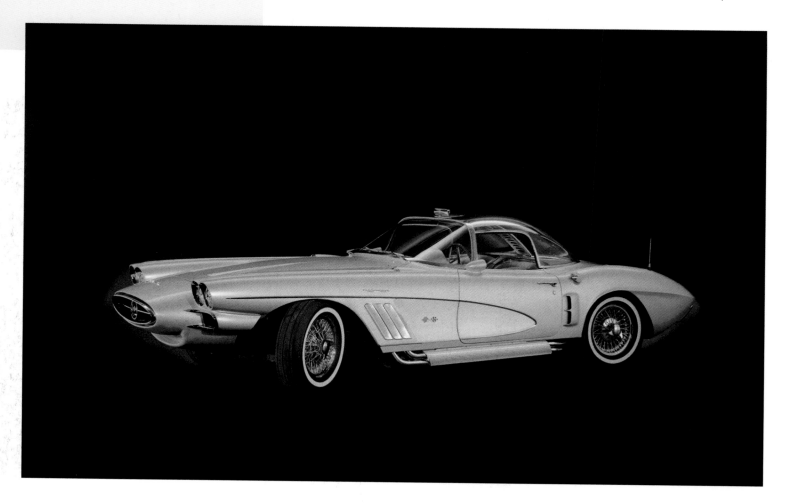

Opposite
The XP-700 appeared in the spring of 1959 with a truly wild nose and a double-bubble roof.

Above
While most of the XP-700 features represented pure flights of fancy, its tail treatment did foretell the upcoming 1961 restyle.

RPO 684's asking price dropped by nearly half in 1959, as all the brake-cooling ductwork used in 1957 and 1958 was deleted in favor of simpler vented backing plates at all four corners. Meanwhile, spring rates for the suspension half of the 684 package were increased to compensate for the extra weight the Corvette had gained in 1958 from its quad-headlight nose job.

Another new enhancement, limited-production option (LPO) 1625, was announced in March 1959. Included in this little-known deal was an oversized fuel tank that upped the fuel load from the stock 16.4 gallons to 24. Reportedly, Chevrolet had

installed as many as seven enlarged 21-gallon fuel tanks in 1957 Corvette racers, but these cars were meant only for the track. LPO 1625 made it possible for John Q. Public to enhance his Corvette's range in everyday use, although he obviously also could've used this extra travel time to run longer between pit stops on a race course if he so desired. Remember, Chevrolet wasn't supposed to be directly involved in racing, according to the AMA edict of 1957 barring such activities. But no one said Chevy people couldn't keep competition-conscious parts coming for supposedly independent racers who took their own Corvettes to the track.

Filling up more space than usual behind the '59 Corvette's bucket seats, the big-tank option required installation of RPO 419, the removable hardtop, because there was no room left to include the standard folding roof in its typical location. Another mandated modification involved the standard gas cap. The protruding tab supplied as a handle on this cap conflicted with the fuel filler door after the filler neck was extended to compensate for the larger tank. Making things fit was, in assembly-manual words, simply a matter of "removing [the] handle or bending it over to make it flat with [the] surface of [the] cap."

No one knows exactly how many big-tank solid-axle Corvettes were built, with estimates claiming less than 200 hit the streets between 1959 and 1962. For that latter year, the option code changed from LPO 1625 to RPO 488,

and it is known that 65 RPO 488 installations
were made.

The cap clearance problem was dealt with
differently beginning in 1961, when a lengthened
neck simply poked through a holed filler door that
was sealed to the body. A chrome cap topped
that filler neck, making it relatively easy to spot
a rare big-tank Corvette built in 1961 or 1962.
But very few exposed-cap cars are known, as
some owners cut down the neck and reinstalled
the working filler door.

1959 Stingray™ racer

Harley Earl, the Corvette's true father, stepped
down as head of GM Styling in December 1958.
In his place came William Mitchell, who, like his
mentor, loved his toys. He also loved racing, and in
1956 had, again like Earl, commissioned the
construction of an SR-2 competition Corvette for
his very own. Two years later, endowed with even
more executive privilege, Mitchell put his men to
work on yet another personalized hot rod, this one

Left
The Stingray tours the Elkhart Lake road course while on public display in 1962.

Below
GM exec Bill Mitchell loved his toys. And, yes, he did drive them. Here, he pilots his Stingray on the way to work.

based on the Corvette SS mule's chassis, left over after Chevrolet's overt racing projects were shut down by the AMA in June 1957.

During the winter of 1958–1959, Mitchell's right-hand man, Larry Shinoda, fashioned a new fiberglass shell for the SS mule that featured much of the Q-Corvette's shape and thus foretold the upcoming 1963 restyle. Foretelling the future as well was the name chosen for Mitchell's second personalized Corvette: "Stingray." Most mechanicals, at least early on, were SS carryovers, including the aluminum-head 283 fuelie V-8, which in this case was rated at about 280 horsepower. New for the Stingray was a prototype version of the aluminum Harrison radiator that would appear for the hottest Corvette V-8s in 1960.

Supposedly financed and campaigned solely by Mitchell himself, the gloriously red

Stingray first hit a track in anger at Maryland's Marlboro Raceway on April 18, 1959. The "Flying Dentist," Dr. Dick Thompson, drove the car that day to a fourth-place finish, a nice start in the minds of most witnesses, including the car owner's. Zora Duntov, however, wasn't at all happy about Mitchell's revival of his dream machine and never acknowledged the car in any way. He had envisioned his SS as a world-class champion, not an American road race special.

Road racing across the United States nonetheless proved to be Mitchell's plan, as was winning an SCCA championship. But his Stingray was at first too heavy to compete effectively, and those problem-plagued SS brakes also hindered progress. The original cerametallix stoppers were exchanged for sintered-metallic linings during the summer of 1959, and a lighter body (painted

metallic silver) was fabricated by November, bringing overall weight down by about 75 pounds. Stiffer springs were added in preparation of the 1960 racing season.

A third-place finish at Marlboro in April 1960 was just the beginning for Dick Thompson and Mitchell's Stingray. By year's end, Thompson had won the SCCA C-Modified division with 48 points—30 more than the runner-up.

The Stingray became a show car the following year, appearing at Chicago's McCormick Place in February 1961. Soon, Mitchell was driving it to work, and later improvements included the addition of disc brakes and the substitution of a Weber-carbureted 427-cubic-inch big-block V-8. Red paint temporarily returned before Mitchell opted to bring back the silver metallic paint, in honor of the Stingray's best days as an SCCA racing champion.

1960

01

1960

Specifications	1960
Model availability	convertible, with optional removable hardtop
Wheelbase	102 inches
Length	177.2 inches
Width	72.8 inches
Height	51.09 inches (top up); 51 inches (with removable hardtop)
Shipping weight	2,890 pounds (standard drivetrain)
Tread (front/rear, in inches)	57/59
Tires	6.70x15 four-ply
Brakes	11-inch drums
Wheels	5Kx15
Fuel tank	16.4 gallons
Front suspension	independent short and long wishbones, coil springs, and stabilizer bar
Rear suspension	solid axle with longitudinal leaf springs; tubular shock absorbers
Steering	Saginaw recirculating ball (16.0:1 ratio; 16.3:1 adapter option available)
Standard drivetrain	230-horsepower 283-ci V-8, three-speed manual transmission, 3.70:1 axle ratio (3.55:1 ratio standard behind optional Powerglide automatic)
Optional engine	245-horsepower 283-ci V-8, dual four-barrel carburetors, hydraulic lifters
Optional engine	250-horsepower 283-ci V-8, fuel injection, hydraulic lifters
Optional engine	270-horsepower 283-ci V-8, dual four-barrel carburetors, solid lifters
Optional engine	290-horsepower 283-ci V-8, fuel injection, solid lifters
Note	fuel-injected V-8s were initially advertised with aluminum heads, rated at 275 and 315 horsepower; carryover iron heads actually used and 1959's ratings remained
Optional transmission	Powerglide automatic (not available behind solid-lifter V-8s)
Optional transmission	four-speed manual
Optional gear ratios	4.11:1, 4.56:1, both with Posi-Traction (Posi differential also available for 3.70:1 axle)

Telling the 1960 apart from the 1959 was best done by looking inside, where pleats in the seats switched from horizontal to vertical.

The toothy grille used since the beginning last appeared on the 1960 Corvette. Corvette production surpassed 10,000 for the first time that year.

1960

"We predict that this will be the year of the big changes for the Corvette," claimed a report in the January 1959 issue of *Road & Track*. "The changes to the car in the last six model years are not so great as we think will come about in 1960." But John Bond and the rest of the *R&T* staff were left wearing a bit of egg on their faces when the 1960 Corvette appeared looking almost identical to its 1959 forerunner. Telling the two apart was

best done by looking inside, where pleats in the seats switched from horizontal to vertical.

Prime inspiration for *Road & Track*'s January 1959 forecast had come from the Q-Corvette project, kicked off late in 1957. Apparently, this proposal indeed was considered as a production possibility for 1960, and would have made some radical changes that year. Early mockups featured an innovative driveline incorporating an aluminum V-8 sending torque

to a transaxle located at the rear wheels. Such flights of fancy did foretell the future, just not the near future. An all-aluminum V-8 first found its way between fiberglass fenders in 1969, while relocating the transmission to the rear happened nearly 30 years later as part of the C5 redesign.

One Q-code experiment nearly did make its way into production for 1960. Initially, both fuel-injected 283 V-8s offered that year, RPOs 579

The 1960 Corvette also was the last to feature the curvaceous tail introduced in 1956. *Mike Mueller*

(with hydraulic lifters) and 579D (with solid lifters), featured weight-saving cylinder heads with revised combustion chambers and larger intake valves. Cast from aluminum, these hot heads helped delete 53 unwanted pounds. And, combined with an enlarged injection plenum and more compression (11:1 instead of 10.5:1), they also boosted RPO 579D output from 290 horsepower to 315. Retaining 1959's compression ratio (9.5:1), the aluminum-head hydraulic-cam 283 was uprated from 250 horses to 275.

These bigger numbers, however, appeared only on paper, as casting irregularities shelved the aluminum heads before they made it into production. Duntov's engineers were forced to fall back on the same 250- and 290-horse injected 283s used in 1959. Both fuelie V-8s were limited to four-speed installations in 1960, as the Powerglide automatic was no longer available with RPO 579, as it had been previously.

Despite the cylinder head setback, other aluminum pieces showed up elsewhere on the 1960 Corvette. A new aluminum bell housing cut off 18 pounds in four-speed applications, while a little more weight melted away from sold-lifter V-8s thanks to the addition of an aluminum Harrison radiator. Hydraulic-cam Corvette V-8s used conventional copper-core radiators in 1960.

Additional mechanical upgrades appeared underneath. Introducing a rear stabilizer bar and thickening its counterpart in front meant stiffened springs were no longer needed. In turn, the heavy-duty brake/suspension package (RPO 684) failed to return for 1960. In its place was RPO 687, which included stiffer shocks, a quick-steering adapter, and finned brake drums with vented backing plates and cooling scoops, called "elephant ears." Gone were the gnarly cerametallix brake linings, replaced in the new 687 deal by the sintered-metallic shoes used in the RPO 686 package. Also included in RPO 687 were 24-blade cooling fans mounted inside each brake drum.

CERV I

With his ill-fated SS racer relegated to the history books and the highly advanced Q-Corvette project

An open-wheel machine that looked every bit like an Indy-style racer, Duntov's CERV I made its public debut at Riverside, California, in November 1960.

The large aircraft-style openings below the headlights were purely ornamental in most cases. They became functional in 1958, when the heavy-duty brakes and suspension package (RPO 684) was ordered, serving as intakes for the rear-brake cooling duct work. However, all that ducting was deleted early in 1959. A 1960 Corvette nose is shown here. *Mike Mueller*

derailed, Zora Duntov refocused his innovative efforts as the 1960s dawned on his Chevrolet Experimental Research Vehicle, or "CERV I," a name that only came about after a second CERV testbed appeared in 1963. An open-wheel machine that looked every bit like an Indy-style racer, Duntov's CERV I made its public debut at Riverside, California, in November 1960. Notably not in the business of building race cars, at least not officially, Chevrolet was quick to diplomatically describe CERV I as "a research tool for Chevrolet's continuous investigations into automotive ride and handling phenomena under the most realistic conditions."

Innovative CERV I features included an aluminum V-8 mounted directly behind the driver,

a tubular space frame, a specially constructed lightweight fiberglass body, and independent rear suspension (IRS) with inboard aluminum brake drums. The work of Duntov and his senior engineers, Harold Krieger and Walt Zeyte, this relatively simple IRS design featured a three-link arrangement that used the U-jointed half shafts as upper locating members. Typical chrome-moly tubes handled lower linking duties, while a boxed-steel combination hub carrier/radius arm on each side supplied the all-important horizontal third link, which transferred forward thrust to the frame.

IRS advantages include the obvious ability of both wheels to respond separately to changing road conditions. Depending on the design, an IRS setup also can be adjusted for negative camber,

meaning the tires lean in slightly on top. Negative camber translates into better adhesion for the outside tire during hard cornering, since more of the tread remains planted as the car rolls away from the turn. Standard solid-axle suspensions tend to lift the tread's footprint off the road during hard turns, as the outside rear tire is forced to lean out. IRS designs also considerably reduce unsprung weight, since a heavy axle housing is no longer around to tax the springs.

Too much unsprung weight (mass not supported by the springs: tires, wheels, brake components, axle housing, etc.) relative to the amount of sprung weight (body, frame, engine and transmission, passengers, fuel, luggage) translates into severe vertical wheel motion under harsh driving conditions. Simply put, sprung weight must be substantial enough to dampen its unsprung counterpart's natural tendency to react proportionally to bumps, shocks, and body roll. Reducing unsprung weight not only helps handling, it also greatly improves general ride quality.

Duntov hoped to transfer both the CERV I's IRS and its midengine layout into the Corvette equation sometime in the future, but only the former feature carried over, this as part of the Sting Ray redesign for 1963. As for the CERV I itself, it did its research thing quietly for a few years, then went through various collectors' hands like so many other unforgettable pieces of Corvette history.

Right
Shown here is Zora
Duntov with his
CERV I prototype.
That the CERV I
looked like a racer
was no coincidence.
Plans to put it on
the track were
considered, but
the machine never
served anything
other than testing
purposes. It, too,
was designed by
Larry Shinoda.

Below
The CERV I debuted
at Riverside in
November 1960.
Its most notable
contribution to the
Corvette bloodline
involved development
of the independent
rear suspension that
appeared beneath the
1963 Sting Ray.

1961

Specifications	1961
Model availability	convertible, with optional removable hardtop
Wheelbase	102 inches
Length	177.7 inches
Width	70.4 inches
Height	51.6 inches (top up); 51.5 inches (with removable hardtop)
Shipping weight	2,905 pounds (standard drivetrain)
Tread (front/rear, in inches)	57/59
Tires	6.70x15 four-ply
Brakes	11-inch drums
Wheels	5Kx15
Fuel tank	16.4 gallons
Front suspension i	ndependent short and long wishbones, coil springs, and stabilizer bar
Rear suspension	solid axle with longitudinal leaf springs; tubular shock absorbers
Steering	Saginaw recirculating ball (16.0:1 ratio; 16.3:1 adapter available option)
Standard drivetrain	230-horsepower 283-ci V-8, three-speed manual transmission, 3.36:1 axle ratio (3.70:1 standard behind optional four-speed manual, 3.55:1 ratio standard behind optional Powerglide automatic)
Optional engine	245-horsepower 283-ci V-8, dual four-barrel carburetors, hydraulic lifters
Optional engine	275-horsepower 283-ci V-8, fuel injection, hydraulic lifters
Optional engine	270-horsepower 283-ci V-8, dual four-barrel carburetors, solid lifters
Optional engine	315-horsepower 283-ci V-8, fuel injection, solid lifters
Optional transmission	Powerglide automatic (available with base V-8 and 245-horsepower 283)
Optional transmission	four-speed manual (available with all V-8s)
Optional gear ratios	4.11:1, 4.56:1

The tail design first proposed on the Q-Corvette was morphed into reality for 1961. Notice the Bugatti roadster posing with this 1961 Corvette.

1961

Road & Track wasn't the only source to predict an all-new Corvette for 1960, and many of these incorrect forecasts were inspired by the XP-700, another executive toy fashioned for Bill Mitchell, this one coming early in 1959. Many members of the press figured the XP-700 dream machine represented a styling practice for the new body that was supposedly arriving the next year. Though they were wrong, they weren't 100 percent wrong.

Like Dave McLellan's engineers later on in the 1980s, Bill Mitchell's styling crew let Corvette buyers take a peek into the crystal ball in 1961. Mitchell's men simply grafted the XP-700's rear bodywork onto the existing Corvette shell. From the front, the '61 Corvette carried the same quad

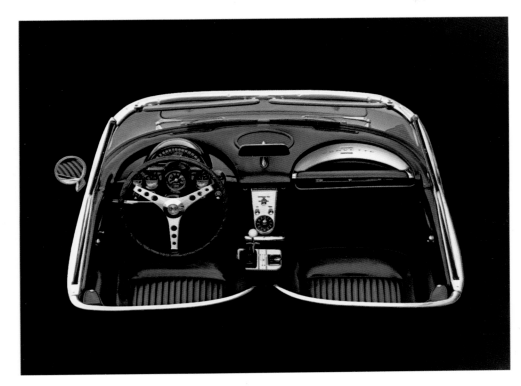

According to
Sports Car Illustrated,
the new exhausts
"rumble with a truly
musical motorboat
tone and beat a
tattoo on the sides
of the cars you pass."

Left
While the interior's basic layout carried over from
1960, the 1961 Corvette cockpit did feature extra
leg room thanks to a revised floorpan that
incorporated a narrowed transmission tunnel.

headlights, complemented with new painted
bezels instead of chromed units. But in back,
those familiar curves were traded for a crisper,
uplifted tail fitted with two pairs of small, round
taillights, a look that would carry over through
1962 and into the Sting Ray era.

That "boat-tail" rear not only appeared more
modern, it also backed up its warmed-over form
with a well-received functional upgrade—trunk
space was increased without even a smidgen
being tacked on to the existing solid-axle
platform's 177.2-inch length. Additional changes
in back involved rerouting the dual exhausts,
which now dumped out just behind the rear tires.
According to *Sports Car Illustrated*, the new
exhausts "rumble with a truly musical motorboat
tone and beat a tattoo on the sides of the cars
you pass." New up front was a toothless grille
featuring an anodized rectangular mesh.

More optional power appeared in 1961, as
the aluminum heads tried the previous year were
recast in iron, leading to the belated introduction
of the 275- and 315-horsepower fuel-injected
V-8s. Revised option codes also were introduced:
RPO 353 for the former, RPO 354 for the latter.
While the hydraulic-cam, dual-carb 245-horse 283
carried over into 1961 still wearing the RPO 469
tag used the previous year, its solid-lifter 270-
horse running mate was retagged RPO 468.

More weight-saving metal surfaced in 1961,
as the optional four-speed (RPO 685) was
treated to an aluminum case and an aluminum
radiator became standard with all engines.
Included with the latter equipment was a remote
surge tank (in place of the integral header tank
used in 1960) that looked like a mini beer keg.
Not all 1961 Corvettes had this remote tank,
however, as leftover supplies of 1960's header-
tank radiators had to be exhausted first.

A revised grille sans teeth set the
1961 Corvette apart from its 1960
predecessor. Body-colored headlight
bezels also appeared this year.

Like Dave McLellan's
engineers later on in the 1980s,
Bill Mitchell's styling crew
let Corvette buyers take
a peek into the crystal ball in 1961.

Below
Various one-hit wonder finishes were offered over the years.
Jewel Blue was seen only in 1961. Note the exhaust exiting
behind the rear wheel—a new feature for 1961. *Mike Mueller*

Mako Shark I

Bill Mitchell just couldn't collect enough toys. After having his Stingray racer built in 1959, he followed it up with yet another personal ride, the Shark, or XP-755, in 1961. Built atop a mildly modified 1961 Corvette frame, the Shark was viewed by some at the time as a precursor to the all-new Corvette then being readied for its 1963 debut. Indeed, like Mitchell's other personal customizations, it did foretell many of the upcoming Sting Ray's lines and curves. But what most witnesses didn't know was that the Sting Ray's form had already been finalized when Larry Shinoda drew up XP-755. In this case, the boss simply wanted to update his collection, and Shinoda complied.

Mitchell's request (make that demand) concerning XP-755's looks were explicit: he wanted it painted to match a mako shark he'd caught off Bimini, which he had mounted on his office wall—thus the "Shark" name. But reproducing that blue-fading-into-white shade proved quite difficult, so much so that the GM paint crew reportedly snuck in one night to respray the fish to match the car, fooling the main man in the process.

Snazzy side exhausts and either wire wheels or Halibrand mags complemented that finish. The curious double-bubble roof used atop the XP-700 Corvette in 1959 was applied, too, with some modifications. Power, meanwhile, came from a supercharged 327 small-block V-8 fed by four side-draft Weber carburetors.

The Shark was completed in only a few months, just in time to take a tour around the Road America track during the summer of 1961. It followed that up with auto show appearances in 1962, while also serving as Mitchell's occasional driver. More than one upgrade was made over the years, including a switch to big-block power, which the car still carries today.

Opposite, top
Mounting the optional big tank behind a 1961 Corvette's seat meant the removable hardtop had to be installed because there was no longer room for the standard folding roof. *Mike Mueller*

Opposite, bottom
The top engine option in 1961 was the 315-horsepower fuel-injected 283 V-8. *Mike Mueller*

Below
Like XP-700, XP-755 too showed off the boat-tail treatment that became a regular-production feature in 1961. The Shark is pictured in 1995 on display at the National Corvette Museum. *Mike Mueller*

Inset
Race-ready brakes were available in 1961 via RPO 687. The option included vented backing plates with elephant-ear ducts, finned drums with internal cooling fans, and sintered-metallic linings. The correct metallic linings appear here on the ground; the owner saves these valuable pieces from unwanted wear, using standard shoes while driving his big-brake Corvette. *Mike Mueller*

A name change occurred along the way, after another prototype was created in 1965 sporting a similar paint job. Predicting the third-generation Corvette that debuted for 1968, this Shinoda-drawn machine was at first called the Mako Shark. The official moniker became Mako Shark II after it was decided to retroactively rename XP-755 Mako Shark I.

Above
The Mako Shark I made various auto show appearances, as well as on-track demonstrations. Here, it runs around Road America in 1962.

Left
Created early in 1961, XP-755 was originally called "the Shark." It was later renamed Mako Shark I after the Mako Shark II appeared in 1965.

A totally blacked-out grille was new for 1962. Corvette production that year was 14,531.

1962

Specifications	1962
Model availability	convertible, with optional removable hardtop
Wheelbase	102 inches
Length	177.7 inches
Width	70.4 inches
Height	51.6 inches (top up); 51.5 inches (with removable hardtop)
Shipping weight	2,905 pounds (standard drivetrain)
Tread (front/rear, in inches)	57/59
Tires	6.70x15 four-ply
Brakes	11-inch drums
Wheels	5Kx15
Fuel tank	16.4 gallons
Front suspension	independent short and long wishbones, coil springs, and stabilizer bar
Rear suspension	solid axle with longitudinal leaf springs; tubular shock absorbers
Steering	Saginaw recirculating ball (16.0:1 ratio; 16.3:1 adapter available option)
Standard drivetrain	250-horsepower 327-ci V-8, three-speed manual transmission, 3.36:1 axle ratio
Optional engine	300-horsepower 327-ci V-8, four-barrel carburetor, hydraulic lifters
Optional engine	340-horsepower 327-ci V-8, four-barrel carburetor, solid lifters
Optional engine	360-horsepower 327-ci V-8, fuel injection, solid lifters
Optional transmission	Powerglide automatic (available with base V-8 and 300-horsepower 327)
Optional transmission	four-speed manual (2.54:1 low with base V-8 and 300-horsepower 327; 2.20:1 low with 340-horsepower and 360-horsepower V-8s)
Optional gear ratios	3.08:1, 3.55:1, 3.70:1, 4.11:1, 4.56:1

1962

At $4,038, the 1962 base price was the Corvette's first to bash the four-grand barrier. But in exchange for all that dough, a customer got what ads called the "finest, fiercest yet."

Although exterior refinements were few, they still stood out. A tasteful blacked-out grille led the way up front, and another consolation to simplicity involved the deletion of the chrome trim around the traditional bodyside coves, which in turn meant that two-tone paint was no longer possible. Completing 1962's trim package were revised grilles for the cove panels' simulated vents and new rocker panel

Above
Rocker moldings were added in 1962, while cove panel trim was deleted, meaning two-tone paint schemes were no longer possible.

Left
The year 1962 marked the last time a Corvette body was dropped onto a solid-axle chassis.

moldings. A few updated emblems, restyled door panels, and slightly revised seat upholstery, and there you had it, the 1962 Corvette.

Major changes came beneath the hood, beginning with a bigger small block, a bored and stroked 283 that now displaced 327 cubic inches. Dual carburetors were dropped after 1961, leaving three four-barrel 327s and the top-dog fuelie V-8 as the only power choices.

The '62 Corvette's base 327 used a more potent hydraulic cam, 10.5:1 compression, and small-valve (1.72-inch intakes) cylinder heads to make 20 more horses than its 283 forerunner. Adding a larger Carter four-barrel and big-valve (1.94-inch intakes) heads resulted in the 300-horsepower 327, RPO 583. The most potent 327s both relied on the solid-lifter Duntov cam, big-valve heads, and 11.25:1 compression. The Carter-fed version, RPO 396, was rated at 340 horsepower, while its injected counterpart, RPO 582, produced 360 horses, all ready, willing, and able, in advertisement's words, to "please the wildest wind-in-the-face sports car type."

The Carter-fed version produced 360 horses, all ready, willing, and able, in advertisement's words, to "please the wildest wind-in-the-face sports car type."

Left
A 1962 Corvette undergoes final inspection before leaving the St. Louis assembly line.

Bottom left
Heaters became standard Corvette equipment for the first time in 1962 but could have been deleted for racing applications by way of RPO 610.

Bottom right
The small-block Chevy V-8 grew again in 1962, this time to 327 cubic inches. The 1962 Corvette's standard engine was this 250-horsepower 327. *Mike Mueller*

Additional drivetrain upgrades for 1962 included a new weight-conscious aluminum case for the optional Powerglide automatic transmission, RPO 313, which was available only behind the two hydraulic-cam 327s. A three-speed manual was standard issue, and this tame little gearbox again lost ground in the popularity race with its optional counterparts. By the time the tire smoke cleared in 1962, sales of four-speed Corvette models had soared to 11,318, representing 78 percent of the total run. Two different T-10 four-speeds, both listed under RPO 685, were offered in 1962, another first. The existing close-ratio box was available behind the two solid-lifter 327s, while a new wide-ratio four-speed was optional for the two hydraulic-cam V-8s.

Other optional firsts for 1962 included off-road straight-through mufflers (RPO 441), positive crankcase ventilation (RPO 242, mandatory on '62 Corvettes delivered in California), and narrow whitewall tires (RPO 1832) that replaced the antiquated wide whites used up through 1961.

From building only 300 Corvettes in 1953, Chevrolet managed to up the production ante to 14,531 by 1962, the last year for the venerable solid-axle models, and the last year for a Corvette trunk until the C5 convertible debuted in 1998. But nary a tear was shed as the car's first generation came to a close; far better things waited in the wings.

Above
Output for the fuel-injected 327 soared to 360 horsepower in 1962. *Mike Mueller*

Left
Dual carburetors became a thing of the past beneath Corvette hoods in 1962. Optional engines included two single-carb 327s and the top-shelf fuel-injected V-8. Shown here is the 340-horse 327 (RPO 396). *Mike Mueller*

Right
Solid-axle Corvettes dominated SCCA road racing in America during the late 1950s and early 1960s.

Nary a tear was shed as the car's first generation came to a close; far better things waited in the wings.

02

Above
Topless Corvette models remained popular in 1964, outnumbering the coupe counterparts 13,925 to 8,304.

Middle
The Sting Ray grille was revised in 1965 with blacked-out horizontal bars surrounded by bright trim. The entire grille had been chromed in 1963 and 1964.

Right
Two midengine GS-II prototype racers were built in 1964, one with a steel chassis, the other with an alloy foundation.

Enter the Sting Ray

C2
1963–1967

→ First enclosed coupe body style and hideaway headlights (1963)
→ Independent rear suspension (IRS) introduced (1963)
→ Wheelbase cut to 98 inches (1963)
→ Optional air conditioning introduced (1963)
→ Split-window styling appears for one year only (1963)
→ New RPO code system introduced (1963)
→ Last fuel-injected V-8 until 1982 (1965)
→ Four-wheel disc brakes become standard (1965)
→ First big-block V-8 (1965)
→ Optional teakwood steering wheel and telescopic steering column introduced (1965)
→ Big-block V-8 displacement goes from 396 cubic inches to 427 (1966)
→ Triple-carburetor induction introduced for 427 V-8 (1967)
→ Aluminum heads become an option (RPO L88) for 427 V-8 (1967)

For years sports car purists pooh-poohed the Corvette, claiming that it no way, no how belonged in the international sporting fraternity. In their humble opinion, the car always has been, among other things, too big, too heavy, too convenient . . . or, plain and simply, too American. But such stones have been thrown less and less often as Chevrolet's fantastic plastic plaything has matured over the years.

By the time the C5 model debuted for 1997, no one doubted the Corvette's proven place among the world's best sports cars, and for the price you simply couldn't do any better. Today's C6 is not only this planet's biggest bang for the buck, it's also able to run circles around performance machines costing many, many thousands more. If only Zora was still here to see it.

Duntov often found himself defending his baby against those slings and arrows during the solid-axle years, and, in many cases, detractors did have a case. While first-generation Corvette models unquestionably were the hottest things running on American streets during the 1950s, they never could quite get over the hump when compared to Europe's best, especially so on the international

racing stage. Under-hood affairs matched up well with all but the most exotic foreign sports cars; it was the chassis that needed some serious work.

Enter the Sting Ray—the new model that had Duntov beaming in the fall of 1962. "For the first time, I now have a Corvette I can be proud to drive in Europe," he said, while introducing Chevrolet's second-generation two-seater to the press. Beneath that beautiful body, penned by Larry Shinoda, was a radically revised foundation featuring innovative independent rear suspension (IRS), a layout first tested beneath the CERV I experimental vehicle in 1960.

Similar in layout to the CERV I design, save for springing, the 1963 Sting Ray's IRS relied on each U-jointed half shaft to play the part of an upper locating link running from the differential to the hubs. Typical control rods made up the lateral lower links, from differential to hub carriers, with the latter coming at the end of a pair of boxed-steel trailing arms that supplied the longitudinal third link to the frame on each side. Space constraints ruled out the CERV I's coil-over shock absorbers, forcing Duntov to use what he called an "anachronistic feature"—a transverse multi-leaf spring mounted below and behind the differential.

Clearly representing the only feature ever shared by a Model T Ford and a Corvette, this nine-leaf buggy spring may have appeared antiquated at a glance, but it did the job in lieu of the more expensive coil-over shocks.

Combined with improved suspension geometry up front, IRS helped transform the Sting Ray into a more complete sporting package. "This is a *modern* sports car," wrote *Motor Trend's* Roger Huntington. "In most ways, it's as advanced as the

latest dual-purpose sports/luxury cars from Europe. The new Corvette doesn't have to take a back seat to any of them, in looks, performance, handling, or ride."

Sting Ray roots date back to 1957, when Duntov's team began work on the "Q-Corvette," a radical departure initially proposed for regular production in 1960. Q-code features included an innovative rear-transaxle layout with independent suspension and inboard drum brakes. By

Left
Zora Arkus-Duntov and his beloved Sting Ray: "For the first time, I now have a Corvette I can be proud to drive in Europe."

Opposite, top
Stylist Robert McLean's first clay mockup of the Q-Corvette proposal was completed in November 1957.

Opposite, bottom
The Q-Corvette mockup versus the regular-production 1958 Corvette in December 1957.

"This is a *modern* sports car," wrote *Motor Trend*'s Roger Huntington.

relocating the transmission to the rear while keeping the engine up front, designers hoped to move closer to a preferred tail-heavy weight distribution, something all but impossible in a car carrying a big V-8 in its nose. Duntov's ideal design, of course, involved a supremely balanced midengine layout, but the Q-code proposal was as close as he could get to such a high-minded goal back in the 1950s.

Duntov planned a unit-body chassis on an extremely short 94-inch wheelbase (down 8 inches from the existing model) for the

Q-Corvette. Stylist Bob McLean then fashioned a coupe body standing only 46 inches tall. Slated for production in steel, McLean's startlingly sleek shell debuted full-scale in clay in November 1957. Slim and compact with pop-up headlights, a pointed fastback roofline, and stylish bulges atop each wheel opening, the body eventually would carry over into regular-production reality even though the Q-Corvette never made it past the mock-up stage. Chevrolet quickly gave up on the Q concept once retooling costs were determined to be too great.

Above
Designer Larry Shinoda went to work for GM late in 1956 and quickly became Bill Mitchell's favored son. Shinoda styled Mitchell's Stingray racer and then went to work on XP-720. He also was responsible for CERV I, CERV II, and both Mako Shark show cars. *Mike Mueller*

Right
Work on the XP-720 began late in 1959, with this clay caught on film in October that year. Larry Shinoda's touch is clear; XP-720 looked much like Bill Mitchell's Stingray racer with a roof.

Above
An XP-720 mockup poses in April 1960 with a standard 1960 Corvette.

Left
Much of the final Sting Ray shape was formed by the spring of 1960. This XP-720 clay was painted and trimmed out for executive review that April.

Above
Designers even considered a stretched, four-passenger proposal during the XP-720 styling exercise.

Left
A 1/4-scale Sting Ray model is readied for wind tunnel testing.

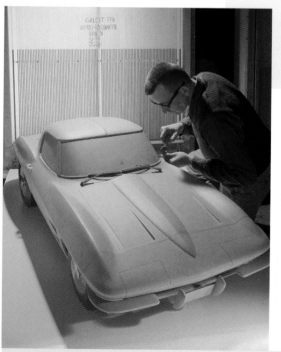

Though Duntov did have his dreams, he also recognized the budgetary realities that controlled his hand. The Q-Corvette was simply too big a step ahead; improving the car would have to happen in smaller doses, and to that end he wrote the following memo to engineer Harry Barr in December 1957:

"We can attempt to arrive at the general concept of [a new] car on the basis of our experience, and in relationship to the present Corvette. We would like to have better driver and passenger accommodation, better luggage space, better ride, better handling, and higher performance.

Superficially, it would seem that the comfort requirements indicate a larger car than the present Corvette. However, this is not so. With a new chassis concept and thoughtful body engineering and styling, the car may be bigger internally and somewhat smaller [externally] than the present Corvette. Consideration of cost spells the use of a large number of passenger car components, which indicates that the chassis cannot become so small that [those components] cannot be used."

While Duntov battled with bean counts, Bill Mitchell's stylists were hard at work fashioning the final shape for the next-generation Corvette to

> ## "For the first time, I now have a Corvette I can be proud to drive in Europe."
> *–Zora Arkus-Duntov*

come. Public previews showed up in the form of Mitchell's own Stringray racer, the 1958 XP-700, and the 1961 XP-755 Shark, all of which were created in the Q-Corvette's image. The actual working model for the 1963 Corvette form was XP-720, born in the fall of 1959 in a cramped basement area at GM Styling known as "Studio X," home to Mitchell's right-hand man, Larry Shinoda.

A concession to comfort, transforming the Corvette into a coupe also was key to the Sting Ray image. That tapered roof in back served as an extension for Bill Mitchell's stinger concept, a styling queue that began as a blade-shaped bulge on the hood dubbed "Mitchell's phallic symbol" by Shinoda. The bulge was followed by a sharp ridge running up over the roof, and that ridge continued

The St. Louis plant started rolling out Sting Rays in September 1962.

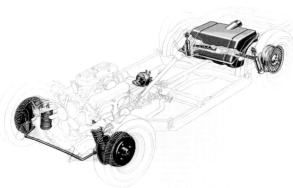

Left
Overall, the second-generation Corvette cut through the wind like no other American car, but it created way too much aerodynamic lift up front.

Above
Widely spaced perimeter frame rails allowed the Sting Ray's passenger compartment to ride low to the ground.

Left
Nicknamed "the birdcage," this welded-steel reinforcement allowed for the use of thinner fiberglass panels that remained strong.

Below
While the Sting Ray's front suspension remained of conventional design (with revised geometry), the rear of the car was supported independently.

on to the tail, creating the famed split-window theme in the process. Representing a clear case of function falling victim to form, the split rear window didn't work at all for Duntov, who questioned its negative impact on rear visibility. Mitchell, however, was adamant. "If you take that off, you might as well forget the whole thing," Mitchell said. The stinger stayed, but not for long. It was gone, to the delight of most drivers, when the 1964 Corvette debuted.

As for the package as a whole, it wowed witnesses, both in America and overseas, like no Corvette before. And the so-called midyear models stuck around for five years, one more than planned. Mitchell, Duntov, and crew originally had hoped to have a third-generation Corvette up and running for 1967, but technical difficulties delayed that introduction until 1968. Critics who still believe that the '67 Sting Ray represented one of the finest of the breed remain thankful.

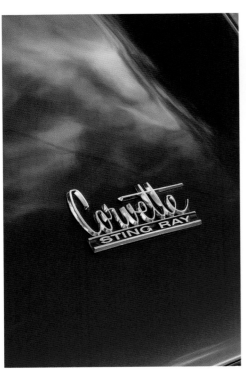

Clockwise, from left
The split-window theme appeared only once, for 1963, before it was replaced by one-piece rear glass in the best interests of maximizing rearward visibility. *Mike Mueller*

Telling the five second-generation Corvette models apart is a simple task if you know your fuel filler doors. Shown here is the 1963 style. *Mike Mueller*

Standard 1963 Sting Ray wheel covers featured simulated knock-off spinners. *Mike Mueller*

A new coupe body and a new name debuted for 1963. All midyear Corvettes, with or without a top, were Sting Rays. *Mike Mueller*

1963

1963

Specifications	1963
Model availability	coupe and convertible (optional removable hardtop)
Wheelbase	98 inches
Length	175.3 inches
Width	69.6 inches
Height	49.8 inches, in all cases
Tread (front/rear, in inches)	56.25/57
Tires	6.70x15 four-ply
Brakes	four-wheel drums
Fuel tank	20 gallons
Front suspension	parallel A-arms with coil springs
Rear suspension	independent three-link with transverse leaf spring
Standard drivetrain	250-horsepower 327-ci V-8, backed by a Saginaw three-speed manual transmission and 3.36:1 rear axle
Optional engine	300-horsepower 327-ci V-8 (L75)
Optional engine	340-horsepower 327-ci V-8 (L76)
Optional engine	360-horsepower 327-ci fuel-injected V8 (L84)
Optional transmission	M35 Powerglide automatic (limited to base 327 and L75 only)
Optional transmission	M20 wide-ratio four-speed manual with 2.54:1 low (limited to base 327 and L75 only)
Optional transmission	M20 close-ratio four-speed manual with 2.20:1 low (limited to L76 and L84 V-8s only)
Optional gear ratios	ranged from 3.08:1 to 4.56:1, with or without optional Posi-Traction (4.11:1 and 4.56:1 were Posi-Traction only)

Two body styles were offered for the first time in 1963. Coupe production that year was 10,594, compared to 10,919 convertibles.

1963

Available for the first time in two body styles, coupe or convertible, the 1963 Corvette rolled on a revised ladder-type frame (with five lateral crossmembers) that was 50 percent more rigid than the antiquated X-member unit it replaced. And along with being much stronger, the new frame's widely spaced boxed perimeter rails allowed designers to lower the Sting Ray's floorpan, which in turn meant the roofline could be dropped without cutting headroom.

Wheelbase also was reduced, from 102 inches to 98, and Duntov managed to favorably redistribute the car's weight by relocating the engine and passenger compartment rearward on that shortened hub-to-hub stretch. Better balance and less unsprung weight in back (200 pounds, compared to 300 in 1962), thanks to the new IRS layout, made the Sting Ray the best-handling, nicest-riding Corvette to date.

Steering precision was improved, as were brakes. Although drum diameters stayed at 11

inches at all four corners, width increased—from 2 inches to 2.75 in front, and from 1.75 inches to 2 in back. Optional power assist (RPO J50) for those brakes debuted for 1963, as did optional power steering (RPO N40). The standard steering ratio was 20.2:1; a faster 17.6:1 ratio was optional. Steering wheel turns, lock to lock, were 3.4 for the former, 2.92 for the latter.

Further enhancing the newfound solid feel was the body's welded-steel birdcage, an internal reinforcing structure that weighed nearly twice as

Thoroughly modern styling touches for 1963 included the hideaway headlights that would remain a Corvette trademark up through 2004 and aircraft-style doors that were cut into the roofline to aid entry and exit.

Sting Ray doors were cut aircraft-style into the coupe's low roof, an idea that looked cool and made entry and exit a little less hairy.

02

much as the minimal steel skeleton backing up the 1962 Corvette's fiberglass shell. Thoroughly modern styling touches for 1963 included the hideaway headlights that would remain a Corvette trademark up through 2004 and aircraft-style doors that were cut into the roofline to aid entry and exit. The two vents in the hood were nonfunctional, though initial plans had them working. The idea was dropped after engineers determined that the hot under-hood air exiting those vents would flow directly into the passenger compartment's cowl intakes.

Above
This vacuum-assisted, dual-circuit master cylinder was unique to the Z06 package. It wasn't the same unit used in the J50 power brake option. *Mike Mueller*

Opposite, clockwise from upper left
Optional leather seats debuted along with the Sting Ray in 1963. Black plastic doorknobs were used that year. *Mike Mueller*

Along with the L84 327, the Z06 package included special brakes with finned drums for improved cooling. Also notice the holes in the Z06 drum's face—these allowed an escape route for overheated internal air. *Mike Mueller*

Segmented linings and a cooling fan were incorporated inside the Z06's finned drums. The elephant ear on the ground attached to the inside of the backing plate to funnel cooling air into the brakes. *Mike Mueller*

The top engine option in 1963 was again the fuel-injected 327 V-8 (RPO L84), rated at 360 horsepower. Standard power came from a 250-horse 327. *Mike Mueller*

Above
Base price for the 1963 Sting Ray coupe was $4,252. Its convertible running mate cost $4,037.

Powertrain packages carried over unchanged from 1962, with the 250-horsepower 327 backed by a three-speed manual transmission as standard fare. All the hot performance options of the previous year also returned wearing Chevrolet's new RPO codes: metallic brakes and the Posi-Traction differential were listed under RPOs J65 and G81, respectively. Another new option, the N11 off-road exhaust system, was announced for 1963 but apparently didn't show up until 1964.

Last, but certainly not least, on the 1963 RPO list was Z06, the Special Performance Equipment group package. Chevrolet's original Z06 package (it would return in 2001) was introduced at

Riverside, California, on October 13, 1962, when the first six Z06 Sting Rays built went directly into prominent racers' hands. SCCA production-class competition represented the Z06's reason for being—hence the inclusion of every hot piece on the Corvette parts shelf.

The L84 327 close-ratio four-speed and Posi-Traction rear were mandatory additions with the Special Performance Equipment package. Initially listed as part of the Z06 deal were a heavy-duty suspension, special heavy-duty power brakes, an oversized 36.5-gallon fiberglass fuel tank, and five cast-aluminum knock-off wheels. Typical road-worthy upgrades made up the track-

Introduced in October 1962, the Z06 racing package was created just before GM execs ordered Chevrolet to cease all competition activities. Veteran Corvette racer Bob Bondurant was among the first to put a 1963 Z06 Sting Ray into action. The number on his car, 614, was the street address of his sponsor, Washburn Chevrolet.

ready suspension: stiffer shocks, beefier springs, and a thickened front stabilizer bar.

Not so typical was the brake equipment, which included a vacuum-assisted, dual-circuit master cylinder unique to the Z06 application—not the standard J50 setup as is often concluded. Unique too were the Z06's sintered cerametallix brakes shoes. They measured 11.75 inches long, compared to their 11-inch sintered metallic J65 counterparts.

Z06 brakes also featured special cooling equipment. Like the J65 units, the Z06's drums were finned to aid cooling. Additionally, five holes were opened up in the Z06 drums' faces, and special vented backing plates were used. In between, an internal fan kept a steady breeze blowing through those parts. Rubber elephant-ear scoops completed the package, attached to the backing plates' backsides to direct cooling air into the special vents.

Originally priced at a whopping $1,818.45, the Z06 package was trimmed a bit in December 1962 after the knock-off wheels and big tank were dropped from the deal. The tank still could have been added to a '63 Sting Ray after December 1962 by checking off RPO N03. Customers fond of the new knock-offs, however, weren't so lucky. Reportedly the result of Corvette racer and Gulf Oil executive Grady Davis' request

for a quick-change road-racing wheel, the rims measured 15x6 inches and included a special hub adapter that allowed attachment by a single three-pronged threaded spinner (early prototypes used a two-eared spinner) in place of the typical five lugs. But nearly all wheels produced for 1963 leaked air, resulting in the option's quick cancellation. Some did make it into public hands before dealers began turning down requests for the desired option. Exactly how many remains unknown.

Another change made to the Z06 option in December 1962 involved availability. Like the N03 fuel tank, RPO Z06 was initially only offered for coupes. Plain and simple, the oversized tank could not be located in a topless Sting Ray. That exception disappeared after the big tank was dropped from the Z06 lineup, and thus the Special Performance Equipment package became listed as an option for the convertible too. That is, at least according to a distribution bulletin dated December 14. Apparently all 199 of the '63 Z06 Sting Rays known are coupes.

Originally known simply as the "lightweight Corvette," Duntov's latest racing machine was officially titled "Grand Sport."

1963 Grand Sport

Chevrolet wasn't supposed to be involved in racing in 1963, at least according to the infamous ban on factory-backed competition projects announced by the AMA in the summer of 1957. Yet Zora Duntov was again working on a special-edition racing Corvette—a car he hoped would pick up where his ill-fated SS had left off in 1957. Originally known simply as the "lightweight Corvette," Duntov's latest racing machine was officially titled "Grand Sport."

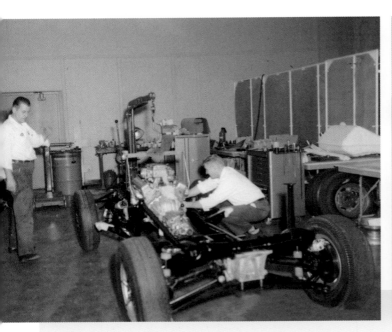

Zora Duntov's Grand Sport project was kicked off in the summer of 1962. This lightweight racing Corvette was based on a tubular steel frame that weighed 94 pounds less than the standard String Ray foundation.

Although the Grand Sport's original bodywork looked stock at a glance, various dimensions differed compared to a garden-variety 1963 Sting Ray, and panel thicknesses were decreased to reduce weight. Fixed headlights also were incorporated.

Above
Unlike standard 1963 Sting Rays, Grand Sports featured deck lids in back to comply with prototype-class racing rules that mandated a spare tire and a trunk to carry it. Also notice the competition-type fuel filler above the rear wheel.

Above
Texan John Mecom took three Grand Sports to the Bahamas in November 1963 for the Nassau Speed Week races. By then, the cars had been heavily modified with various scoops, vents, and flairs, the latter items added to help house wider wheels and tires.

Below
Initial plans called for this all-aluminum 377-cubic-inch V-8 to power the Grand Sports, but it wasn't ready in time, leaving the cars to race early on with basically stock fuel-injected 327s. *Mike Mueller*

Duntov's engineering team kicked off the Grand Sport project in the summer of 1962, beginning with a tubular-steel frame that weighed 94 pounds less than the stock foundation and incorporated mounting points for a full roll cage. With its transverse leaf spring and three-link layout, the Grand Sport's independent rear suspension looked familiar, but it was beefed up considerably. Unwanted pounds, meanwhile, were trimmed by using modified sheet-steel trailing-arm hub carriers drilled with lightening holes. Other weight-saving components included an aluminum steering box, special sheet-steel A-arms up front, and a set of 15x6 Halibrand magnesium knock-off wheels. Solid 11.75-inch Girling disc brakes with three-piston calipers were mounted at all four corners. Heavy-duty front coil springs, various reinforced steering pieces, and stiff Delco shocks completed the chassis.

On top of that purpose-built platform went a one-piece fiberglass shell with superthin panels to save even more weight. Other measurements here and there—a lower, narrowed roofline and slightly more windshield slope, for example—differed from stock specs as designers tried to improve on the Sting Ray's surprisingly poor aerodynamics. The

1963 Grand Sport

Specifications	1963 Grand Sport
Model availability	coupe and roadster
Body	specially molded lightweight fiberglass panels with trunk lid for spare tire access
Wheelbase	98 inches
Chassis	tubular steel
Brakes	Girling 11.75-inch discs
Wheels	Halibrand magnesium knock-offs
Fuel tank	36.5 gallons
Front suspension	independent with sheet-steel A-arms and coil springs
Rear suspension	independent with sheet-steel trailing arms, aluminum differential housing, and transverse leaf spring
Engine (proposed)	377-ci aluminum small-block V-8 with four Weber two-barrel carburetors and tube headers
Transmission	four-speed manual

Above
Zora Duntov hoped to build as many as 125 Grand Sport racers in 1963, but GM's anti-racing edict, sent down in January that year, squelched his plan. *Mike Mueller*

Left
Original Grand Sport interiors represented a strange mix of regular-production pieces and purposeful racing equipment. *Mike Mueller*

car looked slick, but it remained a veritable brick in the wind. Frontal area was much too large for a race car, and body lift at high speeds was akin to an airplane. That unwanted lift plagued all Corvettes built from 1963 to 1967.

Additional differences between the standard Sting Ray shell and its flimsy Grand Sport counterpart included enlarged wheelhouses (to make room for more rubber), a rear deck lid for spare tire access, fixed headlights mounted behind clear plexiglass in place of the heavy hideaway units, and aluminum underbody reinforcement instead of the conventional steel birdcage. All windows, save for the windshield, were made of plexiglass, and Mitchell's stinger was deleted in back.

Initial plans had the Grand Sport powered by an exotic 377-cubic-inch small block made entirely of aluminum and topped by four Weber 58-mm two-barrel carburetors, but the engine wasn't ready in time. The first Grand Sport was fitted with

an aluminum version of the Sting Ray's fuel-injected 327 V-8 and sent out for testing at Sebring in December 1962.

Grand Sport number 001 was the first of 125 planned lightweight Corvette racers. That plan, however, barely got off the ground before GM execs issued their own ban on factory racing in January 1963. Those same corporate officers had looked the other way while Chevrolet continued supporting competition projects after the AMA edict had gone into effect, but enough was enough. The Grand Sport was history even before it could make history at the track.

The aluminum 377 V-8 never made it into production and only five Grand Sport chassis were completed before the project was canceled. Or at least that's what the experts thought up until 2003, when evidence surfaced that a sixth might have been built but destroyed in 1964 or 1965 by order of GM officers who weren't happy about even one Grand Sport getting built. Whatever the case, the

five Grand Sports known to exist today managed to find their way out of Chevrolet Engineering in 1963 and into supposedly private hands.

Once in the wild, all five Grand Sports began sprouting various louvers, holes, and vents for added cooling. Spoilers, huge hood scoops, and enormous fender flares were also added, and the transparent headlight shields were quickly replaced by solid covers. Various engines were tried over the years, including the 427 Mk. IV big block.

But the most noticeable modification involved the first two coupes, GS numbers 001 and 002. They were later converted into roadsters in the hopes of improving on the lackluster aerodynamics. But the topless Grand Sports didn't get the chance to prove their merits, at least not immediately, after their conversions in early 1964.

GM officials once again laid down the law after reading all about the Grand Sport coupes, which had been making mucho noise at various racing venues in 1963, including a wild foray to

A Grand Sport coupe (number 004) toured a big-time track, Daytona, in anger for the last time in February 1967.

Introduced at the same time as Chevrolet's Z06 Corvette, Carroll Shelby's Ford-powered Cobra quickly ran away from the new Sting Ray in stock-class racing early in 1963. But Shelby's sneaky snakes were no match for Mecom Racing's Grand Sports during the Nassau Speed Week events.

the Bahamas for the Nassau Speed Weeks in November. Texan John Mecom (who now claims he bought all six Grand Sports that year) fielded the team with much help from Chevrolet. When the dust had cleared, Mecom's Grand Sports had thoroughly embarrassed Carroll Shelby's Cobras. They also had mortified GM execs who were sure they had ordered the Grand Sport Corvette racers scrapped. Another upper office edict came down, this one telling Chevy people to steer clear of the

Grand Sports or else, and no other high-profile appearances followed for Duntov's lightweight Corvette racers.

From there, the cars went through various racers' hands and competed with so-so success. The last major on-track appearance for a roadster (number 002) came in June 1966 at Mosport in Ontario. A Grand Sport coupe (number 004) toured a big-time track, Daytona, in anger for the last time in February 1967.

Below
Two Grand Sports entered the week's first race, the Tourist Cup, but failed to finish after their differentials seized. All three cars were then modified with rear-axle coolers for the last two events. Dick Thompson drove his Grand Sport to a fourth-place finish (again, well ahead of the Cobras) for the finale, the Nassau Trophy race.

Left
Three events were run at Nassau in 1963, and the three Grand Sports were driven by legendary racers Dick Thompson, Jim Hall, Roger Penske, and Augie Pabst. All three cars finished in the top 10 for the week's second race, the Governor's Cup, while the Cobras were nowhere in sight.

Below
Grand Sports competed in various guises for various teams during the early 1960s, and both small-block and big-block engines were installed. The breed's last major appearance came at Daytona in February 1967.

1964

Specifications	1964
Model availability	coupe and convertible (optional removable hardtop)
Wheelbase	98 inches
Length	175.3 inches
Width	69.6 inches
Height	49.8 inches, coupe and convertible; 49.3 inches, with removable hardtop
Tread (front/rear, in inches)	56.3/57
Tires	6.70x15 four-ply
Brakes	four-wheel drums
Fuel tank	20 gallons
Front suspension	parallel A-arms with coil springs
Rear suspension	independent three-link with transverse leaf spring
Standard drivetrain	250-horsepower 327-ci V-8, backed by a Saginaw three-speed manual transmission and 3.36:1 rear axle
Optional engine	300-horsepower 327-ci V-8 (L75)
Optional engine	365-horsepower 327-ci V-8 (L76)
Optional engine	375-horsepower 327-ci fuel-injected V-8 (L84)
Optional transmission	M35 Powerglide automatic (limited to base 327 and L75 only)
Optional transmission	M20 wide-ratio four-speed manual with 2.56:1 low (limited to base 327 and L75 only)
Optional transmission	M20 close-ratio four-speed manual with 2.20:1 low (limited to L76 and L84 V-8s only)
Optional gear ratios	ranged from 3.08:1 to 4.56:1, with or without optional Posi-Traction (4.11:1 and 4.56:1 were Posi-Traction only)

Among the few changes made for 1964 was the deletion of Bill Mitchell's beloved stinger in back. Second-edition Sting Ray coupes featured a one-piece rear window.

1964

The Z06 Corvette didn't return for 1964, even though dealers had begun taking orders for them in the fall of 1963. Instead of the Special Performance Equipment group, Chevrolet simply offered the various components separately, with the heavy-duty suspension listed as RPO F40 and the gnarly metallic brakes found under RPO J56. The knock-off wheels (P48) and 36.5-gallon gas tank (N03) were brought back individually, too, and the off-road exhaust system (N11) mentioned in 1963 was officially introduced for 1964. Another new option, the K66 transistorized ignition, also debuted.

Once again, the 250-horsepower 327 backed by a three-speed manual transmission was standard beneath the hood. A 300-horse L75 V-8 and two improved 327s followed. The peak option

The removable hardtop was a $236.75 option in 1964. Production that year was 7,023.

was the L84 fuelie, by then rated at 375 horsepower, thanks to revised heads with bigger valves (2.02-inch intakes, 1.60-inch exhausts) and a new mechanical cam with more lift and longer duration. Since the extra lift meant the valves would intrude farther into the combustion chamber, machined reliefs were required for the piston tops, which in turn translated into a slight compression cut to 11:1. Basically an L84 V-8 with a big Holley four-barrel carburetor in place of the Ramjet fuel-injection setup, the L76 small block was advertised at 365 horsepower, the highest output Chevrolet would record for a noninjected 327.

Save for the removal of Mitchell's beloved stinger from the rear window, updates to the 1964 Sting Ray body were minor, and restyled wheel covers represented a notable change. Harder to spot, the revamped rocker moldings only sported three black stripes instead of eight. The fake grilles were removed from the hood, but their indentations remained. The fake air outlets behind the coupe's doors were restyled too, and the driver-side outlets became functional after an electric motor and ductwork were added to help ventilate the interior.

And let's not forget the gas cap—a restyled lid was introduced each year during the C2 run.

Clockwise, from top
Revised seats and chromed doorknobs set the 1964 interior apart from its 1963 predecessor. *Mike Mueller*

A restyled, frosted wheel cover appeared for 1964. *Mike Mueller*

The two indentations remained in the 1964 Corvette's hood, but the fake grilles seen the year before were deleted. *Mike Mueller*

02

SECTION 02: C2

CERV II

Chevrolet wasn't supposed to be racing, but that didn't stop Zora Duntov from building another prototype race car immediately after his Grand Sport plan was shot down by corporate party-poopers in 1963. Originally proposed in the summer of 1962, the CERV II two-seater was built in 1964 with hopes of competing in Sports Prototype classes at Le Mans, Daytona, and Sebring. Like its CERV I forerunner, CERV II featured a midengine layout, but its all-wheel-drive design was truly unique, made possible by installing two torque converters—one for the front wheels, another for the back.

After initials plans for a tubular space frame were cast aside, the CERV II was constructed

Above
The optional L76 327 debuted for 1964. Basically an L84 V-8 with a single four-barrel carburetor in place of the Ramjet fuel injection system, the solid-lifter L76 produced 365 horsepower.

Upper right
A new fuel filler door adorned the 1964 Corvette's tail. *Mike Mueller*

Right
An AM/FM radio (RPO U69) was a popular $176.50 option in 1964. U69 installations numbered 20,934 that year. *Mike Mueller*

using boxed aluminum chassis members on a wheelbase measuring 92 inches from hub to hub. Original specifications called for a downsized 240-cubic-inch small-block V-8 to stay within the 4.5-liter displacement limit then in place for international endurance racing. Reportedly, one prototype CERV II was to be followed by six actual competition machines; three would be raced, three would serve as backups.

Only the prototype was built, however, as corporate killjoys again stepped in before Duntov could take the fiberglass-bodied two-seater racing. From then on, the company line read: the lone CERV II was created solely as an engineering testbed. Putting tires to task then briefly became its job before it soon faded into obscurity. Along the way, an all-aluminum 427 big-block V-8 was installed.

Again like its CERV I predecessor, CERV II survived the crusher and has passed through various collectors' hands over the years.

Above
Constructed in 1964, the attractive XP-819 Corvette featured a rear-mounted V-8 beneath a flip-up tail section. Its curvaceous body, penned by Larry Shinoda, previewed much of the upcoming third-generation Corvette's look.

Left
The midengine CERV II made the scene in 1964 with all-wheel drive and a boxed-aluminum chassis.

1965

Specifications

Specifications	1965
Model availability	coupe and convertible (optional removable hardtop)
Wheelbase	98 inches
Length	175.3 inches
Width	69.6 inches
Height	49.8 inches, coupe and convertible; 49.3 inches with removable hardtop
Tread (front/rear, in inches)	56.3/57
Tires	7.75x15 four-ply
Brakes	four-wheel discs (drums available as credit option)
Fuel tank	20 gallons
Front suspension	parallel A-arms with coil springs
Rear suspension	independent three-link with transverse leaf spring
Standard drivetrain	250-horsepower 327-ci V-8, backed by a Saginaw three-speed manual transmission and 3.36:1 rear axle
Optional engine	300-horsepower 327-ci V-8 (L75)
Optional engine	350-horsepower 327-ci V-8 (L79)
Optional engine	365-horsepower 327-ci V-8 (L76)
Optional engine	375-horsepower 327-ci fuel-injected V-8 (L84)
Optional engine	425-horsepower 396-ci V-8 (L78)
Optional transmission	M35 Powerglide automatic (limited to base 327 and L75 only)
Optional transmission	M20 wide-ratio four-speed manual with 2.56:1 low (limited to base 327 and L75 only)
Optional transmission	M20 close-ratio four-speed manual with 2.20:1 low (limited to L76, L78, L79, and L84 V-8s only)
Optional gear ratios	ranged from 3.08:1 to 4.56:1, with or without optional Posi-Traction

Top
The gap between coupe and convertible grew in 1965. Production for the former was 8,186 and 15,387 for the latter.

Right
New fender louvers for 1965 featured three vertical openings, which were nonfunctional.

1965

Minor exterior upgrades for 1965 included a revised, blacked-out grille and a reformed hood devoid of those disliked indentations present in 1963 and 1964. Three functional vertical louvers graced the fenders, new mag-style wheel covers went on at the corners, and restyled trim (with one long black stripe) covered the rocker panels. More-supportive vinyl bucket seats went inside, as did flat-faced instruments (in place of 1964's conical units), seatbelt retractors, and new molded door panels with integral armrests.

In big news at the corners, four-wheel disc brakes became standard equipment in 1965. The new system featured 11.75-inch rotors squeezed by four-piston calipers. Buyers who preferred less stopping power could order the old drums (at a $64.50 credit), but only 316 did.

Making even more headlines was a new optional engine, the 396-cubic-inch Mk. IV V-8.

Beauty beneath the '65 Corvette's skin included four-wheel disc brakes, a new standard feature.

The 350-horsepower 327 (RPO L79) appeared for 1965 as a more civilized alternative to the solid-lifter L76. The L79 used maintenance-free hydraulic lifters.

Minor exterior upgrades for 1965 included a revised, blacked-out grille and a reformed hood devoid of those disliked indentations present in 1963 and 1964.

Clockwise, from above
Yet another restyled fuel filler door showed up in 1965.
Mike Mueller

Optional side-mount exhausts debuted for the 1965 Sting
Ray. *Mike Mueller*

A four-speed stick was the only choice behind the optional
L79 327, as was the case with the two solid-lifter small
blocks, the L76 and L84, in 1965. *Mike Mueller*

Listed under RPO L78, the big-block baby
featured free-breathing cylinder heads with
staggered valves laid out in a seemingly
haphazard fashion, reminiscent of a porcupine's
quills—thus the nickname "porcupine motor."
Mk. IV intake valves were located up high near
their ports and inclined slightly, making for a
straighter flow from intake manifold to combustion
chamber. An opposite inclination was applied
(to a slightly lesser degree) on the exhaust end to

Clockwise, from above
This legendary badge made its final appearance on fiberglass flanks in 1965. *Mike Mueller*

A classy teakwood steering wheel became a Corvette option in 1965. *Mike Mueller*

Cast-aluminum knock-off wheels were first offered as part of the Z06 package in 1963, but quality problems led to their recall that year. They returned, problem-free, in 1964. *Mike Mueller*

Rated at 360 horsepower in 1963, the fuel-injected L84 327 was muscled up to 375 horses the following year. The rating remained the same for the last fuelie V-8, offered for 1965 Corvette models. *Mike Mueller*

the same effect. Along with exceptional breathing characteristics, the inclined valve setup also offered slightly more room for bigger valves—Mk. IV units were truly big, with 2.19-inch intakes and 1.72-inch exhausts.

A serious solid-lifter cam activated those valves, a big Holley four-barrel fed the beast, and a mandatory K66 transistorized ignition supplied the spark. Inside the bores, impact-extruded aluminum

pistons squeezed the mixture to an octane-intensive 11:1 ratio. The sum of the parts equaled a potent 425-horsepower big block that helped many among the fiberglass faithful forget all about the 327 fuelie V-8, which was then in its last year.

Another new engine appeared in 1965, the L79 small block. More or less an L76 327 with a slightly milder hydraulic cam in place of the solid-lifter stick, the L79 was rated at 350 horsepower. The L79 was identical to the L76 on the outside with its chromed air cleaner (atop the same Holley four-barrel) and finned cast-aluminum valve covers. Compression, at 11:1, was also the same. Priced a little lower than the L76, the L79 was easier to live with in everyday operation thanks to those hydraulic lifters.

Left
Redesigned seats and restyled instrument faces represented the main changes to the Corvette interior in 1965. *Mike Mueller*

Bottom left
The 396 Turbo Jet was a one-hit wonder in the Corvette world. In 1966, it was replaced by its bigger, badder 427 Turbo Jet cousin. *Mike Mueller*

Below
With its bulging hood, a 396 Corvette was tough to miss in 1965.

1965 Mako Shark II

Specifications	1965 Mako Shark II

Body style	two-door fastback coupe with lift-up roof and tilt front end
Wheelbase	98 inches
Length	184.5 inches
Width	69.1 inches
Height	46.5 inches
Tires	8.80/9.15
Wheels	7.50x15 cast-aluminum knock-offs
Engine	427-ci V-8
Transmission	Turbo Hydra-matic automatic

Mako Shark II

Bill Mitchell first got serious about the next-generation Corvette image midway through 1964. He instructed Larry Shinoda to have a suitable preview ready in time for the New York International Auto Show, scheduled for April 1965. Shinoda's team rolled out a full-size mockup for press release photography in March—rolled out because, even though the hood said "Mark IV 396," there was no engine residing beneath. Originally labeled "Mako Shark," the moniker was soon changed to "Mako Shark II" after it was decided to retroactively rename the XP-755 prototype "Mako Shark I." A fully functional Mako Shark II followed, fitted with a 427-cubic-inch Mk. IV big-block V-8.

With or without an engine, the car looked fast. A sharply pointed prow led the way, followed by a domed hood that signified power. The bulging wheelhouses at all four corners looked ready to explode, their flared openings barely able to contain the fat Firestones within. Adding to the

Top
While the fuel-injected small block was on its way out in 1965, few tears were shed considering its replacement: the new king of the Corvettes was the breed's first big-block model, powered by Chevrolet's new 396-cubic-inch Mk. IV V-8.

Above
Chevy's Mk. IV big block was nicknamed "the porcupine," due to the seemingly haphazard fashion in which its valve stems protruded upward from its cylinder heads. Those canted valves helped the 396 breathe with ease; making 425 horsepower was no problem.

Top right
A one-piece, lift-off roof topped the Mako Shark II.

Right
Electric switches abounded inside the Mako Shark II. Along with power locks and windows, the car also featured hideaway wipers and rear window louvers that were both controlled electrically.

The original Mako Shark (in back) was retroactively renamed Mako Shark I after the Mako Shark II (front) was unveiled in 1965. Both show cars were drawn up by Larry Shinoda.

Measuring 3 inches lower than the existing Sting Ray, the Mako Shark II featured a sleek roofline that rolled back into a tapered exclamation point.

Shown here is the nonrunning Mako Shark II mockup. The finned side exhausts weren't used on the running example.

mockup's image were cast-aluminum side exhausts that exited the empty engine room halfway up the front fenders. The finned sidepipes were painted in crackle black with the edges of the fins remaining polished bright. The paint was removed after the New York showing, and the pipes were fully polished. Side exhausts were then deleted altogether on the functional Mako Shark II once its 427 big block went in place.

Measuring 3 inches lower than the existing Sting Ray, the Mako Shark II featured a sleek

roofline that rolled back into a tapered exclamation point. A pronounced ducktail brought up the rear, and the whole works were painted dark down to light (Firefrost Midnight Blue, to lighter blue, to light gray).

The seats were fixed inside, as the foot pedals adjusted electrically to match the driver's reach. Equally unconventional, the aircraft-style steering wheel looked like a rectangle squeezed in slightly on the bottom.

Like those impractical side exhausts, the futuristic steering wheel was left off of the Mako

Shark's functional alter ego, which was already in the works while the mockup was wowing New Yorkers in April 1965. When the 427-powered Mako was shown to the press on October 5, it had a typical round steering wheel. In place of the sidepipes was a conventional full-length exhaust

117

system exiting through two highly stylized rectangular tips at the car's tail.

Gizmos and gimmicks, most of them electrical, abounded throughout the car. In all, there were 17 remote power units added to control all the toys, which included two spoilers in back that could've been raised some 4 inches at the flick of a switch. Also predicting things to come were digital readouts for the clock, fuel gauge, and speedometer.

After its press introduction, the 427-powered Mako Shark II was flown to France for an appearance at the Paris Automobile Salon on October 7, 1965. From there, it went to London, Turin, Brussels, and Geneva, before returning to America for the New York Auto Show in April 1966. Though some critics at home didn't think much of the car's eccentricities, overall opinions around the world were positive, and the sensationally sexy Mako Shark II image evolved into the third-generation Corvette, now known as the "Shark" model.

Left
The Mako Shark II's entire nose flipped forward to allow engine access.

Below
While the mockup wore "Mark IV 396" badges, the functional machine was first powered by a 427-cubic-inch big block.

1966

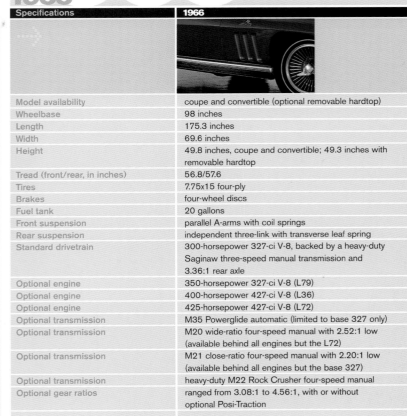

Specifications	1966
Model availability	coupe and convertible (optional removable hardtop)
Wheelbase	98 inches
Length	175.3 inches
Width	69.6 inches
Height	49.8 inches, coupe and convertible; 49.3 inches with removable hardtop
Tread (front/rear, in inches)	56.8/57.6
Tires	7.75x15 four-ply
Brakes	four-wheel discs
Fuel tank	20 gallons
Front suspension	parallel A-arms with coil springs
Rear suspension	independent three-link with transverse leaf spring
Standard drivetrain	300-horsepower 327-ci V-8, backed by a heavy-duty Saginaw three-speed manual transmission and 3.36:1 rear axle
Optional engine	350-horsepower 327-ci V-8 (L79)
Optional engine	400-horsepower 427-ci V-8 (L36)
Optional engine	425-horsepower 427-ci V-8 (L72)
Optional transmission	M35 Powerglide automatic (limited to base 327 only)
Optional transmission	M20 wide-ratio four-speed manual with 2.52:1 low (available behind all engines but the L72)
Optional transmission	M21 close-ratio four-speed manual with 2.20:1 low (available behind all engines but the base 327)
Optional transmission	heavy-duty M22 Rock Crusher four-speed manual
Optional gear ratios	ranged from 3.08:1 to 4.56:1, with or without optional Posi-Traction

1966

Powertrain updates again made the most noise in 1966, as the 250-horsepower 327 was dropped in favor of a new standard engine, the 300-horse L75. Behind the V-8 was a new, stronger Saginaw three-speed manual transmission.

The optional 365-horse L76 too was cancelled, but the more civilized L79 327 remained. The two small blocks were then joined by a new big block, as the 396 was bored out to 427 cubic inches. Two 427 options were offered in 1966: the comparatively mild, hydraulic-cam L36, rated at 390 horsepower, and the truly awesome L72. Like its L78 forerunner, the L72 427 was stuffed full of 11:1 pistons, compared to 10.25:1 slugs for the L36. The L72 mechanical cam, however, was even lumpier than that of the

Above
A new egg-crate-style grille appeared in 1966. *Mike Mueller*

Right
If you identified this fuel filler door as the 1966 edition, you'd be right on. *Mike Mueller*

L78, meaning even more horsepower was waiting beneath a '66 big-block hood. After being initially rated at an unheard-of 450 horses, the L72 was given a token 425-horsepower label. But anyone who believed that number needed only to drop the hammer one time on an L72 Corvette.

"Chevrolet insists that there are only 425 horses in there, and we'll just have to take their word for it," explained a *Car and Driver* report, which went on to mention the only numbers that really counted, anyway: 0–60 in 5.4 seconds and

Top
Two optional 427 V-8s were offered for 1966: the 390-horse L36 and 425-horse L72. The former featured a hydraulic cam, the latter solid lifters. *Mike Mueller*

Above
Extra pleats were added to the Sting Ray's bucket seats in 1966. *Mike Mueller*

Right
External changes for 1966 included deleting the vents formerly seen on the 1963–1965 coupe's roof pillar behind the doors.

"Chevrolet insists that there are only 425 horses in there, and we'll just have to take their word for it," explained a *Car and Driver* report.

Right
The optional Powerglide automatic transmission was only available behind the standard 300-horsepower 327 small block in 1966. *Mike Mueller*

Below
Big-block Corvettes wore the same hood in 1966, but beneath the bulge that year was the 427-cubic-inch V-8, created by boring out the 396. *Mike Mueller*

Convertibles outnumbered coupes 17,762 to 9,958 in 1966. The convertible base price was $4,084, compared to $4,295 for the coupe.

the quarter-mile in 12.8 seconds at 112 miles per hour. "Unreal" was *Car and Driver*'s understated conclusion.

Among other new options for 1966 were the J56 brake package and F41 sport suspension. Included in J56 were metallic linings and a dual-circuit master cylinder with power assist. F41 parts consisted of typically beefed-up springs and a thickened front stabilizer bar.

Basic exterior changes were limited to different rocker trim, restyled wheel covers, and a revised grille, this one featuring an attractive egg-crate design. Less-noticeable upgrades included adding "Corvette Sting Ray" script to the hood, and designers finally deleted the roof vents

behind the doors, dropping the electric interior ventilation system too. Reupholstered seats, a vinyl-covered foam headliner in place of the previously used fiberboard, chrome door-pull handles, and standard backup lights were new as well for 1966.

1967

Specifications	1967

Model availability	coupe and convertible (optional removable hardtop)
Wheelbase	98 inches
Length	175.1 inches
Width	69.6 inches
Height	49.8 inches, coupe and convertible; 49.3 inches with removable hardtop
Tread (front/rear, in inches)	57.56/58.36
Tires	7.75x15 four-ply
Brakes	four-wheel discs
Fuel tank	20 gallons
Front suspension	parallel A-arms with coil springs
Rear suspension	independent three-link with transverse leaf spring
Standard drivetrain	300-horsepower 327-ci V-8, backed by a heavy-duty Saginaw three-speed manual transmission and 3.36:1 rear axle
Optional engine	350-horsepower 327-ci V-8 (L79)
Optional engine	390-horsepower 427-ci V-8 (L36)
Optional engine	400-horsepower 427-ci 3x2 V-8 (L68)
Optional engine	435-horsepower 427-ci 3x2 V-8 (L71)
Optional engine	430-horsepower 427-ci V-8 (L88)
Note	aluminum heads (L89) were available for the L71; output did not change with this installation
Optional transmission	M35 Powerglide automatic (available behind base 327, L36 and L68 427s)
Optional transmission	M20 wide-ratio four-speed manual with 2.52:1 low (available behind all engines except the L71 and L88)
Optional transmission	M21 close-ratio four-speed manual with 2.20:1 low (available behind all engines except the base 327)
Optional transmission	heavy-duty M22 Rocker Crusher four-speed manual (for L88 427)
Optional gear ratios	ranged from 3.08:1 to 4.56:1, with or without optional Posi-Traction

Above
Excess trim was deleted in 1967, and restyled fender louvers became functional.

1967

Originally scheduled for 1966, the C2's closing act had most critics raving in 1967. This unintended encore resulted in what many still feel was the best Corvette of the short midyear run—as well as one of the best of all time. Even *Road & Track*'s ever-critical testers approved: "The Sting Ray is in its fifth and probably last year with that name and body style, and it finally looks the way we thought it should have in the first place."

Exterior modifications included stripping all identification off the fenders, which looked cleaner thanks to small, modernized louvers with a slight forward rake. Along the body's lower edge were new rocker moldings that were nearly completely blacked out. The traditional crossed-flag emblem

up front was smaller, and the Corvette script seen on 1966 hoods was deleted. The whole works were complemented by a new standard wheel, the popular Rally rim with its brake cooling slots, trim ring, and center cap.

But easily the most prominent upgrade was the bold, new big-block hood, a marked improvement over the somewhat crude bulges used in 1965 and 1966. Complementing its sleek stinger shape was a set of paint stripes that varied in color depending on the exterior and interior shades chosen. For example, a black '67 Sting Ray with a black or red interior received red striping, while a black car with saddle or green appointments inside was adorned with a white

Left
The 427 Corvette remained one of the hottest things running on American roads in 1967.

Below, starting at left
Chevrolet's popular Rally wheel debuted as the standard rim for the 1967 Corvette. *Mike Mueller*

Another new fuel filler door for the 1967 Sting Ray. *Mike Mueller*

Notice that the 1967's fuel filler door was color-keyed to match the exterior paint choice. *Mike Mueller*

scoop. In addition to the red and white stripes, hood scoops were also painted black, dark teal blue, or medium bright blue. And thanks to problems perfecting the painting process, some early '67 427 Corvettes were delivered with no stripes at all. Another problem—this one involving a mishap with the molds for the familiar, flat small-block hood—resulted in some stinger scoops appearing on 327 Corvettes in 1967. Apparently some dealers made this swap too.

Standard power beneath a '67 Corvette hood was once more the 300-horsepower 327, and the L79 small block and L36 big block (then rated at 390 horsepower) were again optional. But an even meaner 427 was available in 1967, topped by three Holley two-barrel carburetors and crowned by a triangular air cleaner. This 3x2 L71 V-8 was rated at 435 horsepower, the highest rating ever stuck on a Corvette big block. Everything that made the L72 so tough—four-bolt

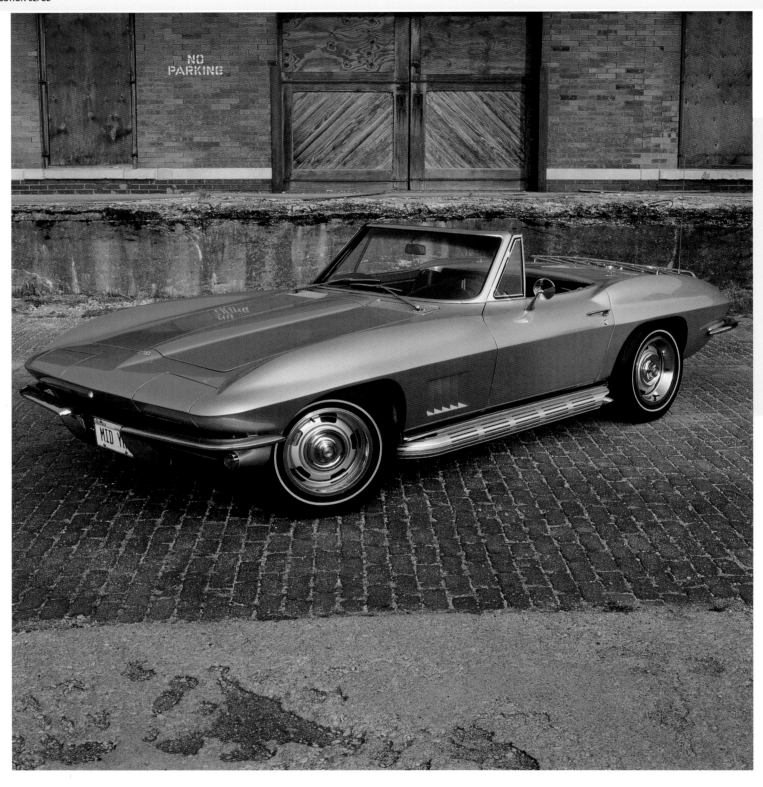

Opposite
Convertibles still dominated in 1967: production was 14,436. Coupe production was 8,504. *Mike Mueller*

Right
The 390-horse L36 carried over into 1967, fed again by a single four-barrel. Two triple-carb 427s also were offered: one at 400 horsepower, the other at 435. *Mike Mueller*

Below
Conventional bolt-on cast-aluminum wheels replaced the knock-off option offered in 1966. An ornamental center cap hid the bolt-on apparatus.

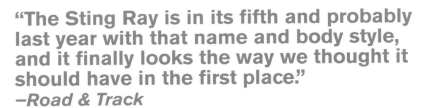

"The Sting Ray is in its fifth and probably last year with that name and body style, and it finally looks the way we thought it should have in the first place."
—*Road & Track*

main bearing caps, a lumpy solid-lifter cam, 11:1 compression, big valve heads, K66 transistorized ignition—was in the L71 package, save, of course, for that big 780-cfm Holley four-barrel.

Chevrolet's 3x2 induction setup began with an aluminum intake manifold. The center carb atop that manifold served as the primary fuel-feeder during normal operation, as throttle plates in the two secondary Holleys' venturi remained closed until revs reached roughly 2,000 rpm. Then a mass-air vacuum signal sent directly from the primary carb's venturi (as opposed to a typical central vacuum source) brought the front and rear two-barrels into the fray in a progression relative to the weight of the driver's foot. By the time engine speeds hit 4,000 rpm, all three throats were wailing away. The best published quarter-mile time for the L71 Corvette was a sizzling 12.90 seconds.

Chevrolet offered two triple-carb 427s in 1967, the other being the milder 400-horse L68. Despite a major price difference ($437.10 for 435

A new big-block hood complemented the 1967
Sting Ray's cleaner exterior but was nonfunctional.

horses, $305.50 for 400), the L71 outsold the L68 by nearly a two-to-one margin. Production totals for the L68 and its L71 big brother amounted to 2,101 and 3,754, respectively.

Much rarer was another new big-block option, L88. Only 20 of these were built in 1967, and all were meant to go right to the track despite GM's claim that it wasn't involved in racing. Zora Duntov simply wouldn't be denied, and he had kicked off yet another competition-conscious project in 1965 based on a collection of regular-production options.

At the heart of it all was the fabled L88 427, conservatively rated at 430 horsepower. Introduced in the spring of 1967, the first L88 Corvette didn't exactly set the racing world afire, thanks primarily to early durability problems involving overheating and an inherently weak lower end. Nonetheless, it was no slouch when it came to scorching a racetrack. At Le Mans in June 1967, an L88 topped 170 miles per hour on the Mulsanne Straight before a connecting rod disconnected during the night to end the Corvette's pursuit of the legendary 24-hour laurels.

Plain and simple, this uncivilized beast was never intended for use on the street, although some brave souls did try. What these Walter Mitty types probably noticed first were the blank covers in place of both the radio and heater/defroster controls normally found in the center of a '67 Corvette's dash. RPO C48, the heater/defroster delete credit introduced in 1963, was included as part of the L88 deal. Options like a radio and power windows were off-limits, and a convenient automatic choke was not installed, although a retrofit hand-choke kit was available from Chevrolet.

Another feature common to street cars, a fan shroud to aid cooling, was also missing on the L88, as was any semblance of emissions controls. A typical PCV valve wasn't even present; instead, the L88 427 used an obsolete road-draft tube that vented crankcase vapors directly into the atmosphere via the driver-side valve cover. Anything that wasn't needed on a racetrack and anything that added unwanted extra pounds wasn't included in the L88 package, an off-road option if there ever was one.

The 435-horse L71 427's triple Holley carburetors used vacuum operation for a truly smooth power boost. Compression was 11:1. The L71 big block also could've been fitted with optional aluminum heads (RPO L89) to save weight.

Below
The Corvette's familiar passenger-side grab handle was deleted for 1967, and a parking brake lever was added to the console. Notice the headrests; this option debuted in 1966.
Mike Mueller

While L88
production would
carry over into
1968, the midyear
Corvette retired
at the end of 1967
to, in many minds,
a standing ovation.

Only 20 L88 Corvette models were built in 1967, with this curious concoction being one of the earliest, if not the first. Used for testing, it features various unique touches, including prototype L88 decals on the hood and valve covers. Its 8-inch-wide Rally wheels were prototypes for the rims introduced on 1968 Corvettes. *Mike Mueller*

Left
The 1967 big-block hood was functional in the L88's case. The air cleaner fit into ductwork on the hood's underside that allowed cooler, denser atmosphere an easy route from the base of the car's windshield to the carburetor below. *Mike Mueller*

Below
Both the radio and heater were deleted as part of the L88 deal. *Mike Mueller*

What was included was an impressive list of purpose-built, heavy-duty hardware. For starters, the L88 427 big block featured weight-saving aluminum cylinder heads atop a typical Mk. IV four-bolt iron block. The L88's crankshaft was specially forged out of 5140 alloy steel, then cross-drilled for sure lubrication and Tuftrided for hardness. Attached to that crank by shot-peened, Magnafluxed connecting rods were eight forged-aluminum pop-up pistons that squeezed the air/fuel mixture at a molecule-mashing 12.5:1 ratio. As it turned out, the L88's connecting rods were its weakest links. High-rpm failures convinced engineers to reinforce the L88's lower end in 1968 with beefier rods featuring heavier 7/16-inch bolts.

Those lightweight heads were fitted with big valves: 2.19 inches on the intake side, 1.84 inches on the exhaust. The same aluminum heads were also available in 1967 as RPO L89, which was offered exclusively atop the L71 427. Only 16 pairs of L89 heads were sold in 1967.

Supplying air/fuel to the L88 427 was a huge 850-cfm Holley four-barrel. The special high-rise aluminum intake below that four-holer had its internal partition machined down to create an open plenum for maximum high-rpm performance. Designed by Denny Davis, the L88's solid-lifter cam was radical to say the least, with 337 degrees intake duration, 340 degrees exhaust. Valve lift was 0.5365-inch intake, 0.5560 exhaust. Pushrods were thick 7/16-inch pieces with hardened ends. On top, special long-slot stamped-steel rockers rocked on heat-treated, hardened ball studs. Heavy-duty valve springs were held in place by beefed-up retainers and locks.

On the L88's breathing end, a unique "air cleaner" (using the term very loosely) fit into the

Zora Duntov poses proudly with an L88 427 during dyno testing in the summer of 1966. The engine's 430-horsepower rating was a token.

Left
A huge 850-cfm Holley four-barrel carburetor fed the L88 427 through a special aluminum open-plenum manifold. Compression was a crushing 12.5:1. *Mike Mueller*

hood's underside. Looking little like an air cleaner at all, the L88 unit featured an open pan mounted atop that big Holley. In the center of the pan was a small screen; around its edge was a foam gasket. With the hood closed, the gasket sealed the pan to a duct than ran back to the rear edge of the Corvette's normally nonfunctional stinger scoop. By making that scoop functional, engineers allowed the L88 to breathe in from the denser air mass that typically gathers at the base of a car's windshield at speed—a clever idea that had proven itself under Chevrolet hoods during the Daytona 500 in 1963.

Bolted up between the L88 427 and M22 trans was an appropriate heavy-duty clutch mated to a small 12.75-inch-diameter flywheel, the latter added in the best interests of increasing rpm potential by reducing reciprocating mass. A Harrison heavy-duty cross-flow radiator handled cooling chores.

The L88's sky-high compression left Chevrolet officials no choice but to warn owners about their use of fuel. "This unit operates on Sunoco 260 or equivalent gas of very high octane," read delivery paperwork. "Under no circumstances should regular gasoline be used."

Another label inside the car repeated this caveat. "Warning: Vehicle must operate on a fuel having a minimum of 103 research octane and 95 motor octane or engine damage may result."

Remaining standard features contributed further to a nasty nature. All L88s built in 1967 were fitted with such mandatory options as the stiff F41 suspension, G81 Posi-Traction differential, J56 power-assisted metallic brakes, and M22 Rock Crusher four-speed manual transmission. RPO K66, the transistorized ignition, was also a specified option. Living with the J56 brakes alone in everyday operation was not for the faint of heart. The fade-resistant clampers worked famously once warmed up. But when cold, they were about as effective as Fred Flintstone's feet.

While L88 production would carry over into 1968, the midyear Corvette retired at the end of 1967 to, in many minds, a standing ovation.

03

Above
Total Corvette production reached an all-new high of 28,566 in 1968. Of that figure, 9,936 were coupes and 18,630 were convertibles.

Middle
There were no optional engines in 1982, nor was a four-speed manual transmission available—all 25,407 Corvettes built that year featured four-speed automatics. Of that total, 18,648 were conventional sport coupes and 6,759 were Collector Edition hatchbacks.

Right
Four round taillights—a Corvette tradition from 1961—remained a part of the plan for 1968.

Third Time's a Charm

C3
1968–1982

- → C3 generation was the Corvette's longest (15 model runs)
- → Zora Arkus-Duntov officially made Corvette chief engineer (1968)
- → Stingray name tag (now as one word) returns after one-year hiatus (1969)
- → Last L88 built (1969)
- → All-aluminum ZL-1 V-8 built for one year only (1969)
- → Annual production surpasses 30,000 for first time (1969)
- → Base price surpasses $5,000 for first time (1970)
- → Original LT-1 V-8 introduced (1970)
- → Original ZR-1™ options package introduced (1970)
- → Advertised horsepower drops for first time (1971)
- → Original LS6 V-8 introduced (1971)
- → Crash-proof plastic front bumper debuts (1973)
- → Crash-proof plastic rear bumper follows (1974)
- → Catalytic converters appear (1974)

- → Last big-block Corvette built (1974)
- → Dave McLellan becomes second Corvette chief engineer (1975)
- → Last Corvette convertible built until 1986 (1975)
- → Stingray badge last used (1976)
- → Annual production surpasses 40,000 for first time (1976)
- → St. Louis plant builds Chevrolet's 500,000th Corvette (1977)
- → All 1978 Corvettes were 25th Anniversary models
- → Two-tone Silver Anniversary paint option offered (1978)
- → Corvette paces the Indianapolis 500 for first time (1978)
- → Base sticker price surpasses $10,000 for first time (1979)
- → All-time production record (53,807) established (1979)
- → St. Louis assembly line closes, Bowling Green plant opens (1981)
- → Two-tone paint option returns (1981)
- → Collector Edition offered (1982)

Like your best girl in school, the Corvette has never been able to make it downstairs on time for the big date. Consider the C5. Initial plans called for a 1993 debut, but various gremlins helped push that intro back to 1997. And who can forget 1983? Chevrolet decision-makers apparently did–they delayed the C4's unveiling by more than six months, resulting in a model-year jump from 1982 directly to 1984.

Yet another perceived delay had occurred some 25 years earlier when the rumor mill had the public anxiously awaiting a radically redesigned second-generation Corvette for 1960. But Zora Duntov and Bill Mitchell simply would sell no Sting Ray before its time, and that moment didn't arrive until 1963.

As exciting as the first Sting Ray was, it still was doomed to a short life from the outset. The first-generation solid-axle Corvette had carried on for 10 years—far longer, in many critics' minds, than it should have. No way Duntov, Mitchell, and the gang were going to let things go that stale

again. They began working on the next best 'Vette yet even as the paint was drying on the first of the second-generation midyear models. Four years and out was the plan, as was topping a classic. Literally. Developing the original Sting Ray had already cost a boatload; busting the bank again only a few years later was out of the question. Developing the C3 was then left primarily to Mitchell's stylists, as placing an exciting new body atop the existing platform became the only choice. And the coming-out party for this new look initially was scheduled for 1967.

Opposite
LT-1 production (coupes and convertibles) was 1,949 in 1971. LT-1 350 output went down (to 330 horsepower) that year as its price went up (to $483).

Above
Coupe production was 20,496 in 1972. Base price was $5,533.

Above
A full-size clay shows off the nearly finalized third-generation form on a GM Styling studio patio.

Below
Cutting aerodynamic front-end lift was a major goal of the C3 design project. Mako Shark II ties are clearly evident in the profile.

the original Sting Ray coupe. A one-piece, lift-off Targa top—an idea unashamedly borrowed from the European sports car scene—crowned things.

Making the Mako dream a reality, however, hit a hitch once Duntov's engineers began their tasks of mating function to form. The prototype C3 looked great, but it floundered in real-world tests as driver visibility, engine ventilation, and aerodynamics fell well below acceptable standards. Shinoda's shape was too curvaceous, too bulging. Those tall fender tops, that low tapered roof, and the big duck tail in back worked in concert to make it almost impossible to see anything other than low-flying airplanes from behind the wheel. The slinky shell was also too close to the ground in front, where its sharp-edged beak limited the amount of cooling air able to reach the engine.

Smoothing things out beneath that oversexed skin required more time than was allotted, thus Duntov requested an extra year to properly prepare the C3 for production. One of the first changes made was to trade that boat-tail roof for

Wouldn't you know it?—late again.

The revamped C3 didn't debut until 1968, leaving the midyear Sting Ray to make an encore appearance for 1967. Not that that was bad—many critics still consider the '67 Sting Ray to be a classic among classics. But Corvette watchers then were anxiously awaiting the next step, especially after many had caught a glimpse of Larry Shinoda's Mako Shark II, which had debuted at New York's International Auto Show in April 1965. *Car Life*'s editors asked if this was the "next Corvette"? "Let's hope Chevrolet's Special Engineering boys land this one by 1967," added *Hot Rod*'s Eric Dahlquist.

While the Mako Shark II was busy turning heads on the show circuit, Shinoda and the rest of Chevrolet's styling team were themselves hustling to finalize the form that would indeed emerge as the C3 Corvette, or "Shark," the nickname devotees prefer. Early prototypes mirrored the Mako Shark II image right down to the tapered roofline, which carried on in the best tradition of

a more practical, more pleasing design also borrowed from Europe—in this case, from the Porsche 904. Vertical rear glass was sandwiched between two parallel flying-buttress C-pillars, a style known as a tunneled window.

A removable roof remained in place atop prototypes until the last minute. But with no fixed roof structure in place to help stiffen the platform, the Targa-top Corvette flexed too much. This pesky twisting not only made the top creak, it also compromised the car's weather-sealing capabilities. Designers had no choice but to add a central reinforcing strut to join the windshield header to the rear roof arch. This in turn meant the one-piece roof had to be separated into two sections—presto, a "T-top."

Additional fixes included cutting down the front fenders to allow the driver a safer look ahead. The rear quarters and roofline were also modified to improve rearward visibility. Downsizing the rear spoiler into a molded-in lip further enhanced the view.

Engine cooling was aided by a reshaped nose that allowed the radiator a more prominent location up front. An air-dam lip that ran beneath the car and up around the front wheel openings was added to better direct cool air toward that radiator. Finally, large fender vents were incorporated to help hot air escape more easily from beneath the hood. Those last two modifications also helped decrease high-speed lift—a problem Duntov had been battling for years.

Though it looked sleek, the original Sting Ray was an aerodynamic disaster when it took off in 1963. In Zora's own words, the second-generation body possessed "just enough lift to be a bad airplane." The Mako Shark II was even worse, leaving the C3 prototype little chance of playing down the Corvette's high-flying reputation.

A third-generation test vehicle was touring GM's Milford Proving Grounds as early as the fall of 1965. A new '65 Corvette also hit the track to serve as a measuring stick. Duntov's "bad airplane" tended to lift at both ends at high speeds. At 120 miles per hour, the '65 Sting Ray's nose rose 2.25 inches, the rear a half-inch. In comparison, Engineering's C3 prototype hunkered down in

Above
A 1968 Chevrolet auto show display featured a wealth of Corvette history, including both Mako Shark show cars, the CERV II, a 1953 model, and a 1963 Sting Ray.

Right
Beneath the 1968 Corvette's restyled skin was basically the same foundation used from 1963 to 1967. The engine lineup also rolled over from 1967.

Below
Stiffer springs and a lowered rear roll center constituted the most notable changes to the C3's carryover chassis. Wheelbase was still 98 inches.

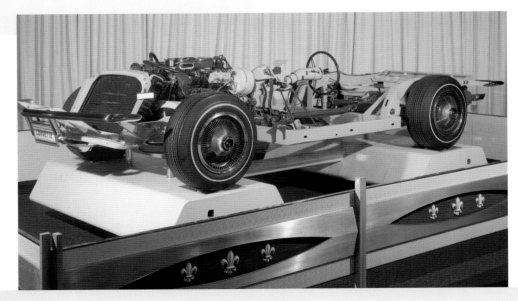

03

Now the new 1968 Corvette was ready to take on the world.

Above
C3 coupe owners could at least pretend they were driving a convertible. Both the car's T-tops and rear window could be removed to let the wind muss whatever hair was left.

Below
The beat went on at St. Louis in 1968 as the Corvette's third generation began. Notice the Turbo Hydra-matic automatic transmission, which replaced the old Powerglide on the RPO list that year.

back at speed, thanks to that large rear spoiler. At 120 miles per hour, its tail dropped a quarter-inch. This depression, in turn, helped raise the nose, a task the car could already handle well enough on its own. Front-end lift at 120 miles per hour measured 3.75 inches.

Reducing this lift was first achieved by venting the front fenders. These vents (which, as mentioned, also aided cooling) allowed trapped airflow up front a quicker exit, which helped bring the prototype's aerodynamics down close to stock '65 Sting Ray levels. Adding a chin spoiler up front decreased top-end lift even further, to a measly five-eighths of an inch.

Case closed? Not exactly.

Excessive under-hood heat continued to plague the Shark right up to its press introduction in August 1967. All Duntov needed was one tour in the blue big-block coupe then being readied for

journalists' scrutiny to recognize that the car would never keep its cool under the magnifying glass. Big-block Corvettes had always run hot, and this particular prototype was no exception. In truth, it was even more so due to the fact that all that cast iron was stuffed into stuffier confines. Cooling air still couldn't find its way into the radiator.

Duntov's quick fix saved the day. He opened up two oblong vents beneath the car's low-slung nose just ahead of the chin spoiler, then enlarged that spoiler to help increase the pressure, forcing the airflow up into those openings. From there, the rush of air could only flow through the radiator as all gaps to either side were closed up. The big-block prototype ran all day long in 85-degree heat at the Milford Proving Grounds during the press introduction, and the temperature gauge remained calm. Now the new 1968 Corvette was ready to take on the world.

1968

Base price for a 1968 Corvette sport coupe was $4,663. The convertible base sticker was $4,320.
Mike Mueller

Specifications	1968
Model availability	sport coupe and convertible (optional removable hardtop)
Wheelbase	98 inches
Length	182.5 inches
Width	68.9 inches
Height	47.76 inches (sport coupe), 47.88 inches (convertible, top up), 47.78 inches (convertible, with hardtop)
Shipping weight	3,055 pounds (coupe), 3,070 pounds (convertible)
Tread (front/rear, in inches)	58.23/59
Tires	F70-15
Brakes	11.75-inch discs
Wheels	15x7 Rally rims with trim rings and center caps
Fuel tank	20 gallons
Front suspension	parallel A-arms with coil springs
Rear suspension	independent three-link with transverse leaf spring
Steering	recirculating ball, 20.2:1 ratio (17.6:1 with fast steering adjustment)
Standard drivetrain	300-horsepower 327-ci V-8 with single four-barrel carburetor, three-speed manual transmission, 3.36:1 axle ratio
Optional engine	350-horsepower 327-ci V-8 (L79) with four-barrel carburetor, hydraulic lifters (four-speed manual transmission only)
Optional engine	390-horsepower 427-ci V-8 (L36) with four-barrel carburetor, hydraulic lifters
Optional engine	400-horsepower 427-ci V-8 (L68) with three two-barrel carburetors, hydraulic lifters
Optional engine	435-horsepower 427-ci V-8 (L71) with three two-barrel carburetors, solid lifters (close-ratio four-speed transmission only)
Optional engine	430-horsepower 427-ci V-8 (L88) with four-barrel carburetor, aluminum heads, solid lifters (heavy-duty M22 four-speed transmission only)
Optional transmission	Turbo Hydra-matic automatic (with 3.08:1 axle ratio)
Optional transmission	wide-ratio four-speed manual
Optional transmission	close-ratio four-speed manual
Optional transmission	heavy-duty four-speed manual (M22), L88 only
Optional gear ratios	2.73:1, 3.55:1, 3.70:1, 4.11:1, 4.56:1

1968

Corvette customers were no strangers to fiberglass imperfections, as body-finish quality had fluctuated considerably during the midyear run. But it had never been as bad as it was in 1968. Yet even with its obvious quality-control problems, the first Shark by no means flopped. Corvette sales for 1968 hit 28,566, a new record. And even though more than one press source was willing to point out the body's blemishes, other critics looked past those pimples to the C3's inner beauty.

Car Life called the 1968 Corvette "the excitement generator," and rightly so. Along with quickening pulses every bit as easily as the Mako Shark II had done three years before, Chevy's newest two-seater also did a decent job of cheating the wind, although most critics pointed out that much of the car's aerodynamic performance remained a mirage; less so, however, than in 1967. Test figures for drag and high-speed lift were, according to *Sports Car Graphic*'s Paul Van Valkenburgh in 1970, "very respectable considering that the shape was dictated by GM Styling, and Chevrolet engineers had to sweat acid

trying to keep the nose on the ground at speeds over 150."

Although the C3 gained some high-speed abilities, it lost a little ground on the scales, where it weighed in at about 3,440 pounds, roughly 200 more than the '67 Sting Ray. It was also 7 inches longer overall at 182.5 inches. At 69 inches, width was two-tenths less than in 1967, while height dropped from 49.6 inches to 47.8. Those last two measurements, working in concert with the radically increased tumble-home of the rounded Shark body sides, translated into a considerable reduction in interior space.

Left
Widened 15x7 Rally wheels became standard at the corners in 1968. Red-stripe F70x15 tires were optional. *Mike Mueller*

Left, below
The thoroughly modernized 1968 interior featured Astro ventilation, which drew cooling breezes in through the cowl and directed them back out through grilles located in the rear deck behind the rear window. *Mike Mueller*

Below
Full instrumentation was standard in 1968, while an AM/FM radio was an option. Notice the radio's knobs—they were unique to 1968 Corvettes. *Mike Mueller*

A sleek shape and claustrophobic cockpit weren't the only things to carry over from the Mako Shark II. Among features shared by the show car and the production model were a fiber-optic warning-light system and hidden windshield wipers. The latter rested below a vacuum-operated panel that popped open on demand. Like the Mako Shark II, the '68 Corvette also arrived without vent windows. In their place was Chevrolet's new Astro ventilation system, which routed fresh breezes in through the cowl, around interior airspace, and out through grilles located in the rear deck right behind the back window. Like those T-tops, that rear window also could be removed for maximum ventilation.

Most engineering features were carryovers as well. Beneath the '68 Corvette was basically the same chassis introduced in 1963, with its 98-inch wheelbase and independent rear suspension. Though familiar to any '63–'67 Sting Ray owner, the '68 suspension did receive a couple of nice tweaks, these performed to address another problem inherent to midyear models. Prior to 1968, mashing the go-pedal on a Corvette instantly pitched the nose up, which then threw

Left
As in 1967, the L89 aluminum-head option was available for the L71 427 V-8 in 1968. Only 624 pairs of L89 heads were ordered that year. Another 390 L89/L71 combos followed in 1969. *Mike Mueller*

Above
The 390-horsepower L36 427 big-block V-8 was a $200.15 option in 1968. L36 production that year was 7,717. *Mike Mueller*

Below
Discounting the exotic L88 and ZL-1 V-8s, the 435-horsepower L71 427 remained the hottest engine option in 1968 and 1969. L71 output remained at 435 horsepower.

front wheel geometry out of whack. The end result was a tendency for the car to wander at a time when precise control was preferred more than ever. To correct this, spring rates were stiffened, and the rear roll center was dropped from 7.56 inches above the ground to 4.71 inches by lowering the inner pivot points of the lateral suspension arms.

To compensate for the increased understeer dialed in by these changes, widened 7-inch Rally wheels were added to allow the use of fatter F70x15 tires. More rubber on the ground meant more resistance to lateral g forces. Maximum lateral acceleration measured 0.84 g for the Shark, compared to 0.74 for the midyear Corvette.

Did these modifications do the trick? Even *Road & Track*'s ever-critical critics were impressed: "No question about it, the Corvette is

one of the best-handling front-engine production cars in the world."

The '68 Corvette's standard drivetrain was a complete midyear carryover: the same tried-and-true, 300-horse 327 small block backed by a three-speed manual gearbox. And 1968's optional engines list was identical, too. At the bottom was the L79 327, rated at 350 horses. Next came the 427 big blocks: the 390-horsepower L36 and its triple-carb running mates, the 400-horse L68 and 435-horse L71. Topping things off were the L88 and the L89 aluminum-head package for the L71.

All 427s, save for the L88, were fitted with new low-rise intake manifolds designed to allow the carburetor (or carburetors) ample clearance beneath the third-generation Corvette's low, low

hood. Efficient intake flow was preserved by sinking the manifold's underside into the big block's lifter valley.

Changes to the outrageous L88 427 in 1968 included the addition of smog controls, including a PCV valve and Chevrolet's air injection reaction (AIR) system. Beefier connecting rods and various

new cams also were installed, as were Chevy's famed open-chamber heads midway into the year. L88 production for 1968 jumped to 80, all again featuring M22 Rocker Crusher four-speeds.

Optional transmissions rolled over from 1967 with one exception. The Powerglide automatic was finally replaced by Chevrolet's three-speed Turbo Hydra-matic, introduced in 1965. Bringing up the rear in 1968 was the Posi-Traction (RPO G81) differential in most cases. The G81 axle was a mandatory extra-cost choice behind all engine/trans combos, save for the manual-shifted 327s.

XP-882

From his earliest days working with Chevrolet's sporty two-seater, Zora Duntov envisioned an ideal design based on a chassis that located its engine amidships. Advantages to the midengine idea vary, not the least of which involves getting all that weight off the nose. Reducing pressure on the front wheels lightens up steering effort. This means faster manual steering ratios can be used without overtaxing the driver's arms. And moving the engine to the middle not only better balances

the load, it also can translate into a preferred lower center of gravity, because all that motive mass can be mounted closer to the road with no steering or suspension components barring the way. The cockpit, too, can be lowered, primarily because the pilot doesn't have to look over a big V-8.

Duntov reportedly first proposed relocating the Corvette's engine rearward in 1954. His idea wasn't really considered until 1959, but no one on the street paid all that much attention when the midengine CERV I appeared the following year. Much the same could've been said when the all-wheel-drive CERV II followed in 1964.

Duntov proposed another midengine racer, the GS 3, in April 1964, and at the same time began drawing up a production-based counterpart. Meanwhile, R&D engineer Frank Winchell was hard at work on his rear-engine XP-819 to prove that Corvair technology could work wearing Corvette carb. Track tests proved otherwise.

Winchell returned to the drawing board in 1967, resulting in the sleek XP-880. This midengine machine was running by February

Research and development engineer Frank Winchell began work on his XP-880 in 1967, and the midengine prototype was running by February 1968. It was named "Astro II" once it started appearing on auto show stages.

1968, and was officially named "Astro II" in preparation for a public introduction at the New York Auto Show that April.

Picking up where Winchell's XP-880 left off was XP-882, which Duntov began putting together early in 1968. Unlike previous prototypes, XP-882 featured a transverse-mounted engine, in this case a 400-cubic-inch small-block V-8. Power was transferred by a chain to an automatic transmission, where it was redirected 90 degrees to a differential. Wheelbase was a scant 95.5 inches, and total vehicle weight was a tidy 2,595 pounds.

This unique vehicle was nearing testing stages early in 1969 when new Chevrolet General Manager John DeLorean cancelled the project. He directed designers instead to try a less-expensive course using a more conventional platform based on the Camaro® chassis then being readied for 1970.

Zora Duntov created another midengine experimental, XP-882, early in 1968. It featured a transverse-mounted small-block V-8.

Below
Wheelbase for the XP-882 was a tidy 95.5 inches. Weight was 2,595 pounds.

Fortunately, this "Cormaro" idea was itself quickly cancelled after it was learned that both Ford and American Motors would be showing up at the 52nd annual New York Auto Show in April 1970 with their own midengine proposals, the Pantera and AMX/3, respectively. In response, Chevrolet revived the XP-882 project and put together its own 1970 exhibit labeled simply "Corvette prototype."

"We'll stake our reputation on this being the Corvette of the future," announced a July 1970 *Road & Track* report, "but don't expect it until 1972 at the earliest." Six months later, *R&T*'s Ron Wakefield explored the midengine proposal further. "We have now established beyond a doubt that the car was indeed a prototype for future production—1973, to be exact—and can report full details on the 1973 Corvette," he wrote in the January 1971 issue.

XP-882, however, was just the first in a short line of midengine experiments that never made it past the dream stage.

1969

1969

Specifications	1969
Model availability	sport coupe and convertible (optional removable hardtop)
Wheelbase	98 inches
Length	182.5 inches
Width	69 inches
Height	47.8 inches (sport coupe), 47.9 inches (convertible, top up), 47.8 inches (convertible, with hardtop)
Shipping weight	3,091 pounds (coupe), 3,096 pounds (convertible)
Tread (front/rear, in inches)	58.7/59.4
Tires	F70-15
Brakes	11.75-inch discs
Wheels	15x8 Rally rims with trim rings and center caps
Fuel tank	20 gallons
Front suspension	parallel A-arms with coil springs
Rear suspension	independent three-link with transverse leaf spring
Steering	recirculating ball, 20.2:1 ratio (17.6:1 with fast steering adjustment)
Standard drivetrain	300-horsepower 350-ci V-8 with single four-barrel carburetor, three-speed manual transmission, 3.36:1 axle ratio
Optional engine	350-horsepower 350-ci V-8 (L46) with four-barrel carburetor, hydraulic lifters (close- or wide-ratio four-speed manual transmissions only)
Optional engine	390-horsepower 427-ci V-8 (L36) with four-barrel carburetor, hydraulic lifters
Optional engine	400-horsepower 427-ci V-8 (L68) with three two-barrel carburetors, hydraulic lifters
Optional engine	435-horsepower 427-ci V-8 (L71) with three two-barrel carburetors, solid lifters (optional aluminum-head L89 available)
Optional engine	430-horsepower 427-ci V-8 (L88) with aluminum heads, four-barrel carburetor, solid lifters
Optional engine	430-horsepower 427-ci V-8 (ZL-1) with aluminum heads and cylinder block, four-barrel carburetor, solid lifters
Note	370-horsepower 350-ci LT-1 V-8 initially listed but wasn't offered until 1970
Optional transmission	Turbo Hydra-matic automatic (with 3.08:1 axle ratio) available with all engines except L46 350
Optional transmission	wide-ratio four-speed manual
Optional transmission	close-ratio four-speed manual
Optional transmission	heavy-duty four-speed manual (M22)
Optional gear ratios	2.73:1, 3.55:1, 3.70:1, 4.11:1, 4.56:1

Far and away the meanest, nastiest engine to ever make an RPO list, the exotic ZL-1 was purely and plainly a racing mill let loose on the street.

Above
The familiar Stingray (now one word) badge returned to Corvette fenders in 1969 after a one-year hiatus.

Below
Total Corvette production surpassed 30,000 for the first time in 1969. This was the last year for the optional 427 big-block V-8.

1969

Like the midyear models it replaced, the third-generation Corvette's initial body style rolled on in essentially identical form through five model runs, and two more five-year plans followed the first before the C3 run finally came to a close. Among other things, the basic profile, those cool T-tops, and the coupe's removable rear window all carried over unchanged from 1968 to 1972. Much the same could be said for the original Shark's standard wheels. Though widened from 7 inches to 8 in 1969, the Corvette's 15-inch Rally rims retained the same style each year up through 1972, as did the optional full wheel covers.

Most casual witnesses still find it difficult to readily differentiate between those first five Sharks. Perhaps the easiest clues in 1969 involved badging. Although the Sting Ray nameplate used from 1963 to 1967 didn't reappear in 1968, it did show up on 1969 fenders, this time spelled as one word.

Furthermore, push-button door releases, individual square backup lights, and a dash-mounted ignition switch were all unique to 1968 models. In 1969, the ignition was moved to the steering column, the doors' pushbuttons were deleted, and the backup lights were moved up into the center of the inner pair of taillights. Additional 1969 giveaways included two noticeable options offered for that year only: side-mount exhausts (RPO N14) and bright trim (RPO TJ2) for the car's fender louvers.

Much less noticeable in 1969 was a new standard engine, a 350-cubic-inch small block originally created in 1967 by stretching the 327's 3.25-inch stroke to 3.48 inches while retaining the 4.00-inch bore. All other numbers carried over from the Corvette's 327 to the new base 350 as compression remained at 10.25:1 and output stayed at 300 horsepower.

A new code on the options list, RPO L46, emerged to mark the popular 350-horse small block's evolution from 327 cubic inches to 350—out with L79, in with L46. A second code first seen in 1969, ZL-1, identified an entirely new breed of big block, an all-aluminum 427. All the other optional 427s—they with their cast-iron blocks—rolled over from 1968, as did the L89 aluminum-head option.

Far and away the meanest, nastiest engine to ever make an RPO list, the exotic ZL-1 was purely

Top
Bright trim for the fender louvers was an option for only one year: 1969. *Mike Mueller*

Above
Optional side-mount exhausts were offered for the third-generation Corvette in 1969 only. *Mike Mueller*

Left
Corvette convertibles outsold coupes from 1963 to 1968, but the tables were turned in 1969 as coupe production soared to 22,129, compared to 16,633 for the topless counterpart.

and plainly a racing mill let loose on the street. Once again, Chevrolet wasn't supposed to be in racing, but there was performance products chief Vince Piggins lobbying for an all-aluminum big-block engine in 1968, with intentions being to support, among others, Bruce McLaren's successful Canadian-American (Can-Am) Challenge Cup team. Small-block Chevy-powered McLaren racers had begun their domination of the Can-Am series in 1967. Then Jim Hall built an aluminum big block for his Chaparral race team, inspiring McLaren to threaten to look to Ford for a comparable lightweight big block to power his 1968 Can-Am cars. Piggins stepped in, promised Bruce his aluminum big blocks, and the rest is racing history. Armed with the ZL-1, McLaren destroyed all Can-Am comers from 1968 to 1971, winning 32 of 37 events.

Thoroughly baptized by fire on the 1968 Can-Am circuit, the ZL-1 427 then made its way in 1969 onto the Corvette's RPO list, as well as into GM's central office production order (COPO) pipeline. Although some references identified the ZL-1 V-8 as a "special L88," creating the king of

Above
After building only 20 L88 Corvettes in 1967, Chevrolet came back with 80 in 1968 and 116 in 1969. Shown here is the latter rendition. *Mike Mueller*

Left
The aluminum-head L88 427 remained conservatively rated at 430 horsepower in 1968 and 1969 (shown here). New for the L88 in 1968 were emission controls. *Mike Mueller*

the 427s was by no means a simple matter of trading cast iron for aluminum to make the cylinder block match those lightweight heads. While the ZL-1 and L88 wore similar heads in 1969, the block was a truly unique piece of engineering.

Duntov turned to Fred Frincke for the expertise needed to fashion a high-performance engine completely out of aluminum. Casting was Frincke's forte; he knew his way around a foundry. Winters Foundry was responsible for casting the

ZL-1's block, heads, and intake. Machining work and assembly were then completed at Tonawanda under a "100-percent parts inspection" policy in production areas that Duntov described as being "surgically clean."

Frincke chose heat-treated 356 T-6 alloy for the block, which was cast with thickened walls and beefed-up main webs to compensate for the aluminum's weaker nature. The heads trapped the eight cast-iron cylinder sleeves in the aluminum block's bores. At the bottom end was a fully nitrided, forged-steel crank held in place by four-bolt main bearing caps. The same Magnafluxed connecting rods, introduced midyear in 1968 for the L88, were used, with their beefed 7/16-inch bolts, full-floating wrist pins, and Spiralock washers.

ZL-1's heads, also cast from 356 T-6 aluminum, were based on the open-chamber units introduced midway through 1968 for the L88. Combustion chambers in those heads were opened up (thus the name) around the spark plug. Results of this change included a drop in compression (from 12.5:1 to 12:1) for the "second-design" L88 because chamber volume increased. Breathing, on the other hand, went up by a reported 30 percent, thanks to the revised open chamber's closer relation to the exhaust port.

Revised ports also contributed greatly to the open-chamber head's superior breathing. Although the large rectangular intake passages remained the same size as the first-generation L88's, they were recontoured internally to help speed the air/fuel mixture into those open chambers. Exhaust ports were radically reshaped from rectangles into round passages to match up to the tube headers that racers would quickly bolt up in place of the mismatched, rectangular-passage iron manifolds delivered from the factory.

Like the open-chamber L88 head, the ZL-1 unit featured 2.19-inch intake valves and enlarged 1.88-inch exhausts. The ZL-1, however, was fitted with new TRW forged-aluminum pistons with extra-thick tops and strengthened pin bosses. These beefier slugs not only proved more durable than the L88 units, they also reinstated the aluminum-head 427's original 12.5:1 compression by way of increased dome area.

Above
Only two documented ZL-1 Corvettes are known for 1969.
Mike Mueller

Right
Like the L88, the all-aluminum ZL-1 427 was laughingly rated at 430 horsepower. Actual output was more like 525 horses. *Mike Mueller*

The ZL-1 427's solid-lifter cam was even more radical than the L88's, at least as far as lift was concerned. Intake valve lift was 0.560 inch, exhaust was 0.600. Tests, however, demonstrated that decreased durations cooperated better with those free-flowing, sewer-sized ports. The resulting shorter-duration cam, working in concert with the various reinforced internals, helped the ZL-1 wind out like no big block on this planet. Seven grand on the tach was no problem, and Chevrolet engineers claimed short bursts to 7,600 were within reason. Keeping the juices flowing during those high-rpm trips was a huge 850-cfm Holley four-barrel.

As was the case with the L88, the ZL-1 was given a bogus output rating of 430 horsepower. Reportedly, 525 horsepower was more like it, and engineers claimed 600 horses were possible with only a little tweaking.

Not until the new Z06 was unleashed in 2006 has Chevrolet dared deliver so much raw power to the people. Yes, John Q. Public could have walked into his nearest Chevy dealership in 1969 and rolled out in a street-legal, emissions-controlled, aluminum-engine Corvette able to break not simply into the 13-second bracket, nor the 12—breaking the sound barrier was more like it.

"The ZL-1 doesn't just accelerate, because the word 'accelerate' is inadequate for this car," wrote *Motor Trend*'s Eric Dahlquist after a wild ride in the most outrageous Corvette ever built. "It tears its way through the air and across the black pavement like all the modern big-inch racing machines you have ever seen."

The great white whale of a Corvette that Dahlquist raved about screamed through the quarter-mile in 12.1 seconds at 116 miles per hour. Shorter rear gears easily would have translated into 11 seconds in the quarter-mile, if not less. A second ZL-1 test mule present on the day Dahlquist took his ride managed a 10.89-second pass at 130 miles per hour. Not only was that ridiculously fast, it was ridiculously easy. "The fact that almost anybody who knows how to drive could jump in and duplicate this run after run may be the most shattering aspect of all," concluded a *Motor Trend* report entitled "The 10-second Trip."

Why anyone in his right mind would want to travel from point A to B that quickly also begged the question of what type of maniac in 1969 would fall in line to buy a ZL-1 Corvette. "First, he will have a lot of money," answered Duntov. The all-aluminum 427 big block alone wore a $4,718.35 price tag. A complete ZL-1 Corvette cost more than $9,000, and it was this intimidating total that explains why only two documented examples are known today.

Already 9 inches longer than a production Stingray, the reshaped Mako Shark II body grew even more after the Manta Ray transformation, shown on display in 1994 at the National Corvette Museum. *Mike Mueller*

Explaining how others appeared over the years is easy enough. Reportedly, as many as a dozen mules or executive toys might've been built. The race-ready ZL-1 427 also was offered on its own, in a crate, and any number of these could have found their way into street-going Corvettes. According to Fred Frincke, Chevrolet's Mk. IV engine facility in Tonawanda, New York, built 154 ZL-1 427s.

Tonawanda plant man and diehard big-block researcher Fran Preve claims a different score. His search through Chevrolet's official "Summary of Engines Shipped" papers uncovered 94 ZL-1s manufactured for Y-body Corvette applications: 80 for four-speeds, 14 for M40 automatics. Add to that another 90 all-aluminum 427s built for F-body Camaros. Sixty-nine ZL-1 Camaros rolled out of Chevrolet's back door in 1969 thanks to Vince Piggins' clever use of the COPO loophole. Along with the two recorded factory installations in Corvettes, one other ZL-1 big block went into the Mako Shark II when it was restyled into the Manta Ray show car in 1969.

Like 1969's engine lineup, that year's transmission list looked familiar, with one notable change as the tough Turbo Hydra-matic (RPO M40) became available behind the two solid-lifter 427s, and not a moment too soon in some minds. "The Turbo Hydro is the best thing that's happened

The Mako Shark II show car was reborn in 1969 as the Manta Ray, powered by Chevy's all-aluminum ZL-1 427 big-block V-8.

to big-engined Corvettes since high-octane gas," wrote *Hot Rod*'s Steve Kelly. "Those who can overcome the four-speed mystique are in for a surprise," claimed *Car Life*'s Corvette fans. "The Turbo Hydra-matic fitted to the high-performance 427s is magnificent. It slips from gear to gear in traffic without so much as a nudge. Power tightens the shifts into a series of iron hands, strong enough to light the tires at every change."

When ordered behind the base 350 that year, the M40 trans was priced at $221.80. It cost $290.40 when mated to the L71 or L88. "In the mild engine, the M40 was set to shift up quickly," continued *Car Life*'s July 1969 L88/automatic review. "In the wild engines, the transmission stays in the lower gear until the driver lifts his foot, right up to redline." Of the 116 L88 Corvettes built for 1969, 17 featured the Turbo Hydra-matic.

Manta Ray show car

Once off the auto show circuit, the Mako Shark II paced a few races and also, like other Corvette show cars, served time as Bill Mitchell's personal driver. Then, in 1969, it took on a new identity when it was restyled into the Manta Ray.

Already measuring some 9 inches longer than a standard Stingray, the Mako Shark length grew even more after the Manta Ray conversion. Extra inches came by way of a restyled, stretched tail that took on a tapered look from a profile perspective. The point of that tail was protected by a body-colored Endura bumper. Among other updates were a chin spoiler up front and a repaint

that played down the shark shading. Sidepipes were later added, as were small mirrors mounted up high on the windshield pillars. The biggest news, though, was the Manta Ray's new power source. In place of the iron-block 427 used by the Mako Shark II was Chevrolet's all-aluminum ZL-1 427, an exotic mill more befitting of such an exotic, one-of-a-kind show car.

Estimates put the price tag for the original 427-powered Mako Shark II at as much as $2.5 million. Reportedly, that bill may have even hit $3 million by the time the ZL-1 Manta Ray transformation was complete.

1970

Specifications	1970
Model availability	sport coupe and convertible (optional removable hardtop)
Wheelbase	98 inches
Length	182.5 inches
Width	69 inches
Height	47.8 inches (sport coupe), 47.9 inches (convertible, top up), 47.8 inches (convertible, with hardtop)
Shipping weight	3,153 pounds (coupe), 3,167 pounds (convertible)
Tread (front/rear, in inches)	58.7/59.4
Tires	F70-15
Brakes	11.75-inch discs
Wheels	15x8 Rally rims with trim rings and center caps
Fuel tank	20 gallons (California emissions tank, 17 gallons)
Front suspension	parallel A-arms with coil springs
Rear suspension	independent three-link with transverse leaf spring
Steering	recirculating ball, 20.2:1 ratio (17.6:1 with fast steering adjustment)
Standard drivetrain	300-horsepower 350-ci V-8 with single four-barrel carburetor, four-speed manual transmission, 3.36:1 axle ratio
Optional engine	350-horsepower 350-ci V-8 (L46) with four-barrel carburetor, hydraulic lifters (close- or wide-ratio four-speed manual transmissions only)
Optional engine	370-horsepower 350-ci V-8 (LT-1) with four-barrel carburetor, solid lifters (close- or wide-ratio four-speed manual transmission only)
Optional engine	390-horsepower 454-ci V-8 (LS5) with four-barrel carburetor, hydraulic lifters
Note	460-horsepower (or 465-horsepower) 454-ci LS7 V-8 initially listed but cancelled before reaching production
Optional transmission	Turbo Hydra-matic automatic (with 3.08:1 axle ratio), not available with L46 or LT-1 350-ci V-8
Optional transmission	wide-ratio four-speed manual
Optional transmission	close-ratio four-speed manual
Optional transmission	heavy-duty four-speed manual (M22), ZR1 option only
Optional gear ratios	2.73:1, 3.55:1, 3.70:1, 4.11:1

Motor Trend's Chuck Koch almost couldn't believe his eyes. "The Corvette was just as fast, if not faster, through the corners as the Porsche."

Coupes were again most popular in 1970, with 10,668 built. Convertible production was 6,648. *Mike Mueller*

1970

Corvette production first surpassed the 20,000 level in 1963 and stayed there up through 1969, the year the annual figure topped 30,000 for the first time on the way to a new all-time high of 38,762 cars. It needs to be said, however, that this record came about partially because Chevrolet General Manager John DeLorean allowed the 1969 model year to run over into December after

a strike had delayed production for two months earlier in the year. This extension in turn then took a bite out of the following model run, resulting in only 17,316 1970 Corvettes being released by the St. Louis plant, representing its lowest effort since 1962.

The 1970 Corvette included flares added to the wheel openings to reduce bodywork damage created by debris tossed up by the fat tires in

1968 and 1969. Revised fender vents wearing crosshatch grilles appeared in 1970 and stuck around through 1972, as did rectangular exhaust tips, which replaced the round units used previously. The round turn signal lamps and small side marker lights seen in 1968 and 1969 were replaced by larger side markers and rectangular turn signals, and these items carried on unchanged through 1972.

Posi-Traction and the M20 wide-ratio four-speed transmission were added into the standard package. G81 installations had been on the rise throughout the 1960s and by 1968 were found on 94.5 percent of that year's cars. Meanwhile, the reverse was happening concerning deliveries of the standard three-speed manual trans, which had made up 67.5 percent of the mix in 1957, the first year for the four-speed option. That figure fell to a microscopic 4.3 percent in 1963, followed by only 1.1 percent five years later. No more three-speeds were seen after 1969.

Both the close-ratio M21 manual box and the Turbo Hydra-matic automatic could've been ordered in place of the M20 at no extra cost in 1970. Yet another former option, tinted glass all around, also was tossed in as part of the standard deal that year.

Of course, adding extra standard equipment meant that Chevrolet had to ask more for base Corvette coupes and convertibles in 1970. After increasing only 2.5 percent from 1968 to 1969, the Corvette coupe's bottom line jumped 8.6 percent in 1970, surpassing $5,000 for the first time in the process. The convertible's standard sticker first breached the five-grand plateau in 1971.

Standard power again came from the 300-horse 350, and the 350-horse L46 returned on the options list. But all other optional engines were

Strength in numbers for 1970— 300, 350, 370, 390, 460 hp.

Every Corvette is built tough right from the start. Our basic V8, the 300-hp Turbo-Fire 350, features a 10.25:1 compression ratio, a 4-barrel carb, cast aluminum alloy pistons and a precision-formed crank. With this, and all other Corvette engines, you get Corvette's dual exhausts with new rectangular outlets and Positraction rear axle standard.

Go one step up to the 350-hp Turbo-Fire 350, and you get an 11.0:1 compression ratio, impact-extruded aluminum alloy pistons, finned aluminum rocker covers, a high-performance cam and a forged steel alloy crank. Our 370-hp 350 features the same hardware as the 350-hp version plus an aluminum intake manifold, domed hood, special cam, special exhaust and mechanical lifters. Next step up. Our 390-

hp 454-cu.-in. Turbo-Jet V8. This engine uses a cast aluminum alloy intake manifold, chromed air cleaner and rocker covers and an extra-large oil pan. You also get a high-domed hood, heavier duty front springs, a larger diameter front stabilizer bar, rear suspension stabilizer bar, a larger capacity radiator, dual pulleys for

the fan and water pump and a higher performance starter motor.
Also available: our 460-hp Turbo-Jet 454 with a large 4-barrel carb, high-performance cam, mechanical lifters, aluminum cylinder heads and full-transistor ignition system.
Transmissions: standard gearbox is a floor-mounted, wide-range 4-speed, 2.52:1 low gear. Also available, a close-ratio version with a 2.20:1 low (close ratio not available with 300-hp engine, wide range not available with 460-hp engine).
With the 300-, 390- and 460-hp engines, you can order Turbo Hydra-matic. Just sit back and let this 3-range fully automatic transmission shift for itself; or upshift and downshift through the 1-2-3 quadrant yourself with all the benefits of a stick and none of the legwork.

Chevrolet Corvette Stingray Convertible with removable hardtop.

Above
Early 1970 Corvette ads mentioned the 460-horsepower LS7 454 V-8 as an option. Magazines even road-tested one of these beasts. But the engine was cancelled before it could escape into the wild.

In 1969, the 350-horsepower L46 V-8 picked up where the L79 left off after the Corvette small block grew from 327 cubic inches to 350. The L46 350 cost $131.65 in 1970. Production that year was 12,846. *Mike Mueller*

Left
In place of the vertical slots seen in 1968 and 1969 was this mesh-style fender louver, which stuck around up through 1972. *Mike Mueller*

dropped in favor of two new V-8s—one small block, one big block, respectively known as "mouse" and "rat" motors among the Chevy faithful. The new rat came about after engineers stroked the Mk. IV V-8 (from 3.76 to 4.00 inches) to raise displacement to 454 cubic inches. At 4.25 inches, the LS5's bore remained constant, as did compression (10.25:1) and base output (390 horsepower). Torque, on the other hand, was a whopping 500 ft-lbs, 40 more than the L36 427 turned out in 1969.

While it could melt a Wide Oval with the best of 'em and gulp a gallon of ethyl quicker than you

could pump 'er in, the high-compression LS5 still could've been considered user friendly, thanks in part to its hydraulic cam. "It is by far the most tractable big-engine Corvette unit we've tried," claimed *Road & Track*.

As for the new optional small block, it too impressed witnesses, and to much greater degrees. Labeled LT-1, this 350-cubic-inch mouse motor relied on a solid-lifter cam to help produce a whopping 370 horsepower, meaning it easily could slug it out with engines displacing many more cubes. Built from 1970 to 1972, the LT-1 Corvette combined rat-like muscle with the nimbleness no big-block driver ever knew. "As you would expect, the personalities of the LS5 and the LT-1 are worlds apart," explained *Car and Driver*. "In performance, however, they are neck and neck."

RPO LT-1 was initially listed in Corvette paperwork in 1969 but didn't actually appear until the following year, priced at $447.60, compared to $289.65 for the LS5 big block. Among LT-1 features were big-valve heads (2.02-inch intakes, 1.60 exhausts), an aggressive cam, 11.1:1 forged-aluminum TRW pistons, and a forged crank held in

place by four-bolt main bearing caps. On top was an aluminum high-rise dual-plane intake mounting an 800-cfm Holley four-barrel.

All these hot parts translated into a 0–60 run of 5.7 seconds according to *Car Life*. Quarter-mile time was 14.17 seconds. But pure speed wasn't necessarily the goal. Supreme overall performance was, and to that end the LT-1 also came standard with a stiffened suspension, inspiring *Car Life* to call it "the best of all possible Corvettes."

"Corvette handling is superior with any engine," continued *Car Life*, "and the LT-1 is the best of the bunch. The weight balance is a perfect 50/50 with the small-block engine." After pairing the LT-1 up against a Porsche 911E, *Motor Trend*'s Chuck Koch almost couldn't believe his eyes. "The Corvette was just as fast, if not faster, through the corners as the Porsche."

Neither air conditioning nor the Turbo Hydra-matic could be installed when the 370-horse 350 was ordered. LT-1 buyers in 1970 could have chosen between two four-speeds: the wide-ratio M20 or its close-ratio M21 cousin.

The M22 Rock Crusher was also available but only by way of Chevrolet's original ZR-1 package, which cost an intimidating $965.95 in 1970. Along with the LT-1 V-8 and M22 gearbox, this expensive deal included heavy-duty power brakes, an even stiffer suspension, and an aluminum radiator with metal fan shroud.

Three items were exclusive to the ZR-1 Corvette, and all three were carryovers from the

Top
Vinyl covering (RPO C08) for the Corvette convertible's optional removable top first appeared in 1967. In 1970, the C08 option cost $63.20. It was installed on 832 auxiliary hardtops (RPO C07) that year. *Mike Mueller*

Left
Turning on a Corvette's headlights from 1963 on always represented a compromise from an aesthetic point of view, as well as an aerodynamic negative. Thus, designers chose to finally do away with hideaway headlamps when the time came to fashion the new C6, introduced for 2005. *Mike Mueller*

L88s of 1967–1969: the M22 trans, F41 special suspension, and J56 heavy-duty brakes. The F41 suspension consisted of shorter, stiffer coils up front, a seven-leaf spring in back, and heavy-duty stabilizer bars at both ends, at least on paper. Officially listed early on, that rear stabilizer bar apparently didn't make it beneath any ZR-1 cars in 1970.

The special J56 brakes included the J50 power booster, heavy-duty Delco Moraine four-piston calipers, and fade-resistant metallic linings. Front pads were fixed more firmly in place by two mounting pins each, compared to the rear pads that typically only used one pin. Cast-iron caliper mount braces were added up front to restrict vibration during hard stops. This brake system was all but identical to the L88's, save for the fact that its dual-circuit master cylinder didn't incorporate a proportioning valve.

Although it did finally appear in Corvette brochures the following year, the purposeful ZR-1 option wasn't promoted at all in 1970. Offered along with the LT-1 up through 1972, it attracted only 25 buyers in 1970, followed by 8 in 1971 and 20 in 1972.

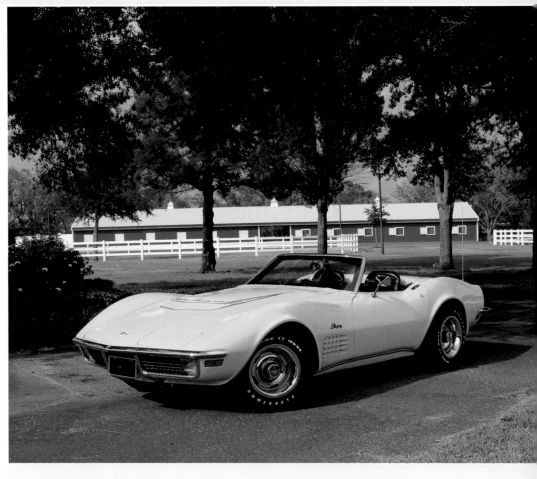

The $447.60 LT-1 engine package was available for both coupes and convertibles in 1970. Total LT-1 Corvette production that first year was 1,287. *Mike Mueller*

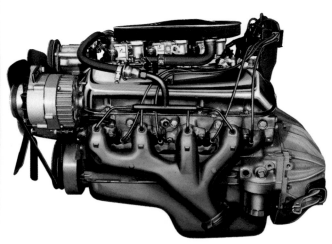

Far left
Originally listed as a 1969 Corvette option, the 350-cubic-inch LT-1 small block officially debuted in 1970 at 370 horsepower. A 360-horse LT-1 also appeared as the heart of the 1970-1/2 Z/28 Camaro.

Left
The LS7 V-8 wasn't 1970's only stillborn engine. Chevrolet engineers that year planned to retain the optional Corvette engine packages offered in 1969 using 454 cubic inches instead of 427. That triple-carb 454 would have superseded the 435-horsepower L71 427.

Specifications	1971

Model availability	sport coupe and convertible (optional removable hardtop)
Wheelbase	98 inches
Length	182.5 inches
Width	69 inches
Height	47.8 inches (sport coupe), 47.9 inches (convertible, top up), 47.8 inches (convertible, with hardtop)
Shipping weight	3,153 pounds (coupe), 3,167 pounds (convertible)
Tread (front/rear, in inches)	58.7/59.5
Tires	F70-15
Brakes	11.75-inch discs
Wheels	15x8 Rally rims with trim rings and center caps
Fuel tank	18 gallons
Front suspension	parallel A-arms with coil springs
Rear suspension	independent three-link with transverse leaf spring
Steering	recirculating ball, 20.2:1 ratio (17.6:1 with fast steering adjustment)
Standard drivetrain	270-horsepower 350-ci V-8 with single four-barrel carburetor, four-speed manual transmission, 3.36:1 axle ratio
Optional engine	330-horsepower 350-ci V-8 (LT-1) with four-barrel carburetor, solid lifters (close- or wide-ratio four-speed manual transmission only)
Optional engine	360-horsepower 454-ci V-8 (LS5) with four-barrel carburetor, hydraulic lifters
Optional engine	425-horsepower 454-ci V-8 (LS6) with four-barrel carburetor, aluminum heads, solid lifters
Optional transmission	Turbo Hydra-matic automatic (with 3.08 1 axle ratio), not available with LT-1 350-ci V-8
Optional transmission	wide-ratio four-speed manual
Optional transmission	close-ratio four-speed manual
Optional transmission	heavy-duty four-speed manual (M22) included with ZR1 and ZR2 options, available with LS6 V-8
Optional gear ratios	3.36:1, 3.55:1, 3.70:1, 4.11:1

Coupes outnumbered convertibles two to one in 1971. Production for the latter was 7,121 and 14,680 for the former.

1971

From 1965 to 1969, the Corvette reigned supreme as Chevrolet's most powerful production car. And it would have remained so again in 1970 had the awesome LS7 454 V-8 appeared as planned. More or less an enlarged L88, this aluminum-head big block was actually listed in brochures and assembly manuals early in the year, rated at 460 or 465 horsepower, depending on your source. One LS7 Corvette was even road tested by *Motor Trend* and *Sports Car Graphic*, the latter reporting quarter-mile performance of 13.8 seconds at 108 miles per hour, "with full fuel, passenger, and luggage for two." Not to mention full exhausts, street tires, a smog pump, radio, heater, etc.

"We close with the old Texas proverb," concluded *SCG*'s Paul Van Valkenburgh after his thrilling LS7 ride. "If you care who's quickest, don't get caught shoveling manure behind someone else's 465 horses."

But it was Duntov's engineers who ended up doing the shoveling, as they were forced to send the LS7 to an early grave before it ever got the chance to live it up on American streets. What happened? Coupled with GM efforts to tone down performance in 1970 were Chevy officials' decisions to cut back on costly options that complicated assembly lines. "De-pro" was the company jargon for this de-proliferation program, and both the LS7 and L46 small block ended up being de-pro victims in 1970. While Duntov's

"If you care who's quickest, don't get caught shoveling manure behind someone else's 465 horses."
–Paul Van Valkenburgh
Sports Car Graphic

The 1971 Corvette looked essentially identical to its 1970 forerunner. Standard small-block power dropped from 300 horsepower to 270. Engine options included the 330-horse LT-1 350, 365-horse LS5 454 (shown), and 425-horse LS6 454. *Mike Mueller*

Below
This deluxe wheel cover was a $63 option (RPO P02) in 1971. *Mike Mueller*

Below, right
Chevrolet built 5,097 1971 Corvette coupes and convertibles fitted with the LS5 454 big-block V-8.

greatest disappointment came in the mid-1970s when GM finally squelched his midengine proposals, he later expressed every bit as much dismay concerning the LS7's cancellation in 1970.

With the LS7 gone, its 450-horsepower LS6 454 brother became Chevy's hottest V-8 in 1970. But it was only installed in SS 454 Chevelles that year, resulting in what many still believe was the muscle car era's supreme machine. Like the LS7, a second-edition LS6 Chevelle was road tested and then cancelled early on in 1971. Meanwhile, the hottest Corvette for 1970 was the 390-horse LS5.

And if that wasn't enough, new for 1971 were the first power cutbacks in Corvette history. Standard output dropped from 300 horses to 270 as compression was slashed (from 10.25:1 to a tidy 8.5:1) as part of GM's response to Washington's crackdown on engine emissions.

The LT-1, too, lost ground, to 330 horsepower, as its compression also was cut to 9:1. Same for the LS5 big block: compression went from 10.25:1 to 9:1, dropping advertised output to 365 horsepower.

Fortunately, not all was lost. While the LS6 was dropped from the A-body Chevelle line, it was added to the Y-body Corvette lineup for 1971. It didn't escape the compression axe (the squeeze went from 11.25:1 to 9:1), but it remained strong at 425 horsepower, putting the Corvette back on top where it belonged.

Another difference between the 1970 LS6 and the 1971 edition involved the cylinder heads— they were made of iron for A-body applications, aluminum for Y-body installations. Valve sizes were 2.19 inches intake, 1.88 exhaust; pistons were TRW forged-aluminum pieces, and rods were forged-steel units with big 7/16-inch bolts. A potent solid-lifter cam went inside, and a 780-cfm Holley four-barrel mounted on a low-rise, dual-plane aluminum intake went on top.

Like its Chevelle predecessor, the LS6 Corvette wasn't cheap. The aluminum-head 454's asking price was a hefty $1,220, leaving little wonder why only 188 customers chose the LS6 in 1971. "It's Duntov's favorite engine and he's tortured because few customers can afford it," claimed a *Car and Driver* report. But this time Zora's pain may have been self-inflicted. "Maybe for street engine I make mistake," he admitted to *Car and Driver*. "Aluminum heads are expensive and that weight doesn't matter on the street."

Even more expensive was RPO ZR2, the special-purpose turbo-jet 454 option, which mirrored the ZR-1 racing package offered for the 1970–1972 LT-1 small block. The bottom line for RPO ZR2 was $1,747. A mere 12 were sold in 1971.

Even without the track-ready ZR2 package, the LS6 was a big winner on the street, running 0–60 in 5.3 seconds, according to a *Car and Driver* test. Quarter-mile performance was listed at 13.8 seconds at 104.65 miles per hour; quite notable considering the car was equipped with a less-than-desirable 3.36:1 economy axle.

Car Craft magazine went a step further, adding headers, stump-pulling 4.56:1 gears, and racing slicks, resulting in a 12.64-second quarter-mile pass at 114.21 miles per hour. Not long after this sizzling pass, one of *Car Craft*'s less experienced lead-footers put a couple of the LS6's rods through its oil pan—a somewhat fitting exclamation point for a story entitled "Goodbye Forever, LS6." *Car Craft*'s crew knew even as they were flogging one of the strongest Corvettes ever built that they would probably never see such speed and power again. Chevrolet officials had made it clear that the option wouldn't return for 1972.

XP-895

Further toying with the existing midengine XP-882 chassis in 1971 resulted in the more pleasing XP-895. But as much as this steel-bodied prototype looked like the next step into the future, the XP-895 still weighed every bit as much as a regular-production Corvette. Cutting the car's weight was significant to the midengine prototype ideal, so to breach this hurdle, John DeLorean's people turned to the Reynolds Metals Company in 1972. Reynolds created an aluminum copy of the

Top
John Greenwood put together some of the hottest racing Corvettes during the 1970s. This L88-powered Greenwood roadster copped SCCA championships in 1970 and 1971. It finished first in the GT class at Sebring in 1971 with comedian Dick Smothers co-driving.

Above
In 1971, the XP-882 chassis was morphed into the XP-895 midengine machine, which initially featured a steel body. That car was then refitted in 1972 with a weight-saving aluminum shell (shown) supplied by the Reynolds Metals Company.

XP-895 body, painted silver like its heavier sibling, and delivered it to Chevrolet Engineering. A year or so later, Chevy engineers used that lightweight shell to create an XP-895 variant that weighed about 500 pounds less than the original.

According to Reynolds' officials, the running XP-895 machine represented "an important

milestone in the application of aluminum in auto-body construction." And beneath that lightweight skin was much of the same innovative mechanical makeup demonstrated earlier by XP-882. But the costs of producing the "Reynolds Corvette" in suitable numbers proved prohibitive, and this experiment also ended up on the shelf.

1972

Specifications	1972

Model availability	sport coupe and convertible (optional removable hardtop)
Wheelbase	98 inches
Length	182.5 inches
Width	69 inches
Height	47.8 inches (sport coupe), 47.9 inches (convertible, top up), 47.8 inches (convertible, with hardtop)
Shipping weight	3,215 pounds
Tread (front/rear, in inches)	58.7/59.5
Tires	F70-15
Brakes	11.75-inch discs
Wheels	15x8 Rally rims with trim rings and center caps
Fuel tank	18 gallons
Front suspension	parallel A-arms with coil springs
Rear suspension	independent three-link with transverse leaf spring
Steering	recirculating ball, 20.2:1 ratio
Standard drivetrain	200-horsepower 350-ci V-8 with single four-barrel carburetor, four-speed manual transmission, 3.36:1 axle ratio
Optional engine	255-horsepower 350-ci V-8 (LT-1) with four-barrel carburetor, solid lifters (close- or wide-ratio four-speed manual transmission only)
Optional engine	270-horsepower 454-ci V-8 (LS5) with four-barrel carburetor, hydraulic lifters
Optional transmission	Turbo Hydra-matic automatic (with 3.08:1 axle ratio), not available with LT-1 350-ci V-8
Optional transmission	wide-ratio four-speed manual
Optional transmission	close-ratio four-speed manual
Optional transmission	heavy-duty four-speed manual (M22), included with ZR1 option
Optional gear ratios	3.36:1, 3.55:1, 3.70:1, 4.11:1

The 1972 Corvette coupe was the last to feature a removable rear window.

1972

While ever-tightening federal emissions standards would cut horsepower even more soon enough, advertised outputs for all GM engines plummeted further in 1972 when gross ratings were traded for SAE net figures per an industry-wide trend. The '72 Corvette's standard 350 was listed at a paltry 200 horsepower. New net ratings for the two optional de-pro survivors, the LT-1 small block and LS5 big block, were 255 and 270 horsepower, respectively.

That latter figure apparently embarrassed engineers so much they failed to stick an output label on the LS5 air cleaner lid, making it the first time that a big block went out in public incognito.

California customers were none the wiser because they never even got a look at a 1972 LS5. Chevrolet officials that year didn't bother to put the LS5 through that state's stringent emissions testing, meaning it failed to meet certification for sale there. This wouldn't be the last time that a Corvette engine would be banned on the West Coast.

Among various far-less-obvious changes made for 1972 was the deletion of transistorized ignition and the optic-fiber warning light system. In exchange for the latter, buyers received a standard horn-honking burglar alarm system, which was previously an option (RPO UA6) for 1968–1971 Corvettes.

LT-1 buyers were treated to one last surprise as their favorite ride rolled on in its final year. With its lowered compression, the LT-1 350 was not nearly the same hothead it had been in 1970, so engineers were able to add optional air conditioning into the equation. The cool C60 option was installed on as many as 240 LT-1 Corvettes during the last four months of 1972 production.

The LT-1 production tally for the three-year run read 1,287 in 1970, 1,949 in 1971, and 1,741 in 1972. Some press reports mentioned a fourth LT-1 Corvette for 1973, but most witnesses, critical or otherwise, had already noticed the handwriting on the wall. Two years later, it was

In June 1971, Ed Cole gave the go-ahead to the XP-897GT project. Wearing a Pinanfarina body atop that same transverse-engine chassis, this car, the so-called Two-Rotor Corvette, debuted in September 1973.

painfully clear that the days of clattering lifters and big, thirsty Holley carbs were done. The mouse that roared would roar no more.

Rotary Corvettes

Duntov's midengine ideal was struck down more than once, but his XP-882 platform just wouldn't die. Yet another resurrection followed after GM bought out the patent rights to the Wankel rotary engine in November 1970. In June 1971, Ed Cole gave the go-ahead to the XP-897GT project. Wearing a Pinanfarina body atop that same transverse-engine chassis, this car, the so-called Two-Rotor Corvette, debuted in September 1973. Duntov never did like the rotary Corvette idea, but he had no choice in the matter.

"Ed Cole was enamored with the Wankel engine," said Zora in a 1980 *AutoWeek* interview. "And he kept twisting my arm. 'What about a rotary Corvette?' Then DeLorean comes to Styling and looks at the midengine Corvette. He knows already that the decision has been made to produce this Corvette, but with the Wankel engine.

Top
The XP-882 chassis was reborn yet again in 1973, that time powered by a Wankel rotary engine. The Two-Rotor Corvette was Ed Cole's baby; Zora Duntov never did approve of the rotary Corvette idea.

Left
The Four-Rotor Corvette followed its Wankel-powered predecessor but was cancelled late in 1974. Even so, more than one member of the automotive press continued to predict the upcoming introduction of a midengine Corvette.

I told him it was not powerful enough, and he lost his composure. 'You're some genius!' he shouted. 'Invent something!'"

Duntov turned to Gib Hufstader, who then did the Two-Rotor job two better. Hufstader's much more powerful "Four-Rotor" Corvette debuted one month after the XP-897GT. Using two Wankel engines coupled together, this truly fast gullwinged beauty was, according to *Car and Driver*, "the betting-man's choice to replace the Stingray." All bets were off, however, after

Cole announced in September 1974 that GM was postponing the use of the Wankel rotary engine after running into problems getting it emissions certified.

Two years later, the Four-Rotor Corvette's Wankel was replaced by a conventional small-block V-8, as the name was changed to "Aerovette." The body remained the same, as did those tired, old rumors. According to a February 1977 *Road & Track* prediction, the Aerovette would become the 1980 Corvette. Too bad

Clockwise from above
The last LT-1 Corvette appeared in 1972. Production that year was 1,741. *Mike Mueller*

This seat upholstery pattern was unique to the 1972 Corvette. *Mike Mueller*

The 1972 Corvette's standard drivetrain featured this 200-horsepower 350 small block backed by a four-speed manual transmission. *Mike Mueller*

LT-1 V-8 output dropped to 255 net-rated horses in 1972. Notice the optional air conditioning—1972 was the only year it could have been combined with RPO LT-1. Also note the autographed air cleaner lid. *Mike Mueller*

Chevrolet was still selling conventional Corvettes like there was no tomorrow.

Duntov's dreams for the perfectly balanced, lightweight Corvette had been dashed about three years before that last *Road & Track* prophecy hit the stands. GM execs' opinion of his plan was plain and simple: why fix something that wasn't broken? Chevrolet held a captive audience for its fiberglass two-seater (with its front-mounted engine) during the 1970s, and everyone from DeLorean on up knew it. Even so, Duntov was allowed to dream on almost right up to his retirement early in 1975.

When GM once and for all squelched the midengine Corvette proposal in 1974, it resulted in easily the greatest defeat Duntov encountered during his stay at GM. "Until 1970, 90 percent of what I intended to do, I accomplished," added the Corvette's first chief engineer in that *AutoWeek* interview. "In 1972, a midship car was touch and go. It was all designed." But it still wasn't to be.

LS5 454 output dropped to 270 horsepower in 1972. LS5 Corvette production (coupes and convertibles) that year was 3,913.

Dave Heinz and Bob Johnson drove this '69 Corvette to a fourth overall finish at Sebring in 1972. Here, the car runs at Rochester, Michigan, that year.

Specifications	1973

Specifications	1973
Model availability	sport coupe and convertible (optional removable hardtop)
Wheelbase	98 inches
Length	184.7 inches
Width	69 inches
Height	47.7 inches (sport coupe), 47.9 inches (convertible, top up), 47.7 inches (convertible, with hardtop)
Shipping weight	3,407 pounds
Tread (front/rear, in inches)	58.7/59.5
Tires	GR70-15
Brakes	11.75-inch discs
Wheels	15x8 Rally rims with trim rings and center caps
Fuel tank	18 gallons
Front suspension	parallel A-arms with coil springs
Rear suspension	independent three-link with transverse leaf spring
Steering	recirculating ball, 20.2:1 ratio
Standard drivetrain	190-horsepower 350-ci V-8 (L48) with single four-barrel carburetor, four-speed manual transmission, 3.36:1 axle ratio
Optional engine	250-horsepower 350-ci V-8 (L82) with four-barrel carburetor
Optional engine	275-horsepower 454-ci V-8 (LS5) with four-barrel carburetor
Optional transmission	Turbo Hydra-matic automatic (with 3.08:1 axle ratio)
Optional transmission	close-ratio four-speed manual
Optional transmission	wide-ratio four-speed manual
Optional gear ratios	3.36:1, 3.55:1, 3.70:1

Chrome front bumpers and an egg-crate grille were last seen on the 1972 Corvette. Convertible production fell to 6,058 that year.

1973

This year's Corvette became the first of the breed to break the 30,000-unit sales barrier—in a standard 12-month model run, that is. Remember, John DeLorean had cheated in 1969. Two months after the former Pontiac chief took over as Chevrolet general manager on February 1, the St. Louis assembly line was shut down by a strike. Once the Corvette line restarted, DeLorean decided to make up for lost ground. Normally, 1970 production would have begun in September

1969, but he put 1970's startup on hold and let the 1969 run continue until December. After 1970's limited run, annual production didn't drop again until 1978.

That year commenced the third of the Shark's three five-year design trends. Recognizing this trio is easy enough: the first, spanning 1968 to 1972, had traditional chrome bumpers at both ends, while the last, running from 1978 to 1982, showed off a large, fastback glass in back. In the middle, the 1973 to 1977 Corvettes introduced body-color, crash-proof bumper systems, first at the nose in 1973, then at the tail beginning in 1974.

Trading that classic chrome front bumper for a urethane-covered, energy-absorbent nose was the result of new federal automotive safety standards

that specified that all 1973 cars be able to bounce back from 5-mile-per-hour impacts. Further safety enhancement was found inside the '73 Corvette's doors, where steel guard beams were added to protect occupants from side impacts.

Amazingly, all this extra reinforcement, steel or otherwise, didn't add on nearly as many pounds as most detractors feared early on. Reportedly, that plastic-covered bumper system up front—which stretched total length by 3 inches—only increased overall weight by 35 pounds in 1973. Typical 1973–1977 curb weights went up about 250 pounds compared to those of 1968–1972.

The 1973 nose job also included a new hood that incorporated duct work to draw in cooler, denser air from the high-pressure area at the base

Above
A urethane-covered nose appeared in 1973. The body-colored bumper system could survive 5-mile-per-hour impacts, per federal automotive safety specifications.

Left
The 1973 Corvette's energy-absorbing nose helped stretch overall length by 3 inches and added 35 pounds to total weight.

of the windshield. Once a heavy foot depressed the throttle linkage beyond a certain point, a switch activated a solenoid, which in turn opened a flap hidden beneath a grille at the hood's trailing edge. Opening this flap allowed denser air to whistle directly into the air cleaner, which was sealed to the hood's underside by a rubber doughnut.

This new standard hood also did away with a Shark feature that had had many witnesses shaking their heads from its introduction in 1968. The 1973 hood ran all the way back to the windshield uninterrupted, hiding the wiper arms below its rear lip. Gone was the clunky pop-up panel that didn't always work and added unwanted extra weight.

The Four-Rotor Corvette's Wankel engine was replaced by a small-block V-8 in 1976, and the name was changed to Aerovette. The Aerovette was displayed during the National Corvette Museum's grand opening in September 1994. *Mike Mueller*

Gone, too, was the removable rear window included on all 1968–1972 Corvettes. Duntov claimed this deletion was done not to cut costs but to eliminate an unwanted back draft that would occur at high speeds with windows up and roof panels removed.

Among other upgrades were larger mufflers (to tone down the exhaust note) and extra sound deadener beneath the hood and in the interior cabin's floor and side panels. New rubber-cushioned body mounts were added to reduce the vibrations transferred from the road to the driver through the frame, and ride harshness

was reduced by making steel-belted radial tires standard.

Customers in 1973 again had three V-8s to choose from. Joining the base 190-horse 350 small block and the optional LS4 454 big block was a new RPO code—L82. Though it filled in for the LT-1, the L82 350 was actually a descendant of the hydraulic-lifter L46. Featuring 9:1 compression, big-valve heads, and a relatively aggressive hydraulic cam, the L82 produced 250 horses. L82 compression never slipped during the 1973–1977 run and in fact topped all Corvette engines built in those years. Even with its low

Chevrolet officials claimed a 40 percent decrease in noise infiltration inside the 1973 Corvette, thanks to the addition of extra sound-deadening insulation.

This year's Corvette became the first of the breed to break the 30,000-unit sales barrier–in a standard 12-month model run, that is.

The L82 350 was rated at 250 horsepower in 1973. It cost $299. Production was 5,710.

The 275-horse LS4 454 big block replaced the LS5 on the 1973 Corvette's RPO list. LS4 price was $250. Production was 4,412.

Traditional chrome bumpers remained in back in 1973. Side-impact beams were added inside the doors of all 1973 models.

A new hood in 1973 incorporated cowl-induction duct work and did away with the clunky pop-up panel that hid the wiper arms on previous C3 Corvettes.

Below, right
A 190-horsepower 350 small-block V-8 was standard for the 1973 Corvette. Functional cowl induction was standard, too, atop all three available engines that year. *Mike Mueller*

8.25:1 compression, the LS4 remained the top power choice at 275 horsepower.

New on the 1973 options list was the off-road suspension and brake package, RPO Z07. Offered up through 1975, the Z07 deal included considerably stiffer springs and shocks at both ends, a thicker front sway bar (a rear sway bar was also listed), and heavy-duty power brakes with dual-pin-mounted pads up front and fade-resistant metallic linings all around. The M21 close-ratio four-speed was mandatory, and neither air conditioning nor the base 350 could've been included along with RPO Z07.

1974

Specifications	1974
Model availability	sport coupe and convertible (optional removable hardtop)
Wheelbase	98 inches
Length	185.5 inches
Width	69 inches
Height	47.7 inches (sport coupe), 47.9 inches (convertible, top up), 47.7 inches (convertible, with hardtop)
Shipping weight	3,532 pounds
Tread (front/rear, in inches)	58.7/59.5
Tires	GR70-15
Brakes	11.75-inch discs
Wheels	15x8 Rally rims with trim rings and center caps
Fuel tank	18 gallons
Front suspension	parallel A-arms with coil springs
Rear suspension	independent three-link with transverse leaf spring
Steering	recirculating ball, 20.2:1 ratio (17.6:1 with optional power steering)
Standard drivetrain	195-horsepower 350-ci V-8 (L48) with single four-barrel carburetor, four-speed manual transmission, 3.36:1 axle ratio
Optional engine	250-horsepower 350-ci V-8 (L82) with four-barrel carburetor
Optional engine	270-horsepower 454-ci V-8 (LS5) with four-barrel carburetor
Optional transmission	Turbo Hydra-matic automatic (with 3.08:1 axle ratio)
Optional transmission	close-ratio four-speed manual
Optional transmission	wide-ratio four-speed manual
Optional gear ratios	3.36:1, 3.55:1, 3.70:1

Top
Coupe production soared to a new all-time high in 1974: 32,028. Base price ($6,001.50) topped six grand for the first time.

Right
Only minor details changed inside the 1974 Corvette. The same gauge cluster surround panel was used from 1973 to 1976.

1974

More crash protection was added in 1974 when 1973's energy-absorbing nose design was repeated in back. In place of that familiar duck-tail rear and twin chrome bumpers was another resilient plastic cap, this one molded in two pieces. Further evidence of the Corvette's ever-softening nature appeared in the exhaust system, where two small resonators were added to additionally tone down the car's growl.

Standard output rose slightly to 195 horses, while the optional L82 remained at 250 horsepower and the LS4 dipped to 270. This was the big block's swan song, as the painful realities of 50-cent gallons of low-lead and insurance premiums as heavy as car payments forced the 454 into retirement at 1974's end.

New options for 1974 initially included a lightweight aluminum wheel deal (RPO YJ8) to

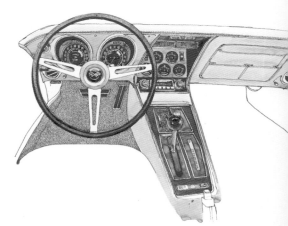

complement the radial tires and help offset some of that federally mandated, safety-supplying excess fat. Each YJ8 rim would have cut off 8 pounds of unsprung weight, but manufacturing gremlins forced a recall after a couple hundred poor-quality sets were cast. Chevy paperwork showed that as many as four 1974 Corvettes apparently were delivered with YJ8 wheels before the option was withdrawn.

More plentiful was another new option, the gymkhana suspension package (RPO FE7), which simply added a thickened front sway bar and higher-rate springs. No ordering restrictions or mandatory equipment were specified when FE7 was chosen.

An energy-absorbing body-colored bumper was introduced for 1974. It also was the last year for an optional Corvette big block. Shown here is one of 3,494 454 Corvettes built in 1974. *Mike Mueller*

1975

Specifications	1975
Model availability	sport coupe and convertible (optional removable hardtop)
Wheelbase	98 inches
Length	185.2 inches
Width	69 inches
Height	48.1 inches (sport coupe)
Shipping weight	3,532 pounds
Tread (front/rear, in inches)	58.7/59.5
Tires	GR70-15
Brakes	11.75-inch discs
Wheels	15x8 Rally rims with trim rings and center caps
Fuel tank	18 gallons
Front suspension	parallel A-arms with coil springs
Rear suspension	independent three-link with transverse leaf spring
Steering	recirculating ball, 20.2:1 ratio (17.6:1 with optional power steering)
Standard drivetrain	165-horsepower 350-ci V-8 (L48) with single four-barrel carburetor, four-speed manual transmission, 3.36:1 axle ratio
Optional engine	205-horsepower 350-ci V-8 (L82) with four-barrel carburetor
Optional transmission	Turbo Hydra-matic 400 automatic (with 3.08:1 axle ratio)
Optional transmission	close-ratio four-speed manual
Optional transmission	wide-ratio four-speed manual
Optional gear ratios	2.73:1, 3.36:1, 3.55:1, 3.70:1

Convertible production for 1975 was 4,629. Catalytic converters appeared on all models that year.

1975

An end of an era came in 1975, as 65-year-old Zora Arkus-Duntov retired on January 1 after 21 years and seven months with General Motors. Two decades before, he had boldly written Ed Cole about a job after seeing the Corvette prototype on GM's Motorama stage; after "fiddling on the side" (his words) at Chevrolet in 1953 and 1954, Duntov was named the division's director of high-performance vehicle design and development in 1956. He wasn't officially tabbed the Corvette's chief engineer until 1968, this after some bureaucratic bumbling had temporarily cut him out

of the loop late in the C3 development process. By then, nonetheless, he already was well known as the "father of the Corvette."

For those who've always wondered, Zora got his surname as a result of having two dads. Born Zora Arkus, his name was lengthened after his Russian mother divorced and remarried Josef Duntov. Though his hyphenated moniker was official, he was most often called Duntov, or, more

An end of an era came in 1975, as 65-year-old Zora Arkus-Duntov retired on January 1 after 21 years and seven months with General Motors.

1975 was the last year for a Corvette convertible until 1986. And it was the last time a topless model cost less than a hardtop. Base price for the former was $6,550.10 and $6,810.10 for the latter.

affectionately, simply Zora. A bold race driver, a dashing, unforgettably handsome man who knew how to show off with style, an engineering genius with few equals—if there was anything bad to say about him no one was talking following his death in April 1996.

"I was impressed with his continental poise, sophistication, and his honesty and dedication to performance and to his work as an engineer," began fellow Chevy engineer Gib Hufstader's respectful homage. "He appreciated people who were very dedicated to doing a good job, to getting the job done. For some of us, it was a dream come true to work with him."

How did a mere mortal pick up where a living legend left off in 1975? The man handed the task of keeping the dream alive was David Ramsay McLellan, who basically had been groomed for the job after joining GM in 1959. He spent most of 1973 and 1974 at the Massachusetts Institute of Technology's Sloan School of Management on GM's dime, then, with his master's degree in hand, he returned to Chevrolet as one of Duntov's staff engineers. Six months later, Zora stepped down and McLellan rose to the post that he already knew was his for the taking. His influence, however, wouldn't be truly noted until the C4 debuted eight years later.

Coupe production established another record in 1975 as 33,836 were built.

Both energy-absorbing bumpers were redesigned slightly in 1975, with the rear unit featuring a one-piece covering in place of the split unit used the previous year.

The last Corvette convertible until 1986, driven by general inspection foreman Bob Shell, leaves the St. Louis plant on July 31, 1975.

In the meantime, the Shark sailed on in typical fashion. Changes were few for 1975, with a new plastic honeycomb framework beneath that soft nose (to supply additional low-speed cushioning) leading the way. In back, a new body-colored end cap was redone in one piece without that telltale seam down the middle. Beneath the solid cap, a new aluminum bumper bar was attached to the frame with twin hydraulic cylinders. Chevrolet's breaker-less high-energy ignition—with its hotter, more-reliable spark—also became standard.

With the 454 in the archives, the engine lineup was left with only the standard 350 and the optional L82 in 1975—the first time in 20 years that only two power sources were offered. Output for the former was now a paltry 165 horsepower, 205 for the latter. These power cuts were due to

the inclusion of contaminant-burning catalytic converters, introduced to help meet more-restrictive emissions standards.

The 1975 Corvette's revised exhaust system featured a single large-capacity converter after a design featuring two smaller units had failed durability tests. Two Y-pipes were used to at least preserve the appearance of a sporty dual-exhaust system. The first one funneled exhaust flow from both sides of the engine together into one tube to enter the converter. From there, a reversed Y-pipe did the opposite in back to deliver the cleansed spent gases to typical twin mufflers at the tail. True duals wouldn't make a comeback until the LT5-powered ZR-1 debuted for 1990. Mainstream Corvettes wouldn't be refitted with a real dual-exhaust system until the second-generation LT1 appeared for 1992.

Horsepower wasn't the only thing to fade away in 1975. One year after the last big-block Corvette rolled into the sunset, the same thing happened to the convertible model. GM's explanation this time involved both safety concerns and nose-diving demand. The convertible's hunk of the Corvette pie sank from 38.4 percent in 1970 to 16.2 in 1973, and the last 4,629 ragtops built in 1975 represented a mere 12 percent of that year's total production run. Another end of an era? Fortunately not: topless Corvettes returned to center stage in 1986.

1976

Specifications	1976

Model availability	sport coupe
Wheelbase	98 inches
Length	185.2 inches
Width	69 inches
Height	48.1 inches
Shipping weight	3,445 pounds
Tread (front/rear, in inches)	58.7/59.5
Tires	GR70-15
Brakes	11.75-inch discs
Wheels	15x8 Rally rims with trim rings and center caps
Fuel tank	18 gallons
Front suspension	parallel A-arms with coil springs
Rear suspension	independent three-link with transverse leaf spring
Steering	recirculating ball, 20.2:1 ratio (17.6:1 with optional power steering)
Standard drivetrain	180-horsepower 350-ci V-8 (L48) with single four-barrel carburetor, four-speed manual transmission, 3.36:1 axle ratio
Optional engine	210-horsepower 350-ci V-8 (L82) with four-barrel carburetor
Optional transmission	Turbo Hydra-matic 350 automatic (with 3.08:1 axle ratio), L48 only
Optional transmission	Turbo Hydra-matic 400 automatic 350 (3.36:1 axle ratio), L82 only
Optional transmission	close-ratio four-speed manual
Optional transmission	wide-ratio four-speed manual
Optional gear ratios	3.08:1, 3.55:1, 3.70:1

The standard vinyl upholstery came in four colors in 1976: black, Firethorn, Buckskin, and white. Upholstery patterns varied with the optional leather seats included with the custom interior.

1976

Modifications in 1976 did away with the C3 hood's cowl flap, which apparently whistled too loudly for most drivers. In place of the solenoid-activated induction setup was a simpler system that rammed in airflow through a duct that ran forward over the radiator support to pick up some of the radiator's cooling breezes. Even though this hood no longer used the cowl-induction equipment, it still kept the intake grille. This opening wasn't deleted until 1977.

A partial underpan made of steel was added in 1976 to increase rigidity and improve heat insulation, and a lighter (13 pounds so), maintenance-free Delco Freedom battery also joined the standard equipment list. The Astro ventilation system used since 1968 was dropped in 1976, meaning the vents previously found behind the rear window were deleted too. A new sport steering wheel, shared with, of all things, Chevrolet's compact Vega, was added inside.

A little tinkering helped standard output rise to 180 horsepower, and the optional L82 also improved to 210 horses. The L82, however, wasn't offered in California in 1976 and 1977 because it didn't meet that state's tougher emissions standards. Four-speed transmissions were also banned out west for those years.

The automatic transmission limited to Californians in 1976 and 1977 wasn't the Turbo Hydra-matic 400 previously used behind all

A tilt-telescopic steering column was a C3 option (RPO N37) from the beginning and became standard in 1980. Shown here is the 1976 tilt wheel, priced at $95.

Left
The St. Louis plant rolled out a whopping 46,558 Corvettes in 1976, a new record by far. Base price was $7,604.85.

Below left
Two rear bumper styles appeared in 1976: the first with small recessed "Corvette" lettering, the second with larger lettering that wasn't recessed.

Corvette engines. Mandated behind the base 350 during those years was the mundane TH 350 automatic, as product planners opted not to waste the more expensive, heavy-duty Turbo Hydra-matic on engines that didn't put out enough punishment to merit its use. The TH 400 remained the weapon of choice whenever an L82 buyer forked over the extra cash for the M40 automatic transmission in 1976 and 1977, while the lighter TH 350 was a no-cost option behind the 210-horse 350.

The lightweight YJ8 rims were finally perfected in 1976, and this package included four aluminum wheels (supplied by Kelsey-Hayes) with a standard steel spare to keep the cost down. Listed as options early on, power steering, power brakes, and the custom interior trim group (with its leather seats) became part of the base package midyear, mandating a bottom-line increase. All Corvettes built for 1976 featured power brakes, while only 173 hit the streets without power steering.

The 1976 Corvette also was the last to wear the familiar Stingray badge.

1977

Specifications

	1977

Model availability	sport coupe
Wheelbase	98 inches
Length	185.2 inches
Width	69 inches
Height	48.1 inches
Shipping weight	3,448 pounds
Tread (front/rear, in inches)	58.7/59.5
Tires	GR70-15
Brakes	11.75-inch discs
Wheels	15x8 Rally rims with trim rings and center caps
Fuel tank	18 gallons
Front suspension	parallel A-arms with coil springs
Rear suspension	independent three-link with transverse leaf spring
Steering	recirculating ball, 20.2:1 ratio (17.6:1 with optional power steering)
Standard drivetrain	180-horsepower 350-ci V-8 (L48) with single four-barrel carburetor, four-speed manual transmission, 3.36:1 axle ratio
Optional engine	210-horsepower 350-ci V-8 (L82) with four-barrel carburetor
Optional transmission	Turbo Hydra-matic 350 automatic (3.08:1 axle ratio), L48 only
Optional transmission	Turbo Hydra-matic 400 automatic (3.55:1 axle ratio), L82 only
Optional transmission	close-ratio four-speed manual (3.70:1 axle ratio)
Optional transmission	wide-ratio four-speed manual (3.70:1 axle ratio)
Optional gear ratios	3.08:1, 3.55:1, 3.70:1 (with L82 four-speeds only)

A revised console and steering column appeared for 1977. The latter relocated the steering wheel 2 inches closer to the dash.

1977

It took Chevrolet 15 years to build its first quarter-million Corvettes. Hitting the half-million mark required only eight more years. The 250,000th, a Riverside Gold convertible, was built on November 7, 1969. The 500,000th, a white coupe, was driven off the line by Robert Lund on March 15, 1977.

It seemed nothing could deter the fiberglass faithful as popularity continued growing stronger even as the car's price soared. In 1974, the base sticker had edged beyond $6,000 for the first time, and this was only the beginning. It jumped to $6,810.10 in 1975 and then hit $7,604.85 the following year. In 1977, it was a whopping $8,647.65, due to the inclusion of so many standard comfort and convenience features.

Production, meanwhile, kept rolling on, with 33,836 Corvettes built for 1975, followed by a whopping 46,558 in 1976 to establish a new record, which was then broken by 1977's 49,213 tally.

Most Corvettes built during the 1970s wore even higher price tags as popularity of various options also went on the rise. When introduced in 1963, air conditioning attracted only 278 customers, equal to 1.3 percent of the first Sting Ray run. By 1968, C60 installations made up 19.8 percent of the production run, and that figure was 82.8 percent by 1975. In 1977, 45,249 of the 49,213 cars built were air conditioned, adding an extra $553 to the sticker.

Assisted side glass installations, too, went on the rise. Introduced in 1956, power windows still were found on only 17.6 percent of the Corvettes built for 1967. But by 1973, the cut was 46 percent, followed by 90.1 in 1977, when the A31 option cost $116. Also popular that year were the tilt-telescopic steering wheel (46,487 sold at $165) and no-cost M40 automatic transmission (41,231 specified).

Only 2,060 four-speed transmissions were sold in 1977, and production of the optional L82 V-8 (still rated at 210 horsepower) was a mere 6,148. While buyers seemed willing to spend tons on frills, they apparently couldn't justify shelling out an extra $495 for 30 more horses.

Above
Another new
production record—
49,213—was
established in 1977.
Base price soared to
$8,647.65 as various
options became
standard equipment.

Left
Chevrolet General
Manager Robert
Lund drove the
500,000th Corvette,
a white coupe,
off the St. Louis
assembly line on
March 15, 1977.

1978

1978

Specifications	1978
Model availability	sport coupe
Wheelbase	98 inches
Length	185.2 inches
Width	69 inches
Height	48 inches
Shipping weight	3,401 pounds
Tread (front/rear, in inches)	58.7/59.5
Tires	P225/70R-15; P255/60R-15 included with Indy Pace Car replica
Brakes	11.75-inch discs
Wheels	15x8 Rally rims with trim rings and center caps; 15x8 cast-aluminum wheels included with Silver Anniversary and Indy Pace Car models
Fuel tank	23.7 gallons
Front suspension	parallel A-arms with coil springs
Rear suspension	independent three-link with transverse leaf spring
Steering	recirculating ball, 20.2:1 ratio (17.6:1 with optional power steering)
Standard drivetrain	185-horsepower 350-ci V-8 (L48) with single four-barrel carburetor, four-speed manual transmission, 3.36:1 axle ratio
Note	175-horsepower V-8 with Turbo Hydra-matic 350 automatic transmission and 3.55 1 axle ratio only available in California and high altitudes
Optional engine	220-horsepower 350-ci V-8 (L82) with four-barrel carburetor, not available in California and high altitudes
Optional transmission	Turbo Hydra-matic 350 automatic (with 3.08:1 axle ratio with L48, 3.55:1 ratio with L82 and California/high-altitude V-8s)
Optional gear ratios	3.36:1, 3.70:1, with L82 four-speeds only

The Silver Anniversary Corvette.

25 years of men, machines, and memories.

It stands alone today as it has since the summer of 1953, a truly unique and finely machined two-seater. America's only true production sports car.

The legend lives on and improves, as legends do, with the passage of time.

The Silver Anniversary Corvette: Twenty-five years in the making, and we've enjoyed every minute of it.

And now, if you will, please join us in a round of applause for the Corvette founding fathers, that spirited corps of doers and dreamers who created the legend, brought it to life, and kept it there.

Also for the countless men and women who've had a hand in building and refining Corvettes over the years. For everyone who has ever owned a Corvette, driven one, loved one. Or dreamed about owning one someday.

Which, we'd imagine, includes just about everybody.

SEE WHAT'S NEW TODAY IN A CHEVROLET.

Chevrolet

Chevrolet commemorated 25 years of Corvette history with a special Silver Anniversary model in 1978. Exclusive paint, sport mirrors, and aluminum wheels were included in the package.

1978

Demand dropped slightly in 1978, as the St. Louis plant rolled out 46,774 Corvettes, all fitted with new swooping rear glass that *Car and Driver* called "a universally appreciated Good Move." "The large rear window freshened up the Corvette's profile, and it also added space and light to help relieve the claustrophobia inside this, the most tightly coupled car known to man."

The new window improved rearward visibility as well as glass area, expanded from 392 square inches up to a whopping 1,425. But while extra cargo space represented a benefit, accessing that space still required reaching behind the seats.

Making that huge glass sheet a hinged, lift-up roof would have been cool. Dave McLellan, however, opted not to complicate matters, at least not until he rolled out his Collector Edition hatchback model for 1982.

New for 1978 were special 25th Anniversary badges on all cars. And along with those badges, a customer could have further honored a quarter-century of Corvette history by checking off RPO B2Z, the Silver Anniversary paint option, which added an exclusive two-tone paint scheme done in light silver over dark silver. Dual sport mirrors and aluminum wheels were required

extra-cost features on all 1978 Silver Anniversary Corvettes.

A second special model, the Limited Edition Corvette, helped commemorate both the car's 25 years and its appearance in 1978 as the prestigious pacer for the Indianapolis 500. Along with being a first for Chevrolet's two-seater, this year's Indy 500 performance also represented the first time that an unmodified, truly stock machine paced the annual Memorial Day race. The Corvette that led the way for Tom Sneva, Danny Ongais, Rick Mears, and the 30 other drivers on May 28, 1978, was all but identical to

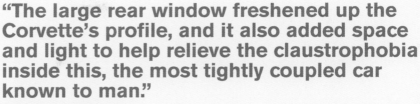

"The large rear window freshened up the Corvette's profile, and it also added space and light to help relieve the claustrophobia inside this, the most tightly coupled car known to man."
—*Car and Driver*

the car John Q. Public drove that year, save for the two openings made in back for the requisite flag poles.

When the checkered flag dropped that day, Al Unser Sr. had collected his third Indy 500 win. At the same time, Chevrolet officials were busy capitalizing on the event by, among other things, calling May "Pacesetter Month." Dealers, meanwhile, put on pacesetter promotions, with the star of their shows being the limited-edition pace car replica.

As the name implied, Chevrolet's original plan was to make this package a limited-edition collectors' piece. Building only 300 was at first the goal. *The Wall Street Journal* even went so far as to print a cover story in March 1978 touting the Indy pace car Corvette as a sure-fire ride to riches. Those lucky enough to get their hands on one of these rare machines reportedly would be able to turn it around for many times its original sales price after only a matter of months. Initial window stickers read $13,653.21, $4,300 more than a

Above, left
This refashioned front fender was considered for 1978 production.

Left
All 1978 Corvettes were treated to a new fastback rear window. Standard Corvette coupe production that year was 40,274.

In 1978, 6,502 Limited Edition models were sold to mark the Corvette's first appearance as the prestigious pace car for the Indianapolis 500.

base 25th Anniversary Corvette coupe. But once word got around, the going price soared as high as $30,000. Those unlucky enough to buy at that price soon found out that some old adages never lie: if it sounds too good to be true, it probably is.

All speculation ran right down the drain after Chevy's litigation-shy decision-makers chose to build at least one pace car replica for every dealer in America. Apparently, the idea was to avoid any lawsuits from potential buyers or dealers (translated: opportunistic exploiters) left in the

lurch with nothing save for complaints of unfair, monopolistic sales practices. Whatever the case, the final "limited-edition" count for the '78 Indy pace car reached 6,502. Most (if not all) of those who originally jumped on the Limited Edition Corvette bandwagon 20-plus years ago are still waiting to make hay today.

Included in the Limited Edition's original astronomical price was a long list of options combined with a heavy dose of special treatments. On the outside was an exclusive black-over-silver

two-tone paint scheme accented by red pinstriping. Official Indy 500 decals were expected. A front air dam, rear spoiler, aluminum wheels (also with red pinstripes), and glass T-tops were part of the deal as well. Inside was an exclusive leather interior done in a silver-gray shade called "smoke." Lightweight buckets were also exclusive to the Limited Edition's interior. Additional extras included power windows, door locks, and antenna; a rear window defogger; air conditioning; sport mirrors; a tilt-telescopic

Dave McLellan (far left) poses proudly with the car that some forecasters predicted (incorrectly) would become a valued collectors' item. Robert Lund is on the far right; next to him is Bob Stempel.

steering column; white-letter P225/60R15 tires; a heavy-duty battery; AM/FM eight-track stereo with dual rear speakers; and the Convenience Group. Included in that last collection, RPO ZX2, were a dome light delay, headlight warning buzzer, under-hood light, low-fuel warning light, interior courtesy light, floor mats, intermittent wipers, and passenger-side vanity mirror on the visor.

Powertrain pieces were the same offered for all other Corvettes in 1978. The base package was a 185-horsepower 350 backed by a wide-ratio four-speed manual. The top-shelf 220-horse L82 was optional, as was the close-ratio M21 four-speed and MX1 TH 400 automatic. Adding the

FE7 sport suspension allowed a Limited Edition buyer to outfit his replica in identical fashion to the actual Indy pace car.

Increasing L82 output from 210 to 220 horsepower was done by adding a less restrictive exhaust system and a dual-snorkel air induction

Left
Chevrolet officials were especially proud that their 1978 Corvette needed no modifications (save for adding flags at the tail) to lead the pace lap at Indy.

Below
Former Indy 500 champion Jim Rathmann drove the pace car at Indy in May 1978, making it the fifth time he'd led the field around the Brickyard.

setup that improved breathing on the top end. And even the standard L48 350 got five more horses, but L48s sold in California and high altitudes that year were rated at 175 horsepower instead of 185.

Either way, the quarter-century-old two-seater was a real hot rod once more, or so claimed *Car and Driver*. "After a number of recent Corvette editions that prompted us to mourn the steady decline of both performance and quality in this once-proud marque, we can happily report the twenty-fifth example of the Corvette is much improved across the board. Not only will it run

faster now—the L82 version with four-speed is certainly the fastest American production car, while the base L48 automatic is no slouch—but the general drivability and road manners are of a high order as well." L48 performance was quoted at 7.8 seconds for the 0–60 run, 123 miles per hour on the top end. The L82 reportedly could reach 133 miles per hour.

Clockwise, from above
All Corvettes built for 1978 featured commemorative exterior badges . . . and all were fitted with anniversary horn buttons. *Mike Mueller*

The original idea was to limit the Indy pace car replica's production, thus explaining the investment frenzy that resulted after the car's release. But Limited Edition proved to be a misnomer. *Mike Mueller*

Aluminum wheels (with red stripes) were included in the Limited Edition deal, as were removable glass roof panels. *Mike Mueller*

A CB radio was a Corvette option from 1978 to 1985. The AM/FM stereo with Citizens Band feature (RPO UP6) cost a healthy $638 in 1978. Nonetheless, 7,138 UP6 radios were sold that year. *Mike Mueller*

Clockwise, from top left
An AM/FM stereo with eight-track player (RPO UM2) cost $419 in 1978. UM2 production was 20,899 that year. The UM2 option first appeared in 1977 and was last offered in 1982. *Mike Mueller*

Seats and upholstery were unique to the 1978 Limited Edition Corvette. Air conditioning and a tilt-telescopic steering wheel were among the various options included in the $13,653.21 Limited Edition package. *Mike Mueller*

A 185-horsepower 350 small block was standard for the 1978 Corvette. *Mike Mueller*

Specifications	1979

Model availability	sport coupe
Wheelbase	98 inches
Length	185.2 inches
Width	69 inches
Height	48 inches
Shipping weight	3,372 pounds
Tread (front/rear, in inches)	58.7/59.5
Tires	P225/70R-15
Brakes	11.75-inch discs
Wheels	15x8 Rally rims with trim rings and center caps
Fuel tank	23.7 gallons
Front suspension	parallel A-arms with coil springs
Rear suspension	independent three-link with transverse leaf spring
Steering	recirculating ball, 20.2:1 ratio (17.6:1 with optional power steering)
Standard drivetrain	195-horsepower 350-ci V-8 (L48) with single four-barrel carburetor, four-speed manual transmission, 3.36:1 axle ratio
Note	California and high-altitude V-8 also rated at 195 horsepower; both only available with Turbo Hydra-matic 350 automatic transmission
Optional engine	225-horsepower 350-ci V-8 (L82) with four-barrel carburetor, not available in California and high altitudes
Optional transmission	Turbo Hydra-matic 350 automatic (with 3.55:1 axle ratio)
Optional gear ratios	3.36:1, 3.70:1, with L82 four-speeds only

Corvette production peaked at 53,807 in 1979, a record that undoubtedly will never be broken.

1979

Corvettes were rolling off the line at dizzying paces during the late 1970s. "The St. Louis plant is operating two nine-hour shifts daily and working overtime two Saturdays a month just to meet sales demand," said Chevrolet General Manager Robert Lund in March 1977. "Current demand is running more than 29 percent ahead of last year." Predicting yet another Corvette sales record that year was easier than spotting an SUV today.

But once again that record didn't stick around long. After dipping a bit in 1978, Corvette production soared the following year to 53,807, a feat that undoubtedly will never be repeated, or even approached.

That year's Corvette also established a new base price record by surpassing $10,000 for the first time. As before, adding more features into the standard deal contributed to this all-time high. The Limited Edition Corvette's high-back bucket seats and the previously optional AM/FM radio became standard equipment in 1979, but that was just a start, as product planners once again took note of customer preferences and responded accordingly.

Of the 46,774 Corvettes sold in 1978, 37,858 had tilt-telescopic steering columns, 37,638 were fitted with air conditioning, and 36,931 featured power windows. All told, these three options cost $910 in 1978 and $966 the following year. Then, effective May 7, 1979, this trio was made part of the standard package, raising the base price by

After dipping a bit in 1978, Corvette production soared the following year to 53,807, a feat that undoubtedly will never be repeated, or even approached.

Clockwise, from left
Priced at $565, the optional L82 V-8 produced 225 horsepower in 1979. L82 production that year totaled 14,516.

Optional aluminum wheels (RPO N90) cost $380. N90 production was 33,741. *Mike Mueller*

A four-speed manual transmission was again standard in 1979. Installations of the no-cost automatic transmission numbered 41,545 that year. *Mike Mueller*

The high-back bucket seats exclusive to the Limited Edition Corvette in 1978 became standard equipment on all 1979 models. *Mike Mueller*

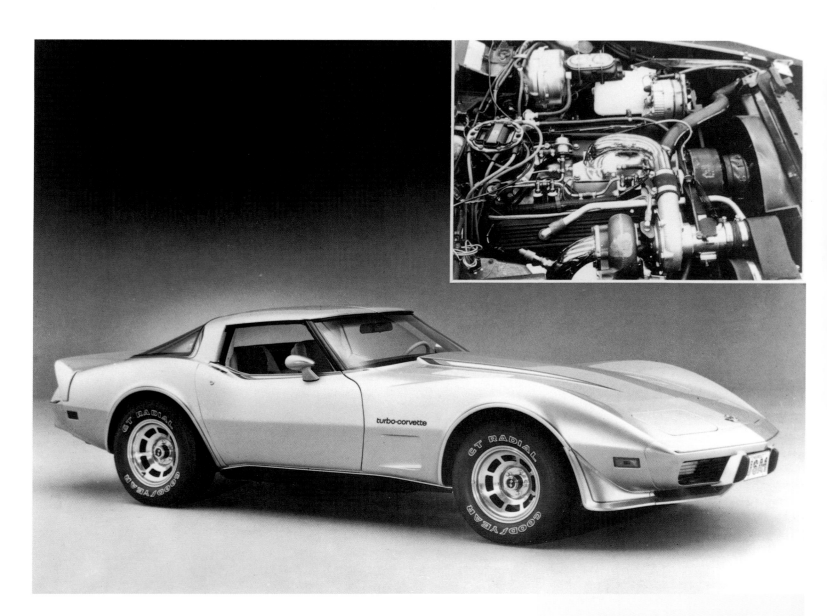

Dave McLellan's engineers created this show car in 1979 to experiment with a new Corvette power source: turbocharging. About 290 horsepower resulted.

$706. Various other additions eventually helped hike the 1979 bottom line to $12,313.23.

Two other pace car features, front and rear spoilers, became optional (listed together under RPO D80) for all 1979 Corvettes and went a long way toward reducing unwanted drag. The optional L82 V-8 was tweaked up to 225 horsepower, and its dual-snorkel induction and open-flow mufflers were passed down to the L48, boosting it to 195 horses, a rating shared by the L48s sold in high altitudes and on the West Coast in 1979.

1980

1980

Specifications	1980

Model availability	sport coupe
Wheelbase	98 inches
Length	185.2 inches
Width	69 inches
Height	48 inches
Shipping weight	3,206 pounds
Tread (front/rear, in inches)	58.7/59.5
Tires	P22570R-15
Brakes	11.75-inch discs
Wheels	15x8 Rally rims with trim rings and center caps
Fuel tank	23.7 gallons
Front suspension	parallel A-arms with coil springs
Rear suspension	independent three-link with transverse leaf spring
Steering	recirculating ball, 20.2:1 ratio (17.6:1 with optional power steering)
Standard drivetrain	190-horsepower 350-ci V-8 (L48) with single four-barrel carburetor, four-speed manual transmission, 3.07:1 axle ratio
Standard California drivetrain	180-horsepower 305-ci V-8 (LG4) with single four-barrel carburetor, Turbo Hydra-matic automatic transmission, 3.07:2 axle ratio
Optional engine	230-horsepower 350-ci V-8 (L82) with four-barrel carburetor, not available in California
Optional transmission	Turbo Hydra-matic 350 automatic (with 3.07:1 axle ratio)

1980

Base output was 190 horsepower in 1980, except on the West Coast. California's tough smog standards had limited Corvette customers in that state to one engine only, the L48, since 1976. Then that state's extra-strict emissions standards tightened even further for 1980. Chevrolet didn't even bother to certify the 350 V-8 for use there that year, meaning a stand-in was needed.

In place of the L48, and in exchange for a $50 credit, California Corvettes in 1980 were fitted with the 305-cubic-inch LG4 V-8. Although it came right off the mundane passenger car parts shelf, the LG4 still produced only 10 fewer horses than the L48, thanks to the use of stainless-steel tubular headers and a "computer command control" system that automatically adjusted carburetor mixture and ignition timing on demand.

Various weight-saving measures made the 1980 Corvette lighter on its feet; this after the car had steadily put on pounds during the 1970s.

California's tough smog standards had limited Corvette customers in that state to one engine only, the L48, since 1976.

The L82 was boosted to 230 horsepower for 1980, but this was as good as it got for the Corvette's last optional "high-perf" V-8. Engineers were never able to certify this so-called high-compression (9:1) small block for California use, and demand dropped off considerably in remaining states after 1979. Thus, the L82 was cancelled at 1980's end.

In other news, the 1980 body was treated to front and rear body caps featuring integral spoilers, as opposed to the optional add-on spoilers offered the year before. Reportedly, these modifications improved the drag coefficient from 0.503 (for the spoiled 1979 model) to 0.443.

Another performance upgrade involved weight savings, something McLellan paid special attention to. A lighter differential housing and corresponding frame crossmember, both made of aluminum, were introduced in 1980. And adding the L82's aluminum intake manifold to the base L48 cut a few more pounds.

Corvette production fell to 40,614 in 1980, still an impressive result. Front and rear integral spoilers were new that year.

Above
Base price for the 1980 Corvette was $13,140.24, at least early in the year. By year's end, it had jumped to $14,345.24 as more standard features were added on.

Right
Power windows, air conditioning, and the tilt-telescopic steering wheel, all options in 1979, became standard inside the 1980 Corvette.

1981

Specifications	1981
Model availability	sport coupe
Wheelbase	98 inches
Length	185.2 inches
Width	69 inches
Height	48 inches
Shipping weight	3,206 pounds
Tread (front/rear, in inches)	58.7/59.5
Tires	P225/70R-15
Brakes	11.75-inch discs
Wheels	15x8 Rally rims with trim rings and center caps
Fuel tank	23.7 gallons
Front suspension	parallel A-arms with coil springs
Rear suspension	independent three-link with transverse leaf spring
Steering	recirculating ball, 20.2:1 ratio (17.6:1 with optional power steering)
Standard drivetrain	190-horsepower 350-ci V-8 (L48) with single four-barrel carburetor, four-speed manual transmission, 2.72:1 axle ratio
Optional transmission	Turbo Hydra-matic 350 automatic (with 2.87:1 axle ratio)

Slightly restyled emblems set the 1981 Corvette apart from its 1980 predecessor. Rally wheels were still standard in 1981. *Mike Mueller*

1981

They passed like those two proverbial ships in the night: the Corvette's old plant and its new Kentucky home. Roughly 27 years and eight months after it started working, the Corvette assembly line in Chevrolet's Fisher Mill Building, located on Natural Bridge Avenue in St. Louis, rolled out its last 'glass-bodied two-seater. Earlier, on June 1, a new line began moving Corvettes out the door in Bowling Green, and for two months the plants worked in tandem to meet some of the heaviest demand ever experienced during the car's long career. Of the 40,606 Corvettes built for 1981, 8,955 began life in the Bluegrass State.

Rumors of a move to a larger, more modern plant began circulating along the Mississippi River as early as 1973. Reportedly, this talk was the result of an increasing flow of bad blood between labor and management. GM officials denied such rumors and also shot down claims that they were looking for a way out. "We can say categorically that we have no plans for closing the assembly plant in St. Louis, and any rumors to that effect are without foundation," wrote GM Vice President Robert Magill in a letter to a Missouri congressman in the early 1970s. Whether or not Magill's office truly didn't have a relocation plan in

mind then, it was fairly obvious to many that the St. Louis line couldn't be long for this world.

Age was clearly a factor. Completed in 1920, Chevrolet's St. Louis plant was not only archaic, it was also lacking in size and scope. Expansion on the site was out of the question. Things, of course, were different in late 1953, when GM officials opted to relocate Corvette production from its temporary assembly line in Flint, Michigan, to a more promising home in Missouri.

"We selected St. Louis as the exclusive source of Corvette manufacture because the city has a central location and excellent shipping facilities,

Corvette production relocated from Missouri to Bowling Green, Kentucky, in 1981. The last fiberglass two-seater rolled out of the old, cramped St. Louis assembly facility on June 31, 1981.

and we have always found here an ample supply of competent labor," said Edward Kelly, Chevrolet Motor Division's general manufacturing manager. The Flint line ceased operation on December 24, 1953. After Christmas, workers on the new line down in Missouri began assembling their first Corvette on December 28.

About a quarter-century later, the rumor mill began churning early in 1979, this after Environmental Protection Agency (EPA) clean-air cops started hounding St. Louis officials about their paint facilities, which were in violation of federal air-quality standards. GM people then did admit that they were considering relocating Corvette production to a plant able to house a roomier, modernized painting section. Official announcement of an impending move finally came down from Michigan on March 26, 1979.

What GM execs didn't announce was that two St. Louis plant managers had been quietly sent to Bowling Green in 1978 to shop for the Corvette's new home. There they toured a 550,000-square-foot complex formerly used by the Fedders Corporation and the Air Temp Division of Chrysler Corporation. After a deal was cut, the plant was expanded to 1 million square feet, and improved state-of-the-art assembly equipment was installed. Furthermore, the facility would be dedicated solely to one vehicle, unlike the St. Louis plant, which was home to various Chevrolet models during its lifetime.

"The Bowling Green facility, which will build Corvettes exclusively, is an investment in Corvette's future," claimed a 1981 brochure. "It represents the experience and knowledge learned over all those years [in St. Louis]."

Kentucky Governor John Brown drove the first Corvette off the Bowling Green line in 1981.

One of the factors that led to the Corvette's move to Kentucky involved the St. Louis plant's archaic paint facilities. State-of-the-art painting processes awaited new models at Bowling Green.

Bowling Green officials showed off their modernized paint facility by offering two-tone paint schemes in 1981. Four combinations were applied: Silver/Dark Blue, Silver/Charcoal, Beige/Dark Bronze, and Autumn Red/Dark Claret. *Mike Mueller*

"We selected St. Louis as the exclusive source of Corvette manufacture because the city has a central location and excellent shipping facilities, and we have always found here an ample supply of competent labor," said Edward Kelly, Chevrolet Motor Division's general manufacturing manager.

Above
An optional driver-side power seat (RPO A42) appeared for the first time in 1981. *Mike Mueller*

Above right
How times had changed. Chevrolet began phasing in 85-mile-per-hour speedometers in 1979—by 1981, the wimpy unit was an accepted reality. *Mike Mueller*

Right
The 190-horsepower L81 350 V-8 was the only available power source in 1981. *Mike Mueller*

Marvin Lloyd, an 18-year veteran at the St. Louis plant, assists the body drop on the last Missouri-built Corvette in July 1981.

A few months later, the new plant was producing Corvettes at a rate of 15 per hour. The best the St. Louis line had ever managed was 10 cars an hour.

Quantity, however, was not the main priority. Higher standards of quality were established in Bowling Green, most importantly concerning finishing the product. New base-coat/clear-coat enamel paint was put into use at the Kentucky plant instead of the lacquer paint used at St. Louis right up until the end. Advantages of the clear-coated enamel finish included superior clarity and

mirror-like gleaming depth. The days of streaky, uneven metallic finishes were over.

Chevrolet officials were proud of their new paint processes at Bowling Green, so much so that they chose to show them off with a special presentation. A distinctive two-tone paint option, RPO D84, was offered for the 1981 Corvette. The majority of the cars built that first year in Kentucky featured two-tone paint.

Four combinations were offered—Beige/Dark Red, Silver/Dark Blue, Silver/Charcoal, and

Autumn Red/Dark Claret—with sales of those combinations totaling 5,352. Another 4,871 D84 cars followed in 1982 (in White/Silver, Silver/Dark Claret, Silver Blue/Dark Blue, and Silver/Charcoal) before the option was cancelled, due both to lukewarm popularity and less-than-complimentary critical reviews.

Only one engine was offered in 1981, the 190-horsepower L81 350, a cleaner-running small block that finally made the emissions grade in all 50 states. No California-specific V-8, no optional engines—1981 was the first time since the Corvette's earliest days that all models built relied on the same power source. And the L81 also could've been mated to a four-speed in California, meaning manual-trans Corvettes could be sold in that state for the first time since 1975.

Making the L81 legal in California was simply a matter of incorporating the lightweight tube headers (with oxygen-sensor smog controls) and

Above
Chevrolet's new Bowling Green plant began turning out Corvettes on June 1, 1981. Of the 40,606 cars built for 1981, 8,955 originated in Kentucky.

Opposite
All 1981 Corvettes were fitted with the same engine: the 190-horsepower L81 350 small-block V-8. Total production that year was a whopping 40,606.

"The Bowling Green facility, which will build Corvettes exclusively, is an investment in Corvette's future," claimed a 1981 brochure. "It represents the experience and knowledge learned over all those years [in St. Louis]."

computer controls used by the LG4 V-8 in 1980. Weight-saving magnesium valve covers were also added, and additional fat was trimmed by introducing a mono-leaf fiberglass spring in back. Added to automatic-transmission Corvettes with standard suspensions, this plastic spring weighed only 8 pounds, compared to the 44-pound steel leaf spring used in 1980.

Choosing between the automatic or manual transmissions required no extra dollars in 1981, after which time the four-speed was temporarily dropped. Not since 1954 had a complete model-year run been limited only to automatic installations, as was the case in 1982.

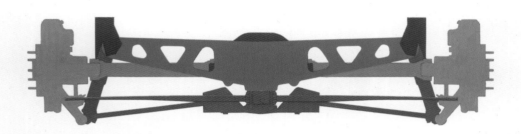

Left
Dave McLellan made various weight-cutting moves during the C3's lifetime. A lightened differential housing and corresponding frame member, both made of aluminum, were introduced beneath the 1980 Corvette. Shown here is the 1981 car's rear axle.

Below
An exploded view of the 1981 Corvette's energy-absorbing nose.

1982

Leather/vinyl or cloth/vinyl upholstery was standard inside the 1982 Corvette. Popular options included power door locks and driver's seat, cruise control, rear window defogger, and an AM/FM cassette stereo.

Specifications	1982
Model availability	sport coupe (Collector Edition featured exclusive hatchback rear glass)
Wheelbase	98 inches
Length	185.2 inches
Width	69 inches
Height	48 inches
Shipping weight	3,213 pounds (3,222 pounds, Collector Edition)
Tread (front/rear, in inches)	58.7/59.5
Tires	P225/70R-15; P225/60R-15 included with Collector Edition
Brakes	11.75-inch discs
Wheels	15x8 Rally rims with trim rings and center caps; 15x8 cast-alloy turbine rims included with Collector Edition
Fuel tank	23.7 gallons
Front suspension	parallel A-arms with coil springs
Rear suspension	independent three-link with transverse leaf spring
Steering	recirculating ball, 20.2:1 ratio (17.6:1 with optional power steering)
Standard drivetrain	200-horsepower 350-ci V-8 (L83) with Cross-Fire Injection, four-speed Turbo Hydra-matic 700-R4 automatic transmission, 2.72:1 axle ratio (2.87:1 axle ratio with Collector Edition)

1982

The fiberglass mono-leaf spring seen in 1981 was one of various upcoming C4 features that Dave McLellan let leak out beforehand. Easily the most prominent of these came in 1982, when an intriguing new drivetrain appeared for the final C3.

"It's a harbinger of things to come," said McLellan about the car that preceded his sport coupe de grace. "For the 1982 model is more than just the last of a generation; it's stage one of a two-stage production. We're doing the power team this year. Next year, we add complete new styling and other innovations."

While Corvette fans would have to wait more than half a year to finally see the redesigned C4, they got to try out the new car's engine and transmission some 18 months before. Designated L83, the 1982 Corvette's 350 V-8 used refined versions of the tubular-header exhaust system and computer command control equipment that first appeared along with the LG4 California V-8 in

1980. And like 1981's L81, the L83 also used weight-saving magnesium valve covers.

Topping it all off was the new Cross-Fire Injection system. To many, the setup looked very much like the rare twin-carb option used on some Z/28™ 203 Camaros in 1969. But those weren't carburetors beneath that cool-looking air cleaner. They were two computer-controlled Rochester throttle-body fuel injectors mounted diagonally on an aluminum cross-ram intake manifold. Making this throttle body injection (TBI) system work was an electronic control module (ECM) that was capable of dealing with up to 80 variable (ignition timing, air/fuel mixture, idle speed, etc.) adjustments per second to maximize performance and efficiency, and offer something fuelie fans had been missing since 1965: instant throttle response.

Enhancing overall response even further was the new 700-R4 four-speed automatic

transmission, which was electronically linked to the ECM. Shifts and the torque converter's lockup clutch feature were precisely controlled by the ECM, depending on varying speed and load data inputs. This power team combo clearly was as high as high-tech had ever been beneath a fiberglass hood to that point. Yet even with all that techno-wizardry, the 1982 small block still only produced 10 more horsepower than 1981's L81.

To both showcase all this new technology and mark the end of the Shark era, Chevrolet, in 1982, put together another special model, the Collector Edition, which, in Dave McLellan's words, was "a unique combination of color, equipment, and innovation [resulting in] one of the most comprehensive packages ever offered to the Corvette buyer."

At about $18,000, a base Corvette in 1982 was already expensive enough. But carrying a full load of features like 1978's Limited Edition model,

the Collector Edition became the first Corvette to crack the $20,000 realm. The exact suggested price was $22,537.59. Helping hike that bottom line up were exclusive turbine alloy wheels wearing white-letter P255/60R15 Goodyear Eagle GT rubber, glass roof panels done in unique bronze tinting, a rear window defogger, a power antenna, and special identification inside and out.

Also included was unique paint—a silver-beige finish accented by graduated gray decals and accent striping. That exclusive color carried over inside, where silver-beige leather was found on the seats and door panels. Leather wrapping also

went onto the steering wheel, and luxurious, extra-deep pile carpeting covered the floor. Bringing up the rear was another harbinger, a frameless window hinged to technically expand Corvette body style choices to two—coupe and hatchback—for the first time since the convertible departed after 1975.

A suitable closing chapter for the Shark tale, the Collector Edition was offered for 1982 only. As for the old St. Louis plant, it was boarded up in the fall of 1987 after building 13 million Chevrolet cars and trucks—including about a half million Corvettes.

Priced at $22,537.59, the 1982 Collector Edition hatchback features such exclusive touches as special paint and bodyside decals, unique alloy wheels, and a lavish interior.

Cross-Fire Injection debuted atop the standard Corvette L83 V-8 in 1982, resulting in an output increase to 200 horsepower.

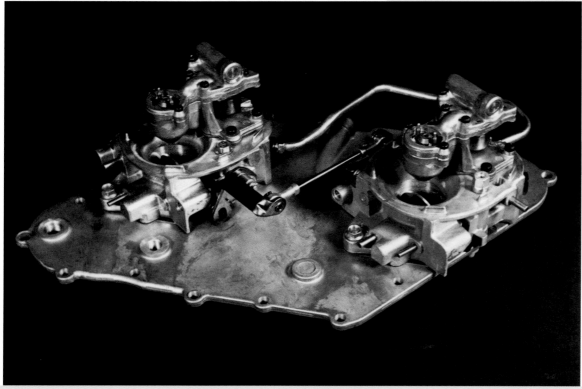

The Cross-Fire Injection manifold was styled after the rare cross-ram intake used by the 1969 Z/28 Camaro. Two throttle-body injectors were used in this case instead of carburetors.

A suitable closing chapter for the Shark tale, the Collector Edition was offered for 1982 only.

The 1982 Collector Edition Corvette was the only C3 model to feature a working glass hatchback. *Mike Mueller*

Above
Silver-beige leather abounded inside the Collector Edition. Luxury carpeting, appropriate badges, and a leather-wrapped steering wheel were also included. *Mike Mueller*

Below
The Collector Edition's exclusive silver-beige paint was accented with graduating decals on the hood and down the body sides. *Mike Mueller*

04

Above
The hot performance option from 1991 to 1995 was the Z07 adjustable suspension package, available for coupes only. In 1995, RPO X07 cost $2,045.

Center
A power delay was added in 1991 that allowed the stereo and power windows to still operate after the ignition was turned off.
Everything shut down after 15 minutes or if the driver's door was opened, whichever came first.

Right
While John Cafaro was busy drawing up the C5 Corvette, John Schinella's Advanced Concepts Center in California was preparing its gorgeous Sting Ray III, unveiled to the public in January 1992.

Better Late than Never

04

C4
1984–1996

By 1982, the Shark had grown old beyond its years. Its bulging body had been around for a decade and a half, but its foundation dated all the way back to 1963. Obviously, a change was long overdue.

Various factors contributed to the C3's marathon run, not the least of which involved its record sales successes. Annual production went up each year from 1970 to 1977, surpassing 40,000 for the first time in 1976 and staying above that level through 1981 despite a national recession. Why fix something that plainly wasn't broken?

Although GM execs were pleased as punch about all the dough the Shark brought home each year, there was an understanding among the Corvette team that the old, tired St. Louis assembly line had seen its best days. The Missouri plant could roll out a lot of C3 Corvettes, but it never would be able to handle production of a new-and-improved next-generation model. A substantially modernized C4 Corvette couldn't appear until a larger, substantially modernized facility opened for business, and that didn't occur until the Bowling Green line got rolling in June 1981.

The fourth-generation Corvette, like its predecessor, then showed up a little late for its own coming-out party. Dating back to 1977,

the C4 project originally involved a 1982 model-year debut. But Bowling Green officials were far too busy ironing out bugs in 1981 to worry about retooling the line for fourth-generation assembly, and the new car was far from ready then. Dave McLellan didn't actually get upper-office approval for his beloved baby until April 22, 1980, and by that stage a 1983 introduction was proposed. Additional stumbling blocks pushed that unveiling back further, resulting in the first dealer showings coming in March 1983. Though Chevrolet officials could've used a midyear "1983-1/2" label, General Manager Robert Stempel chose instead to forego that year entirely, leaving the first C4 to emerge as

Opposite
Convertible production for 1995 was 4,971. An optional removable roof was still around on the options list (RPO CC2) but rarely ordered: CC2 production was only 459 that year.

Above
Convertibles built in any color for 1986 were considered Indy pace car replicas, but yellow was the real choice if a buyer wanted to correctly commemorate the car that hit the Bricks in May 1986.

a 1984 model. No 1983 Corvettes were sold to the public.

Appearing as it did in the spring of 1983, the first C4 then enjoyed an extended production run, allowing it to approach 1979's sales record. The 51,547 Corvettes built in Kentucky for 1984 stand second only to the 53,807 models born alongside the Mississippi River during John DeLorean's lengthened 1979 run.

Dave McLellan had been chief engineer for four years by the time the Corvette reached its all-time high in 1979. But the cars he was engineering were still Zora Duntov's, and much the same could've been said about early redesign proposals. Duntov was retired, yet he still dropped by McLellan's offices in Warren, Michigan, regularly during the late 1970s. The father not only couldn't walk away from his baby, he also couldn't quite forget his one dream that never came to be.

GM execs could shoot down Duntov's midengine ideal again and again, but it just wouldn't die, nor would his intriguing XP-882 platform. Late in 1976, Ed Cole's favored Wankel

engine was pulled from the XP-882 chassis and replaced by a Yankee-friendly V-8, resulting in the critically acclaimed Aerovette, a gorgeous concoction that *Road & Track* described as "The 1980 Corvette."

The Corvette team continued dabbling with midengine experiments even though it was reasonably clear that GM execs wouldn't change their minds, at least not then. So it was that when McLellan and crew went before the GM approval board in April 1980, their C4 proposal involved a traditional engine placement, leaving Duntov

Above
The new C4 Corvette was introduced in the spring of 1983 as a 1984 model. No 1983 models, though built in prototype and pilot forms, were released to the public. *Mike Mueller*

Left
An early C4 clay is precisely sculpted using a computer-controlled milling machine.

"Performance, luxury, comfort–the new Corvette is a paragon of all the things which the only true American sports car has come to stand for," bragged the car's chief engineer in February 1983.

1983 CORVETTE ROADSTER

1983 CORVETTE

disappointed yet again. Zora's dream, however, was revived in 1985 when Chevy's Advanced Engineering team began work on two other middies—the Corvette Indy and CERV III—once more leading the automotive press to proclaim the coming of a truly new era. And once more the powerplant remained rooted up front when the next all-new Corvette showed up in 1997.

Duntov's hopes might have been dashed when the C4 emerged with a conventional drivetrain layout, but Dave McLellan almost couldn't say enough about how happy he was with the results. "Performance, luxury, comfort—the new Corvette is a paragon of all the things which the only true American sports car has come to stand for," bragged the car's chief engineer in February 1983. "Even in base suspension configuration, the new Corvette is a sports car absolutely superior to any production vehicle in its part of the market. To find even a peer to this vehicle, you have to look at cars produced in extremely limited numbers and at prices traditionally two or more times that of the Corvette. This car will be at home and respected on the interstate, the autobahn, or any highway in the world."

"In terms of technical innovation, we've taken a great leap forward with this new model," added Development Engineer Fred Schaafsma. Most innovative was the chassis, which featured rack-and-pinion steering, transverse mono-leaf springs front and rear, Girlock disc brakes, revised suspension locations at both ends, a five-link independent rear suspension (in place of the old three-link design), and various lightweight components.

McLellan had released some of the C4's weight-saving components early, with the first—an

Above
The 1984 Corvette was the first car developed in GM's wind tunnel facility, which opened in 1980.

Above right
The birdcage idea first seen in 1963 carried over into the fourth generation, but that second time the body/frame structure was an integral unit welded up in one piece for added strength and rigidity.

Below
As opposed to the third-generation Corvette, the C4 was every bit as new underneath its restyled skin, save for its powertrain, which debuted in 1982.

upgraded differential housing and its frame member mount—coming in 1980. Switching these parts to aluminum reportedly shaved off 300 pounds from that year's Shark. The 1984 Corvette's mono-leaf springs also were made of fiberglass, a weight-conscious idea first tried as part of the 1981 C3 platform.

Corvette customers also had been tipped off to the C4's drivetrain, which McLellan chose to unveil in 1982. For 1984, the L83 Cross-Fire Injection V-8 put out 5 more horsepower (205) and could've been mated to a four-speed manual transmission, a warmly welcomed addition after buyers were forced to stick with the 700-R4 four-speed automatic in 1982. As innovative as its automatic running mate, this new four-speed, supplied by Doug Nash, incorporated computer-controlled overdrive operation in its top three gears—thus its "4+3" moniker.

Along with the C4's technical innovation, its small block also exhibited unprecedented high style as designer Jerry Palmer opted to not let beauty run only skin deep. "We made sure the engine compartment would be just as pleasant to look at as the rest of the car," he said early in 1983. "I remember lengthy discussions concerning the eventual color of the high-tension

cable leading to the spark plugs. We even asked Delco for a new black-and-gray battery, so it would go with the rest of the hardware." Black was the color of choice for the L83's cylinder block and heads.

At the time, Palmer was head of GM Design Staff's Chevy 3 studio, which had been home to both Camaro (F-body) and Corvette (Y-body) styling development since 1974. It was the Design Staff group that promoted Duntov's ideal, while Chevrolet Engineering people preferred to stick with the status quo, leaving Palmer squared off against his close coworker and friend, Dave McLellan.

"In the early Seventies, we were thinking along the lines of a midengine sports car as our next Corvette," explained Palmer in February 1983. "Work on such a car accelerated when the rotary engine was being viewed as a promising powerplant for a sport machine." Palmer's Chevy 3 team proposed a smaller midengine Corvette powered by a V-6, and they even built a running mule using a Porsche 914 platform as a base.

Then a funny thing happened on the way to the drawing board. In the summer of 1977, Porsche unveiled its new 928 with a front-mounted V-8, a conventional rear-driver that came

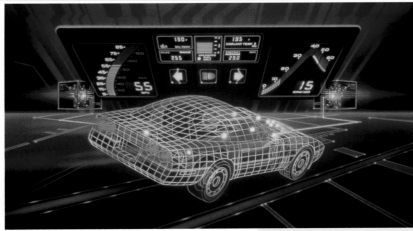

High-tech C4 touches included this out-of-this-world electronic instrument panel, which used liquid crystal displays to put on one heck of a colorful light show.

The 350-cubic-inch L83 Cross-Fire Injection V-8 carried over from 1982 but produced 205 horsepower instead of 200.

about reportedly after engineers and designers in Germany had evaluated a 1976 Corvette. Chevrolet Engineering officials had already concluded that a V-6 would never do between fiberglass fenders; after Porsche's Corvette copycat appeared, the deal was done. No way the C4 would rely on anything other than a V-8 delivering torque to the rear wheels. Palmer then complied with a suitable body to match the conventional chassis layout engineered by McLellan.

On the C4's clean side, Chevy 3's totally fresh restyle incorporated improved function into its form by way of a large clamshell hood that allowed easier engine access. Created by John Cafaro, then new to Palmer's studio, this idea was made possible by Cafaro's addition of a parting line running completely around the car, separating the body into upper and lower halves. In front, this parting groove served as a break between the lower fenders and the forward-hinged clamshell. Overall, the groove made for easier body construction by doing away with the pesky, often-unsightly bonding seams required previously. A rub molding installed into the groove hid the joint between upper and lower C4 body panels.

On top of the C4 was a one-piece lift roof panel; in back was a hatchback rear window that at the time represented the largest piece of compound glass ever fitted to an American car. Front glass sloped back 65 degrees, making it the most rakish windshield in Detroit history. Wind tunnel tests of this low, sleek shape resulted in a superb drag coefficient of 0.34.

While overall width increased 2 inches, wheelbase (96.2 inches) went down 2, length dropped 8.8, and height fell by 1.1. The lowered stance in turn lowered the C4's center of gravity, and that aspect, working in concert with a revised engine location (moved rearward) and widened front and rear tracks, translated into noticeably improved handling. While promotional people claimed the car's added width made for more interior room, some of those gains were negated (mostly in the footwells) by the wider transmission tunnel required to make room for the L83's exhaust system.

Overall looks were certainly fresh, yet still honored the past. "I really believe we've designed a car without compromises," said Palmer. "But we've managed to retain Corvette identity. The first time that people see this car, they're going to know what it is. They're going to say, 'Hey! That's a new Corvette!'"

Dave McLellan introduced his pride and joy to the press at the Riverside International Raceway in California in December 1982. The first C4 wearing a 1984 vehicle identification number (VIN) rolled

out of its Kentucky home on January 6, 1983. Before that, 43 Corvettes wearing 1983 VINs were built: 33 pilot cars and 10 prototypes. All were supposedly scrapped, but one miraculously later showed up in the National Corvette Museum in Bowling Green. Reportedly, those 43 cars cost Chevrolet about $500,000 apiece.

The 1984 run began at serial number 00002, and the first 69 C4s built were engineering cars used for testing. The officially tagged 00001 car was actually put together after 00070 and donated to the National Council of Corvette Clubs to be raffled off as part of a fund raiser to help fight spina bifida.

Although most engineering cars eventually found private homes, serial number 00071 was the first 1984 Corvette sold to the public through traditional channels. It and the following 678 cars were shipped from Bowling Green to California in February 1983 to take part in the model's first dealer introductions, held March 24. Buyers elsewhere across America got their initial looks on April 21.

1984

1984

Specifications	1984
Model availability	sport coupe with rear hatchback glass
Construction	fiberglass body on steel skeleton chassis, perimeter rail frame
Wheelbase	96.2 inches
Length	176.5 inches
Width	71 inches
Height	46.7 inches
Shipping weight	3,088 pounds
Tread (front/rear, in inches)	59.6/60.4
Tires	Goodyear Eagle GT P255/50VR-16
Brakes	11.5-inch discs
Wheels	alloy, 16x8.5 inches front, 16x9.5 inches rear
Fuel tank	20 gallons
Front suspension	independent short and long arms, transverse fiberglass leaf spring, stabilizer bar, tubular shock absorbers
Rear suspension	independent five-link layout with upper and lower control arms, tie rods, half shafts, and transverse fiberglass leaf spring; stabilizer bar; tubular shocks
Steering	rack and pinion
Engine	205-horsepower 350-ci V-8 (L83) with Cross-Fire Injection
Transmission	Turbo Hydra-matic 700-R4 automatic transmission
Optional transmission (no cost)	four-speed manual

Above
All four Corvette generations tour a test track in 1984.

Below
Thoroughly modern rack-and-pinion steering debuted in 1984. Steering ratio was a fast 15.5:1.

1984

In the mad rush to proclaim the C5 as the best 'Vette yet, few witnesses in 1997 seemed to recall a similar sensation nearly 15 years earlier. Like the all-new fifth-generation Corvette, the first C4 garnered *Motor Trend*'s prestigious "Car of the Year" award, and rightly so. Okay, the C5's trophy didn't come until the convertible version was introduced in 1998, but that's only because the Targa-topped sport coupe appeared too late to make *Motor Trend*'s 1997 balloting.

While honoring the C4, *Motor Trend* claimed it "has the highest EQ [excitement quotient] of anything to come out of an American factory. Ever. Its handling goes beyond mere competence; call it superb, call it leading edge, call it world class. *We* certainly do."

Early paperwork had specified 15-inch alloy wheels wearing P215/65ZR rubber for the 1984 Corvette, but these were superseded in regular

RACK AND PINION STEERING

- **LOW-FRICTION DESIGN**
- **POWER-ASSISTED**
- **EQUAL TURNING EFFORT**
- **PRECISE CONTROL**
- **TILT-TELESCOPING**

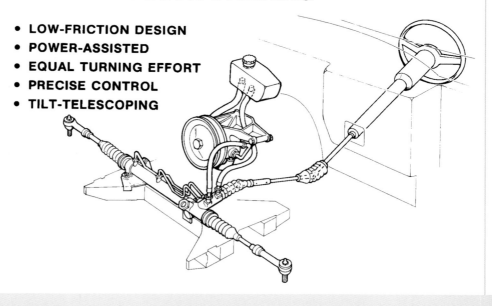

Like the all-new fifth-generation Corvette, the first C4 garnered *Motor Trend*'s prestigious "Car of the Year" award, and rightly so.

Top
Various C4 features were released early during the third-generation run, including the 1984 Corvette's engine and transmission, which debuted in 1982. That year's Collector Edition also featured the breed's first hatchback roof, which remained a standard item on all 1984 Corvettes.

Above
New C4 Corvettes began rolling off the Bowling Green line in Kentucky on January 6, 1983.

Right
Chevrolet's 750,000th Corvette was built in Bowling Green on October 26, 1983.

production by P255/50VR-16 tires on truly large (for the time) wheels measuring 16x8.5 inches in front, 16x9.5 in back. Initially listed as an individual option (RPO QZD), these wheels and tires also were included in the new Z51 performance handling package, which featured heavy-duty springs, shocks, and bushings; stiffened stabilizer bars; quicker steering; an engine oil cooler; and a second cooling fan that pushed air into the radiator, which incorporated aluminum fins and plastic reservoirs. The oil cooler could've been ordered separately (RPO KC4), as could the heavy-duty Delco-Bilstein shock absorbers (RPO FG3).

Certainly new inside was the C4's electronic instrumentation, which featured digital readouts and liquid-crystal graphic displays in place of a conventional speedometer and tach. While some critics soon would knock this so-called "arcade" design, *Motor Trend*'s Kevin Smith apparently liked what he saw early on. "The light show can get fairly spectacular," he wrote, "and while we still fail to see any advantage over old-fashioned round dials, the Corvette's is the first digital panel that we can at least imagine coming to accept." Some compliment.

Above
Performance improved in all facets for 1984, making this truly the best 'Vette yet.

Right
Cloth seats were standard inside the 1984 Corvette. Optional sport seats (in cloth) were offered, as was leather upholstery for the base seats.

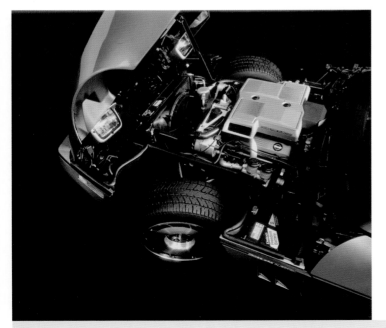

Left
Access to the 1984 Corvette's L83 V-8 was made relatively easy, thanks to John Cafaro's clamshell hood design.

Right
Some wags made jokes about the Cross-Fire name. Fortunately, Corvette drivers only had to endure those slings and arrows during 1982 and 1984. *Mike Mueller*

While honoring the C4, *Motor Trend* claimed it "has the highest EQ [excitement quotient] of anything to come out of an American factory. Ever."

Top right
The C4's powertrain and suspension components were assembled as a unit. Notice the longitudinal beam tying the transmission and differential together.

Above
The 1984 Corvette wheels featured black accents in their centers, and this style carried over into 1985. Wheel centers for 1986 were left with a natural aluminum finish.
Mike Mueller

Right
The 1984 Corvette wearing serial number 00001 was donated to the National Council of Corvette Clubs, which then raffled it off to raise funds to help fight spina bifida.
Mike Mueller

1985

1985

Specifications	1985
Model availability	sport coupe with rear hatchback glass
Construction	fiberglass body on steel skeleton chassis, perimeter rail frame
Wheelbase	96.2 inches
Length	176.5
Width	71 inches
Height	46.4 inches
Shipping weight	3,088 pounds
Tread (front/rear, in inches)	59.6/60.4
Tires	Goodyear Eagle GT P255/50VR-16
Brakes	11.5-inch discs
Wheels	alloy, 16x8.5 inches front, 16x9.5 inches rear
Fuel tank	20 gallons
Front suspension	independent short and long arms, transverse fiberglass leaf spring, stabilizer bar, tubular shock absorbers
Rear suspension	independent five-link layout with upper and lower control arms, tie rods, half shafts, and transverse fiberglass leaf spring; stabilizer bar; tubular shocks
Steering	rack and pinion
Engine	230-horsepower 350-ci V-8 (L98) with tuned-port injection
Transmission	Turbo Hydra-matic 700-R4 automatic transmission
Optional transmission (no cost)	four-speed manual

Below
Few changes set the 1985 Corvette apart from its 1984 forerunner. Spring rates were softened front and rear to appease drivers who had complained about the first C4's rough ride.

Above
After building 51,547 Corvettes for 1984, production for 1985 remained high, totaling 39,729. Base price was $24,403.

1985

The second-edition C4 served as a showcase for Chevrolet's first electronic fuel injection (EFI) system, called tuned-port injection (TPI). A major step up compared to the TBI setup used in 1982 and 1984, TPI was kind to both the environment and the pocketbook, but at the same time was downright mean when it came to making muscle. Bringing back serious performance was the goal this time around, and the TPI-equipped L98 V-8 did not disappoint. Its 230 newfound horses inspired *Car and Driver* to call the new L98 Corvette the "king of the road, reborn." Torque was 330 ft-lbs, compared to 290 for 1984's L83.

"This engine is stronger than dirt," began *Car and Driver*'s Rich Ceppos in praise of the L98. "The white golf shirts that the Corvette guys handed out with a grin at Chevrolet's 1985 press preview say it all. Stenciled over the left breast are the Corvette crossed-flags insignia and the words

The 1985 Corvette's new L98 small-block V-8 made 230 horsepower using a true fuel injection system called tuned-port injection (TPI).

Above
Car and Driver magazine honored the 1985 Corvette as America's fastest production car. Its top end was 150 miles per hour.

Left
Created by Bosch, the L98's TPI system featured eight individual injectors, one at each intake port. Up front was a mass airflow sensor that led to eight precisely tuned (thus the name) intake runners.

The injected L98 was hot, for sure, but it also looked so damned cool.

'Life Begins at 150.' Yes, that's *miles per*, and yes, for the first time in more than a decade, Chevy's plastic bi-seater will hit the magic one-five-oh mark. How sweet it is."

"No need to speculate, the car is definitely quicker," added *Road & Track*. "And what numbers! With the automatic transmission [L98], we ran off 0 to 60 mph in 6.2 seconds and the quarter-mile in 14.6 sec, both of which represent a good second off our previous times."

Now a true fuel-injection system (in some minds, the L83's twin throttle-body injectors were little more than force-feeding carburetors), TPI featured eight individual Bosch injectors, one at

each intake port. Up front was a mass airflow sensor that directed ambient atmosphere into a large-capacity aluminum plenum. From there, the flow was separated into eight precisely tuned (thus the name) intake runners that curved somewhat elegantly down to the ports in the cylinder heads. These tubular runners helped ram the air stack into the combustion chamber when the intake valve opened. And a pair of high-pressure fuel rails, one stretched along each bank of intake ports, supplied the go-juice to those eight injectors.

The injected L98 was hot, for sure, but it also looked so damned cool. According to Rich

Ceppos, the TPI equipment "makes the scenery under the clamshell hood as pretty as anything you'll find in a Porsche or BMW."

Few other changes were made for 1985. Springs were softened by 26 percent in front, 25 in back, to answer customer complaints concerning the 1984 Corvette's harsh ride. The Z51 package made for even rougher seat-of-the-pants responses, so its springs were undone too, by 16 percent in front, 25 in back. Thicker stabilizer bars were added to the Z51 option to compensate for these weaker transverse leafs. New to that year's Z51 deal was the V08 heavy-duty cooling equipment.

Inside, revisions included less colorful speedometer and tachometer graphics and larger digits for the liquid-crystal displays. The sport seat option, which was cloth in 1984, was done in leather beginning midyear.

1986

1986

Specifications	1986
Model availability	sport coupe (with rear hatchback glass) and convertible
Construction	fiberglass body on steel skeleton chassis, perimeter rail frame
Wheelbase	96.2 inches
Length	176.5 inches
Width	71 inches
Height	46.4 inches
Shipping weight	3,086 (coupe)
Tread (front/rear, in inches)	59.6/60.4
Tires	Goodyear Eagle GT P255/50VR-16
Brakes	11.5-inch discs with ABS
Wheels	alloy, 16x9.5 inches
Fuel tank	20 gallons
Front suspension	independent short and long arms, transverse fiberglass leaf spring, stabilizer bar, tubular shock absorbers
Rear suspension	independent five-link layout with upper and lower control arms, tie rods, half shafts, and transverse fiberglass leaf spring; stabilizer bar; tubular shocks
Steering	rack and pinion
Engine	230-horsepower 350-ci V-8 (L98) with tuned-port injection and cast-iron cylinder heads (235 horsepower with aluminum heads)
Transmission	Turbo Hydra-matic 700-R4 automatic transmission
Optional transmission (no cost)	four-speed manual

1986

Big news in 1986 involved the standard application of a Bosch-supplied anti-lock brake system (ABS) and the return of a Corvette convertible, absent since 1975. Center high-mount stoplights (CHMS) also appeared high on the coupe's roof, at the top of the convertible's rear fascia. Wheels changed slightly as their center caps' black finish was dropped, leaving a natural metal tone.

L98 enhancements included aluminum cylinder heads, though not in all cases. Early faulty castings delayed the installation of weight-saving heads until 1986 production was well under way. Beginning midyear as well, the reborn convertible was fitted with aluminum heads from start to finish. But the majority of coupes that year were delivered with typical cast-iron heads. Aluminum-

Above
A long list of paint choices greeted Corvette customers in 1986, including four two-tone finishes. Bright red was most popular that year, followed by black and white.

Right
The 230-horsepower L98 V-8 backed by a four-speed automatic transmission was again standard in 1986. A four-speed manual trans (shown) was a no-cost option.

head L98 V-8s were rated at 235 horsepower, 5 more than their iron-headed counterparts.

The new convertible became the second Corvette to pace the Indianapolis 500, and Chevrolet that year was more than proud that its two-seater again (like its 1978 forerunner) needed

no special engineering modifications to help bring Rick Mears, Danny Sullivan, Michael Andretti, and the rest up to speed. Save for the safety-conscious strobe lights, five-point harness, and onboard fire system, the yellow, 230-horsepower ragtop that led the pace lap on May 31, 1986,

A Corvette paced the Indianapolis 500 for the second time in 1986. Veteran fighter ace and test pilot Chuck Yeager drove the car on race day in May that year.

was basically identical to all other '86 Corvette convertibles sold to the public.

Retired U.S. Air Force Brigadier General Chuck Yeager, a man familiar with setting the pace, was the celebrity driver in 1986. Yeager, of course, was the first man to surpass the speed of sound, that achievement coming in October 1947. Flying much lower and slower, Bobby Rahal won the Indy 500 in May 1986.

After the race, civilian drivers were typically offered pace car replicas. But this time, Chevrolet considered every Corvette convertible built in 1986, 7,315 in all, to be a street-going Indy pacer, regardless of color. No special limited-edition package was offered; it simply was left up to the buyer to add a dealer-offered commemorative decal to the doors of his or her '86 drop top. Most didn't.

The Z51 Corvette remained the hottest thing rolling, but came only in coupe form. Even with its integral X-member reinforcement, the convertible chassis was no match for the beefed, bone-chattering Z51 suspension. The 1986 Z51 package also included a heavy-duty radiator (RPO V01) and boost fan (B4P), along with all the hot parts of previous years.

A warmly welcomed convertible returned to the Corvette lineup in 1986. Drop-top production that year was 7,315, compared to 27,794 coupes.

Corvette Indy

In 1985, Chevrolet's Advanced Engineering team hooked up with Lotus in Hethel, England, to build two experimental Corvettes, one targeted for the auto show stage, the other for the test track. The former was the Corvette Indy; the latter was CERV III.

The Corvette Indy showed up first, at the Detroit auto show in January 1986. Its name came from its power source: the 2.65-liter Ilmore Indy Car twin-turbo V-8. This mighty mite was mounted transversely behind a severely cramped cockpit. It existed there, however, only for display purposes—Chevy people didn't call this nonrunning mockup the "pushmobile" for nothing. Warren's latest midengine wonder didn't actually work until the Chevrolet-Ilmore V-8 was traded for the 32-valve, DOHC LT5 V-8 then being developed by Lotus for the upcoming ZR-1. A Toronado transmission was mated to the LT5 to

allow for its transverse location, and the package was offered to journalists to drive at Lotus in 1988.

Futuristic simply wasn't a big enough word in this sexy two-seater's case. Sensationally sleek on the outside, the Corvette Indy, in many minds, predicted the shape of things to come, although that super-low-sloping canopy would've never made do in real-world applications. Its advanced mechanicals, however, were certainly feasible. Both its drive-by-wire throttle control and its monocoque chassis' central backbone (in this case done in Kevlar and carbon fiber) reappeared later as part of the C5's makeup.

Additional innovations included all-wheel drive with traction control, four-wheel steering, anti-lock brakes, and a definitely advanced active suspension system designed by Lotus. The latter did away with conventional springs, shocks, and stabilizer bars, relying instead on computer-

controlled hydraulics at each wheel to instantly adjust ride and handling characteristics per changing road conditions. Some witnesses felt this feature could eventually reach production but not until, as *Road & Track's* Joe Rusz explained it, such "futuristic concepts can be assimilated into the world of mass production. The prototype active suspension system costs perhaps $100,000," he continued. "Mass produced, it could cost only a few hundred dollars."

Still others were sure that the Corvette Indy signified that Zora Duntov's dream of a midengine redesign wasn't dead. By 1993, claimed some publications, the next new Corvette would also feature a midship-mounted V-8, perhaps additionally fitted with twin turbos like the original Corvette Indy. Wishful thinking again.

The Corvette Indy concept car with all three Corvette chief engineers: (left to right) David Hill, Zora Arkus-Duntov, and Dave McLellan.

Chevrolet's Advanced Engineering group teamed up with Lotus in England to create the midengine Corvette Indy in 1985. A nonrunning mockup appeared at the Detroit auto show in January 1986 with a transverse-mounted Ilmore Indy car V-8, thus the experimental machine's name. Two fully functional models followed, powered by Chevy small-block V-8s.

1987

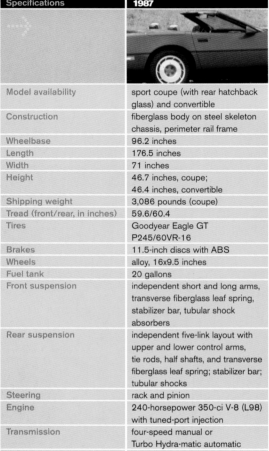

Specifications	1987
Model availability	sport coupe (with rear hatchback glass) and convertible
Construction	fiberglass body on steel skeleton chassis, perimeter rail frame
Wheelbase	96.2 inches
Length	176.5 inches
Width	71 inches
Height	46.7 inches, coupe; 46.4 inches, convertible
Shipping weight	3,086 pounds (coupe)
Tread (front/rear, in inches)	59.6/60.4
Tires	Goodyear Eagle GT P245/60VR-16
Brakes	11.5-inch discs with ABS
Wheels	alloy, 16x9.5 inches
Fuel tank	20 gallons
Front suspension	independent short and long arms, transverse fiberglass leaf spring, stabilizer bar, tubular shock absorbers
Rear suspension	independent five-link layout with upper and lower control arms, tie rods, half shafts, and transverse fiberglass leaf spring; stabilizer bar; tubular shocks
Steering	rack and pinion
Engine	240-horsepower 350-ci V-8 (L98) with tuned-port injection
Transmission	four-speed manual or Turbo Hydra-matic automatic

For 1984 and 1985, the wheel's center cap and radial slots were painted black. In 1986, only the slots wore black paint. In 1987, both cap and slots were treated to argent gray coloring.

A 1987 Corvette convertible carried a $33,172 base sticker; the coupe's base price was $27,999.

1987

Identifying a new Corvette in 1987 was made somewhat easy by a revised wheel finish. For 1984 and 1985, the wheel's center cap and radial slots were painted black. In 1986, only the slots wore black paint. In 1987, both cap and slots were treated to argent gray coloring.

New beneath the C4 clamshell were 240 horses, which resulted from a switch to friction-reducing roller lifters. Additional performance enhancements included a finned power-steering cooler and convertible-style structural reinforcements for the Z51 package, then limited to four-speed manual installations

in coupes.

Another chassis upgrade came by way of RPO Z52, introduced for 1987 with all the Z51 stuff save for its raucous springs. Called the sport handing package, the Z52 deal relied on the softer standard springing, and thus was available on both coupes and convertibles. There was no transmission limitation, either.

A second new-for-1986 option briefly came and went due to technical difficulties. A low-tire-pressure indicator (RPO UJ6) appeared early that year wearing a hefty $325 price tag. But some of

the units were able to trigger the warning alarms in other UJ6-equipped Corvettes if they wandered too close. Reportedly, 46 UJ6 installations were made before the faulty option was withdrawn and sent back to the drawing board. It would return in fine shape in 1989.

An existing option, electronic air conditioning (RPO C68), became available in coupes and convertibles in 1987. Originally announced as a late 1985 option but not released until the following year, C68 had been limited to coupes in 1986.

Production totals for the 1987 coupe and convertible were 20,007 and 10,625, respectively.

Left
New friction-cutting roller lifters helped the 1987 L98 produce 240 horsepower.

Right
A one-piece, body-colored lift-off roof was a standard feature on all C4 coupes. Dual removable panels were optional, as were tinted see-through one-piece tops.

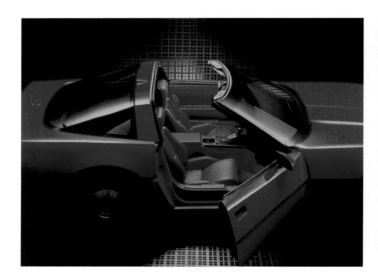

1988

Specifications	1988
Model availability	sport coupe (with rear hatchback glass) and convertible
Construction	fiberglass body on steel skeleton chassis, perimeter rail frame
Wheelbase	96.2 inches
Length	176.5 inches
Width	71 inches
Height	46.7 inches, coupe; 46.4 inches, convertible
Shipping weight	3,229 pounds
Tread (front/rear, in inches)	59.6/60.4
Tires	Goodyear Eagle GT P255/50ZR-16
Brakes	11.5-inch discs with ABS
Wheels	alloy, 16x9.5 inches
Fuel tank	20 gallons
Front suspension	independent short and long arms, transverse fiberglass leaf spring, stabilizer bar, tubular shock absorbers
Rear suspension	independent five-link layout with upper and lower control arms, tie rods, half shafts, and transverse fiberglass leaf spring; stabilizer bar; tubular shocks
Steering	rack and pinion
Engine	240-horsepower (or 245 horses, depending on mufflers) 350-ci V-8 (L98) with tuned-port injection
Transmission	four-speed manual or Turbo Hydra-matic automatic

Left
New six-slot wheels appeared for 1988 coupes and convertibles. Brakes and the front suspension also were improved.

Below
The Corvette's optional manual transmission from 1984 to 1988 was the so-called 4+3 gearbox, with computer-controlled overdrives for the top three gears. Installations of the 4+3 transmission in 1988 totaled 4,282. *Mike Mueller*

1988

All-new six-slot wheels appeared in 1988, still wearing P255/50ZR-16 rubber. Technical improvements included better brakes and a revised front suspension. The latter was redesigned to reduce unwanted steering wheel actions induced by brake torque and varying road condition inputs. The former featured new, dual-piston brake calipers and an upgraded parking brake system that relied on the rear disc pads instead of the separate small drums used

previously. Larger calipers and rotors (12.9-inch fronts, 11.9-inch rears) were added to the Z51 package, as were bigger (17x9.5 inches) 12-slot wheels shod in P275/40ZR tires.

Less-restrictive mufflers (for coupes with the optional 3.07:1 performance axle only) in 1988 boosted L98 output to 245 horsepower. Deemed too loud for convertibles (and coupes with taller 2.59:1 gears), these mufflers didn't go behind some L98s that year, resulting in a repeat of 1987's 240-horse rating in those cases.

Representing the biggest news for 1988 was the Corvette's second anniversary model, the 35th special edition package, RPO Z01. Available for coupes only, this option added exclusive white paint (accented by a black roof bow), white wheels, appropriate exterior badges, and a console-mounted anniversary plaque. Inside, the steering wheel was covered in white leather, and more white cowhide graced the seats, which featured anniversary embroidery on their headrests. Various options (electronic air conditioning, Z52 suspension, etc.) were thrown in as part of the Z01 deal, explaining its hefty asking price of $4,795. Z01 production was 2,050.

Corvette GTP

In 1980, the International Motor Sports Association (IMSA) created a new racing class for

Grand Touring Prototype (GTP) cars, truly exotic machines able to run well beyond 200 miles per hour. Corvettes by then were no strangers to IMSA events, but in lower, slower, production-based classes. Competing at such a high level in front of far more fans would surely provide far

Wheels on the 35th Anniversary Corvette were painted white too. *Mike Mueller*

more publicity for Chevrolet's two-seater, or so thought some company officials. Thus came the Corvette GTP, one of the wildest vehicles to tour an IMSA track during the 1980s.

The Bowtie banner was first carried onto the GTP battlefield by the Chevy-powered Lola T-600, a midengine coupe that first ran in May 1981. Inspired by the T-600's successes, Chevrolet people—no longer afraid to admit to participating in racing—aspired to morph the powerful package into a competition vehicle that fans would directly associate with Chevy's hottest street-going product.

About the same time, performance product promotion chief Vince Piggins had engine builder Ryan Falconer working on a competition V-6 that Piggins first planned to take racing at Indy. But plans for the Brickyard fell flat, leaving Falconer to suggest that Chevrolet put his turbocharged V-6 to work on the IMSA circuit. The idea then became to plant the V-6 into a modified T-600 chassis and wrap it up with bodywork resembling that of the existing Corvette.

In 1980, the International Motor Sports Association (IMSA) created a new racing class for Grand Touring Prototype (GTP) cars, truly exotic machines able to run well beyond 200 miles per hour.

The steering wheel of the 1988 35th Anniversary Corvette was wrapped in white leather. *Mike Mueller*

Jerry Palmer's GM design studio supplied the body, which looked somewhat like a Corvette up front, but from the doors back was a pure prototype racer. Lola delivered the 10th of 12 T-600 platforms built, and the vehicle became Chevrolet's first Corvette GTP. Created for show purposes only, the racer-in-name-alone debuted at the Detroit Grand Prix Expo in June 1983. Lotus handled chassis refinement and testing, and one Corvette GTP was later fitted with the British firm's innovative active suspension.

Lola's one-and-only T-710 chassis served as a base for the Hendrick Motorsports GM Goodwrench Corvette GTP, the first of the breed to actually race. Powered by a 3.4-liter turbo V-6, the Hendrick car debuted at Road America in Elkhart Lake, Wisconsin, on August 25, 1985, completing 69 of 125 laps to finish 33rd. Later honors included a lap-speed record at Daytona in December that year and a victory, in record time, at Road Atlanta in April 1986.

Although Hendrick put in the bulk of the Corvette GTP's track time, other teams also contributed. After Hendrick Motorsports took delivery of its first GTP car in May 1984, Lee Racing brought home one of its own later that December. Peerless Automotive accepted a V-8-powered Corvette GTP in May 1988, by

Z01 interiors featured leather upholstery, a console-mounted anniversary plaque, and this commemorative embroidery on the seats' headrests. *Mike Mueller*

which point the breed's time in the sun was waning. The No. 76 Peerless car, driven by Jacques Villeneuve and Scott Goodyear, was the last Corvette GTP to race, finishing 11th at Watkins Glen in July 1989.

While track records and awesome speeds were relatively plentiful during the Corvette GTP's short, happy career, victories weren't.

Based on the 10th of 12 Lola T-600 chassis built, this Corvette GTP prototype was created for display purposes only in 1983.

Hendrick Motorsports campaigned various GM Goodwrench Corvette GTP racers during the 1980s, with the first running in August 1985. Early cars used turbocharged V-6 engines; later versions were fitted with V-8s.

1989

Specifications	1989
Model availability	sport coupe (with rear hatchback glass) and convertible
Construction	fiberglass body on steel skeleton chassis, perimeter rail frame
Wheelbase	96.2 inches
Length	176.5 inches
Width	71 inches
Height	46.7 inches, coupe; 46.4 inches, convertible
Shipping weight	3,229 pounds (coupe), 3,269 pounds (convertible)
Tread (front/rear, in inches)	59.6/60.4
Tires	Goodyear Eagle GT P275/40VR-17
Brakes	11.5-inch discs with ABS
Wheels	alloy, 17x9.5 inches
Fuel tank	20 gallons
Front suspension	independent short and long arms, transverse fiberglass leaf spring, stabilizer bar, tubular shock absorbers
Rear suspension	independent five-link layout with upper and lower control arms, tie rods, half shafts, and transverse fiberglass leaf spring; stabilizer bar; tubular shocks
Steering	rack and pinion
Engine	240-horsepower (or 245 horses, depending on mufflers) 350-ci V-8 (L98) with tuned-port injection
Transmission	four-speed manual or Turbo Hydra-matic automatic
Optional transmission	six-speed manual

Above
The most noticeable difference between the 1984 Corvette (right) and the 1989 rendition (left) involved redesigned wheels. A center high-mount stoplight (CHMS) was also added to the coupe's roof (barely visible here) in 1986. *Mike Mueller*

Below
Base price for the Corvette coupe in 1989 was $31,545. Production was 16,663.

1989

The 17-inch 12-slot wheels included in the Z51 and Z52 packages in 1988 were bolted on to all Corvettes for 1989. Standard power was again either 240 or 245 horses, depending on the exhaust system installed.

New behind the L98 for 1989 was a Zahnradfabrik Friedrichshafen (ZF) six-speed manual, a no-cost option that replaced the oft-maligned 4+3 Doug Nash gearbox. The ZF transmission incorporated computer-aided gear

selection (CAGS), an innovation that also attracted detractors. According to *Road & Track*'s Douglas Kott, "The best thing about [CAGS] is that it goes unnoticed most of the time."

In loafing-rpm situations, CAGS activated a shifter detent to bypass second and third. Below 19 miles per hour, a driver was forced to shift from first to fourth, with the idea to improve fuel economy by limiting engine revs when they weren't needed. Like Kott, more than one owner complained about this nuisance, but avoiding it was simply a matter of surpassing 19 miles per hour in first or blipping the throttle lightly while attempting a low-speed shift into second.

A selective ride and handling package (RPO FX3), priced at $1,695, appeared on 1989's options list, while the Z52 suspension disappeared. Available only on Z51 Corvettes, the electronic FX3 system adjusted shock damping per suspension firmness levels specified by a console-mounted switch. Three modes were available: touring, sport, or competition. Once again, the Z51 option was offered only for manual-transmission coupes. Furthermore, optional sport leather seats (RPO AQ9) were installed only in Z51 cars.

Corvette Challenge racers

Corvettes dominated SCCA Showroom Stock racing during the early 1980s, so much so that SCCA officials in 1987 basically asked Chevrolet to take its two-seater home after running four straight years without a loss.

Left
An optional removable hardtop, priced at $1,995, returned for Corvette convertibles in 1989.

Above
Identically equipped Corvettes competed against each other in 1988 and 1989 in the Corvette Challenge series. Chevrolet built 56 Corvette Challenge cars that first year, followed by another 60 in 1989.

Right
This wheel first appeared as part of the Z51 and Z52 options packages in 1988. In 1989, it became the standard Corvette rim. *Mike Mueller*

The Corvette Challenge series then followed, organized by Canadian race promoter John Powell and fully supported by Chevrolet. Powell's plan called for pitting 50 identical L98 Corvettes against each other in competition for a $1 million purse. Ten Corvette Challenge events were run in 1988; another 12 followed in 1989 before the popular series ran its course. Bill Cooper claimed the first purse; Stu Hayner copped the championship in 1989.

Chevrolet built 56 street-legal Corvette Challenge cars that first year, featuring engines specially assembled in Flint and delivered in sealed fashion to Bowling Green for installation. Fifty of these cars were then shipped to Protofab in Wixom, Michigan, to be fitted with roll bars and other competition-conscious equipment.

Another 60 Challenge cars followed in 1989, all equipped with standard engines. However, 30 of these were soon refitted with higher-horsepower V-8s especially created by CPC's Flint Engine facility. After assembly, these engines were sent to Specialized Vehicles Inc. (SVI), in Troy, Michigan, where each was sealed after being equalized for power output. Cars and SVI engines then met at Powell Development America, in Wixom, Michigan, where roll bars and other safety gear were installed and the original V-8s were swapped for their warmed-up counterparts. Reportedly, those original engines were later returned to each car owner at season's end.

Although there was no Corvette Challenge after 1989, Chevrolet still offered a special race package in 1990 intended for the SCCA World Challenge series. Listed under merchandising code R9G, the deal involved various heavy-duty deviations from typical build specifications. Reportedly, 23 R9G Corvettes were built for 1990.

1990

Above
An interior restyle represented the major change for 1990. Convertible production that year was 7,630.

Left
The 1990 Corvette's new interior looked more like a jet fighter cockpit. Gauges were both analog and digital.

Specifications	1990
Model availability	sport coupe (with rear hatchback glass) and convertible
Construction	fiberglass body on steel skeleton chassis, perimeter rail frame
Wheelbase	96.2 inches
Length	176.5 inches
Width	71 inches
Height	46.7 inches, coupe; 46.4 inches, convertible
Shipping weight	3,223 pounds (coupe), 3,263 pounds (convertible)
Tread (front/rear, in inches)	59.6/60.4
Tires	Goodyear Eagle GT P275/40VR-17
Brakes	11.5-inch discs with ABS
Wheels	alloy, 17x9.5 inches
Fuel tank	20 gallons
Front suspension	independent short and long arms, transverse fiberglass leaf spring, stabilizer bar, tubular shock absorbers
Rear suspension	independent five-link layout with upper and lower control arms, tie rods, half shafts, and transverse fiberglass leaf spring; stabilizer bar; tubular shocks
Steering	rack and pinion
Engine	245-horsepower (or 250 horses, depending on mufflers) 350-ci V-8 (L98) with tuned-port injection
Transmission	four-speed manual or Turbo Hydra-matic automatic
Optional transmission	six-speed manual

1990

A modernized interior appeared in 1990 with an instrument panel that toned down at least some of the snickers heard concerning the arcade dash. While digital graphics remained for the speedometer, all other readouts went back to analog. New, too, were a supplemental inflatable restraint (SIR) air bag system on the driver's side and a glove box on the passenger's.

The standard ABS system was improved, a more efficient radiator was installed, and optional leather sports seats became available for all 1990 models. That radiator worked so well there was no longer a need for the optional boost fan (RPO B24) offered from 1986 to 1989. Additional changes on the 1990 options list included widening FX3's scope (it was no longer limited to Z51 cars) and the introduction of a 200-watt premium Delco-Bose stereo system (RPO U1F)

priced at $1,219. The U1F stereo featured a compact disc player. Only one stereo option (without a CD system) was listed in 1989.

L98 output went up 5 horses (again depending on the exhausts installed) to 245 and 250 horsepower. More cam, more compression, and a switch from mass-air to speed-density controls helped free up those extra ponies. These two ratings then rolled over into 1991, the year the L98 finally retired.

CERV III

Specifications	**CERV III**
Body style and construction	midengine two-seater with Kevlar/carbon-fiber/Nomex shell
Drag coefficient	0.277
Wheelbase	97.6 inches
Chassis	carbon-fiber monocoque with central backbone
Length	193.6 inches
Width	80 inches
Height	45.2 inches
Curb weight	3,400 pounds
Tread (front/rear, in inches)	66.1/66.1
Tires	275/40ZR-17, front; 315/35ZR-17, rear
Brakes	twin discs at each wheel with ABS
Wheels	cast magnesium; 17x9.5 inches, front; 17x11 inches, rear
Fuel tank	23.3 gallons
Suspension	upper and lower A-arms with coil springs and hydraulic actuators, front and rear
Steering	power-assisted rack and pinion at both ends
Engine	transverse-mounted 32-valve DOHC LT5 V-8 with twin turbos and intercoolers
Transmission	custom two-speed automatic and three-speed Turbo Hydra-matic in tandem

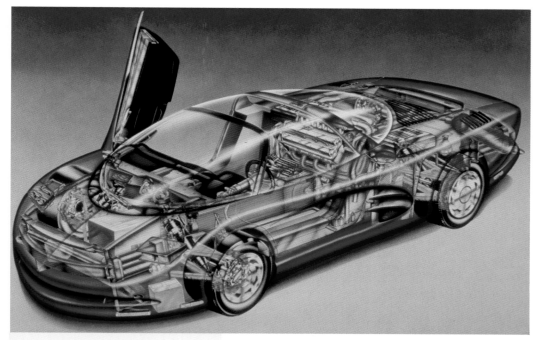

A twin-turbocharged LT5 V-8 powered the
CERV III. Output was 650 horsepower.

CERV III

Chevrolet Chief Engineer Don Runkle and Lotus engineering boss Tony Rudd first discussed building the midengine Corvette Indy in June 1985, in part to showcase the new Indy racing V-8 created for Chevy by Ilmore. Home to the Corvette Indy's futuristic carbon-fiber shell was the Chevy 3 studio, where, as Jerry Palmer told *Road & Track* in 1990, "there was a lot of clay flying around" as the "extremely emotional program" (more Palmer words) progressed.

Lotus handled the innovative mechanicals, while Ken Baker's Advanced Vehicle Engineering (AVE) group was tasked with integrating things. AVE engineer Dick Balsley was the main man behind the Corvette Indy's development, as well as that of the CERV III to follow.

Three Corvette Indy cars were built, the first the nonfunctional Ilmore-equipped model displayed at the Detroit auto show in 1986. A running counterpart, painted white and fitted with an LT5 V-8, was completed at Lotus late in 1986 and served as a pilot car of sorts for a more-refined runner finished in January 1987. A third working midengine Corvette also was up and running by early 1988, and that exceptional machine was given the CERV designation, which at that time stood for "corporate experimental research vehicle."

While CERV III shared all of the Corvette Indy's advanced technologies (all-wheel drive, four-wheel steering, etc.), its overall makeup was redone to make it more practical and less experimental. Initial plans called for secrecy—the public wasn't meant to see this engineering exercise, which was intended to morph the Indy ideal into a reality-friendly prototype that perhaps could become the latest best 'Vette yet, and the various changes made to accomplish this goal explained why CERV III took a little longer to complete compared to its three forerunners. But when GM President Robert Stempel set eyes on the car, he immediately ordered it onto an auto show stage. So it was that CERV III was introduced to show-goers in Detroit in January 1990. By then, it had clocked about 2,000 miles of testing time.

The midengine CERV III debuted at the 1990 Detroit auto show. It was basically a modified Corvette Indy platform featuring a more practical cockpit and hideaway headlights.

First and foremost among CERV III upgrades was a modified, roomier (both taller and wider) greenhouse complemented with Lamborghini-style swing-up doors that incorporated power windows. Remember, the Corvette Indy cockpit was no place for full-sized drivers, thank to its windshield and side glass sloping in so sharply that, according to *Road & Track*'s Joe Rusz, "only a Munchkin can sit [inside] without scraping his head." Like its Indy predecessors, CERV III also was crowned by a removable roof but a predictably larger panel in this case.

Further concessions to real-world realities involved opening up the wheelhouses for 3.5 inches of wheel travel and reshaping the rocker panels to accommodate fuel cells. The nose was reshaped to meet federal guidelines concerning bumper height and headlight locations, and the latter became hideaway units instead of exposed beneath clear covers.

Power was supplied by a muscled-up LT5 fed by two intercooled Garrett T3 turbochargers.

Output was an outrageous 650 horsepower and 655 ft-lbs of torque. Compression dropped to 8.5:1 to deal with the turbos' boost, and beefed connecting rods and Mahle pistons were added to further handle the extra strain.

All that power was transmitted by chain from the engine's torque converter to a compound transmission consisting of a strengthened Turbo Hydra-matic three-speed and a custom-built two-speed box. After that came a bevel-gear differential that turned the horses around a corner, redirecting them both fore and aft to two more differentials, both Posi-Traction units, that supplied the final drive to front and rear wheels. The middle differential relied on computer controls to deliver the power where it was needed most: if the back wheels slipped, the front wheels automatically compensated.

CERV III's top end was estimated at 225 miles per hour. To bring that much performance back to Earth, Dick Balsley specified a unique ABS brake system incorporating two huge disc

rotors at each wheel. Done in carbon fiber, these discs and their pads were supplied by AP Racing, a firm known for its Formula 1 stopping systems.

Suspension pieces included titanium coil springs at the corners, but they were only installed to keep CERV III off the ground when not running. Once the turbocharged LT5 took over, Lotus' hydraulic active suspension handled all supportive chores.

Clearly advanced inside and out, CERV III certainly would have made one helluva real-world Corvette. But all that innovation didn't come cheap. According to Don Runkle, the car would have carried an out-of-this-world price tag in the $300,000 to $400,000 range. As he told *Road & Track*'s John Lamm in 1990, "We did a business case on the CERV III, but the intent was not really to do it for production. Rather, we put production specifications on the design because it's more interesting to build cars like that than to do an Indy. That car is a sculpture and doesn't need any reality to it."

1991

Specifications	1991
Model availability	sport coupe (with rear hatchback glass) and convertible
Construction	fiberglass body on steel skeleton chassis, perimeter rail frame
Wheelbase	96.2 inches
Length	178.6 inches
Width	71 inches
Height	46.7 inches, coupe; 46.4 inches, convertible
Shipping weight	3,223 pounds (coupe), 3,263 pounds (convertible)
Tread (front/rear, in inches)	59.6/60.4
Tires	Goodyear Eagle GT P275/40VR-17
Brakes	11.5-inch discs with ABS
Wheels	alloy, 17x9.5 inches
Fuel tank	20 gallons
Front suspension	independent short and long arms, transverse fiberglass leaf spring, stabilizer bar, tubular shock absorbers
Rear suspension	independent five-link layout with upper and lower control arms, tie rods, half shafts, and transverse fiberglass leaf spring; stabilizer bar; tubular shocks
Steering	rack and pinion
Engine	245-horsepower (or 250 horses, depending on mufflers) 350-ci V-8 (L98) with tuned-port injection
Transmission	four-speed manual or Turbo Hydra-matic automatic
Optional transmission	six-speed manual

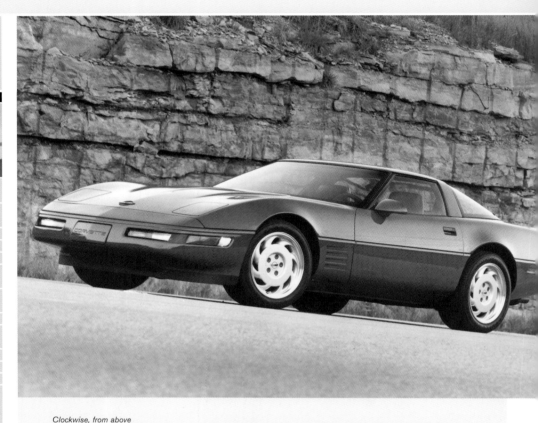

Clockwise, from above
Restyled wheels and new fender louvers announced the 1991 Corvette's arrival. Coupe production that year was 14,967.

Base price for a 1991 Corvette convertible was $38,770.

A driver-side air bag was introduced as part of 1990's interior redesign.

All Corvettes—coupes and convertibles—were treated to the ZR-1-style tail in 1990.

1991

The 1991 C4 shell experienced a major makeover. First, the car's nose was revised with more rounded corners and wraparound parking lights. Fender louvers increased from two to four and were horizontal instead of vertical; the black rub strip was replaced by a wider, body-colored molding; and wheels were redesigned. But most noticeable was the new tail, which borrowed the look from the ZR-1 but was not as wide. All Corvettes that year looked alike at a glance, with only the center high-mount stoplights setting them apart: this extra brake light appeared on the ZR-1's roof but showed up on the restyled rear fascia of L98-powered coupes.

A finned power-steering cooler became standard, as did a power outlet for cell phones and such. Less-restrictive mufflers were installed for improved performance, but advertised L98 output carried over unchanged from 1990.

Nearly all options rolled over, too, with the most prominent exception involving RPO Z51, which was traded in 1990 for the Z07 adjustable suspension package. Priced at an intimidating $2,155, the Z07 deal was similar to the old Z51 package in that it added beefed-up brakes, stiffened underpinnings, and an oil cooler for the L98. The electronic FX3 system also was incorporated. But therein lay the differences. Z51 Corvettes fitted with FX3 in 1989 and 1990 relied on relaxed standard springing to allow ride adjustments, running from soft to firm. The Z07 option, on the other hand, kept the Z51 stiff suspension parts to make for three truly firm adjustable modes. Like the Z51 option, the uncompromising Z07 deal was limited to manual-transmission coupes, though apparently at least one automatic example was built. Z07 production was only 733 in 1991.

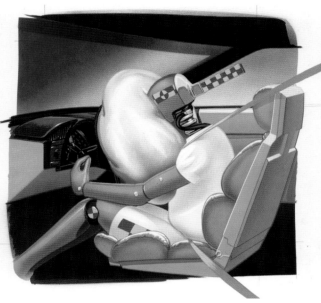

1992

Specifications	1992
Model availability	sport coupe (with rear hatchback glass) and convertible
Construction	fiberglass body on steel skeleton chassis, perimeter rail frame
Wheelbase	96.2 inches
Length	178.6 inches
Width	71 inches
Height	46.3 inches, coupe; 47.3 inches, convertible
Shipping weight	3,223 pounds (coupe), 3,269 pounds (convertible)
Tread (front/rear, in inches)	57.7/59.1
Tires	Goodyear GS-C P275/40ZR-17
Brakes	11.5-inch discs with ABS
Wheels	alloy, 17x9.5 inches
Fuel tank	20 gallons
Front suspension	independent short and long arms, transverse fiberglass leaf spring, stabilizer bar, tubular shock absorbers
Rear suspension	independent five-link layout with upper and lower control arms, tie rods, half shafts, and transverse fiberglass leaf spring; stabilizer bar; tubular shocks
Steering	rack and pinion
Engine	300-horsepower 350-ci (5.7-liter) V-8 (LT1) with multi-port injection
Transmission	four-speed manual or Turbo Hydra-matic automatic
Optional transmission	six-speed manual

"We want to continue to offer a car that people can own as their only car and still do all the things they want to do–go to the golf course or go on a week's vacation."

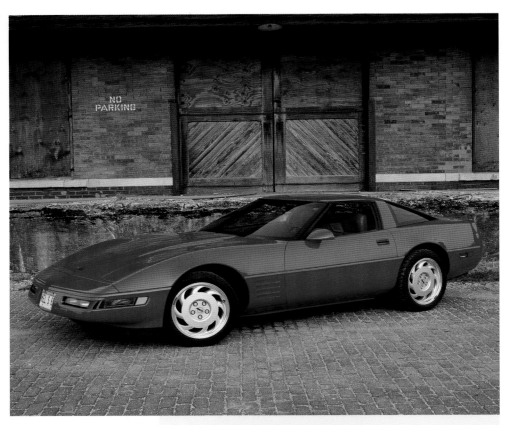

No visible changes marked the arrival of the 1992 Corvette. Coupe production that year was 14,604. *Mike Mueller*

1992

Chevrolet's mouse motor turned 35 in 1990, making it rather young by human standards but certainly venerable in automotive engineering terms. As the 1990s dawned, most anyone could see that the time had come to update the tried-and-true small block, and it was then left to GM Powertrain Assistant Chief Engineer Anil Kulkarni to get the job done.

Kulkarni was issued a somewhat-intimidating list of goals, among which were increased reliability, reduced noise, and minimized external

dimensions. A higher, flatter, longer torque curve was also specified, as was better fuel economy coupled with more performance. Making 50 more horses was what Kulkarni's bosses had in mind.

Kulkarni's resulting design met all those expectations and then some, and represented such a marked improvement that Chevrolet officials chose to announce the coming of a second-generation small block. And to honor the impressive arrival of the aptly named "Gen II" V-8, those same folks also opted to let history repeat

itself, naming this small block "LT1," after the famous LT-1 built from 1970 to 1972.

According to Dave McLellan, the LT1 earned its revered title because of its strength—maximum output was 300 horsepower at 5,000 rpm. Kulkarni had been instructed to better the L98's output by 20 percent and that's exactly what he had done—while also increasing fuel economy by 1 mile per gallon. These numbers aside, it was the seat of your pants that told the true tale. The new LT1 punch literally represented a rebirth for the

Base price for the Corvette coupe in 1992 was $33,635. The convertible base sticker was $40,145.

Right
Bosch-developed traction control, called acceleration slip regulation (ASR), appeared on the 1992 Corvette. The ASR system used spark retard, throttle shut-down, and brake activation to limit wheel spin during hard acceleration. It could be deactivated by a switch on the instrument panel. *Mike Mueller*

Far right
The 1992 Corvette's fender louver layout first appeared in 1991. *Mike Mueller*

As the 1990s dawned,
most anyone could see that the
time had come to update the tried-and-true
small block, and it was then left to
GM Powertrain Assistant Chief Engineer
Anil Kulkarni to get the job done.

Topless Corvette production in 1992 was 5,875.
Folding roof color choices were blue (with white),
beige, black, and white.

Corvette, with published road test results running as low as 4.92 seconds for the 0–60 run and 13.7 seconds (topping out at 103.5 miles per hour) for the quarter-mile.

Chevy's new small block truly was born again. Very little interchanged between LT1 and L98, with carryovers including block height, bore spacing, and displacement. Most everything else was drawn up on a clean sheet of paper, beginning with the iron cylinder block and aluminum heads, which were recast to incorporate a revised reverse-flow cooling system. Gen I coolant typically had been pumped into the block first, then to the heads. But, as Kulkarni explained, cooler heads and warmer cylinder bores are key to maximizing both performance and fuel economy. Thus, the Gen II design sent the coolant

first to the heads, then into the block and back 243to the pump.

That pump also incorporated the crossover passage (used to deliver coolant from head to head) formerly cast into the Gen I's intake manifold, an improvement that essentially allowed engineers to work with more space inside the Gen II's intake while maximizing the all-important air/fuel flow. Removing the coolant crossover from the intake also helped translate into a lower engine silhouette, a major priority considering the Corvette's low, low hoodline. Overall, the LT1 measured almost 3.5 inches shorter than its L98 forerunner.

Working in concert with that low-rise, cast-aluminum intake to reduce engine height was a new induction layout, a multi-port fuel-injection (MPFI) system that did away with the TPI's

exposed long-tube runners. MPFI equipment also delivered the coals to the latest, greatest small block's fire as efficiently as ever. According to Kulkarni, the exact matching of all components—from the low-restriction air snorkel to the bigger, better throttle body; from the short-runner, one-piece intake to the more-precise AC Rochester Multec injectors—was the key to the LT1's newfound performance.

Cylinder heads were massaged for better breathing, compression was boosted up to 10.5:1 (from 9.5:1), and a more-aggressive roller camshaft was installed. Lift increased from the L98 cam's 0.415/0.430 (intake/exhaust) to 0.451/0.450 for the lumpier LT1 unit. Valve specs rolled over from the L98: 1.94-inch intakes, 1.50 exhausts.

The L98's high-energy ignition (HEI) system was exchanged for the new Optispark distributor, located up front where it was driven off the camshaft. This unit used optical signals to govern ignition timing. Light shining through a stainless-

Left
Chevrolet engineers dusted off the LT-1 tag, deleted the hyphen, and used it to announce the rebirth of Corvette performance in 1992. Output for the 1992 5.7-liter LT1 small block was 300 horsepower.

Below
Chevrolet called the 1992 LT1 its Gen II V-8. Born in 1955, the original Gen I small block ran for 37 years.

According to Dave McLellan, the LT1 earned its revered title because of its strength—maximum output was 300 horsepower at 5,000 rpm.

Above
This 1992 coupe served as a paint trial car, in this case testing a shade called Melon Metallic, which didn't make the cut that year. This is not the same color as 1994's rare Copper Metallic. *Mike Mueller*

Right
The Bowling Green plant produced Chevrolet's 1 millionth Corvette—appropriately, a white convertible with red interior—in July 1992. *Mike Mueller*

steel shutter created 360 pulses per crank revolution, and the pulses were translated into electronic signals sent to the powertrain control module (PCM), which then determined spark firing. The most-precise small-block ignition ever was the end result, though some bugs were encountered early on.

Chevrolet engineers filled the LT1 with Mobil 1 synthetic oil and recommended it for continued use throughout each 1992 Corvette's life. Those engineers also determined that synthetic lubricants don't require special cooling, and thus the KC4 oil cooler option was deleted.

Introduced for 1992 were new Goodyear GS-C tires with directional, asymmetrical tread. Acceleration slip regulation (ASR) traction control also became standard that year. Supplied by Bosch, the ASR system could be deactivated by a dash-mounted switch. In operation, it would combine various controls (spark retardation, throttle shutdown, and braking) to avert wheel spin, and a driver knew when it was working by the way the accelerator pushed back on his or her right foot.

Another bit of important Corvette news came in November 1992 as 49-year-old David C. Hill was made the car's third chief engineer, replacing Dave McLellan, who had retired a couple of months prior. Like Ed Cole, Hill came to Chevrolet from Cadillac, where he had spent most of his time after joining GM following his 1965 graduation from Michigan Technological University. He finished a master's degree in engineering at the University of Michigan in 1969 and became chief engineer for the Allante project a dozen years later. By 1992, he was Cadillac's engineering program manager; then came the opening at Chevrolet.

Hill's new job represented a suitable assignment considering his past experience with sports cars. Not long after going to work at GM, he had purchased a 1948 MG TC and restored it. Next, he took a Lotus Super 7 racing in SCCA competition, winning two national events in 1972. By then, his daily driver (as well as his first new car) was a 1970 Corvette coupe, which he toured the country in, piling up 7,500 miles over 13 vacation days.

The Corvette's future fell right into his lap in November 1992, and early on he even considered reviving Duntov's everlasting dream. As he told *Automobile* magazine's Rich Ceppos in 1994, "I myself was not at first satisfied that we shouldn't do a mid-engined car, and I spent some energy on that when I arrived. But cars like the Acura NSX don't have anywhere near the utility of a Corvette. We want to continue to offer a car that people can own as their only car and still do all the things they want to do—go to the golf course or go on a week's vacation."

Of that last aspect, Hill clearly knew from whence he spoke.

Sting Ray III

Early in 1989, Chevy 3 studio's John Cafaro thought he deserved the honor of drawing up a suitably sensational shell for the Corvette's next new generation, the C5. But GM Design chief Charles Jordan didn't quite agree.

At the time, Chevy 3 was busy completing the latest next-generation Camaro. Once that job was done, thought Cafaro, he could give the C5 Y-car project his full attention. But a week before Chevy 3 was to release the new F-body design in January, Chuck Jordan ordered a laundry list of changes inspired by a wild Camaro show car built earlier by John Schinella's Advanced Concepts Center (ACC) in Newbury Park, a northwest suburb of Los Angeles.

Jordan didn't think much of Chevy 3's C5 proposals, anyway, and he told Cafaro if he couldn't do better, Schinella's West Coast boys could. Then he ordered Schinella to sculpt a "California Corvette." Not long afterward, Jordan contacted ACC again, specifying a running car, not just a clay mockup.

Schinella's creation appeared in the spring of 1990. Sweet and sassy, this Black Cherry convertible, nicknamed "the purple car," featured a functional trunk and exposed headlights up front, both features not seen on regular-production Corvettes since 1962. The former showed up on the new C5 convertible in 1998, and the latter reappeared on the C6 in 2005. Another purple car feature, a rear-mounted transmission, also carried over into C5 production.

Coil-over shock absorbers at all four corners suspended this cool convertible, known officially as the Sting Ray III. Wheels were massive: 18x10 in front, 19x10 in back. Mounted on those flashy three-spoke rims were 285/35ZR tires at the nose, 305/35ZR at the tail. Overall, the Sting Ray III was 2 inches shorter than a C4 Corvette, but its wheels were farther apart. Wheelbase was 103 inches, up nearly 7 inches compared to the C4.

Although Cafaro and others back east weren't all that impressed with the Sting Ray III, it was a big hit with the public when it was unveiled at the Detroit International Auto Show in January 1992. Most loved its fresh face. "ACC wrapped all this engineering within an exterior shape that's exciting and aggressive," wrote *Road & Track*'s John Lamm. "With its rear haunches, it looks like a big cat ready to leap. They fitted a soft top that allows the car to look as nice closed as open. And they gave the Sting Ray III those sexy eyes."

Lamm also was impressed with estimates claiming a production Sting Ray III would sell in the $20,000 to $25,000 range. "Come on, Chevrolet!" he continued. "Keep the Corvette out of the technostratosphere and get it back on the asphalt where it belongs: as a Sting Ray III roadster more young Americans—and Europeans and Japanese—can afford."

These pleas, of course, fell on deaf ears. And in the end, John Cafaro did do the bulk of the C5 sketching.

While the Sting Ray III was 2 inches shorter overall compared to a typical C4, its wheelbase was nearly 7 inches longer.

1993

Specifications

	1993
Model availability	sport coupe (with rear hatchback glass) and convertible
Construction	fiberglass body on steel skeleton chassis, perimeter rail frame
Wheelbase	96.2 inches
Length	178.6 inches
Width	70.7 inches
Height	46.3 inches, coupe; 47.3 inches, convertible
Shipping weight	3,333 (coupe), 3,383 (convertible)
Tread (front/rear, in inches)	57.7/59.1
Tires	Goodyear GS-C P255/45ZR-17, front; P285/40ZR-17, rear
Brakes	12-inch discs with ABS
Wheels	alloy; 17x8.5 inches, front; 17x9.5 inches, rear
Fuel tank	20 gallons
Front suspension	independent short and long arms, transverse fiberglass leaf spring, stabilizer bar, tubular shock absorbers
Rear suspension	independent five-link layout with upper and lower control arms, tie rods, half shafts, and transverse fiberglass leaf spring; stabilizer bar; tubular shocks
Steering	rack and pinion
Engine	300-horsepower 350-ci (5.7-liter) V-8 (LT1) with multi-port fuel injection
Transmission	four-speed manual or Turbo Hydra-matic automatic
Optional transmission	six-speed manual

New for 1993 was GM's first passive keyless entry (PKE) system, a neat techno trick that used a mini transmitter in the key fob to automatically lock or unlock the doors whenever the fob moved into or out of range.

The 1993 Corvette rolled over essentially unchanged from 1992. Coupe production that year was 15,898. Base price was $34,595.

1993

Five years after rolling out its white Z01 coupes, Chevrolet returned with its third celebratory Corvette, this one marking 40 years. Listed under RPO Z25, the 40th anniversary package was available for coupes, convertibles, and the fire-breathing ZR-1. This widened scope, combined with an easier-on-the-wallet price ($1,455 compared to $4,795), helped Chevrolet more than triples sales of its latest birthday present; 2,050 35th Anniversary cars were built in 1988, while the Z25 total for 1993 was 6,749, including 4,333 coupes, 2,171 convertibles, and 245 ZR-1s.

Like 1988's Z01, the Z25 Corvette was treated to an exclusive finish: Ruby Red Metallic. Special chrome emblems on the hood and fuel filler door, color-keyed wheel centers, and matching Ruby Red leather seats were also included. Headrests on those seats featured "40th" embroidery, and the same logo appeared in badge form on each fender. All leather seats in 1993 featured anniversary logos (cloth seats did not) even if Z25 wasn't ordered, meaning all ZR-1 coupes featured this stitching inside because all ZR-1s featured leather interiors.

Standard appearance features carried over from 1992 save for a freshened appearance for

the wheels from a revised machining process. Front wheel width also decreased 1 inch for 1993, and tire size correspondingly dropped: in place of 1992's P275/40ZR-17 front rubber were P255/45ZR-17 rollers. Rear tires, meanwhile, got bigger: P285/40ZR-17, compared to 1992's P275/40ZR-17. Z07-equipped Corvettes that year used 17x9.5 wheels and P275/40ZR-17 tires all the way around.

Spring rates were lowered slightly, and various minor upgrades were made beneath the hood. A two-piece heat shield (as opposed to the previous one-piece unit) and polyester (instead of magnesium) valve covers helped quiet the LT1 V-8 down in 1993. Inside, revised cam specs on the exhaust side bumped maximum torque from 330 ft-lbs to 340. Horsepower remained at 300.

New for 1993 was GM's first passive keyless entry (PKE) system, a neat techno trick that used a mini transmitter in the key fob to automatically lock or unlock the doors whenever the fob moved into or out of range. Simply walking up to the car with the keys in your pocket instantly disarmed the theft deterrent system, popped the locks, and turned on interior lights. Walking away reversed the process with a little abbreviated beep from the horn to remind you that your CDs were safe.

Clockwise, from left
Appropriate fender badges graced the 40th Anniversary Corvette. Additional anniversary embroidery appeared inside on the seats' headrests. *Mike Mueller*

The 4+3 manual gearbox was replaced by a ZF six-speed in 1989. Six-speed installations in 1993 numbered 5,330.

Commemorative wheel centers were included in the Z25 deal. *Mike Mueller*

Yet another anniversary package, RPO Z25, appeared in 1993 to help celebrate the Corvette's 40th birthday. Ruby Red paint was exclusive to the Z25 cars, which were offered as LT1 coupes, ZR-1 coupes, or convertibles. The production breakdown was 4,204 coupes, 2,043 convertibles, and 245 ZR-1s. *Mike Mueller*

1994

Specifications	1994
Model availability	sport coupe (with rear hatchback glass) and convertible
Construction	fiberglass body on steel skeleton chassis, perimeter rail frame
Wheelbase	96.2 inches
Length	178.5 inches
Width	70.7 inches
Height	46.3 inches, coupe; 47.3 inches, convertible
Shipping weight	3,317 pounds (coupe), 3,358 pounds (convertible)
Tread (front/rear, in inches)	57.7/59.1
Tires	Goodyear GS-C P255/45ZR-17, front; P285/40ZR-17, rear
Brakes	12-inch discs with ABS
Wheels	alloy; 17x8.5 inches, front; 17x9.5 inches, rear
Fuel tank	20 gallons
Front suspension	independent short and long arms, transverse fiberglass leaf spring, stabilizer bar, tubular shock absorbers
Rear suspension	independent five-link layout with upper and lower control arms, tie rods, half shafts, and transverse fiberglass leaf spring; stabilizer bar; tubular shocks
Steering	rack and pinion
Engine	300-horsepower 350-ci (5.7-liter) V-8 (LT1) with multi-port fuel injection
Transmission	four-speed manual or Turbo Hydra-matic automatic
Optional transmission	six-speed manual

Top
Copper Metallic paint was offered for 1994 only and was applied to a mere 116 Corvette coupes and convertibles. *Mike Mueller*

Above
Next to nothing changed for 1994, save for color choices, which then included Admiral Blue and Copper Metallic. Shown here is Polo Green Metallic. *Mike Mueller*

1994

Appearance features again rolled over, with the only noticeable updates for 1994 involving two new paints: Admiral Blue and Copper Metallic. In the latter's case, compromised finish quality limited applications to only 116 1994 Corvettes, creating an instantly recognized rarity.

Interior upgrades were relatively plentiful: a new passenger-side air bag (that deleted the glove box), an express-down power window on the driver side, revised upholstery and door panels, a redesigned two-spoke steering wheel, and new instrument graphics that went from white to tangerine after dark. All seats in 1994 were leather, as cloth upholstery was dropped, and base and optional sport styles were again available.

Among technical changes was a new transmission, the 4L60-E four-speed automatic, that did the previous 4L60 one better by incorporating electronic controls for improved shifts and seamless operation. Shifting the 4L60-E from park also required depressing the brake pedal, another first.

New powdered-metal connecting rods replaced the forged rods inside 1994's LT1 small block, but most notable that year was a switch to a markedly improved sequential fuel-injection system that used a mass airflow (MAF) sensor in

place of 1993's speed-density system. Working in concert with a more powerful ignition (that improved cold-starting), sequential fuel injected (SFI) equipment in turn enhanced throttle response and idle quality, and lowered emissions. Advertised output remained unchanged.

On the options list, the carryover FX3 selective ride and handling package was fitted with lowered spring rates to soften seat-of-the-pants responses. A new RPO, WY5, added the world's first run-flat rubber, the Goodyear GS-C Extended Mobility Tire (EMT), which could travel up to 200 miles at 55 miles per hour at absolutely zero pressure, allowing the driver to make it safely somewhere after suffering a flat. The low-pressure indicator (RPO UJ6) was mandatory with the EMT option because an airless run-flat tire looks no different from one filled to the brim. RPO WY5 was not available with the Z07 package or on the ZR-1 coupe.

Among technical changes was a new transmission, the 4L60-E four-speed automatic, that did the previous 4L60 one better by incorporating electronic controls for improved shifts and seamless operation.

Right
Interior color choices in 1994 numbered four: black, light beige, light gray, or red. *Mike Mueller*

Below
Yet another anniversary package, RPO Z25, appeared in 1993 to help celebrate the Corvette's 40th birthday. Ruby Red paint was exclusive to the Z25 cars, which were offered as LT1 coupes, ZR-1 coupes, or convertibles. The production breakdown was 4,204 coupes, 2,043 convertibles, and 245 ZR-1s. *Mike Mueller*

Below, right
The long-awaited grand opening for the National Corvette Museum, located nearly next door to the Corvette plant in Bowling Green, Kentucky, finally came on Labor Day weekend in 1994. Literally everyone was on hand, including, of course, Zora Arkus-Duntov, shown here during the VIP dinner the night before the official opening. *Mike Mueller*

Chevrolet built 15,771 coupes for 1995. *Mike Mueller*

Specifications	1995
Model availability	sport coupe (with rear hatchback glass) and convertible
Construction	fiberglass body on steel skeleton chassis, perimeter rail frame
Wheelbase	96.2 inches
Length	178.5 inches
Width	70.7 inches
Height	46.3 inches, coupe; 47.3 inches, convertible
Shipping weight	3,203 pounds (coupe), 3,360 pounds (convertible)
Tread (front/rear, in inches)	57.7/59.1
Tires	Goodyear GS-C P255/45ZR-17, front; P285/40ZR-17, rear
Brakes	13-inch discs, front; 12-inch discs, rear; with ABS
Wheels	alloy; 17x8.5 inches, front; 17x9.5 inches, rear
Fuel tank	20 gallons
Front suspension	independent short and long arms, transverse fiberglass leaf spring, stabilizer bar, tubular shock absorbers
Rear suspension	independent five-link layout with upper and lower control arms, tie rods, half shafts, and transverse fiberglass leaf spring; stabilizer bar; tubular shocks
Steering	rack and pinion
Engine	300-horsepower 350-ci (5.7-liter) V-8 (LT1) with multi-port fuel injection
Transmission	four-speed manual or Turbo Hydra-matic automatic
Optional transmission	six-speed manual

1995

Revised fender vents set 1995's Corvette apart from its forerunners. Truly distinctive were the 527 Indy 500 pace car replicas built to mark the breed's third appearance (this time with Chevy General Manager Jim Perkins driving) at the Brickyard, on May 28, 1995. Listed under RPO Z4Z, that year's pace car convertible wore splashy graphics on a Dark Purple/Arctic White finish and featured special leather seats embroidered with Indianapolis 500 logos. Price for the Z4Z option was an eye-popping $2,816.

Dark Purple Metallic was a new finish that year, filling in where the deleted Copper and Black Rose metallic paints left off. Inside, stronger French seams graced the optional sport seats, and an automatic transmission fluid temperature readout was added to the instrument panel display. The 4L60-E automatic was improved (enhanced clutch controls and a lighter yet stronger torque converter) for smoother shifts and a quieter cooling fan went under the hood. Six-speed manuals were also upgraded with a high-detent operation (in place of 1994's reverse lockout) for easier operation.

New on the options list was RPO N84, made possible by the growing popularity of the EMT run-flat tires. The WY5 rubber basically rendered a traditional spare moot; thus came the N84 spare tire delete deal, which put $100 back into the buyer's pocket. Due to the EMT design's success, the Corvette spare tire was done away with completely when the C5 debuted.

Overall ride was improved by less-stiff De Carbon gas-charged shocks and lower spring rates. Brakes, meanwhile, grew tougher as the big front discs (13x1.1 inches) previously limited to the Z07 option and ZR-1 coupe became standard on all 1995 Corvettes in place of 1994's 12x0.79 rotors. Further enhancing the 1995 Corvette's stopping performance was the new Bosch V ABS system.

Above
A Corvette became the prestigious pace car for the Indianapolis 500 for the third time in 1995. Chevrolet built 527 replica convertibles that year.

Above
Fender louvers were restyled yet again for the 1995 Corvette, which rolled on the same style wheels seen in 1994. *Mike Mueller*

Right
Leather seats and a Delco stereo with cassette player were included in the 1995 Corvette's base price, as had been the case the previous year. *Mike Mueller*

Above
Base prices in 1995 were $36,785 for the coupe and $43,665 for the convertible.

Right
A low-tire-pressure warning indicator (RPO UJ6) was created in preparation for the introduction of Extended Mobility tires (EMT), which would stay up, even when flat, leaving some drivers clueless about a loss of pressure.

Far right
Optional EMT run-flat rubber (RPO WY5) was first offered in 1994. EMT treads allowed a Corvette driver to limp home in the event of a flat. WY5 installations numbered 3,783 in 1995.

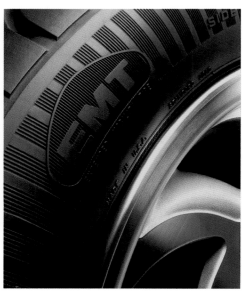

1996

Reminding many of its 1982 ancestor, the 1996 Collector Edition helped honor the end of an era as the curtain closed that year on the C4 run.

Specifications	1996
Model availability	sport coupe (with rear hatchback glass) and convertible (Grand Sport coupe, fender flares to house wider wheels and tires)
Construction	fiberglass body on steel skeleton chassis, perimeter rail frame
Wheelbase	96.2 inches
Length	178.5 inches
Width	70.7 inches
Height	46.3 inches, coupe; 47.3 inches, convertible
Shipping weight	3,298 pounds (coupe), 3,360 pounds (convertible)
Tread (front/rear, in inches)	57.7/59.1
Tires	Goodyear GS-C P255/45ZR-17, front; P285/40ZR-17, rear
Tires (Grand Sport coupe)	Goodyear Eagle GT P275/40ZR-17, front; P315/35ZR-17, rear
Brakes	13-inch discs, front; 12-inch discs, rear; with ABS
Wheels	alloy; 17x8.5 inches, front; 17x9.5 inches, rear
Wheels (Grand Sport coupe)	17x9.5 inches, front; 17x11 inches, rear
Fuel tank	20 gallons
Front suspension	independent short and long arms, transverse fiberglass leaf spring, stabilizer bar, tubular shock absorbers
Rear suspension	independent five-link layout with upper and lower control arms, tie rods, half shafts, and transverse fiberglass leaf spring; stabilizer bar; tubular shocks
Steering	rack and pinion
Engine	300-horsepower 350-ci (5.7-liter) V-8 (LT1) with multi-port fuel injection, only available with automatic transmission
Optional engine	330-horsepower 350-ci (5.7-liter) V-8 (LT4) with multi-port fuel injection (standard with Grand Sport), only available with manual transmission
Optional transmission	six-speed manual, only for LT4

Arctic White was the fourth most popular paint choice in 1996, behind Sebring Silver Metallic, Torch Red, and black. Production of 1996 Corvette coupes was 17,167. *Mike Mueller*

1996

This was the last year for Corvette's Gen II small block, and to honorably mark its farewell tour engineers put together an upgraded version of the LT1, the 330-horsepower LT4. All LT4 V-8s delivered in 1996 were backed by six-speed manuals, while the base 300-horse LT1 was mated only to automatics.

LT4 enhancements began with aluminum cylinder heads, which featured taller ports and bigger valves: 2.00-inch intakes, 1.55-inch exhausts. Those valves had hollow stems to save weight, and they used special oval-wire springs

that could handle more lift without binding. Helping increase the LT4's valve lift were higher-ratio (1.6:1) roller rocker arms supplied by Crane. Revised lift specs were 0.476 inch on intake, 0.479 on exhaust. Cam duration, too, was increased, from 200 degrees to 203 on the intake side and from 207 to 210 on exhaust.

Further LT4 upgrades included a freer-flowing intake (with taller ports to match the heads), a compression increase to 10.8:1, and a roller-type timing chain. The LT4's crank, cam, water-pump drive gear, and main bearing caps were beefed, and premium head gaskets were installed to deal

with the extra compression. Topping things off were various high-profile red engine cover accents.

The LT4/six-speed combo was optional for the coupe, convertible, and a new third concoction, the Collector Edition. The 330-horse package came standard with another special 1996 model, the Grand Sport.

Again, no changes marked a new Corvette's arrival in 1996. Convertible production that year was 4,369. *Mike Mueller*

Top
Base price for the 1996 Corvette convertible was $45,060. The coupe's standard sticker was $37,225.

Above
Interior color choices remained the same in 1996, with red trim standing out like a Yugo in a Grand Prix. *Mike Mueller*

Reminding many of its 1982 ancestor, the 1996 Collector Edition helped honor the end of an era as the curtain closed that year on the C4 run. Priced at $1,250, this package (RPO Z15) included an exclusive Sebring Silver finish, chrome "Collector Edition" badges, silver-painted ZR-1 five-spoke wheels with special centers, black brake calipers with "Corvette" lettering, and perforated sport seats complemented with "Collector Edition" embroidery. Z15 Corvettes came as coupes and convertibles.

Also offered in both body styles, the Grand Sport was listed under RPO Z16, the same code used 31 years earlier for Chevrolet's first SS 396 Chevelle. The idea was to honor the lightweight race cars built by Zora Duntov late in 1962, thus the reasoning behind the red hash marks (or "Sebring stripes") on the left front fender and the white racing stripe accenting the car's exclusive Admiral Blue Metallic paint. Further enhancing the competitive image were blacked-out ZR-1 five-spoke wheels (again with special center caps) wearing big, bad tires measuring P275/40ZR in front, P315/35ZR in back. Grand Sport coupes

The 330-horsepower LT4 small-block V-8 appeared for 1996 only. It was standard for the new Grand Sport model, optional on all other Corvettes. It came only with the six-speed manual transmission. All LT1 Corvettes in 1996 featured automatic transmissions.

All 5.7-liter LT4 V-8s wore special red trim and "Grand Sport" identification, regardless of the application. *Mike Mueller*

were fitted with fender flares in back to better house all that extra rubber. Grand Sport convertibles rolled on smaller tires (P255/45ZR in front, P285/40ZR in back) and therefore didn't require the flares.

Additional Grand Sport flair included black brake calipers with bright "Corvette" lettering, appropriate fender badges, and perforated bucket seats in black or red/black with "Grand Sport" embroidery. A unique serial number also was part of the deal that added $3,250 to a coupe's bottom line, $2,282 to a convertible's. Production was 1,000: 810 coupes, 190 convertibles.

Two new options appeared on the 1996 list, one with a familiar RPO code. From 1984 through 1990, the hottest Corvette available (discounting the ZR-1) was the Z51 with its big brakes and beefed suspension. A Z51 performance handling package returned for 1996, this time with stiff Bilstein shocks, thicker stabilizer bars, higher-rate springs, bigger wheels and tires, and a heavy-duty power steering cooler. Wheels were 17x9.5 ZR-1

Like the last C3 in 1982, the C4's passing in 1996 was honored with a special Collector Edition model, done in Sebring Silver Metallic paint. Listed under RPO Z15, the package cost $1,250 and was available on both coupes and convertibles. *Mike Mueller*

Also offered in both body styles,
the Grand Sport was listed under RPO Z16,
the same code used 31 years earlier for Chevrolet's
first **SS 396** Chevelle. The idea was to honor the
lightweight race cars built by Zora Duntov late in 1962.

five-spokes, front and rear, wearing P275/40ZR Goodyear GS-C tires.

The Z51 deal was limited to coupes, and when ordered for the closed Grand Sport it included the latter's larger rear wheels and tires. When included along with an automatic transmission, RPO Z51 mandated the installation of the 3.07:1 performance axle, RPO G92.

The second newly introduced option was electronic selective real-time damping (RPO F45), which picked up where 1995's FX3 package left off and even carried the same price tag, $1,695. A marked improvement, this driver-adjustable, Delco-supplied ride control system relied on sensors at each wheel and a powertrain control module to deliver data with lightning-quick speed to a central computer that in turn controlled damping rates individually for all four shock absorbers. The FX3 system adjusted the four shocks simultaneously at the same rate. Furthermore, when chassis engineers said "real time," they meant it—maximum damping alterations occurred every 10 to 15 milliseconds, which translated into an F45 Corvette adjusting to each foot of changing road at 60 miles per hour.

Advanced suspensions; a new, hotter small block; and two coveted limited-edition models—what a suitable sendoff for the last of the C4 line.

Top
Collector Edition production in 1996 was 5,413: 4,031 coupes and 1,382 convertibles.

Right
Silver-painted 17-inch ZR-1 wheels were included as part of the Collector Edition package. Black was the only color choice for the top.

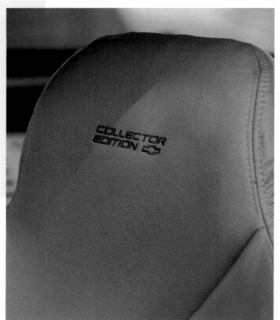

Clockwise from above
Perforated sport seats were standard inside the Collector Edition model. *Mike Mueller*

Appropriate badges predictably adorned the 1996 Collector Edition Corvette. *Mike Mueller*

Collector Edition seats were typically adorned with special embroidery. *Mike Mueller*

Above
The Grand Sport package (RPO Z16) was offered in both coupe and convertible forms in 1996. The Z16 price in coupe applications was $3,250. Z16 coupe production was 810.

Right
Admiral Blue paint with a white accent and red Sebring stripes on the left front fender readily identified the Grand Sport.
Mike Mueller

05

Above
Smoke 'em if you got 'em. According to *Car and Driver*, ZR-1 performance was 0–60 in 4.6 seconds, the quarter-mile in 12.9 clicks at 111 miles per hour.

Middle
Like all Z25 Corvettes, the 40th Anniversary ZR-1 featured wheels with commemorative center caps. *Mike Mueller*

Right
The same dual-exhaust tips used in 1990 carried over into 1991.

Long Live
the King: ZR-1

FYI

→ All ZR-1 Corvettes were coupes with high-mounted brake light on roof

→ All ZR-1 Corvettes featured six-speed manual transmissions

→ A ZR-1 breaks a 50-year-old 24-hour endurance speed record (1990)

→ All Corvettes treated to wide ZR-1 rear bodywork (1991)

→ ZR-1 fender emblems added (1992)

→ Dodge's 400-horsepower Viper appears to wrest away ZR-1's title as America's most powerful production car (1992)

→ LT5 output boosted to 405 horsepower, putting ZR-1 back on top of Detroit's power rankings (1993)

→ 40th Anniversary package (RPO Z25) offered for ZR-1 (1993)

→ Last ZR-1 built at Bowling Green (1995)

ZR-1
1990–1995

General Motors' people began considering the Corvette's near future even as the most advanced example yet, the new C4, was wowing the world in 1984. Most prominent among these forward-thinkers early on was Lloyd Reuss, who that year became GM vice president and general manager of the newly formed Chevrolet-Pontiac-Canada (CPC) group.

A long-time powertrain engineer, Reuss considered keeping Chevy's "halo vehicle" (his words) on top a personal priority, and he was fearful of the growing threat then posed by sports cars made in Japan. American automakers already were being taught a hard lesson in the compact classroom by their Far East rivals; was Chevrolet about to take an after-school beating on the high-performance playground as well?

Building more muscle was Reuss' prime concern, and he then made it Dave McLellan's. Both recognized that the boost from 205 horsepower to 230 in the works for the 1985 Corvette was nowhere near big enough. Three hundred horses was more like it, and to that end McLellan passed the ball on to Powertrain Engineering Director Russ Gee, who in turn put V-type engines' chief engineer Roy Midgley in pursuit of those ponies. Midgley at first

experimented with a turbocharged V-6 before all involved concluded that Corvette customers would never settle for a six. Exhaust-boosted induction couldn't produce acceptable fuel economy (at mandated performance levels) anyway, and this inherent downside also kept an experimental twin-turbo V-8 from getting off the ground.

Further investigation led Gee toward a newly emerging power-boosting, fuel-efficient technology: multi-valve heads with overhead cams. In October 1984, he instituted a program to create new four-valve engines in four-cylinder, V-6, and V-8 forms. But CPC engineers already were buried up to their pocket protectors in multi-port fuel injection development work, leaving Gee to look outside his company for help.

In November 1984, Lotus Cars' Engineering Managing Director Tony Rudd came over from England to Warren, Michigan, for a visit, bringing

Opposite
The ZR-1 was introduced to the world at the Geneva auto show in March 1989. American journalists were flown to Europe to partake in a picturesque debut drive through France and Switzerland.

Above
ASC artistry in the Spyder's case involved a top chop. Windshield pillars were cut down 8 inches, and glass was shortened to match. ASC also fashioned a sleek removable hardtop to further enhance the car's low, low lines. *Mike Mueller*

Chevrolet turned to Lotus in England to design the ZR-1's LT5 V-8. Lotus also tested various 1989 ZR-1 prototypes.

The ZR-1 RPO code was first used in 1970 for a rarely seen race-ready LT-1 Corvette. The code was then dusted off in 1990 for what some inside Chevrolet called the "King of the Hill." *Mike Mueller*

with him some interesting news: at the time, Lotus was making 350 horsepower with a four-liter dual-overhead-cam (DOHC) V-8. Gee got the bright idea to try mating Lotus' four-valve heads atop the existing Chevy V-8 cylinder block. But such a proposal ended up being too wide for the C4 engine compartment, inspiring Rudd in April 1985 to suggest building an entirely new engine top to bottom, an expensive proposition to say the least. Rudd promised he could make as much as 400 horsepower from a more compact DOHC V-8 if he was allowed to construct his own block.

Gee relayed this alarming idea to Reuss that same month, and the corporate VP then relied on his own clout, as well as some powerful support from GM Board Chairman Roger Smith, to help ram Rudd's risky proposal past bean-counting killjoys. The result was a cooperative design deal between GM and Lotus to create what would soon be known as the LT5 V-8, the high-tech, all-aluminum, 32-valve DOHC engine that eventually became the heart of the ZR-1 Corvette.

Initially labeled the "King of the Hill" by Chevrolet Chief Engineer Don Runkle, the ZR-1 was unveiled to the world in March 1989 at the Geneva auto show. The previous June, a prototype had blown past gawking American journalists (at

upward of 150 miles per hour) at Riverside Raceway, leaving many magazines to report that Chevrolet would be unleashing this super-duper Corvette as a 1989 model. Indeed, that was the original plan. But lagging development efforts forced Reuss, McLellan, and the gang to make the same decision made during C4 development. While a public introduction midway into 1989 would be possible, a traditional midyear model designation was out of the question.

The official decision to designate the first ZR-1 a 1990 model came on April 11, 1989, and was announced, along with Chevrolet's best 'Vette yet, to the SAE at Selfridge Air Force Base, north of Detroit, one week later. Up until then, all references to the first ZR-1 inside and outside of GM had used a 1989 tag, including a commonly displayed color cutaway done by noted automotive artist David Kimble. Distributed by Chevrolet earlier that year, a poster made from Kimble's "1989 ZR-1" X-ray view instantly became a collectors' item.

News reports of the 1989 ZR-1's midyear arrival prior to this point had been further substantiated in September 1988, when journalists were allowed an up close and personal look, again at Riverside, at both the King of the

Initially labeled the "King of the Hill" by Chevrolet Chief Engineer Don Runkle, the ZR-1 was unveiled to the world in March 1989 at the Geneva auto show.

Above
Once perfected by Lotus, the LT5 was then manufactured at Mercury Marine's MerCruiser division in Stillwater, Oklahoma.

Below
The ZR-1 was born near the end of Dave McLellan's watch as Corvette chief engineer. McLellan proudly poses here with the heart of the beast, the all-aluminum LT5 V-8.

Hill and its awesome LT5 heart. In the latter's case, the introduction was especially thorough. While Roy Midgley and his comrades from Lotus explained its many merits, two technicians nearby assembled an actual engine—then started it up with nary a hiccup, inspiring an ovation from the audience that resounded nearly as profoundly as the distinctive LT5 exhaust note. One of those highly talented (and well-rehearsed) wrenchmen was Ron Opszynski from CPC. The other was Chris Allen from MerCruiser, the firm GM contracted to build the LT5 after Lotus completed development.

In 1985, the plan was for Lotus to design the LT5 and GM to construct it. However, as Manufacturing Manager Dick Donnelly told Midgley, the corporation's engine people were far too busy to take on such a complicated, small-volume project. Russ Gee instructed Midgley to again seek outside help, and he first considered Lotus and another British firm, Coventry Climax. He even checked the John Deere tractor factory, but none of these facilities offered the required production capabilities.

Midgley next turned to the Mercury Marine division of the Brunswick Corporation in Fond du Lac, Wisconsin. He was interested in Mercury Marine's MerCruiser division, based in Stillwater, Oklahoma. For years, MerCruiser had been GM's best customer as far as special products were concerned, buying engines to go along with its state-of-the-art stern drives and inboard boat construction. The inboard industry's acknowledged leader, MerCruiser surely looked like it could handle the production of land-based powerplants. Midgley first contacted Mercury Marine Vice

President of Manufacturing Joe Anthony, who met with him in Stillwater on January 27, 1986, to ice the deal.

After lining up the many required component suppliers and ironing out tooling bugs, the Oklahoma firm completed its first three production LT5 V-8s on July 13, 1989. Its first pre-production LT5 had sputtered to life at about 7:00 P.M. on Christmas Eve 1987, a suitable gift to engineer Terry Stinson. Stinson had been working feverishly, with able assistance from his Lotus counterparts, for nearly two years to prove that Midgley wasn't wrong in choosing MerCruiser, and to demonstrate to his boss, Bud Agner, that Anthony was right in signing off on this cumbersome, pressure-packed project.

Like MerCruiser, Lotus had required more than a little time to complete its assignment, as creating such a mechanical work of art was no simple task.

One stumbling block appeared right out of the gates in May 1985 after Roy Midgley noted a perceived problem with Lotus' initial design. To fit the valve sizes required to make 400 horsepower, Tony Rudd's engineers had put the new engine's bore centers 4.55 inches apart, as opposed to the existing Chevy V-8's long-running 4.40-inch measurement. Though nothing at all carried over from the traditional small block to the LT5, Midgley was adamant about at least continuing the mouse motor's time-honored "440" legacy, something Chevy's radically redesigned Gen III (LS1) small block also would do in 1997. When Rudd replied that squeezing the cylinders closer together would reduce maximum bore width, which in turn would limit valve diameters and thus output (to no more than 385 horses), Midgley couldn't have cared less—to hell with the consequences, get it done. Meanwhile, displacement, at 5.7 liters, also rolled over in familiar fashion from the conventional small block to the exotic LT5.

Lotus' first working prototype, or "Phase I" engine, was up and running on May 1, 1986. Chevrolet sent various Corvettes, with their L98 V-8s removed, to England for experimental LT5 installations. The first Phase I mule was roaring around Lotus' test track in August. Production of the more-refined Phase II engine (of which about 25 were built) began in March 1987, and one of

The original LT5 made 375 horsepower at 6,000 rpm. Maximum torque from 1990 to 1992 was 370 ft-lbs at 4,800 rpm. Output was boosted to 405 horsepower and 385 ft-lbs of torque in 1993.

With its all-aluminum construction, dual overhead cams, and four valves per cylinder, the LT5 represented high tech at its peak in 1990. Compression was 11:1.

"The ZR-1 is scheduled for early next year, but we won't be surprised if it's delayed a few months," added Csere. "One can hardly blame the Chevrolet Motor Division for wanting to make the world's first 190-mph production sports car as perfect as can be."

the last of these was used in a successful 200-hour nonstop durability run staged in November that year. After passing that test with flying colors, the LT5 graduated to its Phase III stage, with production of these nearly ready-for-prime-time prototype players beginning in January 1988. Further testing and refinement of both engine and car continued throughout most of 1988, reducing the ZR-1's chances for a 1989 model year introduction as each month passed.

Early complete-car testing, both in England and America, involved LT5 installations in stock-bodied Corvettes. But from the outset, Reuss and McLellan knew a new shape would be in order. In Reuss' case, he wanted to make sure the King of the Hill stood out from the crowd even more so than a typical Corvette. McLellan's motivation

involved fewer form considerations and more functionality. Wider rear tires surely would be needed to harness those LT5 horses, meaning that bodywork in back would require modification to house all that extra tread.

McLellan's engineers first met with Goodyear tire guys in December 1985 to discuss suitable rear rubber for the ZR-1. Goodyear's response was a sticky roller measuring 1.5 inches wider than the standard Corvette issue. Bolting on a pair meant that the ZR-1's tail would have to be widened by 3 inches. Enter Studio 3 Director Jerry Palmer and his ace designer, John Cafaro.

Palmer's people recognized that add-on flares would never do. Besides looking tacky, they would require even-less-desirable tack-on modifications to the trailing edge of each door, which opened oh

Engineered in England and built in Oklahoma, the LT5 V-8 finally was mated up with its ZR-1 body on the Bowling Green assembly line. A wider tail was required to house the massive tires needed to deal with the LT5's 375 horses.

Automotive artist David Kimble did this cutaway when a 1989 model year introduction was still the plan. Chevrolet even released posters using this artwork to announce the upcoming "1989" ZR-1.

so close to the rear wheelhouses. Regardless of the extra expense, the only choice was to mold new doors and quarter panels to smoothly incorporate the 3 extra inches in back. The rest of the car, in Palmer's opinion, should remain stock. Although Reuss wanted more distinction, including additional nose treatments, Studio 3's simpler design won out, and widened rear body parts started showing up in Bowling Green for prototype builds in the spring of 1987.

There was no way to miss that fat tail, which was made even more distinctive by trading the C4's existing round taillights for square units. As for further identification, the ZR-1 name wasn't finalized until 1989. Like Kimble's first cutaway, early pilot cars up until then had featured LT5 emblems on the lower right corner of their rear fascias, a no-no after GM execs that year decreed that engine RPO codes could no longer be displayed on the outside of the corporation's products. Codes for performance packages, however, remained fair game. Corvette Development Manager Doug Robinson chose "ZR-1," basically because it was available and it sounded cool. That it also honored the car's heritage—RPO ZR1 had been used from 1970 to 1972—was icing on the cake.

A few of those LT5-badged 1989 models are rolling around today. Reportedly, at least 15 of these preproduction vehicles were built, with perhaps all ending up in Lotus' hands for testing, after which time they were supposed to be destroyed per instructions from Warren. But apparently "destroy" isn't defined the same way in England as it is in the United States. A couple of severely crushed 1989 ZR-1s were salvaged by American collectors with relative ease and painstakingly restored during the 1990s, to the utmost dismay of GM officials who previously were sure that these unauthorized machines had been scattered to the winds.

Identifying an official ZR-1 in 1990 was easy enough thanks to its 3-inch-wider rear end, which also incorporated four exclusive, rectangular exhaust trumpets. Even though the rest of the Corvette line had a ZR-1-style tail in 1991, the ZR-1 still stood out, however mildly, due to it roof-mounted extra brake light, and continued doing so until its demise in 1995. All other Corvettes during that span incorporated this light at the top center of their rear fascias.

Along with the exclusive LT5 V-8, all ZR-1s built from 1990 to 1995 featured CAGS-controlled ZF six-speed manual transmissions, and all were coupes. A few stock-bodied convertible ZR-1s were tested early on, followed by the experimental DR-1 drop top in 1990. A topless ZR-1 proponent from the beginning, Don Runkle that year put Chevy's Advanced Engineering team to work developing his idea, which was transformed into reality by the American Sunroof Company (ASC), a Detroit-area firm known for its convertible conversions. ASC, however, built only the single DR-1 and then teamed up with Advanced Engineering and Studio 3 in 1991 to create the chopped-windshield ZR-1 Spyder, a cool custom convertible assembled on the Bowling Green line. Unfortunately, no regular-production ZR-1 ragtops ever left that line.

From start to finish, the ZR-1 coupe was a fully loaded machine. Options for the car's first

Upper left
Early 1989 prototypes displayed this badge in back. But GM execs no longer wanted to display engine RPO codes, and the ZR-1 tag was used in production. *Mike Mueller*

Above
This ZR-1 prototype also was restored from a crushed wreck. Reportedly 84 1989 ZR-1 Corvettes were built for testing and press review purposes, but none were meant for public consumption. *Mike Mueller*

Left
Note the British license plate and prototype "LT5" badge on the tail of this 1989 ZR-1. *Mike Mueller*

year numbered only two: electronic air conditioning and dual removable roof panels. Beyond the drivetrain, standard features included leather power seats, a specially laminated "solar" windshield, a Delco-Bose CD stereo, a low-tire-pressure warning light, the electronic FX3 selective ride and handling package, and the heavy-duty Z51 suspension. That latter was exclusive to the ZR-1 deal, with softened springs and stabilizer bars compared to the optional Z51 equipment found beneath conventional 1990 Corvettes.

Last, but by no means least, were those Goodyear Eagle Gatorback tires. Mounted on 9.5-inch-wide alloy wheels, the fronts were P275/40ZR-17 units, same as those found on garden-variety L98 Corvettes. But mandating that big butt were huge P315/35 z-rated Goodyears on big 11-inch-wide steam rollers, making the ZR-1 a king of the road in more ways than one.

1990

Minor press mentions of the upcoming new king of the Corvette realm first appeared late in 1986, and journalist Rich Ceppos was among the earliest to discuss this mystery machine at any length (but with few real facts) in *Car and Driver*'s June 1987 issue. *Automobile* followed with a one-page report, simply and appropriately titled "King of the Hill," in its September 1987 edition and correctly identified the car's "Lotus-designed LT5, a 32-valve, 5.7-liter V-8." The report included a Barry Penfound spy photo of an LT5 test mule wearing a bulging hood, which was "thought to be temporarily necessary to clear the sixteen aluminum intake runners" of the innovative multi-valve engine.

Another spy shot, this one squeezed off by veteran undercover lensman Jim Dunne, appeared in the February 1988 issue of *Road & Track*. "Could this be the 400-bhp, aluminum-block, aluminum-head, four-cam V-8 Corvette ZR-1 that General Motors Vice President Lloyd Reuss announced at the Specialty Equipment Manufacturers Association (SEMA) trade show in Las Vegas this past November?" asked *R&T*'s Ron Sessions. "Could be and is."

Another Dunne photo showed up in the May 1988 copy of *Car and Driver* with the

announcement: "Coming soon: the highest-performance production car on the planet." All ZR-1 details were correctly reported by *C/D*'s Csaba Csere, save for GM's early 400-horse prognostication and those horses' expected delivery date.

"The ZR-1 is scheduled for early next year, but we won't be surprised if it's delayed a few months," added Csere. "One can hardly blame the Chevrolet Motor Division for wanting to make the world's first 190-mph production sports car as perfect as can be."

When the ZR-1 finally made it into public hands in 1990, it offered 375 horsepower and

370 ft-lbs of torque—nothing to sneeze at; after all, it still qualified as America's most powerful production car. The Lotus-engineered LT5's externally ribbed aluminum block featured forged-aluminum cylinder liners with Nikasil coating and was beefed up on the bottom end by a bolt-on aluminum girdle that incorporated cast-in nodular-iron main bearing caps. The crank and connecting rods were forged steel, the pistons aluminum. Compression was 11.0:1.

Valve sizes in the twin-cam heads were 1.54 inches for the two intakes, 1.39 for the exhausts. Lift was 0.39 inches on intake and exhaust. Duration was 252 degrees for the eight primary

Specifications	1990
Model availability	coupe
Construction	integral perimeter frame birdcage body in reinforced composite, perimeter-rail frame
Wheelbase	96.2 inches
Length	176.5 inches
Width	74 inches
Height	46.7 inches
Curb weight	3,465 pounds
Tread (front/rear, in inches)	59.6/61.9
Tires	P275/40R-17, front; P315/35ZR-17, rear
Brakes	power-assisted four-wheel vented discs with aluminum calipers and ABS
Brake dimensions	12.9 inches, front; 11.9 inches, rear
Wheels	aluminum-alloy; 17x9.5 inches, front; 17x11 inches, rear
Fuel tank	20 gallons
Front suspension	independent short- and long-arm (SLA) upper and lower control arms and steering knuckles, transverse spring, stabilizer bar, tubular shock absorbers
Rear suspension	independent five-link with U-jointed half shafts and forged-aluminum control links and knuckles, camber adjustment, transverse spring, steel tie rods and stabilizer bar, tubular shocks
Steering	power-assisted rack and pinion, 15.73 1 ratio
Engine	5.7-liter all-aluminum 32-valve DOHC LT5 V-8, designed by Lotus, built by MerCruiser
Induction	Rochester electronic port injection
Bore and stroke	3.90x3.66 inches
Compression	11.0 1
Output	375 horsepower at 6,200 rpm, 370 ft-lbs torque at 4,500 rpm
Transmission	aluminum-case ML9 six-speed manual with CAGS
Production	3,049
RPO ZR1 price	$27,016

intakes, 272 degrees for their secondary counterparts, and 252 degrees for all 16 exhaust valves. Cam drive was by duplex roller chain, while sending voltage to the LT5's centrally located spark plugs was the job of a crank-controlled direct-fire system.

A two-phase electronic injection system shot the juice to those primary intake valves only during calm moments; mashing the pedal to the metal put the other intake valve in each combustion chamber to work after about 3,500 rpm or so. A key-operated switch on the console controlled these two phases. Keeping the key turned to the right on "full" allowed all of the LT5's 16 intake valves to do their stuff as designed; turning it to the left (identified as "reduced" on pilot cars, then "normal" in production) left only the less-aggressive primary intakes and their injectors in action for more economic operation. Putting the key in your pocket after leaving your ZR-1 behind

The 1990 ZR-1 looked like a standard Corvette from the windshield forward, but body panels from the doors back were exclusive pieces created to widen the tail by 3 inches. *Mike Mueller*

Installation of huge 17x11 rear wheels mandated a wider tail. Mounted on those rims were truly fat P315/35ZR tires. *Mike Mueller*

They didn't call it King of the Hill for nothing.

in its half-power mode discouraged any extracurricular activity by the likes of, say, parking attendants—thus the "valet key" nickname.

More than one uninitiated ZR-1 driver early on failed to turn that key to the right, leaving them disappointed with performance as flat as a pancake. But those who didn't suffer brain fade found the results thrilling to say the least.

"The phrase 'in any gear, at any speed' might have been coined for the LT5," began a *Motor Trend* report. "Power flows from the ZR-1 in a Niagara-like rush that makes the slick-shifting six-speed seem ridiculously redundant."

Early estimates claimed a top end of about 170 miles per hour, and a *Car and Driver* test reported 0–60 in 4.6 seconds and the quarter-mile in 12.9 clicks at 111 miles per hour. Such wild, world-class performance, however, came at a price. RPO ZR1, the special performance package, alone cost a whopping $27,016, making it far and away the most expensive option in Detroit history. Throw in a 1990 sport coupe's base price of $31,979, and it became clear that not just anyone would be standing in line to be the first on their block with a King of the Hill Corvette.

Nonetheless, that line was a long one by the time the most eagerly awaited Corvette of all time appeared in showrooms in 1990. So hot was demand that more than one dealer was asking six digits right out of the box—and getting it. Most who rolled out that much dough for a '90 ZR-1 were sure they had themselves a piece of history, and indeed many of these high-priced high rollers were stashed away in climate-controlled storage quicker than you could say "museum piece."

But the boys in Bowling Green just had to rain on the planned parade toward automotive immortality. High demand led to a relatively hefty supply of ZR-1s that first year, 3,049 to be exact. To say the market was flooded is akin to calling a Corvette simply "a car." Yet, within a few years, a '90 ZR-1 could've been had for a typical used car price sometimes running lower than $30,000.

Though it failed as a collector classic, the ZR-1 never let anyone down when it came to rolling up numbers on a speedometer. Truly historic were the figures established by a 1990 ZR-1 specially prepared by Corvette Development

Manager John Heinricy and veteran Corvette racer Tommy Morrison.

In March 1990, this Morrison Motorsports machine took to Firestone's 7.7-mile test track in Stockton, Texas, to challenge a 50-year-old endurance record. In 1940, Ab Jenkins' Mormon Meteor III had run for 24 hours straight on the Bonneville Salt Flats, averaging 161.180 miles per

hour. For years, many challengers tried to eclipse this endurance standard, but all failed. All save for the ZR-1. After 24 hours, the LT5-powered Morrison Corvette had averaged more than 175 miles per hour for 4,200 miles—a new record. In all, the car established three new world endurance records (over varying distances) and 12 class standards.

They didn't call it King of the Hill for nothing.

This valet key allowed a ZR-1 driver to electronically inhibit LT5 performance to discourage hard usage by other drivers—say, parking attendants. *Mike Mueller*

All ZR-1s were equipped with a six-speed manual transmission. *Mike Mueller*

1991

Changes to the ZR-1 were few during its five-year stay, and nearly all were minor, beginning with a revised valet parking key for 1991 that automatically defaulted to the low-power mode when the ignition was switched off. A second revision involved customer preferences. In 1990, only 124 ZR-1 buyers had opted to stick with the standard manually controlled air conditioner, so Chevrolet made the far-more-popular electronic climate control system standard for 1991. And like all Corvettes that year, the second-edition ZR-1 also featured a new wheel design.

But clearly the biggest news involved adding ZR-1-like bodywork to all 1991 Corvettes, obviously diluting the King's distinctiveness in the process. Demand dropped off considerably after 2,044 ZR-1s hit the streets that year. Accountants didn't help matters by hiking the option price to $31,683, bringing the latest bottom line to $64,138.

Different body panels were applied to the 1990 ZR-1. All Corvettes received a similar look in 1991, diluting the ZR-1's exclusive image in the process.

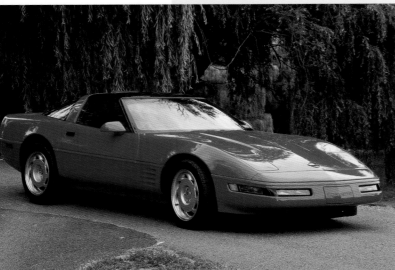

Like all 1991 Corvettes, the second-edition ZR-1 was fitted with restyled wheels. ZR-1 production for 1991 was 2,044, down from 3,049 the year before. *Mike Mueller*

Specifications	1991
Model availability	coupe
Construction	integral perimeter frame birdcage body in reinforced composite, perimeter-rail frame
Wheelbase	96.2 inches
Length	176.5 inches
Width	74 inches
Height	46.7 inches
Curb weight	3,465 pounds
Tread (front/rear, in inches)	59.6/61.9
Tires	P275/40R-17, front; P315/35ZR-17, rear
Brakes	power-assisted four-wheel vented discs with aluminum calipers and ABS
Brake dimensions	12.9 inches, front; 11.9 inches, rear
Wheels	aluminum-alloy; 17x9.5 inches, front; 17x11 inches, rear
Fuel tank	20 gallons
Front suspension	independent short- and long-arm (SLA) upper and lower control arms and steering knuckles, transverse spring, stabilizer bar, tubular shock absorbers
Rear suspension	independent five-link with U-jointed half shafts and forged-aluminum control links and knuckles, camber adjustment, transverse spring, steel tie rods and stabilizer bar, tubular shocks
Steering	power-assisted rack and pinion, 15.73:1 ratio
Engine	5.7-liter all-aluminum 32-valve DOHC LT5 V-8, designed by Lotus, built by MerCruiser
Induction	Rochester electronic port injection
Bore and stroke	3.90x3.66 inches
Compression	11.0 1
Output	375 horsepower at 6,200 rpm, 370 ft-lbs torque at 4,500 rpm
Transmission	aluminum-case ML9 six-speed manual with CAGS
Production	2,044
RPO ZR1 price	$31,683

1991

1992

Specifications	1992
	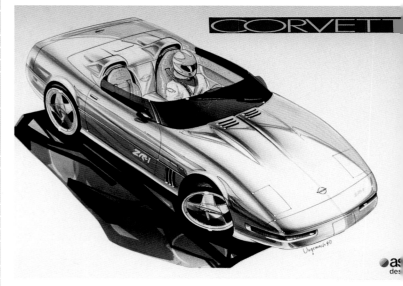
Model availability	coupe
Construction	integral perimeter frame birdcage body in reinforced composite, perimeter-rail frame
Wheelbase	96.2 inches
Length	178.5 inches
Width	73.1 inches
Height	46.3 inches
Curb weight	3,465 pounds
Tread (front/rear, in inches)	57.7/60.6
Tires	Goodyear GS-C; P275/40R-17, front; P315/35ZR-17, rear
Brakes	power-assisted four-wheel vented discs with aluminum calipers and ABS
Brake dimensions	12.9 inches, front; 11.9 inches, rear
Wheels	aluminum-alloy; 17x9.5 inches, front; 17x11 inches, rear
Fuel tank	20 gallons
Front suspension	independent short- and long-arm (SLA) upper and lower control arms and steering knuckles, transverse spring, stabilizer bar, tubular shock absorbers
Rear suspension	independent five-link with U-jointed half shafts and forged-aluminum control links and knuckles, camber adjustment, transverse spring, steel tie rods and stabilizer bar, tubular shocks
Steering	power-assisted rack and pinion, 15.73:1 ratio
Engine	5.7-liter all-aluminum 32-valve DOHC LT5 V-8, designed by Lotus, built by MerCruiser (four-bolt main bearing caps replace previous two-bolt mains)
Induction	Rochester electronic port injection
Bore and stroke	3.90x3.66 inches
Compression	11.0:1
Output	375 horsepower at 6,200 rpm, 370 ft-lbs torque at 4,500 rpm
Transmission	aluminum-case ML9 six-speed manual with CAGS
Production	502
RPO ZR1 price	$31,683

"The new small block is so good it almost makes you wonder why anyone would ante up $30,000 or so for 75 rarely used extra horsepower and 40 lb-ft made by the ZR-1's unchanged LT5," wrote *Motor Trend*'s Mac Demere after driving the new LT1.

Although no ZR-1 convertibles were built, a few experiments did surface, including the ZR-1 Spyder, built in 1991 with the help of the American Sunroof Company (ASC). *Doug Ungemach*

1992

Goodyear GS-C rubber became standard on all 1992 Corvettes, including the ZR-1, as did ASR traction control. And along with those new tires came slightly reduced spring rates front and rear. In back, 1991's quad exhaust tips were traded for two large rectangular trumpets.

Specific ZR-1 changes included appropriate emblems added to the front fenders and a temporary demotion to the options list for the formerly standard six-way power passenger seat. It became part of the basic package again in 1993.

Further dimming the ZR-1 attraction was the introduction of the new LT1 Gen II V-8. The LT1's 300 horsepower, working in concert with the overall package's lighter weight, instantly transformed the regular-issue 1992 Corvette into a machine boasting much of the ZR-1's punch at about half the cost. "The new small block is so good it almost makes you wonder why anyone would ante up $30,000 or so for 75 rarely used extra horsepower and 40 lb-ft made by the ZR-1's unchanged LT5," wrote *Motor Trend*'s Mac Demere after driving the new LT1.

RPO ZR1's asking price carried over from 1991, but an increase in the Corvette coupe's bottom line boosted the total sticker to $65,318. Production, meanwhile, dropped to 502.

The Corvette lineup for 1992 featured (right to left) the convertible, coupe, and awesome ZR-1. ZR-1 fender emblems were new for 1992, as were single-exhaust tips in place of the dual units seen in 1990 and 1991.

Shown here is a 1993 ZR-1.The easiest way to identify a ZR-1 after all Corvettes were fitted with ZR-1 taillamps in 1991 was by the extra brake light, which was mounted on the ZR-1's roof. On garden-variety Corvette coupes, that third lamp was incorporated into the rear fascia.

The beauty beneath the skin was the same in 1991: big brakes, the 375-horsepower LT5, and a ZF six-speed transmission. Optional in 1990, electronic climate control became standard for 1991.

Exclusive fender badges identified a 40th Anniversary ZR-1 coupe in 1993. *Mike Mueller*

Special embroidery on the seats was included on all Z25 models in 1993. *Mike Mueller*

1993

Specifications	1993
Model availability	standard coupe or 40th Anniversary (RPO Z25) coupe
Construction	integral perimeter frame birdcage body in reinforced composite, perimeter-rail frame
Wheelbase	96.2 inches
Length	178.5 inches
Width	73.1 inches
Height	46.3 inches
Curb weight	3,465 pounds
Tread (front/rear, in inches)	57.7/60.6
Tires	Goodyear GS-C; P275/40R-17, front; P315/35ZR-17, rear
Brakes	power-assisted four-wheel vented discs with aluminum calipers and ABS
Brake dimensions	12.9 inches, front; 11.9 inches, rear
Wheels	aluminum-alloy; 17x9.5 inches, front; 17x11 inches, rear
Fuel tank	20 gallons
Front suspension	independent short- and long-arm (SLA) upper and lower control arms and steering knuckles, transverse spring, stabilizer bar, tubular shock absorbers
Rear suspension	independent five-link with U-jointed half shafts and forged-aluminum control links and knuckles, camber adjustment, transverse spring, steel tie rods and stabilizer bar, tubular shocks
Steering	power-assisted rack and pinion, 15.73:1 ratio
Engine	5.7-liter all-aluminum 32-valve DOHC LT5 V-8, designed by Lotus, built by MerCruiser
Induction	Rochester electronic port injection
Bore and stroke	3.90x3.66 inches
Compression	11.0:1
Output	405 horsepower at 5,800 rpm, 385 ft-lbs torque at 4,800 rpm
Transmission	aluminum-case ML9 six-speed manual with CAGS
Production	448 (245 Z25 anniversary models)
RPO ZR1 price	$31,683

1993

During 1990 and 1991, the ZR-1 stood tall as this country's most powerful production car. Then along came Dodge's Viper with its 400-horsepower V-10 in 1992. No problem: Lotus engineers simply went back to their drawing boards and found 30 more ponies for the LT5, making the ZR-1 the king of Detroit's high-performance hill once again in 1993.

This jump up to 405 horsepower came about more or less by massaging the heads for improved flow. And with the aluminum engine making so much more power (torque increased, too, to 385 ft-lbs), more beef was designed in as pistons were strengthened, and the earlier block's two-bolt main bearing caps were replaced by tougher four-bolt pieces. Also new were a Mobil 1 synthetic oil requirement, platinum-tipped

spark plugs, and an electrical linear exhaust gas recirculation (EGR) system that reduced emissions.

Remaining ZR-1 standard features rolled over from 1992. But prominently new on the options list was RPO Z25, the same 40th Anniversary package offered in 1993 for LT1 Corvette coupes and convertibles. Of the 448 ZR-1s built that year, 245 were Ruby Red Metallic

Above
After unleashing only 502 ZR-1s in 1992, the Bowling Green plant rolled out only 448 in 1993. But big news that year involved an increase in LT5 output to 405 horsepower.

Left
The 40th Anniversary package, RPO Z25, was available for all Corvettes in 1993, including the ZR-1 coupe. Of the 448 1993 ZR-1s built, 245 featured the Z25 package and its Ruby Red paint. *Mike Mueller*

The ZR-1's days became numbered after November 23, 1993, when Mercury Marine ceased production of LT5 V-8s.

After falling behind the 400-horsepower Viper in Detroit's horsepower race in 1992, the 405-horse 1993 ZR-1 regained the title of America's most powerful production car. *Mike Mueller*

Z25 models, which added another $1,455 to the already steep base price of $66,278, which included the same amount charged for RPO ZR1 during the two previous years.

The ZR-1's days became numbered after November 23, 1993, when Mercury Marine ceased production of LT5 V-8s. Remaining supplies were shipped to Bowling Green to fulfill predetermined production runs planned for 1994 and 1995. As in 1993, the ZR-1 totals for those last two years numbered 448 cars each.

1994

While the handwriting was clearly on the wall, at least the ZR-1 was treated to exclusive five-spoke wheels in 1994. New, too, was the passenger-side air bag added to all 1994 Corvettes. RPO ZR1's cost this time decreased, to $31,258, but a typical increase in the coupe's base price again translated into a total rise to $67,443.

Above
New, exclusive five-spoke wheels appeared for the 1994 ZR-1

Below
As in 1993, ZR-1 production for 1994 was limited to the number of LT5 engines allotted each year: 448.

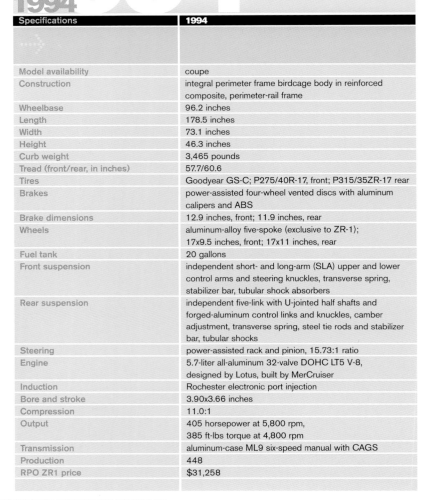

Specifications	1994
Model availability	coupe
Construction	integral perimeter frame birdcage body in reinforced composite, perimeter-rail frame
Wheelbase	96.2 inches
Length	178.5 inches
Width	73.1 inches
Height	46.3 inches
Curb weight	3,465 pounds
Tread (front/rear, in inches)	57.7/60.6
Tires	Goodyear GS-C; P275/40R-17, front; P315/35ZR-17 rear
Brakes	power-assisted four-wheel vented discs with aluminum calipers and ABS
Brake dimensions	12.9 inches, front; 11.9 inches, rear
Wheels	aluminum-alloy five-spoke (exclusive to ZR-1); 17x9.5 inches, front; 17x11 inches, rear
Fuel tank	20 gallons
Front suspension	independent short- and long-arm (SLA) upper and lower control arms and steering knuckles, transverse spring, stabilizer bar, tubular shock absorbers
Rear suspension	independent five-link with U-jointed half shafts and forged-aluminum control links and knuckles, camber adjustment, transverse spring, steel tie rods and stabilizer bar, tubular shocks
Steering	power-assisted rack and pinion, 15.73:1 ratio
Engine	5.7-liter all-aluminum 32-valve DOHC LT5 V-8, designed by Lotus, built by MerCruiser
Induction	Rochester electronic port injection
Bore and stroke	3.90x3.66 inches
Compression	11.0:1
Output	405 horsepower at 5,800 rpm, 385 ft-lbs torque at 4,800 rpm
Transmission	aluminum-case ML9 six-speed manual with CAGS
Production	448
RPO ZR1 price	$31,258

From start to finish, the ZR-1 coupe was a fully loaded machine.

Chevrolet officials knew as early as September 1991 that 1995 would be the ZR-1's final year. The high cost of keeping the LT5 V-8 emissions legal for 1996 was the main reason given for the cancellation. *Mike Mueller*

Specifications	1995
Model availability	coupe
Construction	integral perimeter frame birdcage body in reinforced composite, perimeter-rail frame
Wheelbase	96.2 inches
Length	178.5 inches
Width	73.1 inches
Height	46.3 inches
Curb weight	3,465 pounds
Tread (front/rear, in inches)	57.7/60.6
Tires	Goodyear GS-C; P275/40R-17, front; P315/35ZR-17, rear
Brakes	power-assisted four-wheel vented discs with aluminum calipers and ABS
Brake dimensions	12.9 inches, front; 11.9 inches, rear
Wheels	aluminum-alloy five-spoke (exclusive to ZR-1); 17x9.5 inches, front; 17x11 inches, rear
Fuel tank	20 gallons
Front suspension	independent short- and long-arm (SLA) upper and lower control arms and steering knuckles, transverse spring, stabilizer bar, tubular shock absorbers
Rear suspension	independent five-link with U-jointed half shafts and forged-aluminum control links and knuckles, camber adjustment, transverse spring, steel tie rods and stabilizer bar, tubular shocks
Steering	power-assisted rack and pinion, 15.73:1 ratio
Engine	5.7-liter all-aluminum 32-valve DOHC LT5 V-8, designed by Lotus, built by MerCruiser
Induction	Rochester electronic port injection
Bore and stroke	3.90x3.66 inches
Compression	11.0:1
Output	405 horsepower at 5,800 rpm, 385 ft-lbs torque at 4,800 rpm
Transmission	aluminum-case ML9 six-speed manual with CAGS
Production	448
RPO ZR1 price	$31,258

1995

At 1:12 P.M. on Friday, April 28, 1995, Chevrolet's Bowling Green assembly line came to a halt to honor the passing of a legend. Even though it actually had been built the previous Monday, the 6,939th and last ZR-1 Corvette was paraded off the line that afternoon with plant manager Wil Cooksey and UAW member Billy Jackson on board. Chevrolet General Manager Jim Perkins, with checkered flag in hand, watched over the roll-off, then took the wheel of the Torch Red coupe and drove it across the street to the National Corvette Museum with retired Chief Engineer Dave McLellan along for the ride. Even further closure came that evening at a farewell dinner when Roy Midgley announced his own retirement.

One main reason behind the ZR-1's short but happy life was fairly obvious: the base LT1 Corvette had taken a serious bite out of its big brother's customer base. But Perkins also mentioned a slumping supercar market and the prohibitive costs required to make the ZR-1 meet 1996's tightened emissions standards.

Midgley had visited Lotus in September 1991 to inform his British counterparts that 1995 would be the ZR-1's final year, this after explaining that updating the car's emissions aspects would cost more than $1 million. Reportedly, Lotus engineers had begun work in 1991 on an improved LT5 that would've made between 450 and 475 horsepower, all for naught.

Further nails went into the coffin in 1992 when the car's strongest supporter, Lloyd Reuss, was removed from the GM president's seat given

to him by Board Chairman Robert Stempel two years before. Replacing Reuss was John "Jack" Smith, who contrarily found no soft spot in his heart for such a costly niche-market product as the ZR-1.

And so the axe fell on the killer Corvette that cost $68,603 that last year. Whether it was a good deal or not was argued right up to the end, as some critics still couldn't put the supreme C4 down.

"Forget about the detractors or the sales numbers," began an October 17, 1994, *AutoWeek*

report on the vehicle's downhill slide. "With rocket-sled acceleration, mastiff grip, and right-now brakes, the ZR-1 has the largest performance envelope of any mass-produced American car ever built. It also has the amenities and acceleration of a modern passenger car and none of the temperament of a race car. With a slight tailwind, it will go 180 miles an hour, but it will also trudge through gridlock without complaint, A/C on kill and CD player on loud. We may never see the likes of it again."

Long live the King.

Opposite
The ZR-1's short, happy life came to an end on April 28, 1995. The production tally for that final year was again 448. *Mike Mueller*

Above
The same exclusive wheels rolled over into 1995 for the last ZR-1 Corvette. *Mike Mueller*

Right
The 1995 LT5 looked no different than its 1990 forerunner, but beneath all that aluminum were 405 horses instead of 375. Notice the yellow test vehicle sticker on the radiator. *Mike Mueller*

Long live the King.

06

Above Critics right off the bat complained about the 1997 Corvette's rather abrupt tail. Designers defended the look, claiming the sharp edges and flat back panel were defined by wind tunnel testing.

Center The Corvette's first five generations parade in order in front of the National Corvette Museum in Bowling Green, Kentucky. Bringing up the rear is the all-new C5.

Right A convertible returned to the Corvette lineup in 1998 after a one-year hiatus. Even without a top, the C5 drag coefficient, at 0.32, remained world class.

50 Years and Counting

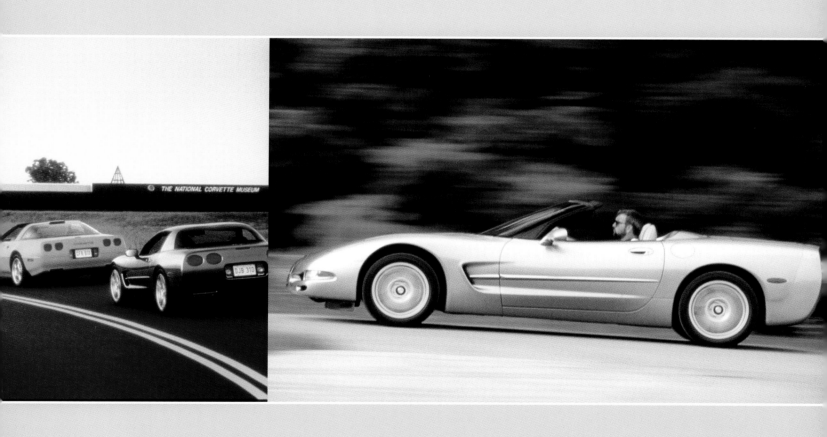

06

C5
1997–2004

→ Chevrolet's Gen III small-block V-8 introduced along with C5 Corvette (1997)
→ Convertible reintroduced to lineup after one-year hiatus (1998)
→ Corvette trunk (last seen in 1962) reintroduced with C5 convertible (1998)
→ Corvette paces the Indianapolis 500 (1998)
→ First time three body styles (coupe, convertible, hardtop) offered (1999)
→ C5-R racing Corvette introduced (1999)
→ Standard LS1 V-8 output boosted from 345 horsepower to 350 (2001)
→ Z06 (powered by new LS6 V-8) introduced (2001)
→ LS6 V-8 output goes from 385 horsepower to 405 (2002)
→ Z06 becomes first Corvette (discounting ZR-1) with a base price beyond $50,000 (2002)
→ A 2003 50th Anniversary coupe paces the Indianapolis 500 (2002)
→ Commemorative Edition package introduced for all Corvette models to honor C5-R racing program (2004)

It's highly unlikely that any future Corvette generation will manage to stay on the scene as long as the C3 did. The C4 lineage came close, falling short by two model runs, but only because it was forced to fill in for a couple more years than planned while the radically redesigned fifth-generation Corvette remained stuck in the works. Like the first Shark in 1968 and Dave McLellan's pride and joy in 1984, the C5 Corvette took its sweet time going from drawing board to the street. Make that seriously sweet.

Dating back to 1988, C5 development initially called for an all-new Corvette to debut for 1993 to help mark the two-seat breed's 40th anniversary. But various cash crunches and delayed decisions pushed the introductory date back repeatedly. In May 1989, the unveiling was rescheduled for 1994 after the engineering budget for the year was slashed, and then the goal changed again to 1995 three months later. In October 1990, the coming out was re-slated for 1996, and by October 1992, it seemed that no one at GM could predict when the C5 really would show.

The prime motivating factor behind the C5's long ride to market involved the severe financial difficulties GM experienced in the early 1990s. Awash in cash in 1988, Detroit's corporate giant found itself losing a record $2 billion two years later, and that was followed by a staggering $24.2 billion worth of red ink in 1992.

Muddying the waters further was the destabilization of corporate leadership that occurred after Chairman of the Board Roger Smith reached mandatory retirement in August 1990. New Chairman Robert Stempel inherited a financial nightmare, and then complicated matters by filling his old president's seat with Lloyd Reuss, a man other board members felt wasn't right for the job. They weren't mistaken. Reuss was shown the door within two years, replaced by Jack Smith,

Opposite
Two Corvette body styles were again available in 1998. Note that the convertible has the optional bodyside moldings; the coupe in back does not.

Above
Though totally fresh, the C5 was a Corvette in no uncertain terms. Production for 1997 was 9,752 coupes. The bodyside moldings seen here were optional.

This early C5 clay model looked too much like a Camaro at the tail.

Chevy 3 studio chief designer John Cafaro was the main man behind the C5 shape.

who was eventually responsible for finally giving the C5 project a green light.

The C5 design team also experienced lineup changes during that time. Dave McLellan retired in 1992 and was replaced that November by former Cadillac engineer David Hill. Stepping down at the same time was the man who had tight-fistedly controlled the C5's early styling developments, GM Design Vice President Charles Jordan. His replacement, Wayne Cherry, was chosen over Jerry Palmer, head of Chevy 3 (the Corvette's studio home since 1974) and the man responsible for the C4 restyle. But while Cherry was officially made design department head in September 1992, his responsibilities involved more business than art—it was Palmer who actually remained in charge of GM studios and thus directly influenced the designs drawn up within. Palmer also oversaw John Cafaro, the designer who ended up riding herd over C5 styling during its evolution.

Jordan first instructed Cafaro to begin sketching a C5 image in a Chevy 3 studio basement in August 1988. But Cafaro's earliest efforts didn't do it for the "Chrome Cobra," as Jordan was known around design department halls. GM's silver-haired exec turned to John Schinella's ACC in California for other options, leading to ACC's creation of its sexy Sting Ray III in 1990. Jordan also ordered Tom Peters in GM's Advanced 4 studio to make it a three-way design contest, all this without informing Cafaro, who,

Below
C5 test cars were labeled "alpha" and "beta." About 30 betas were built, all painted white, after initial bugs were ironed out in alpha tests. Beta tests included enduring heat in the Australian outback and surviving northern Canada winters.

Left
Far more crude compared to their beta successors, the alpha cars were all done in black. This alpha was disguised to throw off spy photographers.

Above
Full frontal imagery was a hotly debated topic throughout the C5 design process.

Lower left
First considered for the Q-Corvette in 1957, a rear-mounted transmission helped balance the C5's weight on all four wheels. Notice the transverse mufflers behind the rear wheels in the upper illustration.

needless to say, wasn't sorry to see Cherry take over in 1992.

In April 1991, Jordan gave his blessing to one of Peters' designs but also directed all involved to blend in many of Cafaro's ideas. Almost a year later, Cafaro came back with his stunning "Black Car," which was based on the C4's birdcage chassis but looked completely new and exciting on the top side. Chevrolet General Manager Jim Perkins was a big fan of the Black Car, which indeed predicted much of the eventual C5 look.

1997

Specifications	1997
Model availability	coupe
Construction	fiberglass body on steel frame with central backbone frame and hydroformed perimeter rails; transmission located at rear axle
Wheelbase	104.5 inches
Length	179.7 inches
Width	73.6 inches
Height	47.7 inches
Curb weight	3,229 pounds (automatic transmission), 3,218 pounds (manual)
Tread (front/rear, in inches)	62/62.1
Tires	Goodyear Extended Mobility; P245/45ZR-17, front; P275/40ZR-18, rear
Brakes	power-assisted four-wheel discs with Bosch ABS
Brake dimensions	11.9 inches, front and rear
Wheels	cast aluminum; 17x8.5 inches, front; 18x9.5 inches, rear
Fuel tank	19.1 gallons
Front suspension	short- and long-arm double wishbone (forged aluminum, top; cast aluminum, bottom), transverse leaf spring, stabilizer bar, monotube shock absorbers
Rear suspension	short- and long-arm double wishbone (cast-aluminum control arms, top and bottom), transverse leaf spring, stabilizer bar, monotube shock absorbers
Steering	speed-sensitive, power-assisted rack and pinion
Engine	5.7-liter OHV V-8 (LS1) with aluminum cylinder block and heads, sequential fuel injection
Bore and stroke	3.90x3.62 inches
Output	345 horsepower at 5,600 rpm; 350 ft-lbs at 4,400 rpm
Transmission	four-speed 4L60-E automatic transmission
Optional transmission	six-speed manual

"If, as they say, God is in the details, then this is the first holy Corvette," gushed *Car and Driver's* Csaba Csere in reverent honor of the first C5.

The C5's superstrong foundation did away with various rattles and shakes inherent to the C4 structure.

Perkins also was responsible for shepherding C5 chassis development through GM's economic quagmire, first creatively charging early work to the existing C4 budget. An official C5 development budget still wasn't in place late in 1992 when Perkins managed to siphon off $1 million for a running test mule, the CERV IV. Unlike its three exotic forerunners, CERV IV was created using as many actually proposed production features as possible. Though its body was a bastardized C4 shell, underneath was a backbone chassis incorporating a rear-mounted transmission—both ideas that were C5 goals from

the outset. An all-new aluminum engine, the proposed Gen III small-block V-8, wasn't ready yet, so power came from another C4 carryover.

Perkins' rolling proposal was clandestinely completed in May 1993, and it was followed by another in January 1994. Called CERV IVb (making its forerunner CERV IVa), the second machine was fitted with an iron-block Gen III V-8 as an aluminum cylinder block had yet to make the grade. Both CERV IV models were followed by more-advanced test cars called "alpha" and "beta" machines. Alphas wore true C5 bodies, and betas demonstrated various improvements dictated by alpha testing.

GM President Jack Smith gave his approval to the project in June 1993. Soon afterward, David Hill decided to concentrate development work on a Targa-top coupe model even though the superstrong C5 chassis was designed with convertible applications first in mind. But little work on a topless body had been completed by August 1993, and if Hill and crew were going to have a new fifth-generation Corvette ready for the latest deadline, 1997, they needed to complete the coupe already well on its way. So it was that a convertible C5 followed its closed running mate one year late, and that duo was then joined by

Wind tunnel tests governed the C5 shape, resulting in a state-of-the-art 0.29 drag coefficient.

A rigid central tunnel served as a base for the C5 frame. Its perimeter rails were created with water pressure in a process known as "hydroforming."

another variety—a hardtop with a trunk—in 1999, making it the first time in Corvette history that buyers could chose from three different body styles.

When finally introduced at Detroit's North American International Auto Show on January 6, 1997, the first C5 stood as Chevrolet's first truly all-new Corvette. Previous next-generation ground breakers in 1963, 1968, and 1984 had brought along at least a little something from their pasts, with carryover powertrains showing up most prominently. Even those Polo White two-seaters in 1953 incorporated many components already familiar to Chevrolet passenger-car buyers.

Next to nothing old or borrowed showed up on the 1997 Corvette coupe, and total components were cut by a third compared to the 1996 model, meaning the C4 had an amazing 1,500 more parts than the C5. This reduction came about as part of a plan to minimize the shakes, rattles, and rolls that inspired common complaints during the C4 era. Fewer pieces also simplified production and maintenance. As Corvette Quality Engineering Manager Rod

Michaelson explained, "The 1,500 parts eliminated equates to 1,500 opportunities for something to go wrong that aren't there any more."

As for the remaining components that made up the C5, they inspired nothing but raves wherever they went.

1997

"If, as they say, God is in the details, then this is the first holy Corvette," gushed Car and Driver's Csaba Csere in reverent honor of the first C5. "The '97 Corvette is a home run in every way," added Automobile's David E. Davis Jr. "Like no Corvette before, [the C5] now possesses the sort of smoothness and refinement that, if it were a scotch, could only be attributed to decades of little lessons learned about distillation and years of quiet aging," concluded a Road & Track review.

Chevrolet people, too, weren't ashamed about bragging a little—or a lot. Describing the C5 as "the best 'Vette yet," David Hill claimed, "You won't find a car in Corvette's price range that provides the same level of quality, power, ride, handling, and

Left
C5 Corvette production started up at the Bowling Green plant late in 1996.

Opposite
The C5 platform was initially designed with convertible applications in mind, but the best 'Vette yet was introduced only in coupe form in 1997. A convertible model followed a year later.

Below
One of the goals established when Chevrolet moved Corvette production from St. Louis to Bowling Green in 1981 was to perfect the car's painting process.

refinement." Indeed, offering nearly 170 miles per hour for about $40,000, the 1997 Corvette ranked right up there with the fastest street-legal production cars for the dollar ever built in America. But sizzling speed wasn't the car's sole attraction.

"We designed the [C5] with a synchronous mindset," added Interior Designer Jon Albert. "We focused on individual goals, such as improved performance, reduced mass, and increased reliability, within the overall framework of the whole car. We evaluated and balanced each change so as to optimize the total car."

So many changes worked together to create that total car. An innovative frame with a rigid center tunnel and hydroformed perimeter rails made the C5's foundation 4.5 times stiffer than the C4's. At the time a new process, hydroforming uses extreme water pressure to literally blow up round steel tubes into desired shapes to exacting specifications. The various welding operations required to build C4 foundations always produced tiny differences from section to section, from frame to frame, meaning you couldn't quite count on suspension precision since overall consistent physical geometry couldn't be guaranteed.

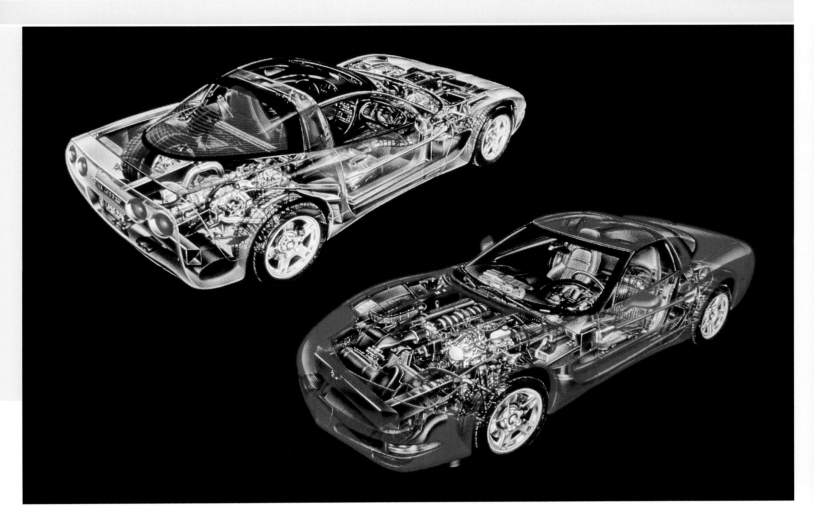

Along with improving both handling and ride, the battleship-strong hydroformed chassis also did away with many of the squeaky gremlins inherent in earlier Corvettes. The C5's rear-mounted transmission improved ride and handling, too. This long-discussed idea not only helped bring weight distribution closer to the preferred 50/50 balance, it also freed up space beneath the passenger compartment, meaning both occupants had more room down there in the footwells to stretch out and ride comfortably. Entry and exit was enhanced as well, thanks to those strengthened frame rails, which traded excess mass for a lower sill height, down 3.7 inches.

Don't forget the new 345-horse Gen III all-aluminum small-block V-8, better brakes and tires, and a more sophisticated suspension. Clearly,

no stones were left unturned during the C5 design process.

"The fifth-generation Corvette is a refined Corvette, in all the right ways," boasted Chief Engineer David Hill in 1997. "It's more user-friendly, it's easier to get in and out of, and it's more ergonomic. It has greater visibility; it's more comfortable and more functional. It provides more sports car for the money than anything in its market segment. It'll pull nearly 1 g, and it starts and stops quicker than you can blink."

Built at GM's engine plant in Romulus, Michigan, the C5's LS1 V-8 at the same time honored previous small blocks and left the past behind. "Based on a timeless design by former Chief Engineer Ed Cole, the 'Gen III' marks a bright new chapter in the highly respected lineage

that GM small blocks have established in more than 40 years," claimed a Chevrolet press release in 1996.

Like all small blocks before it, the LS1 was a traditional pushrod, 16-valve V-8, and it also shared the same time-honored "440" cylinder block layout (measuring 4.40 inches from bore center to bore center) and the familiar 5.7-liter displacement label. "After all," said LS1 Engine Program Manager John Juriga, "some things are sacred." Next to nothing carried over from there, though, as the Gen III represented a real redesign, not just a modernization.

First off, the LS1 relied on revised bore/stroke parameters. Compared to the Gen II, the Gen III V-8's bore (3.90 inches) was less and its stroke (3.62 inches) was more, this adjustment

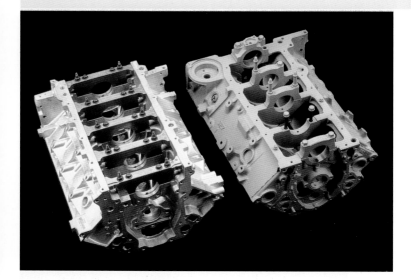

"The fifth-generation Corvette is a refined Corvette, in all the right ways," boasted Chief Engineer David Hill in 1997.

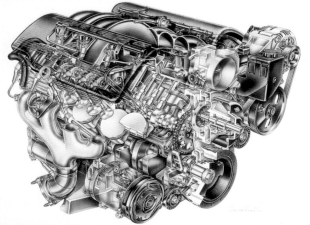

Above
Chevrolet officials claimed the small-block legacy carried on into the C5 era, but nothing interchanged between the 1996 LT1 and 1997 LS1 V-8s. On the right is the conventional-looking LT1 cylinder block; on the left is the cutting-edge LS1 deep-skirt block with its cross-bolted main bearing caps.

Left
The only things the LS1 and LT1 V-8s shared were numbers: both featured the traditional 4.40-inch bore center measurement, and both also displaced 5.7 liters. LS1 output in 1997 was 345 horsepower.

Below
Comfort and convenience issues weren't overlooked by C5 designers. Getting behind the wheel (and out again) was easier in 1997, due primarily to lowered doorsills.

made to allow more cooling space between skinnier cylinders. The Gen II's reverse-flow cooling system was traded for a conventional layout as Gen III coolant was once again pumped into the block first, then to the heads. But easily the most notable innovation was the LS1's lightweight all-aluminum construction, a first for a regular-production Chevy small block.

Gen III development dated back to late 1991. Anil Kulkarni, the man behind the Gen II LT1, was originally in charge of this project, but he stepped aside, giving up control to long-time small-block engineer Ed Koerner. The Gen III program really got cooking in 1993, with testing in early C5 prototypes beginning the following summer using mostly iron-block Gen III pre-runners. Most prototypes were refitted with all-aluminum counterparts by late 1995. Chevrolet then officially introduced the Gen III V-8 to the press in June 1996.

Everything about the LS1 was finely engineered to the limit, beginning with the cast-aluminum cylinder block with its centrifugally cast gray-iron cylinder liners. At only 107 pounds, this aluminum block weighed 53 pounds less than its iron Gen II predecessor, and the entire engine was 88 pounds lighter. Yet at the same time, the LS1 was much stronger, thanks to extensive external stiffening ribs and its deep-skirt construction. Unlike typical V-8 cylinder blocks that end at the crankshaft's centerline, the LS1 block extended below the main bearing caps, encasing the crank in a girdle of aluminum. This extended skirt also made it possible to cross-bolt the main bearing caps for additional rigidity. LS1 bearing caps features six bolts: four in the conventional vertical location on each side of the crank and one each

running through the skirt horizontally into each side of the cap.

Cutting-edge cylinder head design was one of the main keys to the LS1's success. Flow wizard Ron Sperry, who had joined GM Powertrain in late 1987 and had produced the LT1 and LT4 heads, was the man responsible for the LS1 heads, which incorporated replicated ports. Previous small-block ports were located in two closely squeezed siamesed pairs on the intake side, resulting in widely varying internal structures as those passages bent and turned differently with differing volumes, producing varying flow characteristics in the process. Keeping flow rates constant from cylinder to cylinder is vital to maximizing performance, and that's exactly what the replicated-port design accomplished.

Additional features included roller rocker arms and a roller-lifter cam. Intake valves measured 2.00 inches, exhaust valves 1.55. Compression

Jon Albert was the designer in charge of making the C5 the most comfortable Corvette yet.

was 10.2:1. While the LS1's sequential electronic port fuel injection was nothing new, its drive-by-wire electronic throttle control (ETC) was, at least as far as GM gasoline engines were concerned.

The LS1 got its spark from a distributorless ignition system featuring one coil per cylinder. Atop every cylinder, mounted beneath a stylish plastic shield on each valve cover, were eight individual coils and coil-driver assemblies. Once

Though totally fresh, the C5 was a Corvette in no uncertain terms. Production for 1997 was 9,752 coupes. The bodyside moldings seen here were optional.

the spark plugs did their job, spent gases were hauled off by hydroformed tubular exhaust manifolds. Bringing up the LS1's bottom was a bat wing oil pan, a shallow unit created to allow ample road clearance.

An electronic four-speed automatic transmission was standard behind the LS1, with a Borg-Warner six-speed manual available on the C5 options list. Optional carryovers from 1996 included electronic selective real-time damping (RPO F45) and the Z51 performance handling package.

Left
Dura Convertible Systems developed the C5's manual-folding soft top, which went up or down with far less fuss or muss than its C4 forerunner.

Below
Chief Engineer David Hill ruled out a C5 power top mechanism to both keep costs down and preserve space behind the seats for a practical feature Corvette owners hadn't seen since 1962: a trunk.

1998

Although an optional removable hardtop was available beginning in 1956, all Corvettes built before 1963 were convertibles. Then along came the stunning Sting Ray and its sexy coupe shell. Faced with a choice between hardtop and convertible, most Corvette buyers still favored the open-air style until 1969, after which time closed-body sales finally took over. Chevrolet product planners eventually gave up on the topless Corvette after 1975.

Although a drop-top model did return in 1986, convertible popularity has never been as strong as it was during the early Sting Ray years. Open-air C4s numbered only 4,369 in 1996, making up about 20 percent of the total run. But such low numbers didn't deter David Hill and the gang in the least; they knew that a Corvette convertible had to make a second comeback.

The C5 convertible showed up in 1998, just in time to help the latest Corvette cop *Motor Trend*'s coveted Car of the Year trophy. "Like the coupe, this is the best 'Vette yet," bragged Hill again. Calling the new convertible "the most desirable 'Vette since 1967," *Car and Driver*'s Csaba Csere announced that "not even the glorious ZR-1 models had as many of our staffers muttering about owning a Corvette as does this new roadster."

New was the key word. No other convertible in Corvette history could stand up to the 1998 rendition in the way it stood up to the real-world realities of skin-to-the-wind touring, this due to the effort Hill's engineers put into making the C5 chassis as rigid as hell, with or without a roof. "It was critical that we didn't just take the coupe and chop off the top to make a convertible," said Hill. "Corvette's structure has been designed to achieve world-class open-car stability and strength."

Sawing the roof off a Corvette, off any car, has always represented a compromise, as a coupe's top has always played a major role in the structural scheme of things. Removing that structure has always meant additional bracing had to go back in, most commonly in the cowl area. Such bracing helps, but no convertible has ever measured up as solidly as its full-roofed counterparts. Cowl shakes, steering wheel vibrations, and general roughness, rattles, and rumbles have been standard Corvette convertible features from the get-go.

Specifications	1998
Model availability	coupe and convertible
Construction	fiberglass body on steel frame with central backbone frame and hydroformed perimeter rails; transmission located at rear axle
Wheelbase	104.5 inches
Length	179.7 inches
Width	73.6 inches
Height	47.7 inches
Curb weight	3,245 pounds (coupe), 3,246 pounds (convertible)
Tread (front/rear, in inches)	62/62.1
Tires	Goodyear Extended Mobility; P245/45ZR-17, front; P275/40ZR-18, rear
Brakes	power-assisted four-wheel discs with Bosch ABS
Brake dimensions	11.9 inches, front and rear
Wheels	cast aluminum; 17x8.5 inches, front; 18x9.5 inches, rear
Fuel tank	19.1 gallons
Front suspension	short- and long-arm double wishbone (forged aluminum, top; cast aluminum, bottom), transverse leaf spring, stabilizer bar, monotube shock absorbers
Rear suspension	short- and long-arm double wishbone (cast-aluminum control arms, top and bottom), transverse leaf spring, stabilizer bar, monotube shock absorbers
Steering	speed-sensitive, power-assisted rack and pinion
Engine	5.7-liter OHV V-8 (LS1) with aluminum cylinder block and heads, sequential fuel injection
Bore and stroke	3.90x3.62 inches
Output	345 horsepower at 5,600 rpm; 350 ft-lbs at 4,400 rpm
Transmission	four-speed 4L60-E automatic transmission
Optional transmission	six-speed manual

Chevy officials loved to brag about the 1998 C5 convertible's ability to carry two golf bags in its trunk. Storage space was 11.2 cubic feet with the top down, 13.9 with the roof unfolded overhead.

On top of all that, extra bracing had always added more than a few unwanted pounds. And due to this weight handicap, drop-top muscle machines have all been slower than their full-roofed alter egos. Inherent realities of convertible ownership have always included less performance and more annoyance. Not so after 1998.

Beneath that smooth skin was a skeleton that simply refused to bend or flex. Cowl shake and other common convertible maladies were virtually eliminated—without a single extra brace or frame member, or any additional weight. The C5 convertible, at 3,246 pounds, amazingly weighed only 1 pound more than its coupe running mate. It was also 114 pounds lighter than its C4 convertible forerunner.

According to engineers, the new C5 convertible at most only measured 10 percent less torsionally rigid compared to the coupe with its Targa top on and latched down. The topless C5 was so rigid it could be equipped with the tough Z51 suspension package, an option that wasn't offered to C4 convertible buyers. The less-solid C4 frame and hard-as-nails Z51 handling equipment just didn't mix.

Neither did the C5 and a roll bar. A rollover hoop was considered for the '98 convertible, but, according to Hill, observed customer indifference and design complications ruled it out of the C5 plan.

Also ruled out was a power-operated top. Like the C4, the C5's folding roof required two pairs of hands, not just one finger, to put it in its place. As Hill explained, the reasoning behind the choice was simple: keep costs down and available storage space up. As it was, the C5's top folded up so easily it was almost a shame to complain about the power outage.

Simple, lightweight operation, along with a tight seal when up and an equally tight fit when down, were targets of Chevrolet designers. They penciled out what they wanted and then turned to Dura Convertible Systems, Inc., to make it reality. The result was an articulating five-bow pressurized top, pressurized in that when it unfolded, a special linkage in the rearmost fifth bow both squeezed itself down tight against the body and pushed the first four bows upward toward the windshield header, where traditional latches made the seal.

Top
Unlike previous topless Corvettes, the C5 convertible didn't require excess reinforcement to stay strong without a roof in place. Based on a chassis that was 450 percent stiffer than its C4 predecessor, the 1998 convertible weighed only 1 pound more than its coupe counterpart.

Above
The C5 convertible showed up just in time to help the 1998 Corvette garner *Motor Trend*'s Car of the Year trophy. From left to right are David Hill, Chevrolet General Manager John Middlebrook, Petersen Publishing Executive Publisher Lee Kelley, and Corvette Brand Manager Richard Almond.

Opposite
A 1998 convertible became the fourth Corvette to pace the Indianapolis 500. Chevrolet sold 1,163 Indy pace car replicas that year.

Pressure in back was so strong no latching mechanism was required.

The new top also proved exceptionally aerodynamic. The '98 C5 drop top's drag coefficient, at 0.32, was only 0.03 higher than the wind-cheating coupe at a cost of only 0.2 inches of headroom compared to the full-roofed C5.

When down, the C5 top stowed beneath a nicely styled tonneau, reminiscent of high-flying Corvette racing days gone by. More important, the tonneau's double-hump headrest fairings allowed designers that much more room below to hide the top. Once folded, the compact C5 top rested in one helluva tight area, all the better to preserve precious storage space in the new convertible's trunk.

Thirty-six years after a Corvette last brought up its rear with real cargo space, the '98 C5 convertible appeared with a deck lid. The C5's dual-compartment gas tank, deletion of a spare

tire (by making extended-mobility run-flat tires standard), and the compact, nonpower aspects of that folding top all worked in concert to make a trunk possible. The C5 trunk measured 11.2 cubic feet in top-down mode, 13.9 with roof unfolded and in place. Try to imagine two bags of golf clubs nestled in there—that's the suitable analogy Chevrolet's promotional people used to push the point of just how spacious that trunk was.

Among other standard convertible features in 1998 was neat stuff like speed-sensitive steering, the run-flats' tire-pressure monitoring system, a monstrous Bose stereo system, and a driver's power seat. A new option available for the '98 Corvette convertible or coupe was RPO JL4, the active-handling chassis control system. Active handling relied on a system of sensors to read steering inputs, yaw rates, and lateral g forces to better stabilize the car in emergency situations by selectively activating either the ABS or traction

control gear. And it could've been modulated to work without rear-wheel oversteer control for more experienced drivers able to feel their way through the twisties better than the rest of us mere mortals. Called "Bondurant-in-a-box" (in reference to driving school guru and veteran Corvette racer Bob Bondurant) by *Sports Car International*, the well-received active-handling equipment was priced at $500. JL4 installations in 1998 numbered 5,356.

A second new option made the $1,695 selective real-time damping package look like a bargain. Originally designed for 1997 export models, lightweight magnesium wheels, supplied by Speedline in Italy, appeared in 1998 wearing a wallet-wilting price tag of $3,000. These bronze-toned wheels each weighed 8 pounds less than the stock C5 rim. Whether or not those weight savings were worth the cost was up to the individual owner—2,029 apparently thought so in 1998.

"The new hardtop is the ultimate hot sports car, yet it will carry the lowest base price in the Corvette family. Those factors combined should make the consumer appeal for Corvette even greater."

1999

Originally conceived as a low-buck alternative to its flashier Targa-top and convertible counterparts, a C5 hardtop debuted for 1999 priced $400 less than that year's sport coupe. The logic behind its introduction was simple, at least according to Corvette Brand Manager Dick Almond. "Part of our potential customer base really wants a simpler, more elemental, yet high-performance machine," he said in August 1998. "The new hardtop is the ultimate hot sports car, yet it will carry the lowest base price in the Corvette family. Those factors combined should make the consumer appeal for Corvette even greater."

Like the convertible, this hot new hardtop featured a trunk, basically because it was more or less a drop-top model with a roof bolted and molded in place of its much softer, folding counterpart. And, along with being the cheapest of the three 1999 body styles, it was also the lightest, weighing about 80 pounds less than the coupe. At the same time, it was the stiffest of the trio, measuring some 12 percent more rigid than the coupe with its Targa top latched in place. As for performance, according to *Motor Trend*, the slightly lightened 1999 hardtop could run 0–60 in 4.8 seconds. Quarter-mile performance was 13.3 clicks at 108.6 miles per hour.

Plans early on called for cutting costs even further by, among other things, making smaller wheels and tires, manual door locks, and cloth seats standard. Such frugal ideas fortunately fell from grace, allowing black leather seats to eventually become part of the base hardtop package. Other interior color choices weren't offered, and options like sports seats, F45 suspension, and four-speed automatic transmission weren't available, either. Along with the six-speed manual gearbox, the beefy Z51 suspension was included in the standard deal, while exterior paint choices were limited to five of the eight shades listed that year: Arctic White, Light Pewter Metallic, Torch Red, Nassau Blue Metallic, and black.

C5 coupes and convertibles for 1999 also could've been painted Sebring Silver Metallic, Navy Blue Metallic, and Magnetic Red Metallic—the latter finish being an extra-cost ($500) option due to its special clear-coat application. Other than new doorsill trim, improved steering gear, and kinder, gentler, next-generation air bags, all other features represented 1998 rollovers, while new options included a power telescopic steering column (RPO N37) and Twilight Sentinel (T82), which automatically turned the headlights on and

The Corvette lineup expanded to three body styles in 1999 with the arrival of the hardtop (front), which, like the convertible, featured a trunk.

1999

Specifications	1999
Model availability	coupe, hardtop, and convertible
Construction	fiberglass body on steel frame with central backbone frame and hydroformed perimeter rails; transmission located at rear axle
Wheelbase	104.5 inches
Length	179.7 inches
Width	73.6 inches
Height	47.8 inches (coupe), 47.7 inches (convertible), 47.9 inches (hardtop)
Curb weight	3,245 pounds (coupe), 3,246 pounds (convertible), 3,153 pounds (hardtop)
Tread (front/rear, in inches)	62/62.1
Tires	Goodyear Extended Mobility; P245/45ZR-17, front; P275/40ZR-18, rear
Brakes	power-assisted four-wheel discs with Bosch ABS
Brake dimensions	12.6 inches, front; 11.8 inches, rear
Wheels	cast aluminum; 17x8.5 inches, front; 18x9.5 inches, rear
Fuel tank	19.1 gallons
Front suspension	short- and long-arm double wishbone (forged aluminum, top; cast aluminum, bottom), transverse leaf spring, stabilizer bar, monotube shock absorbers
Rear suspension	short- and long-arm double wishbone (cast-aluminum control arms, top and bottom), transverse leaf spring, stabilizer bar, monotube shock absorbers
Steering	speed-sensitive, power-assisted rack and pinion
Engine	5.7-liter OHV V-8 (LS1) with aluminum cylinder block and heads, sequential fuel injection
Bore and stroke	3.90x3.62 inches
Output	345 horsepower at 5,600 rpm; 350 ft-lbs at 4,400 rpm
Transmission	four-speed 4L60-E automatic transmission
Optional transmission	six-speed manual

Above
Coupe production in 1998 was 19,325; 11,849 convertibles were built.

Below
Originally planned as a cost-conscious model with cloth seats and smaller wheels and tires, the hardtop debuted for 1999 fitted out similarly to its coupe and convertible running mates. But it did weigh about 80 pounds less than the coupe, and, at $38,777, was the lowest priced of the three body styles.

off. Both N37 and T82 weren't available on the hardtop model.

Another new option, RPO UV6, was initially limited to coupe and convertible customers early in the year, and then extended to their hardtop comrades later on. UV6 consisted of a heads-up display (HUD) system that projected instrument readouts onto the windshield in front of the driver, making him or her feel much like a jet fighter pilot in the process. This equipment still rates every bit as cool as it is functional.

C5-R racer

Though nearing 50, the Corvette was still running around racetracks like an Olympic sprinter in his prime in 1999, led by the latest in a long line of proud competition cars, the C5-R. But unlike so many of its forerunners, this Corvette racer hit the track with full factory backing. This time around Chevrolet clearly was "in racing."

Obviously a lot has changed since Zora Duntov kept himself busy trying to sneak race-ready Corvettes out of GM's back door. Those

following in Duntov's big shoes today are more than willing to both build race cars and brag about them openly.

"The racing program we have created reinforces and underscores our commitment to the Corvette and its magnificent heritage," explained the breed's marketing director, Rick Baldick, in 2003. "All of us feel a responsibility to preserve and enhance the car's image. The racing program is designed to help us fulfill that responsibility."

Left
The C5's 345-horsepower 5.7-liter LS1 V-8 continued rolling on unchanged into 1999. A 5-horsepower boost came two years later.

Right
Power for the production-based C5-R came from a 600-horsepower bored-and-stroked LS1 V-8. Displacement was 7.0 liters. *Mike Mueller*

Below
Chevrolet announced its factory-backed C5-R Corvette racing team late in 1998. The C5-R first raced in February 1999 at the Rolex 24 at Daytona Beach, finishing third in the GT2 class. On February 3, 2001, a C5-R became the overall winner at that year's Rolex 24.

Left
C5-R Corvettes dominated IMSA's American Le Mans Series (ALMS) from 2001 to 2004. The No. 3 car (driven by Ron Fellows, Johnny O'Connell, and Oliver Gavin) cruises around Road Atlanta in October 2002 on the way to another GTS class win. Corvettes won 9 of 10 ALMS races run that year.
Mike Mueller

Below
The same three body styles appeared again for 2000. Production was 18,113 coupes, 13,479 convertibles, and 2,090 hardtops. A new five-spoke wheel appeared that year.

"It was Zora Duntov's vision in 1953 that Corvette should lead the way with race-ready parts and designs," added GM Racing Group Manager Joe Negri. "I think he would be proud of what has been achieved."

Proud indeed. Announced in 1998, the C5-R went into production the following year using much of the car's existing macho machinery. "We designed the competition engine using as many production parts and processes as possible," said GM Racing engine specialist Ron Sperry. "Powertrain engineers had some prototype block configurations they were studying for future products, and they made some of these available to us for the C5-R engine development program."

A modified LS1 V-8, the C5-R's powerplant was bored and stroked to just a tad short of 7.0 liters. Output was 600 horsepower, more than enough muscle to allow speeds well in excess of 200 miles per hour. Compression was 12.5:1 and oiling was by a typical racing-style dry-sump system. Custom Delphi engine management software controlled this monster mill's electronic fuel injection.

A black-and-silver-painted C5-R made its racing debut early in 1999 at Daytona's Rolex 24, where ace driver Ron Fellows managed an impressive third-place finish. Let loose on unsuspecting GTS competitors in IMSA's American Le Mans Series (ALMS) that year, the C5-R cars quickly built a winning reputation like none ever witnessed during the Corvette's fabled half-century history. An impressive 2001 season kicked off with an overall win at the Rolex 24, "probably the most significant victory in the history of the marque," in GM Racing chief Herb Fishel's opinion. An equally historic 1-2 finish in class followed that summer at Le Mans, and the C5-R team repeated that result in France in 2002. In between, Corvettes ran away with the 2001 ALMS Manufacturer's Championship, winning six of eight races. Two more ALMS titles followed in 2002 and 2003.

"Somewhere, Zora Duntov is smiling, as are more than a million Corvette owners worldwide," said Baldick after the milestone Daytona win in 2001. "This victory signals the Corvette heritage is stronger than ever."

At $45,900, the convertible was the most expensive model in 2000. Base prices for the coupe and hardtop were $39,475 and $38,900, respectively.

2000

Specifications	2000
Model availability	coupe, hardtop, and convertible
Construction	fiberglass body on steel frame with central backbone frame and hydroformed perimeter rails; transmission located at rear axle
Wheelbase	104.5 inches
Length	179.7 inches
Width	73.6 inches
Height	47.7 inches (coupe), 47.7 inches (convertible), 47.8 inches (hardtop)
Curb weight	3,246 pounds (coupe), 3,248 pounds (convertible), 3,173 pounds (hardtop)
Tread (front/rear, in inches)	62.1/62.2
Tires	Goodyear Extended Mobility; P245/45ZR-17, front; P275/40ZR-18, rear
Brakes	power-assisted four-wheel discs with Bosh ABS
Brake dimensions	12.6 inches, front; 11.8 inches, rear
Wheels	cast aluminum; 17x8.5 inches, front; 18x9.5 inches, rear
Fuel tank	18.5 gallons
Front suspension	short- and long-arm double wishbone (forged aluminum, top; cast aluminum, bottom), transverse leaf spring, stabilizer bar, monotube shock absorbers
Rear suspension	short- and long-arm double wishbone (cast-aluminum control arms, top and bottom), transverse leaf spring, stabilizer bar, monotube shock absorbers
Steering	speed-sensitive, power-assisted rack and pinion
Engine	5.7-liter OHV V-8 (LS1) with aluminum cylinder block and heads, sequential fuel injection
Bore and stroke	3.90x3.62 inches
Output	345 horsepower at 5,600 rpm; 350 ft-lbs at 4,400 rpm
Transmission	four-speed 4L60-E automatic transmission
Optional transmission	six-speed manual

As in 1999, only five colors were available for the hardtop in 2000: Arctic White, Light Pewter Metallic, Nassau Blue Metallic, black, and Torch Red.

2000

C5 features carried over nearly unchanged again into 2000, with the most notable difference coming at the corners. A new thin-spoke forged-aluminum wheel wearing a painted finish was now standard. Exchanging paint for polish was possible by checking off RPO QF5, priced at $895. More than 15,000 customers opted for these bright wheels, and this strong demand inspired Chevrolet officials to turn to an outside supplier for another standard rim to preserve its own supply then waiting to be polished. Announced in January 2000, this second standard wheel also featured a painted finish and looked similar to its predecessor, save for slightly thicker spokes.

Optional magnesium wheels rolled over from 1999 but with a lower price tag of $2,000. Other news on the 2000 options list involved improvements to the Z51 suspension package consisting of enlarged stabilizer bars front and rear, and stiffer springs and shocks. New as well was yet another extra-cost paint scheme as the truly radiant Millennium Yellow joined Magnetic Red Metallic, both of which remained limited to coupes and convertibles.

Standard improvements for 2000 included reducing the LS1's emissions and exchanging 1999's passive keyless entry for the new active keyless entry system, which no longer included a backup key lock for the passenger-side door. The same three-body lineup reappeared that year, but demand for the lower-priced hardtop dropped by half. Meanwhile, sales of the most expensive Corvette, the convertible, went up by 21 percent. Go figure.

2001

As impressive as the C5 was from the get-go, David Hill still wasn't satisfied. Looking at the car from a pure performance perspective, he recognized that not all Corvette owners cared about making concessions to comfort and convenience—that some drivers simply wanted to be the baddest in the valley and to heck with everything else. Chevrolet's no-nonsense Corvette hardtop, introduced for 1999, represented an initial step toward appeasing uncompromising customers, but it wasn't quite bad enough, and its cost-conscious nature ruled out any major muscle-maximizing mechanical improvements.

Cost-cutting measures were then thrown out the window in 2001, resulting in the Z06 hardtop, a pumped-up Corvette that was, in Chevrolet's words, "aimed directly at diehard performance enthusiasts at the upper end of the high-performance market." Now the most expensive Corvette offered, priced $500 more than the

The two-car C5-R team first raced at Le Mans in 2000, finishing third and fourth in the GTS class. In 2001, and again in 2002, the C5-R Corvettes finished 1-2 in class at France's fabled 24-hour endurance event. After finishing second and third in 2003, another 1-2 finish came in 2004.

Specifications	2001
Model availability	coupe, Z06 hardtop, and convertible
Construction	fiberglass body on steel frame with central backbone frame and hydroformed perimeter rails; transmission located at rear axle
Wheelbase	104.5 inches
Length	179.7 inches
Width	73.6 inches
Height	47.7 inches (coupe), 47.7 inches (convertible), 47.8 inches (hardtop)
Curb weight	3,246 pounds (coupe), 3,248 pounds (convertible), 3,173 pounds (hardtop)
Tread (front/rear, in inches)	61.9/62; 62.4/62.6, Z06
Tires	Goodyear Eagle F1 GS Extended Mobility; P245/45ZR-17, front; P275/40ZR-18, rear
Z06 tires	Goodyear Eagle F1 SC asymmetric; P265/40ZR-17, front; P295/35ZR-18, rear
Brakes	power-assisted four-wheel discs with Bosch ABS
Brake dimensions	12.6 inches, front ; 11.8 inches, rear
Wheels	cast aluminum; 17x8.5 inches, front; 18x9.5 inches, rear
Z06 wheels	forged aluminum; 17x9.5 inches, front; 18x10.5, rear
Fuel tank	18.5 gallons
Front suspension	short- and long-arm double wishbone (forged aluminum, top; cast aluminum, bottom), transverse leaf spring, stabilizer bar, monotube shock absorbers
Rear suspension	short- and long-arm double wishbone (cast-aluminum control arms, top and bottom), transverse leaf spring, stabilizer bar, monotube shock absorbers
Steering	speed-sensitive, power-assisted rack and pinion
Engine	5.7-liter OHV V-8 (LS1) with aluminum cylinder block and heads, sequential fuel injection
Bore and stroke	3.90x3.62 inches
LS1 output	350 horsepower at 5,600 rpm; 375 ft-lbs at 4,400 rpm
Z06 engine	5.7-liter OHV V-8 (LS6) with aluminum cylinder block and heads
LS6 output	385 horsepower at 6,000 rpm; 385 ft-lbs at 4,800 rpm
Standard transmission (LS1)	four-speed 4L60-E automatic transmission
Standard transmission (LS6)	six-speed manual
Optional transmission (behind LS1)	six-speed manual

2001 convertible, the Z06 apologized to no one for its balls-out, inconsiderate nature. It was nearly every bit as hard on the seat of the pants as it was on the wallet, but it also was, again according to Chevrolet, "simply the quickest, best handling production Corvette ever."

"We've enhanced Corvette's performance persona and broken new ground with the Z06," explained Hill with due pride. "With 0–60 [times] of four seconds flat and more than 1 g of cornering acceleration, the Z06 truly takes Corvette performance to the next level. In fact, the

Right
Base priced at $40,475, the coupe was the lowest-priced Corvette in 2001. Production was 15,681.

Below
Three body styles returned for 2001, only the hardtop was the awesome Z06, a road rocket reminiscent of the race-ready Sting Ray Z06 introduced in 1963.

Corvette Team has begun referring to it as the C5.5, so marked are the improvements we've made and the optimization of the car in every dimension."

"The new Z06 will have great appeal for those who lust after something more—that indefinable thrill that comes from being able to drive competitively at 10/10ths in a car purpose-built do to exactly that," added new Corvette Brand Manager Jim Campbell.

Like its 385-horse LS6 V-8, this lean, mean coupe borrowed its name from a past legend, the one created by Zora Duntov in 1963. Duntov's original Z06 package included Chevrolet's hottest injected small block working in concert with beefed brakes and a seriously stiffened suspension. Hill's plan was similar 38 years later. Standard for the modern Z06 was Chevy's new M12 six-speed manual transmission, wider wheels and tires, special brake-cooling duct work front and rear, and the exclusive FE4 suspension, which featured a larger front stabilizer bar, a stiffer leaf spring in back, and revised camber settings at both ends. Weight was cut throughout the Z06 by about 100 pounds overall compared to a typical 2001 Corvette sport coupe.

Stretched an inch wider than standard C5 rims, the 2001 Z06's wheels measured 17x9.5 inches in front, 18x10.5 inches in back. Mounted on these huge rollers were Goodyear Eagle F1 SC tires, P265/40ZR-17 in front, P295/35ZR-18 in back. C5s in 2001 featured Eagle F1 GS rubber: P245/45ZR-17 at the nose, P275/40ZR-18 at the tail.

Available only with the Z06, the LS6 V-8 took its name from the 425-horse 454 big-block V-8 offered previously beneath Corvette hoods for one year only: 1971. Chevrolet's second-edition LS6 was a muscled-up LS1 small block that looked identical externally, save for red ornamental covers (instead of black) atop each cylinder head. Boosting output to 385 horsepower resulted from more compression (10.5:1), even slicker ports, a freer-flowing intake manifold, a higher-lift cam, and higher-volume injectors. Maximum torque for the 2001 LS6 was 385 ft-lbs at 4,800 rpm, and its redline was 6,500 rpm, compared to 6,000 revs for the LS1.

The LS1, too, received an improved intake in 2001, resulting in an increase from 345 to 350 horsepower. Torque also rose, from 350 to 360 ft-lbs in automatic applications, and to 375 ft-lbs when the optional six-speed manual was installed. Overall performance was improved further by adding second-generation active handling (formerly RPO JL4) into the standard Corvette package.

Nine different exterior colors were offered for 2001 coupes and convertibles, including the two special schemes (Millennium Yellow and Magnetic Red Metallic), now priced at $600. The Z06, on the other hand, was limited to five shades: Speedway White, Quicksilver Metallic, Torch Red, Millennium Yellow, and black.

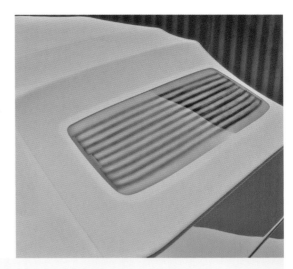

Below
Introduced in 1999, the heads-up instrument display (RPO UV6) became part of new preferred equipment group packaging in 2001.

Above
Refinements for 2001 included a new five-layer convertible top that provided improved sound isolation and a smoother appearance.

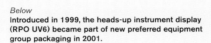

The Z06 was "simply the quickest, best handling production Corvette ever."

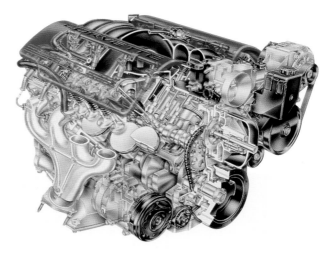

Above
Identified by its red ornamental covers, the 5.7-liter LS6 V-8 produced 385 horsepower in 2001. Like the Z06 tag, the LS6 code also came from the archives; in 1971, it had signified the presence of the Corvette's optional 425-horsepower 454-cubic-inch big-block V-8.

Opposite top
Priced at $47,500, the Z06 hardtop was the most expensive Corvette offered in 2001. Production was 5,773—all equipped with the new LS6 V-8, backed by a six-speed manual transmission.

Above left
Wider wheels and tires, the exclusive FE4 suspension, and special brake-cooling duct work were all standard on the 2001 Z06.

Opposite bottom
Five colors were available for the 2001 Z06: Quicksilver Metallic, Speedway White, Torch Red, black, and the extracost ($600) Millennium Yellow.

Below
Z06 interiors were leather done in black or a black/red combo.

Right
Appropriate embroidery graced the headrests on the Z06's leather seats.

Below
While Z06 instruments featured exclusive italicized numerals, standard Corvette instrumentation retained the traditional style in 2001.

2002

2002

Specifications	2002
Model availability	coupe, Z06 hardtop, and convertible
Construction	fiberglass body on steel frame with central backbone frame and hydroformed perimeter rails; transmission located at rear axle
Wheelbase	104.5 inches
Length	179.7 inches
Width	73.6 inches
Height	47.7 inches (coupe), 47.7 inches (convertible), 47.8 inches (hardtop)
Curb weight	3,246 pounds (coupe), 3,248 pounds (convertible), 3,118 pounds (hardtop)
Tread (front/rear, in inches)	61.9/62; 62.4/62.6, Z06
Tires	Goodyear Eagle F1 GS Extended Mobility; P245/45ZR-17, front; P275/40ZR-18, rear
Z06 tires	Goodyear Eagle F1 SC asymmetric; P265/40ZR-17, front; P295/35ZR-18, rear
Brakes	power-assisted four-wheel discs with Bosch ABS
Brake dimensions	12.6 inches, front; 11.8 inches, rear
Wheels	cast aluminum; 17x8.5 inches, front; 18x9.5 inches, rear
Z06 wheels	forged aluminum; 17x9.5 inches, front; 18x10.5, rear
Fuel tank	18.5 gallons
Front suspension	short- and long-arm double wishbone (forged aluminum, top; cast aluminum, bottom), transverse leaf spring, stabilizer bar, monotube shock absorbers
Rear suspension	short- and long-arm double wishbone (cast-aluminum control arms, top and bottom), transverse leaf spring, stabilizer bar, monotube shock absorbers
Steering	speed-sensitive, power-assisted rack and pinion
Engine	5.7-liter OHV V-8 (LS1) with aluminum cylinder block and heads, sequential fuel injection
Bore and stroke	3.90x3.62 inches
LS1 output	350 horsepower at 5,600 rpm; 375 ft-lbs at 4,400 rpm
Z06 engine	5.7-liter OHV V-8 (LS6) with aluminum cylinder block and heads
LS6 output	405 horsepower at 6,000 rpm; 400 ft-lbs at 4,800 rpm
Standard transmission (LS1)	four-speed 4L60-E automatic transmission
Standard transmission (LS6)	six-speed manual
Optional transmission (behind LS1)	six-speed manual

Top
Those intakes on the Z06's rear flanks were functional: they fed cooling air through ducts to the rear brakes.

Above
Powerful halogen fog lamps were featured in the preferred equipment group packages offered for both coupe and convertible Corvettes in 2002.

Left
The five Z06 colors for 2002 were Quicksilver Metallic, Electron Blue Metallic, Torch Red, black, and the eye-popping Millennium Yellow, which again cost $600 extra.

Below
A new low-restriction air cleaner, a less-restrictive mass airflow sensor, and a more aggressive cam helped the Z06's LS6 V-8 go from 385 to 405 horses in 2002.

2002

Upgrades were minor in 2002, at least as far as base coupes and convertibles were concerned. Most prominent was a switch from stainless steel to aluminum for the automatic transmission cooler case and the inclusion of an AM/FM stereo with in-dash CD player as standard equipment. One new exterior color (Electron Blue Metallic) was added, while two (Dark Bowling Green Metallic and Navy Blue Metallic) were dropped. Available Z06 shades again numbered five, but this time Electron Blue Metallic replaced Speedway White.

Z06 improvements were plentiful, beginning with an increase to 405 horsepower for its exclusive LS6 V-8. Helping make this burst possible was a new low-restriction air cleaner, an even lumpier cam (with the highest lift in small-block history), a less-restrictive mass airflow sensor, and lighter hollow-stem valves. The smaller two of the car's four catalytic converters were removed, a modification that both cut weight and reduced back pressure by 16 percent. Yet even with those missing cats, the 2002 Z06 exhaust system still met federal emissions standards, because the two remaining converters were modified to enhance their efficiency.

The Z06-specific FE4 suspension was upgraded with an enlarged front stabilizer bar,

Above
The Z06 base price hit $50,150 in 2002 and production also rose, to 8,297. Coupe and convertible prices were $41,450 and $47,975, respectively.

Below
Save for more horsepower, the Z06 rolled over nearly unchanged into 2002. Upgrades included recalibrated shocks, a stiffer rear spring, and an enlarged front stabilizer bar. Heads-up instrumentation also became standard Z06 issue that year.

a stiffer rear spring, and recalibrated rear shock absorbers. New front brake linings featured improved durability and fade resistance, and the Z06 aluminum wheels were cast instead of forged. The HUD system became standard Z06 equipment in 2002.

All Z06 hardtops and convertibles with HUD were fitted that year with lighter, thinner (4.8-millimeter) windshields, which shaved off 2.65 pounds per car. All coupes and topless models without HUD featured thicker (5.4-millimeter) windshields.

Above
Chevrolet marked 50 years of Corvette history with a special commemorative C5 model (front) in 2003. All four previous generations appear here: (counterclockwise) C3, C4, C2, and solid-axle C1.

Right
Introduced in 1998, the active handling option (RPO JL4) became standard on all Corvettes in 2001—shown here is the 2002 control switch.

Far right
An in-dash CD player became standard in 2002, making the Corvette's console storage area potentially even more crowded.

Above
Appropriate badges were, of course, also included in the 50th Anniversary edition package.

Below
The Z06 hardtop carried over essentially unchanged for 2003.

"Few vehicles have had the staying power of Corvette," said Rick Baldick, in 2003.

2003

Specifications	2003
Model availability	coupe, Z06 hardtop, and convertible
Construction	fiberglass body on steel frame with central backbone frame and hydroformed perimeter rails; transmission located at rear axle
Wheelbase	104.5 inches
Length	179.7 inches
Width	73.6 inches
Height	47.7 inches (coupe), 47.7 inches (convertible), 47.8 inches (hardtop)
Curb weight	3,246 pounds (coupe), 3,248 pounds (convertible), 3,118 pounds (hardtop)
Tread (front/rear, in inches)	61.9/62; 62.4/62.6, Z06
Tires	Goodyear Eagle F1 GS Extended Mobility; P245/45ZR-17, front; P275/40ZR-18, rear
Z06 tires	Goodyear Eagle F1 SC asymmetric; P265/40ZR-17, front; P295/35ZR-18, rear
Brakes	power-assisted four-wheel discs with Bosch ABS
Brake dimensions	12.6 inches, front; 11.8 inches, rear
Wheels	cast aluminum; 17x8.5 inches, front; 18x9.5 inches, rear
Z06 wheels	forged aluminum; 17x9.5 inches, front; 18x10.5, rear
Fuel tank	18.0 gallons
Front suspension	short- and long-arm double wishbone (forged aluminum, top; cast aluminum, bottom), transverse leaf spring, stabilizer bar, monotube shock absorbers
Rear suspension	short- and long-arm double wishbone (cast-aluminum control arms, top and bottom), transverse leaf spring, stabilizer bar, monotube shock absorbers
Steering	speed-sensitive, power-assisted rack and pinion
Engine	5.7-liter OHV V-8 (LS1) with aluminum cylinder block and heads, sequential fuel injection
Bore and stroke	3.90x3.62 inches
LS1 output	350 horsepower at 5,600 rpm; 375 ft-lbs at 4,400 rpm
Z06 engine	5.7-liter OHV V-8 (LS6) with aluminum cylinder block and heads
LS6 output	405 horsepower at 6,000 rpm; 400 ft-lbs at 4,800 rpm
Standard transmission (LS1)	four-speed 4L60-E automatic transmission
Standard transmission (LS6)	six-speed manual
Optional transmission (behind LS1)	six-speed manual

2003

"Few vehicles have had the staying power of Corvette," said Rick Baldick, in 2003. "We believe much of that success comes from a willingness to embrace advancing technology while remaining true to Corvette's glorious history. As we celebrate our golden anniversary in 2003, we honor our past and cast a bright eye toward the future."

Predictably honoring the Corvette's golden year were 50th Anniversary badges on all 2003 models. And for $5,000, a 2003 coupe or convertible could've been honored further with the 1SC package, a cosmetic addition that wasn't offered to Z06 buyers.

Included in the 1SC deal were unique fender emblems, Anniversary Red "Xirallic crystal" paint,

champagne-colored aluminum wheels, and a Shale-colored interior. Embroidered 50th Anniversary logos appeared on the floor mats and headrests, and convertibles were additionally treated to Shale-colored soft tops. All 50th Anniversary Corvettes were also equipped with magnetic selective ride control, yet another high-tech approach to helping keep the car's dirty side down.

A new option for base coupes and convertibles, magnetic selective ride control (RPO F55) replaced the F45 damping system offered in 2002 and represented a head-and-shoulders improvement. Damping changes in the F45 system were achieved by mechanically controlling the fluid flow within each shock absorber. The F55

system, on the other hand, relied on what was called "magneto-rheological" (MR) fluid, which contained iron particles that could adjust flow rates when acted upon by electrical inputs, and this electronic control could react to changing road conditions in lightning-fast fashion. Reportedly, the new magnetic damping could make as many as 1,000 adjustments per second.

Other options seen the previous year became standard on coupes and convertibles in 2003. Among these were fog lamps, sport seats, power assist for the passenger seat, and dual-zone air conditioning. A parcel net and luggage shade became standard for the coupe. The Z06 hardtop carried over essentially unchanged from 2002.

"We believe much of that success comes from a willingness to embrace advancing technology while remaining true to Corvette's glorious history.
—Rick Baldick

Clockwise, from opposite
Available for coupes and convertibles in 2003, the 50th Anniversary edition option (1SC) was priced at $5,000 in both cases. Anniversary Red Metallic paint was part of the 1SC deal, as were champagne-painted wheels.

A shale-colored interior was included inside the 50th Anniversary Corvette.

Special commemorative embroidery was added to the seats inside the 50th Anniversary Corvette.

A preproduction 2003 Anniversary edition coupe paced the Indianapolis 500 in May 2002 to help kick off the Corvette's 50th birthday celebration.

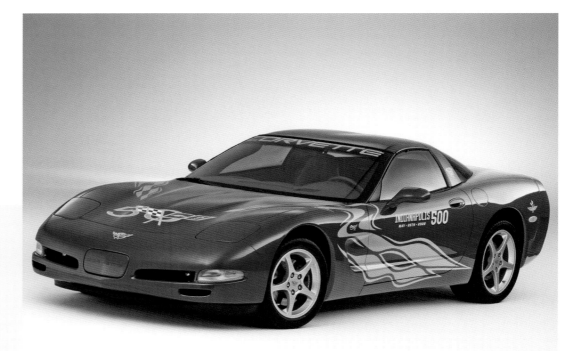

2004

Specifications	2004
Model availability	coupe, Z06 hardtop, and convertible
Construction	fiberglass body on steel frame with central backbone frame and hydroformed perimeter rails; transmission located at rear axle
Wheelbase	104.5 inches
Length	179.7 inches
Width	73.6 inches
Height	47.7 inches (coupe), 47.7 inches (convertible), 47.8 inches (hardtop)
Curb weight	3,246 pounds (coupe), 3,248 pounds (convertible), 3,118 pounds (hardtop)
Tread (front/rear, in inches)	61.9/62; 62.4/62.6, Z06
Tires	Goodyear Eagle F1 GS Extended Mobility; P245/45ZR-17, front; P275/40ZR-18, rear
Z06 tires	Goodyear Eagle F1 SC asymmetric; P265/40ZR-17, front; P295/35ZR-18, rear
Brakes	power-assisted four-wheel discs with Bosch ABS
Brake dimensions	12.6 inches, front; 11.8 inches, rear
Wheels	cast aluminum; 17x8.5 inches, front; 18x9.5 inches, rear
Z06 wheels	forged aluminum; 17x9.5 inches, front; 18x10.5, rear
Fuel tank	18.0 gallons
Front suspension	short- and long-arm double wishbone (forged aluminum, top; cast aluminum, bottom), transverse leaf spring, stabilizer bar, monotube shock absorbers
Rear suspension	short- and long-arm double wishbone (cast-aluminum control arms, top and bottom), transverse leaf spring, stabilizer bar, monotube shock absorbers
Steering	speed-sensitive, power-assisted rack and pinion
Engine	5.7-liter OHV V-8 (LS1) with aluminum cylinder block and heads, sequential fuel injection
Bore and stroke	3.90x3.62 inches
LS1 output	350 horsepower at 5,600 rpm; 375 ft-lbs at 4,400 rpm
Z06 engine	5.7-liter OHV V-8 (LS6) with aluminum cylinder block and heads
LS6 output	405 horsepower at 6,000 rpm; 400 ft-lbs at 4,800 rpm
Standard transmission (LS1)	four-speed 4L60-E automatic transmission
Standard transmission (LS6)	Tremec T56 six-speed manual
Optional transmission (behind LS1)	Tremec T56 six-speed manual

New colors for 2004 included Arctic White, Machine Silver, Magnetic Red, and the Commemorative Edition's Le Mans Blue.

Describing the C5 as "the best 'Vette yet," David Hill claimed, "You won't find a car in Corvette's price range that provides the same level of quality, power, ride, handling, and refinement."

2004

Everything that made the Corvette so great during its 50th anniversary year returned for the last of the C5 models in 2004. As before, three bodies were offered that year: coupe, convertible, and Z06 hardtop. But new for 2004 was a Commemorative Edition package offered for all three models.

Created to honor the C5-R Corvette's racing success, the Commemorative Edition coupes and convertibles featured new Le Mans Blue paint with contrasting Shale interiors, special badges, and polished wheels In the convertible's case, the folding top also was done in Shale. Additional touches on the Commemorative Edition Z06 Corvettes included a special Le Mans stripe accent and a lightweight carbon-fiber hood. All Z06s, commemorative or not, also were treated to revised shock valving that, according to Corvette Product Manager Harlan Charles, made the car feel "more tied down, more glued to the road."

Eight years and out was the C5's fate. But what a great eight they were.

Chevrolet honored its rich racing heritage in 2004 with a Commemorative Edition package, available for all three Corvette models: coupe, convertible, and Z06 hardtop. Included in the deal was exclusive Le Mans Blue paint and polished wheels.

The last of the C5 Corvettes appeared with essentially no changes in 2004. As in 2003, magnetic selective ride control was optional on coupes and convertibles.

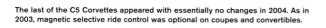

Along with optional Commemorative Edition imagery, the 2004 Z06 hardtop also featured a new carbon-fiber hood and revised shock valving.

Above
The 2006 Z06's carbon-fiber body panels help reduce overall weight to a tidy 3,132 pounds. Rear wheels are huge 19x12 units.

Center
Last offered in 1962, an optional power-operated convertible top returned in 2005. Its operational cycle is only 18 seconds.

Right
The bodacious Z06 returned for 2006 after taking one year off. New for the C6-based Z06 is exclusive bodywork that measures 3 inches wider than a garden-variety 2006 Corvette's shell.

Thoroughly
Modern

07

C6
2005-2006

David Hill wasn't blowing smoke in 1997 when he called Chevrolet's latest Corvette the best 'Vette yet. From nose to tail, from the roof down to the ground, the fabulous C5 was as new and improved as it got. Even so, Hill and his team were already busy working on the next best 'Vette just two years later. According to the Corvette's third chief engineer, various things about the superb C5 needed fixing, and those upgrades could only come about as part of a redesign.

Along with expected performance enhancements, C6 development involved even more refinement, this to make a more-refined customer base happy. That the C5 was arguably the world's best performance buy was only the beginning; its improved comfort and convenience features made the deal as attractive, and classy, as it had ever been during the car's half-century history. Thus, according to Corvette Marketing Director Rick Baldick, a new breed of buyer had emerged, a higher class, if you will. With these more discriminating minds in mind, engineers and designers sought to dial in further comfort, improved overall platform tightness, and extra quietness.

"The C6 represents a comprehensive upgrade to the Corvette," explained David Hill late in 2003. "Our goal is to create a Corvette that does more

things well than any performance car. We've thoroughly improved performance and developed new features and capabilities in many areas, while at the same time systematically searching out and destroying every imperfection we could find." In Hill's opinion, the C5 had been "90 percent perfect." That figure, in his estimation, then became 99 percent for the C6.

Furthermore, Hill claimed that as much as 70 percent of the C6's part numbers were new, a fact that may or may not have proved significant. "We frequently go through this with manufacturers," explained Daniel Pund in *Car and Driver*. "If the suspension control arms look exactly the same but carry a different parts number, are they new? We'll compromise and say the 2005 Corvette is the C5 and 11/16ths."

Opposite
The C6 coupe's removable roof panel is 15 percent larger than its C5 counterpart. A body-colored panel is standard. Options included a dual-roof package and a tinted clear panel.

Above
Like its wheels and tires, the Z06's brakes are equally humongous, with 14-inch rotors in front, 13.4 in back.

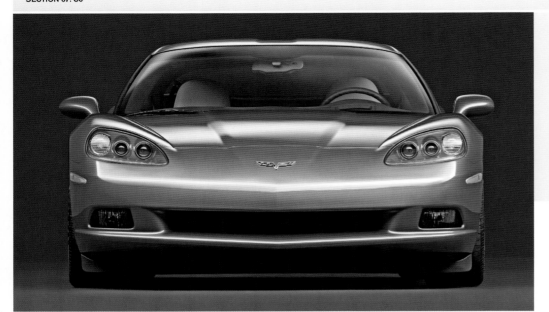

Left
**The C6 Corvette showed up in 2005 with exposed
headlamps, the first for the breed since 1962.**

Below
**Chevrolet's sixth-generation Corvette debuted for
2005 in coupe and convertible forms. The new C6
is both lighter and shorter (by 5 inches) than its
C5 predecessor.**

Initial plans called for the near-perfect, round-numbered C6 to show up in time for the Corvette's 50th birthday celebration in 2003. But then the September 11, 2001, terrorist attacks occurred. Economic aftershocks cut GM budgets to the bone, leaving officials no choice but to hold off on C6 development. When cash began to flow again, the Corvette team resorted to working nights and weekends to have the next-generation machine ready for public sale by the fall of 2004. All told, as many as 200 engineers and 1,000 workers in Bowling Green burned mucho midnight oil to guarantee a 2005 model year debut.

Working long hours under Hill and Assistant Chief Engineer Tadge Juechter were the likes of Bill Nichols, Dave Zimmerman, and Fernando Krambeck. Nichols oversaw powertrain work, Zimmerman did the chassis, and Krambeck handled the interior. Though it wasn't really his j ob, Juechter commonly worked in the wind tunnel, where aerodynamicist Tom Froling reportedly stayed until 8 p.m. many nights to get the job done.

Tom Peters was the designer in charge of giving the C6 a truly new look, which first and foremost involved deleting the hideaway headlights that had been a Corvette tradition since 1963. Like the Sting Ray III, the new C6 featured exposed lamps housed behind cat's-eye clear covers, making more than one thoroughly

entrenched purist cringe. Overall impressions, nonetheless, were hot and were further enhanced by softly rounded contours that help lessen the sharp impact made by the C5. And with a drag coefficient of 0.286, the C6 body ranked as the most aerodynamic Corvette shell yet.

Beneath that slick skin was Chevrolet's latest variation on its small-block theme: the

Gen IV V-8. Tabbed "LS2," this new mouse motor was basically an upgraded, bored-out LS1. It displaced 6.0 liters and produced 400 horsepower, making it the strongest standard Corvette engine to date. It also was nicely fuel efficient, even more so than the 2004 C5's base 350-horse 5.7-liter LS1. Estimated combined city/highway fuel economy

Chief designer Tom Peters was responsible for redrawing the Corvette's shape for 2005.

"The Gen IV is the best example yet of the continuous refinement in performance and efficiency that has been part of the small block's legacy since day one," said engineering chief Sam Winegarden in October 2003.

for the 2005 Corvette was 22.6 mile per gallon, a major plus considering today's high-flying gas prices.

Imagine that—more displacement, more horses, and more miles per gallon. Clearly Chevy engineers knew what the hell they were doing, as had most of their predecessors dating back to 1955.

"The Gen IV is the best example yet of the continuous refinement in performance and efficiency that has been part of the small block's legacy since day one," said engineering chief Sam Winegarden in October 2003. "[This] long history is one of the reasons the new generation of engines is so powerful and efficient. GM has almost 50 years of experience with its valve-in-head design, and that has provided immeasurable detail for keeping the small block a viable, relevant engine for today and the future."

More than one Corvette crazy stood disappointed in 2003 when the C6 failed to appear as the breed's 50th anniversary model. Fortunately, it was dominating magazine covers by the end of the year, and its official public unveiling then came at the Detroit auto show in January 2004.

2005

Nearly all witnesses were well aware that the new C6 wasn't a total redesign, like its C5 forerunner. That wasn't a bad thing, however, considering the long, long list of changes that added up to one thoroughly modern performance package.

"The sixth-generation Corvette blends technical sophistication with expressive style," explained promotional paperwork. "Five inches shorter than the current car, the 2005 Corvette

cuts a tighter, more taut profile—with virtually no loss of usable space. More than just visual, the new dimensions make the car more agile and 'tossable,' with upgrades in handling, acceleration, and braking."

Additional dimensional changes included 1 inch less width and a wheelbase stretch of 1.2 inches. Along with a more sure-footed feel, that latter increase teamed up with the body's decreased overhangs (down 2 inches in front, 3 in back) to produce the aforementioned taut profile. More important was a reduction in weight, down to 3,179 pounds for the coupe, 3,199 for the convertible.

New for 2005 were 18-inch front wheels and 19-inch rears. Widths were 8.5 inches at the nose, 10 inches out back. Goodyear Eagle F1 GS Extended Mobility tires went onto these rims measuring P245/40ZR-18 up front, P285/35ZR-19 at the tail. Bigger, better brakes were standard, too, with the front rotors measuring 12.8 inches across, the backs 12. The C5's suspension layout carried over, but reportedly nearly all components were revised or new.

Boosting LS2 displacement to 6.0 liters (364 cubic inches) was the result of more bore (4.00 inches instead of 3.90 inches) working with the same stroke (3.62 inches) used within the LS1. Helping make those 400 horses was more

2005

2005

Specifications	2005
Model availability	hatchback coupe (with removable roof panel) and convertible
Construction	composite body on hydroformed steel frame with aluminum and magnesium structural components
Wheelbase -	105.7 inches
Length	174.6 inches
Width	72.6 inches
Height	49 inches
Curb weight	3,179 pounds (coupe), 3,199 pounds (convertible)
Tread (front/rear, in inches)	62/1/60.7
Tires	Goodyear Eagle F1 GS Extended Mobility (EMT); P245/40ZR-18, front; P285/35ZR-19, rear
Brakes	power-assisted four-wheel discs with ABS and electronic traction control
Brake dimensions (in inches)	12.8x1.26 front, 12x1 rear
Brake dimensions with Z51 option (in inches)	13.4x1.26, front; 13x1, rear; cross-drilled rotors
Wheels	18x8.5 front, 19x10 rear
Fuel tank	18 gallons
Suspension	short- and long-arm (SLA) double-wishbone cast-aluminum control arms, transverse composite leaf springs, and stabilizer bars front and rear; monotube shock absorbers, active handling electronics (stiffer springs and shocks, thicker stabilizer bars with Z51 option)
Steering	speed-sensitive, magnetic power-assisted rack and pinion (16.1:1 ratio)
Engine	6.0-liter (364 cubic inches) sequential fuel-injected (SFI) LS2 V-8 with overhead valves and cast-aluminum cylinder block and heads
Compression	10.9:1
Bore and stroke	4.00x3.62 inches
Output	400 horsepower at 6,000 rpm, 400 ft-lbs of torque at 4,400 rpm
Standard Transmission	six-speed manual with 2.66:1 low
Optional Transmission	Hydra-matic 4L65E four-speed automatic
Transmission with Z51 option	six-speed manual with 2.97:1 low

demanding that all its divisions cease and desist competition activities. Corvettes still kept racing, and winning, with more than a little support from their makers in Warren, Michigan.

Scoring SCCA championships and endurance victories in the United States was one thing. But from the beginning, Duntov always imagined a much grander legacy for his baby. His 1957 SS was meant not just to win at Sebring, but to move on to bigger, better venues, the most important being Le Mans. AMA action that summer derailed his plan, however, and glory in France continued to elude production-based Corvettes for decades to come.

All that changed in 2001 when C5-R Corvettes finished first and second in the GTS class (8th and 14th overall) at Le Mans. Officially introduced in 1998, the C5-R factory racer first competed in France's fabled 24-hour endurance test in June 2000, placing third and fourth in the GTS field. By 2005, the Corvette Racing team had added three more firsts and a second at Le Mans, as well as three straight Sebring class wins (2001–2003) and five consecutive ALMS championships. All told, Corvette Racing's two cars won 45 of 66 events from 2000 to 2005, including 31 one-two finishes.

compression (10.9:1), a higher-lift cam (with higher-rate valve springs), and intake and exhaust flows improved by 15 and 20 percent, respectively. Overall engine weight, meanwhile, went down by about 15 pounds, courtesy of, among other things, a smaller water pump and thinner-walled exhaust manifolds.

Behind the LS2 was either the four-speed 4L65E Hydra-matic automatic or Tremec T56 six-speed manual. The wide-ratio T56 box used by the 2004 Z06 remained on the options list but only when the Z51 performance package was ordered. Included in the Z51 deal was a stiffer suspension and even bigger (13.4-inch front rotors, 13-inch rears) brakes.

Working together, these parts made for some seriously improved performance. According to Chevrolet officials, a Z51-equipped C6 could nearly match a 2004 Z06's lap time on the test track, a convenient occurrence considering the Z06 didn't carry over into 2005. Thankfully, it did return.

C6.R racer

Corvettes always have been in racing, even if their parent company hasn't. AMA officials could ban factory racing involvement all they wanted in 1957; that didn't stop Zora Duntov from propping Engineering's back door open for racers bent on keeping America's sports car out in front on the track. Then there was GM's 1963 edict

Below
The basic C5 design carried over into the C6 era but with countless new parts and various revised dimensions. "The sixth generation represents a comprehensive upgrade," said Corvette Chief Engineer David Hill.

Opposite
Though noticeably resculpted, the C6 bears considerable resemblance to its C5 forerunner.

C6.R

Specifications	C6.R
Body style	coupe
Construction	composite body on hydroformed steel frame with aluminum and magnesium structural components
Wheelbase	105.7 inches
Length	177.6 inches
Width	78.7 inches
Height	45.8 inches
Tread (front/rear, in inches)	62.2/63.1
Tires	Michelin racing; 290/33-18, front; 310/41-18 ,rear
Brakes	four-wheel discs with monoblock caliper and carbon-fiber rotors and pads
Fuel tank	26.4 gallons
Suspension	independent fabricated steel short- and long-arm double-wishbone, machined aluminum knuckles, coil-over multi-adjustable shocks, anti-roll bar, front and rear
Engine	7.0-liter all-aluminum LS7.R overhead-valve V-8 with electronic sequential fuel injection and dry-sump oiling
Bore and stroke	4.180x3.875 inches
Output	590 horsepower at 5,400 rpm, 640 ft-lbs torque at 4,400 rpm

The two Velocity Yellow machines campaigned by Corvette Racing in 2005 were new C6.R models, which stood head and shoulders above their C5-R forerunners. "We developed this car for a year before it appeared in public, so it had many miles of testing before its first race at Sebring," explained Program Manager Doug Fehan. "You only have to look at the differences between the C5-R and the C6.R—a one-inch-longer wheelbase and five-inch-shorter body—to appreciate how much work had to be done. You can't just re-skin an old car and expect it to win."

"Both the chassis and aerodynamic package changed considerably," added GM Racing road racing group manager Steve Wesoloski. "The new regulations required more extensive use of the production car's chassis structure, retaining items such as the central drivetrain tunnel, the windshield frame, and the rear bumper. We also introduced new low-friction suspension attachments that made the car quicker to react."

Beneath the 2005 C6.R's nose was the 7.0-liter LS7.R V-8, a 590-horsepower, 640-ft-lbs-torque beast that had many Gen IV basics but was lighter than the regular-production LS2. "We took a lot amount of weight out of the engine, helping the balance of the car while improving performance," continued Wesoloski. "Internal components [also] were designed to reduce horsepower losses due to friction and to reduce rotating mass."

Whether or not the C6.R will carry on the C5-R's tire tracks remains to be seen as these words go to press, but most at GM are sure they've got another winner. "History will remember the C5-R as one of the best sports racing cars of all time, and we've raised the bar even higher with the C6.R," said GM Racing Director Mark Kent. "Just when I think the Corvette team has done all that can be done, they surprise me. I just can't wait to see what they do next, and I'm glad that our racing efforts will be part of making the next-generation Corvette even better."

Indeed, apparently racing does improve the breed.

"In many ways, [this] is a racing engine in a street car," added Muscaro.

2006

Specifications	2006
Model availability	coupe (with removable roof panel), convertible, and Z06 coupe (with fixed magnesium roof)
Construction	composite body on hydroformed steel frame with aluminum and magnesium structural components (unique carbon-fiber body panels and hydroformed aluminum frame for Z06)
Wheelbase	105.7 inches
Length	174.6 inches
Length (Z06)	175.6 inches
Width	72.6 inches
Height	49 inches
Curb weight	3,179 pounds (coupe), 3,199 pounds (convertible), 3,132 pounds (Z06)
Tread (front/rear, in inches)	62.1/60 (coupe and convertible); 63.5/62.5 (Z06)
Tires (coupe and convertible)	Goodyear Eagle F1 Supercar Extended Mobility (EMT); P245/40ZR-18, front; P285/35ZR-19, rear
Tires (Z06)	Goodyear Eagle F1 Supercar EMT; P275/35ZR-18, front; P325/30ZR-19, rear
Brakes	power-assisted four-wheel discs with ABS and electronic traction control
Brake dimensions (in inches)	12.8x1.26, front; 12x1, rear
Brake dimensions with Z51 option (in inches)	13.4x1.26, front; 13x1, rear; cross-drilled rotors
Brake dimensions, Z06 (in inches)	14x1.3, front; 13.4x1, rear; cross-drilled rotors
Wheels, coupe and convertible (in inches)	18x8.5, front; 19x10, rear
Wheels, Z06 (in inches)	18x9.5, front; 19x12, back
Fuel tank	18 gallons
Suspension	short- and long-arm (SLA) double-wishbone cast-aluminum control arms, transverse composite leaf springs, and stabilizer bars, front and rear; monotube shock absorbers, active handling electronics (stiffer springs and shocks, thicker stabilizer bars with Z51 option)
Steering	speed-sensitive, magnetic power-assisted rack and pinion (16.1 1 ratio)
Engine (LS2)	6.0-liter (364 cubic inches) sequential fuel-injected (SFI) V-8 with overhead valves and cast-aluminum cylinder block and heads
LS2 compression	10.9 1
LS2 bore and stroke	4.00x3.62 inches
LS2 output	400 horsepower at 6,000 rpm, 400 ft-lbs of torque at 4,400 rpm
Engine (LS7)	7.0-liter (427 cubic inches) SFI V-8 with overhead valves and cast-aluminum cylinder block and heads, dry-sump oiling
LS7 compression	11.0:1
LS7 bore and stroke	4.125x4.00 inches
LS7 output	505 horsepower at 6,300 rpm, 470 ft-lbs of torque at 4,800 rpm
Standard transmission	six-speed manual with 2.66:1 low
Transmission with Z51 option	six-speed manual with 2.97:1 low
Optional transmission	six-speed automatic with paddle shift

2006

The C6 Corvette coupe and convertible rolled over essentially unchanged from 2005 save for one major new optional feature: a six-speed paddle-shift automatic transmission. Featuring clutch-to-clutch operation, an integrated 32-bit electronic controller, and manual-shift capabilities, this advanced gearbox can be switched into three operating modes: drive, sport, and paddle shift. The first two work automatically, with the drive mode concentrating on smoothness, while its sport upgrade makes shifts firmer for improved acceleration. Activating the paddle-shift mode allows drivers to choose gear changes themselves, using manual controls located on the steering wheel.

Yet, as impressive as the paddle-shift option appears, it doesn't represent the really big news for 2006. That honor goes to the new Z06, which is back and better than ever after a one-year hiatus.

Included in the new Z06 deal is the most impressive list yet of unique features, including bad-to-the-bone bodywork that makes the car 3 inches wider than typical C6s. Fashioned from carbon-fiber composites, those fenders and the aluminum frame also help trim overall weight to a reasonably svelte 3,132 pounds. Also part of the deal are huge disc brakes (14-inch rotors in front, 13.4 inches in back) with six-piston calipers at the nose, four-piston units at the tail. Humongous wheels (18x9.5 inches in front, 19x12 inches in back) are at the corners. Coolers for all fluids, even power steering, are included, as is a rear-mounted battery for improved weight distribution.

Last, but obviously not least, is the Z06's main attraction, the LS7 V-8. Along with being the most powerful small block ever, this all-aluminum monster also is the largest. Increasing both the Gen IV's bore and stroke (to 4.125 and 4.00 inches, respectively) has produced 427 cubic inches, which translate into 7.0 liters. While its 505 maximum horses arrive at 6,300 rpm, this big, bad small block can confidently rev up to 7,100

Far left
Included in the C6's optional Z51 performance package are heavy-duty brakes with cross-drilled rotors. Z51 rotors measure 13.4 inches in front, 13 in back. Standard C6 brakes are 12.8 inches in front, 12 in back.

Left, top
Basically a bored-out, upgraded LS1 V-8, the C6's LS2 displaces 6.0 liters and produces 400 horsepower—the highest standard output in Corvette history.

Left, middle
In all 2006 applications—Corvette, SSR pickup, Cadillac CTS-V (shown here)—the 6.0-liter LS2 V-8 was rated at 400 horsepower.

Below
Beneath the C6.R Corvette's hood is the LS7.R V-8, a lightened Gen IV small block that pumps out 590 horsepower and 640 ft-lbs of torque.

rpm, making it one of the world's first regular-production pushrod motors able to regularly breach the seven-grand barrier and return alive. The previous Gen IV V-8 extreme was 6,600 rpm for the LS2.

"For a production engine to run at this high of an rpm blurs the lines even more between [pushrod] and overhead-cam design," said Dave Muscaro, assistant chief engineer for small-block engines. "We took a complete systems approach to achieve the high rpm. We have a tight valvetrain design along with some race-inspired materials for the reciprocating components like titanium intake valves and connecting rods."

Blurred as well by the LS7 is the barrier separating road and track. "In many ways, [this] is a racing engine in a street car," added Muscaro. "We've taken much of what we've learned over the years from the 7.0-liter C5-R racing program and instilled it here. There really has been nothing else like it offered in a GM production vehicle."

LS7 heads, too, look like they came right off a racetrack. "We consulted with our Motorsports group on numerous aspects of the cylinder head design," said Valvetrain Design Engineer Jim Hicks. "We adopted some of the latest ideas that have been successful in the Nextel Cup and the American Le Mans Series, including valve centerline positions, valve angles, valve sizes, and rocker arm ratio."

"The heads are simply works of mechanical art," added Muscaro. "We left nothing on the table when it came to ensuring the best airflow through the engine."

Ports are considerably larger than those in the LS2 heads and have been precisely massaged for exceptionally high flow. Valve sizes are 2.20 inches for the titanium intake unit, 1.61 for its sodium-filled running mate. Valve lift is a ridiculous 0.591 inches for intake and exhaust. Hydroformed stainless-steel headers complete things on the exhaust end.

And like its lightweight yet bulletproof reciprocating mass, the LS7's cylinder block is also unique, being specially cast to preserve strength while making room for all that bore diameter. Pressed-in cylinder sleeves and tough forged-steel cross-bolted main bearing caps also set the LS7 block apart from its LS2 little brother; the latter features cast-in sleeves and powder-metal main caps. LS7 pistons are cast-aluminum flat-top units that bring compression to 11.0:1. On the bottom end is a balanced forged-steel crank, and lubricating all these wildly rotating parts is a competition-type dry-sump oil system, a first for street-going Corvettes.

Building the LS7 is a job as unique as the engine itself. Each engine is hand-assembled with

How much wilder can things get before someone breaks up the party?

Top
In 2005, the C6.R Corvette picked up where the C5-R left off, finishing 1-2 in class (GT1) at Le Mans that summer.

Right
The C6 exterior rolled over nearly unchanged into 2006.

care by a single, specially trained technician at GM Powertrain's new 100,000-square-foot Performance Build Center in Wixom, Michigan. According to this facility's site manager, Timothy Schag, this intriguing process represents "a premium manufacturing technique for premium products. [It] brings a higher level of quality, because each builder is personally involved in every aspect of the assembly."

Only about 30 LS7 V-8s are produced in a day at Wixom, but quantity clearly isn't a priority. "It was important to step away from the high-volume world we all had lived in for so long and soak in the cadence of these specialized environments," continued Schag. "We learned a lot and established a low-volume manufacturing system on par with the world's best niche builders, but we didn't lose sight of the quality practices already in place at GM."

Talk of an even more alarming Z06 is being heard as the LS7 is keeping the neighbors awake well into the night in 2006. But how much wilder can things get before someone breaks up the party?

Above
Chevrolet's SSR™ pickup was fitted with a 400-horsepower version of the Corvette's LS2 V-8 with a manual transmission.

Below
A six-speed paddle-shift automatic transmission debuted in 2006. Paddle-shift controls are on the steering wheel.

Below. left
Powering the 2006 Z06 is a 7.0-liter (427 cubic inches) Gen IV small-block V-8 capable of winding out to a dizzying 7,100 rpm. Output is a whopping 505 horsepower.

2007

C6 changes for 2007 predictably appeared nearly non-existent at a glance. Easily the most noticeable was a truly fresh chromatic finish, Atomic Orange, a shockingly (in some opinions) radioactive shade that cost an extra $750 due to the additional application of a special tint coat that had first shown up atop the 2000 Corvette's optional Millennium Yellow paint. Specially tinted Monterey Red and Velocity Yellow, each also

priced at $750, carried over on the extra-cost palette for the third straight year.

Fashion-conscious customers additionally could've installed Z06-style two-tone upholstery inside their non-Z06 coupes and convertibles— as long as they additionally popped for either the upscale 2LT or 3LT preferred equipment group. Offered separately that year, a power soft top was included as part of the 2007 3LT convertible package.

Whatever the skin color, topless or not, an ought-seven Vette did remain thoroughly identical to its forerunners underneath as Chevy's superb C6 mechanicals kept on keeping on. Four hundred healthy horses reappeared for LS2 coupes and convertibles, five-oh-five was again the norm for the latest Z06's LS7. The most notable technical upgrade arrived on the options list as enlarged cross-drilled brake rotors were added to the carryover F55 magnetic adjustable suspension package. A bit bigger than base brakes, a tad smaller than the Z06's serious stoppers, these drilled discs were only available previously by way of the Z51 deal, which also returned for 2007, again wearing a $1,695 price tag, while the F55 option was $1,995.

Additional sound insulation and a slightly larger glove box came standard inside a 2007 Corvette. New interior options included Bose audio enhancements and steering-wheel-mounted premium stereo controls. OnStar became available for top-shelf 2007 Z06s equipped with the 2LZ preferred equipment group; it had been limited to 3LT coupes/convertibles in 2006. Nostalgic Z06 customers also could've enhanced their cars' hoods with familiar "427" badges, one of many "Genuine Corvette Accessories" offered by dealers in 2007.

Two special-edition Corvettes appeared as well that year; one a plainly pale Z06 coupe, the other a radiant convertible. The former, listed as RPO Z33, was created to honor legendary Chevrolet racer Ron Fellows, hence its full name: the Ron Fellows ALMS GT1 Champion Edition Z06. All 399 Z33 coupes were done in Arctic White paint complemented with a pair of red fender stripes that mimicked the graphics on Fellows' various GT1-class champion Corvettes. Fellows' autograph graced the inside console lid, making this the first "signed" special edition in Corvette history. More would soon follow.

The special 2007 convertible, offered only in Atomic Orange, commemorated the Corvette's ninth appearance (and fourth in a row, both unmatched records) at The Brickyard as the prestigious Indianapolis 500 pace car. Not since 1998 had Chevrolet offered an Indy pace car replica to Walter Mitty types. Commemorative graphics were printed for the 2003 Corvette, but the Memorial Day pace lap tours in 2004, 2005, and 2006 were not replicated in regular

Specifications	2007
Model availability	coupe (with removable roof panel), convertible, and Z06 coupe (with fixed magnesium roof)
Construction	composite body on hydroformed steel frame with aluminum and magnesium structural components (unique carbon-fiber body panels and hydroformed aluminum frame for Z06)
Wheelbase	105.7 inches
Length	174.6 inches (175.6 inches, Z06)
Width	72.6 inches (75.9 inches, Z06)
Height	49 inches
Track (front/rear, in inches)	62.1/60.7 (coupe and convertible); 63.5/62.5 (Z06)
Curb weight	3,179 pounds (coupe), 3,199 pounds (convertible), 3,132 pounds (Z06)
Wheels (coupe and convertible)	18 x 8.5 inches, front; 19 x10 inches rear
Wheels (Z06)	18 x 9.5 inches, front; 19 x 12 inches rear
Tires (coupe and convertible)	Goodyear Eagle F1 Supercar Extended Mobility (EMT); P245/40ZR18 front, P285/35ZR19 rear
Tires (Z06)	Goodyear Eagle F1 Supercar EMT; P275/35ZR18 front, P325/30ZR19 rear
Brakes	power-assisted four-wheel discs with ABS and electronic traction control
Brake dimensions	12.8x1.26 inches, front; 12x1 inches, rear
Brake dimensions with Z51 option	13.4x1.26 inches, front; 13x1 inches, rear; cross-drilled rotors
Brake dimensions, Z06	14x1.3 inches, front; 13.4x1 inches, rear; cross-drilled rotors
Fuel tank	18 gallons
Suspension	short- and long-arm (SLA) double wishbone cast-aluminum control arms, transverse composite leaf springs, stabilizer bars front and rear, monotube shock absorbers, Active Handling electronics (stiffer springs and shocks, thicker stabilizer bars with Z51 option)
Steering	speed-sensitive, magnetic power-assisted rack and pinion (16.1:1 ratio)
Engine (LS2)	6.0L (364 cubic inches) sequential fuel injected (SFI) V8 with overhead valves and cast-aluminum cylinder block and heads, 10.9:1 compression
LS2 bore and stroke	4.00x3.62 inches
LS2 output	400 horsepower at 6,000 rpm, 400 ft-lbs of torque at 4,400 rpm
Engine (LS7)	7.0L (427 cubic inches) SFI V8 with overhead valves and cast-aluminum cylinder block and heads, 11:1 compression, dry-sump oiling
LS7 bore and stroke	4.125x4.00 inches
LS7 output	505 horsepower at 6,300 rpm, 470 ft-lbs of torque at 4,800 rpm
Standard transmission	six-speed manual with 2.66:1 low
Transmission with Z51 option	six-speed manual with 2.97:1 low
Optional transmission	six-speed automatic with paddle shift
Axle ratio	3.42:1 (2.56:1 with paddle-shift automatic)

production. Then in February 2007, Chevy officials announced a run of 500 Z4Z pace car convertibles, all adorned additionally with splashy gold ribbon graphics, expected Indy 500 fender badges and interior embroidery, and a Z06 rear spoiler. A manual-trans LS2 was standard; the paddle-shift automatic was the model's only option. Base price for the 2007 Indy pace car replica was $66,695. Adding the six-speed automatic bumped that number up to $68,245.

2008

A Corvette again paced the annual Indy 500 in May 2008, and Chevrolet again celebrated with a limited run of special-edition Z4Z replicas, this time offered in both coupe and convertible forms. Creating the unprecedented duo was only right considering that Chevy's overall record 19th Indy pace lap honor also represented the first time in Indianapolis Motor Speedway (IMS) history that two different pace cars appeared on race day, in this case a typical ragtop and a unique Z06 concept coupe that ran on eco-friendly E85 ethanol fuel.

"Although not a production FlexFuel vehicle, the Corvette Z06 E85 concept car is a high-performance example of Chevrolet's gas-friendly to gas-free initiative, demonstrating viable fuel solutions," announced Chevy general manager Ed Peper in December 2007. Announced at the same time was the pace car coupe's driver: two-time Indy 500 winner Emerson Fittipaldi, who just happens to be an ethanol refiner back home in Brazil.

"It's only fitting that the Corvette will be the first car to earn the distinction of having two models pace the Indianapolis 500 in the same year," added IMS president and CEO Joie Chitwood. "Chevrolet and Corvette are a vital part of the rich history of 'The Greatest Spectacle in Racing,' and we're honored to have a great champion of the race and of alternative fuels, Emerson Fittipaldi, as this year's pace car driver."

Fittipaldi even signed and numbered every 2008 pace car replica built: 266 convertibles, 234 coupes. Included this time around in the Z4Z package were new chromed five-spoke forged-aluminum wheels, silver checkered-flag graphics on black paint (further honoring the first Indy pace car Corvette from 1978), and a choice between a six-speed stick or paddle-shift automatic. A Z06 spoiler returned, as did requisite "Indy 500" fender badges. All 2008 Z4Z Corvettes also came standard with posh 3LT interior features and a new C6 powerplant, the 6.2-liter LS3 small-block.

Increasing the bore (from 4.00 inches to 4.06) was just the beginning as far as the transformation from LS2 to 376-cid LS3 was concerned. High-flow LS7-style heads worked in concert with, among other things, a lumpier cam, a revised valvetrain (with enlarged intake valves and offset intake rockers), a high-flow intake, and

high-flow injectors (also copped from the Z06's LS7) to up the C6's standard output ante to 430 horsepower. According to Chevrolet, 190 mph was no prob for an off-the-lot LS3 Corvette in 2008. And with a 0–60 clocking of 4.3 seconds, a paddle-shifted LS3 represented the quickest automatic-equipped Corvette ever.

Yet there was more. Installing the optional dual-mode exhaust system (RPO NPP) increased LS3 output further to 436 horsepower. Another LS7-style upgrade, the new dual-mode exhausts came standard beneath the Indy pace car coupes and convertibles. But with or without those 6 extra ponies, the LS3 C6 clearly redefined "best Vette yet."

Opposite top
For the first time in the event's history, two different models paced the Indianapolis 500 race in 2008: a Corvette convertible and a Z06 coupe, the latter a concept vehicle that ran on E85 ethanol fuel.

Opposite bottom
Two-time Indy 500 winner Emerson Fittipaldi poses with Chevrolet's 2008 Indianapolis 500 Pace car replica convertible. The newest Indy 500 commemorative also honored the 30th anniversary of the first Corvette to pace the annual Memorial Day motorsport spectacular.

Below
The Corvette's small-block V-8 was bored up to 6.2 liters (376 cubic inches) for 2008, gaining 30 horsepower in the process. The name also changed from LS2 to LS3. High-flow LS7-style heads were among LS3 upgrades.

According to Chevrolet, 190 mph was no prob for an off-the-lot LS3 Corvette in 2008.

2008

Specifications	2008
Model availability	coupe (with removable roof panel), convertible, and Z06 coupe (with fixed magnesium roof)
Construction	composite body on hydroformed steel frame with aluminum and magnesium structural components (unique carbon-fiber body panels for Z06)
Wheelbase	105.7 inches
Length	174.6 inches (175.6 inches, Z06)
Width	72.6 inches (75.9 inches, Z06)
Height	49 inches
Track (front/rear, in inches)	62.1/60.7 (coupe and convertible); 63.5/62.5 (Z06)
Curb weight	3,179 pounds (coupe), 3,199 pounds (convertible), 3,132 pounds (Z06)
Wheels (coupe and convertible)	18 x 8.5 inches, front; 19 x10 inches, rear
Wheels (Z06)	18 x 9.5 inches, front; 19 x 12 inches, rear
Tires (coupe and convertible)	Goodyear Eagle F1 Supercar Extended Mobility (EMT); P245/40ZR18 front, P285/35ZR19 rear
Tires (Z06)	Goodyear Eagle F1 Supercar EMT; P275/35ZR18 front, P325/30ZR19 rear
Brakes	power-assisted four-wheel discs with ABS and electronic traction control
Brake dimensions	12.8x1.26 inches, front; 12x1 inches, rear
Brake dimensions with Z51 option	13.4x1.26 inches, front; 13x1 inches, rear; cross-drilled rotors
Brake dimensions, Z06	14x1.3 inches, front; 13.4x1 inches, rear; cross-drilled rotors
Fuel tank	18 gallons
Suspension	short- and long-arm (SLA) double wishbone cast-aluminum control arms, transverse composite leaf springs, stabilizer bars front and rear, monotube shock absorbers, Active Handling electronics (stiffer springs and shocks, thicker stabilizer bars with Z51 option)
Steering	speed-sensitive, magnetic power-assisted rack and pinion (16.1:1 ratio)
Engine (LS3)	6.2L (376 cubic inches) sequential fuel injected (SFI) V8 with overhead valves and cast-aluminum cylinder block and heads, 10.7:1 compression
LS3 bore and stroke	4.00x3.62 inches
LS3 output	430 horsepower at 5,900 rpm, 424 lb-ft of torque at 4,600 rpm (436/428 with NPP dual mode exhaust option)
Engine (LS7)	7.0L (427 cubic inches) SFI V8 with overhead valves and cast-aluminum cylinder block and heads, 11:1 compression, dry-sump oiling
LS7 bore and stroke	4.125x4.00 inches
LS7 output	505 horsepower at 6,300 rpm, 470 ft-lbs of torque at 4,800 rpm
Standard transmission	six-speed manual with 2.66:1 low
Transmission with Z51 option	six-speed manual with 2.97:1 low
Optional transmission	six-speed automatic with paddle shift
Axle ratio	3.42:1 (2.56:1 with paddle-shift automatic)

Now the Corvette has improved tactile feel to go with its outrageous performance.

"Corvette is an uncompromising sports car that rewards its owners with impeccable performance and great comfort," bragged Ed Peper. "The changes and enhancements to the 2008 Corvette reflect continual improvements that speak to Chevrolet's unflagging commitment to building the best sports car—and with nearly 55 years of experience, the Corvette just keeps getting better and better."

Technical betterment included improved shift effort for the six-speed manual, quicker shifts for the automatic, and greatly enhanced steering. That latter feature alone was enough to have *Car and Driver's* Larry Webster writing home to ma. "The [latest] Vette no longer has to be muscled through the turn," he scribbled. "It now glides along with far less drama. Now the Corvette has improved tactile feel to go with its outrageous performance."

The latest new C6 also wore new standard wheels, featuring a split-spoke design originally shown off (with a Sterling Silver finish) on the 2007 Indy pace car. Sparkle Silver was the standard finish in 2008; Competition Gray was optional. Polished forged-aluminum wheels were new on the 2008 options list.

Improvements inside consisted of freshened trim for the door sills and instrument panel center plate, joined by a host of new standard equipment: OnStar, XM satellite radio, an auto-dimming rearview mirror (for coupes), and an audio input jack for all radio systems save for those additionally complemented with navigation assistance. Optional interior equipment package choices, first offered in 2001, expanded in 2008 as the 2LT and 3LT groups listed (along with their 2LZ counterparts in Z06 ranks) in 2006 and 2007 were joined by an even tastier 4LT deal.

Among 2LT features were side airbags, leather upholstery, a six-way power seat for the passenger, and a wireless cell phone link. The 3LT option included all this plus head-up instrument display, memory convenience controls, heated seats, a Bose AM/FM stereo with six-disc CD changer, and a tilt-telescopic steering wheel. The new 4LT package added special interior trim and extra leather touches to all this. A 3LZ equipment group also joined the carryover 2LZ option for the 2008 Z06.

Much bigger news on the Z06 front hit the front page midyear in 2008 after production of Chevrolet's "427 Special Edition" Corvette (RPO Z44) commenced. Even though the Z06's LS7 V-8 technically displaced more like 428 cubic inches (427.6), engineers just couldn't help but make the connection between this brute and the vaunted big-block bullies that had made earlier Corvettes kings of the streets from 1966 to 1969. Along with Crystal Red tintcoat paint and exclusive chrome wheels, all 505 Z44 Z06 coupes built for 2008 featured hood/fascia graphics and badges that were plainly reminiscent of the "stinger" hoods seen on the 1967 427 Vette.

"The heritage of the 427 designation with the Corvette is legendary," explained Corvette product manager Harlan Charles. "Recognizing the tie-in of the original 427 engine and the LS7's displacement has been on the Corvette team's mind since the Z06 was introduced, and we're thrilled to express it in this special model."

The Z44 price was $84,195, and for that stack of cash, a customer also received the 3LZ interior accented with a console armrest signed and numbered by Wil Cooksey, who retired in March 2008 after 15 years of shepherding Corvette production in Bowling Green. Chevy's $1,750 navigation system was the only option.

Opposite top
New standard wheels, first shown off on the 2007 Indy pace car wearing a Sterling Silver finish, appeared on the 2008 model, this time done in Sparkle Silver. A Competition Gray finish was optional. A polished forged aluminum wheel was a new option that year.

Opposite bottom
Both OnStar navigation and XM satellite radio became standard features inside the 2008 Corvette. Revised trim for the doors sills and instrument panel center plate appeared too.

Above
Okay, so the Z06's LS7 V-8 technically displaces about 427.6 cubic inches. But Chevy product planners couldn't resist honoring past big-block Corvette glories with their "427 Special Edition" coupe, introduced midyear in 2008 with exclusive chrome wheels, Crystal Red tintcoat paint, unique graphics, and Wil Cooksey's signature. Cooksey retired in March 2008 after 15 years as Bowling Green plant manager.

Right
One of the most eye-catching wheel designs to ever appear on a Vette were these chrome units that came standard on all the '08 505 Z44 Z06 coupes.

Yet another special-edition Corvette made the scene in 2008, this one via Hertz. GM supplied Hertz with 500 "ZHZ" coupes that year, all featuring a black-accented yellow finish to honor the veteran rental car firm. All also were equipped with 436-horse LS3 V-8s backed by paddle-shift automatics. Another 375 similarly adorned ZHZ convertibles were rented out by Hertz in 2009.

2009

On February 11, 2009, Chevrolet introduced its latest Stingray concept vehicle at the Chicago Auto Show. Modeled after Bill Mitchell's sensational show car of the same name, the new Stingray appeared as Sideswipe in the 2009 summer blockbuster *Transformers: Revenge of the Fallen.*

Reportedly on GM Design Center drawing boards for some six years, the 2009 Stingray also reminded some witnesses of Mitchell's regular-production 1963 Sting Ray with its split rear window layout. Ties to Italian exotics were evident as well thanks to its upward-opening, scissor-style, carbon-fiber doors.

Meanwhile, off-stage, "rollover" once again was the big word out of Bowling Green in 2009, as nearly nothing notable marked the arrival of the base fifth-edition C6, save for the introduction of optional Bluetooth phone connectivity for those who apparently had better things to do than fully enjoy the ride in their fantastic plastic two-seaters.

Introduced in the summer of 2008 as a 2009 model, the wretchedly excessive, reborn ZR1 was turning heads everywhere it went, but that story will need to wait for another page or so. Back in the real world, Chevy's 2009 LS3 Corvette looked an awful lot like its predecessor—not a bad thing considering it also still appeared to be one mighty bang for the buck. Same for its 505-horse Z06 running mate, the former cock of the walk now almost lost in the shadow of Chevy's latest biggest, baddest Vette yet.

With further apologies to the new ZR1, about all that remained to report in 2009 was the debut of two more limited-edition models: the Competition Sport Package and GT1 Championship Edition. Specifically created for "enthusiasts who attend driving schools and track events," the Competition Sport option was offered for the Z06 1LZ and 436-horse 1LT coupe, with prices listed at $77,500 and $55,655, respectively.

In both cases, the package included special striping, wheels, and headlamp covers, as well as various Corvette Racing logos inside and out. LS3 versions were painted either Arctic White or Blade Silver; their Z06 running mates came in black or Blade Silver. Added as well to LS3 coupes (along with the dual-mode exhausts) was the Z51 package, a differential cooler, head-up display, red-

2009

Specifications	2009
Model availability	coupe (with removable roof panel), convertible, and Z06 coupe (with fixed magnesium roof)
Construction	composite body on hydroformed steel frame with aluminum and magnesium structural components (unique carbon-fiber body panels and hydroformed aluminum frame for Z06)
Wheelbase	105.7 inches
Length	174.6 inches (175.6 inches, Z06)
Width	72.6 inches (75.9 inches, Z06)
Height	49 inches
Track (front/rear, in inches)	62.1/60.7 (coupe and convertible); 63.5/62.5 (Z06)
Curb weight	3,217 (coupe), 3,246 (convertible), 3,210 pounds (Z06)
Wheels (coupe and convertible)	18 x 8.5 inches, front; 19 x10 inches, rear
Wheels (Z06)	18 x 9.5 inches, front; 19 x 12 inches, rear
Tires (coupe and convertible)	Goodyear Eagle F1 Supercar Extended Mobility (EMT); P245/40ZR18 front, P285/35ZR19 rear
Tires (Z06)	Goodyear Eagle F1 Supercar EMT; P275/35ZR18 front, P325/30ZR19 rear
Brakes	power-assisted four-wheel discs with ABS and electronic traction control
Brake dimensions	12.8x1.26 inches, front; 12x1 inches, rear
Brake dimensions with Z51 option	13.4x1.26 inches, front; 13x1 inches, rear; cross-drilled rotors
Brake dimensions, Z06	14x1.3 inches, front; 13.4x1 inches, rear; cross-drilled rotors
Fuel tank	18 gallons
Suspension	short- and long-arm (SLA) double wishbone cast-aluminum control arms, transverse composite leaf springs, stabilizer bars front and rear, monotube shock absorbers, Active Handling electronics (stiffer springs and shocks, thicker stabilizer bars with Z51 option)
Steering	speed-sensitive, magnetic power-assisted rack and pinion (16.1:1 ratio)
Engine (LS3)	6.2L (376 cubic inches) sequential fuel injected (SFI) V8 with overhead valves and cast-aluminum cylinder block and heads, 10.7:1 compression
LS3 bore and stroke	4.00x3.62 inches
LS3 output	430 horsepower at 5,900 rpm, 424 lb-ft of torque at 4,600 rpm
Engine (LS7)	7.0L (427 cubic inches) SFI V8 with overhead valves and cast-aluminum cylinder block and heads, 11:1 compression, dry-sump oiling
LS7 bore and stroke	4.125x4.00 inches
LS7 output	505 horsepower at 6,300 rpm, 470 ft-lbs of torque at 4,800 rpm
Standard transmission	six-speed manual with 2.66:1 low
Transmission with Z51 option	six-speed manual with 2.97:1 low
Optional transmission	six-speed automatic with paddle shift
Axle ratio	3.42:1 (2.56:1 with paddle-shift automatic)

Above left
The Corvette lineup remained impressive as ever in 2009 with the 505-horsepower Z06 coupe (pictured) still in action, along with the base 430-horse LS3 model, again available with or without a top. The new-for-2009 ZR1 (introduced the year before) represented an outrageous exclamation point to the latest chapter in Chevy's long-running Corvette tale.

Above
Chevrolet introduced the Competition Sport Package for the 2009 Corvette Coupe 1LT and Z06 1LZ models. It included Competition Gray exterior stripes, wheels, and headlamps; Corvette Racing "Jake" and CSR logos on B-pillar, headrest, and center armrest; ebony interior with titanium embroidery; Corvette racing pedals; a special engine cover; and racing style numbers based on build sequence (to be installed by customer).

painted brake calipers, and the Z06 spoiler. Production was 52 for the LS3 Competition Sport, 20 for its 505-horse cousin.

Available in black or Velocity Yellow, the GT1 Championship Edition served as a commemorative exclamation point to 10 years of domination in American Le Mans Series racing, where Corvettes piled up more than 70 wins and scored eight GT1 Manufacturers Championships. Another five GT1-class wins also came in France at the real Le Mans endurance event during that time.

The GT1 package was listed for 4LT coupes/convertibles and 3LZ Z06 coupes, with LS3 versions incorporating the Z51 performance package, dual-mode exhausts, and Z06 spoiler. In all cases, Corvette Racing graphics graced the exterior, chrome wheels went on at the corners, and inside was ebony leather with exclusive yellow accent stitching. "GT1" embroidery complemented the seats, instrument panel, and center armrest, and the engine was topped by a special "carbon pattern" cover sporting yellow "Corvette" lettering.

Pricing was $65,310 for the GT1 LS3 convertible, $71,815 for its topless counterpart, and $86,385 for the Championship Edition Z06. Production was 53, 17, and 55, respectively.

Above
Yet another special model, the GT1 Championship Edition, emerged in 2009 to honor 10 years of domination in American Le Mans Series racing. This package was available for top-shelf 4LT LS3 coupes/convertibles and 3LZ Z06 coupes.

Below left
The GT1 edition's seats, dash, and instrument panel received special "GT1" embroidery as well as the menacing Corvette Racing logo . . .

Below right
. . . while the Corvette's total domination of the ALMS GT1 class was displayed in the form of irrefutable numerical evidence.

2009 ZR1

Specifications	2009ZR1
Model availability	hatchback coupe with fixed magnesium roof
Construction	composite body with carbon-fiber panels on hydroformed aluminum frame with carbon fiber hood, fenders, roof, roof bow, rockers, and splitter
Wheelbase	105.7 inches
Length	176.2 inches
Width	75.9 inches
Height	49 inches
Track (front/rear, in inches)	63.5/62.5
Curb weight	3,350 pounds
Wheels	19 x 10 inches, front; 20 x 12 inches, rear
Tires	Michelin Pilot Sport PS2 ZP; P285/30ZR-19 front, P335/25ZR-20 rear
Brakes	power-assisted four-wheel drilled ceramic discs with ABS and electronic traction control; six-piston calipers front, four-piston calipers rear
Brake dimensions	15.5 inches, front; 15.0 inches, rear
Fuel tank	18 gallons
Suspension	short- and long-arm (SLA) double wishbone cast-aluminum control arms, transverse composite leaf springs, stabilizer bars front and rear, monotube shock absorbers, Magnetic Selective Ride Control
Steering	speed-sensitive, magnetic power-assisted rack and pinion (16.1:1 ratio)
Engine (LS9)	6.2L (376 cubic inches) supercharged SFI V8 with overhead valves and cast-aluminum cylinder block and heads, dry-sump oiling
Bore and stroke	4.06x4.00 inches
Compression	9.1:1
Output	638 horsepower at 6,500 rpm, 604 lb-ft of torque at 3,800 rpm
Standard transmission	close-ratio six-speed manual with 2.29:1 low
Axle ratio	3.42:1

2009 ZR1

In 2006, *AutoWeek* called the Z06 "the best supercar buy of all time." But those words apparently still weren't good enough for General Motors CEO Rick Wagoner. If Chevy could offer so much Corvette for 60 grand, he thought, what could David Hill and right-hand man Tadge Juechter do for 100 Gs? Hill retired in January 2006, leaving his assistant to answer Wagoner's question with the aforementioned world-class ZR1.

Base priced at $106,000, Chevy's latest ZR1 far and away ranked as the most expensive GM product ever. But so what? At an unworldly 638 horsepower, it was also the most powerful, and in turn it didn't take a rocket scientist to determine that all those ponies made this major investment The General's fastest offering of all time.

"The ZR1 is the first Corvette to step up into the rarefied air of truly unearthly performance," claimed *Motor Trend's* Arthur St. Antoine, who additionally reported a 0–60 run of only 3.3 seconds, a quarter-mile pass at a scant 11.2 ticks (at 130.5 miles per hour), and a real top end of 200.4 miles per hour. It went without saying that the last stat also represented a GM first, and it probably wasn't the actual tip-top.

"There's something ridiculous about a street car that can do 66 miles per hour in 1st gear and has a tight-ratio 6-speed that allows for a top speed in excess of 200 miles per hour," added *Road & Track's* Shaun Bailey. "Who can afford the gasoline or the speeding tickets? However, it must be noted that for 'social responsibility,' said chief engineer Tadge Juechter, there is an electronic limiter set for 210 miles per hour. Yet if one disabled the limiter and managed to run the boost beyond 10.5 psi, the ZR1 runs out of gear at 215 mph. It's only a matter of time before a tuned ZR1 breaks that barrier."

Hand-assembled with care along with the Z06's LS7 V-8 at GM's Performance Build Center in Wixom, Michigan, the ZR1's 6.2-liter LS9 V-8 was topped by an Eaton R2300 twin-rotor supercharger specially designed to fit snugly beneath the Corvette's hood. Even with its "dual brick" intercooler system straddling it on both sides, the sixth-generation Eaton blower still stood only slightly taller than the LS3's electronic injection hardware.

On top of that, the ZR1's carbon-fiber hood featured a transparent polycarbonate panel that showed off the LS9's beautiful blue engine cover. The highly visible cover's sparkling color commemorated the "Blue Devil" reference used internally during ZR1 development, itself a nickname reportedly chosen in honor of Wagoner's alma mater, North Carolina's Duke University.

Weight-saving carbon fiber was used throughout the body to help compensate for the nearly 200 pounds of extra weight added beneath that peek-a-boo hood to help make those 638 horses. This race-bred material also made up the widened fenders, roof panel and bows, rocker moldings, and the wind-tunnel-tested splitter added to the Z06-style front fascia. A special clearcoat also was developed to allow body designers to leave the weave patterns inherent to carbon-fiber construction exposed—to further enhance the ZR1's "visual identity"—without any fears of the stuff yellowing or dulling like it normally does upon exposure to ultra violet light.

Additional highlights include a specially tuned suspension capable of more than 1.05g on the skid pad, huge 20-spoke wheels (19-inchers in front, 20s at the rear), massive Michelin Pilot Sport 2 tires, a high-capacity dual-disc clutch, and enormous carbon-ceramic Brembo discs measuring 15.5 inches across at the nose, 15 out back. Like the Z06, the ZR1 came only with a six-speed manual.

Summed up, the ZR1 not only predictably outperformed its Z06 running mate, it also offered a kinder, gentler nature. "The ZR1 is a car anyone can drive confidently and comfortably," claimed Corvette vehicle line executive Tom Wallace. "From the very beginning, refinement, balance, and compliance were targets that were as important as the car's maximum performance." According to chief engineer Juechter, "It's a supercar that doesn't sacrifice ride quality for performance."

Can you say "best buy"?

2010

Visible updates for 2010 were once again minimal, and included an always popular paint choice that returned after a six-year hiatus. Last seen in 2004 (technically speaking, it did show up on one 2005 model), Torch Red again graced the Corvette palette, ending up on 2,249 cars that year, making it 2010's second favorite choice behind black (2,929).

Beneath the skin, side airbags were made standard on all 2010 Corvettes, and the six-speed paddle-shift box was again revised, this time to allow a less fussy return to automatic mode. Easily 2010's top technical story involved the introduction of Launch Control, a system that modulated engine torque up to 100 times per second to help maximize traction during full-throttle take-offs. Launch Control came standard on all manual-trans models. And new for the 2010 ZR1 was Performance Traction Management, which integrated the existing Traction Control, Active Handling, and Selective Ride Control systems to further maximize off-the-line abilities.

Last, but certainly not least, on the new-for-2010 list was yet another revived Corvette legend, this one last seen in 1996. First used in 1963 for Zora Duntov's five all-out competition Corvettes, the "Grand Sport" badge returned 33 years later to both honor those legendary lightweights and help send the retiring C4 breed out with a high-profile bang. A little commemoration was also a part of the plan in 2010, but the main goal involved combining much of the Z06's roadworthiness with as many of the base Corvette's amenities as possible.

For starters, the custom-bodied 2010 Grand Sport was offered as either a removable-roof coupe or convertible; the purposeful Z06 came only as a fixed-roof coupe. Additionally, a Grand Sport customer could've picked either six-speed gearbox, manual, or paddle-shift auto; all Z06 drivers' souls were stirred with a stick. Manual-trans Grand Sports featured a little more standard purpose than their automatic counterparts: they

Specifications	2010
Model availability	coupe (with removable roof panel) and convertible; Grand Sport coupe (with removable roof panel) and convertible; Z06 and ZR1 coupes (with fixed magnesium roof)
Construction	composite body on hydroformed steel frame with aluminum and magnesium structural components (aluminum frame and unique carbon-fiber body panels for Z06/ZR1)
Wheelbase	105.7 inches
Length	174.6 inches (176.2 inches, Z06/ZR1/Grand Sport)
Width	72.6 inches (75.9 inches, Z06/ZR1/Grand Sport)
Height	49 inches (48.7 inches, Grand Sport)
Track (front/rear, in inches)	62.1/60.7 (coupe and convertible); 63.5/62.5 (Z06)
Curb weight	3,217 pounds (coupe), 3,246 pounds (convertible), 3,210 pounds (Z06), 3,350 pounds (ZR1), 3,311 pounds (Grand Sport coupe), 3,289 pounds (Grand Sport convertible)
Wheels (coupe and convertible)	18 x 8.5 inches, front; 19 x10 inches, rear
Wheels (Z06/Grand Sport)	18 x 9.5 inches, front; 19 x 12 inches, rear
Wheels (ZR1)	19 x 10 inches, front; 20 x 12 inches, rear
Tires (coupe and convertible)	Goodyear Eagle F1 Supercar Extended Mobility (EMT); P245/40ZR18 front, P285/35ZR19 rear
Tires (Z06)	Goodyear Eagle F1 Supercar EMT; P275/35ZR18 front, P325/30ZR19 rear
Tires (ZR1)	Michelin Pilot Sport PS2 ZP; P285/30ZR-19 front, P335/25ZR-20 rear
Tires (Grand Sport)	P285/35ZR19 front, P325/30ZR19 rear
Brakes	power-assisted four-wheel discs with ABS and electronic traction control
Brakes (ZR1)	power-assisted four-wheel drilled ceramic discs with ABS and electronic traction control; six-piston calipers front, four-piston calipers rear
Brake dimensions	12.8x1.26 inches, front; 12x1 inches, rear
Brake dimensions (Z06/Grand Sport)	14 x 1.3 inches, front; 13.4 x 1 inches, rear; cross-drilled rotors
Brake dimensions (ZR1)	15.5 inches, front; 15.0 inches, rear
Fuel tank	18 gallons
Suspension	short- and long-arm (SLA) double wishbone cast-aluminum control arms, transverse composite leaf springs, and stabilizer bars front and rear, monotube shock absorbers, Active Handling electronics (Magnetic Selective Ride control with ZR1)
Steering	speed-sensitive, magnetic power-assisted rack and pinion (16.1:1 ratio)
Engine (LS3)	6.2L (376 cubic inches) sequential fuel injected (SFI) V8 with overhead valves and cast-aluminum cylinder block and heads, 10.7:1 compression
LS3 bore and stroke	4.06x3.62 inches
LS3 output	430 horsepower at 5,900 rpm, 424 lb-ft of torque at 4,600 rpm
Engine (LS7)	7.0L (427 cubic inches) SFI V8 with overhead valves and cast-aluminum cylinder block and heads, 11:1 compression, dry-sump oiling
LS7 bore and stroke	4.125x4.00 inches
LS7 output	505 horsepower at 6,300 rpm, 470 ft-lbs of torque at 4,800 rpm
Standard transmission	six-speed manual with 2.66:1 low
Optional transmission	six-speed automatic with paddle shift
Axle ratio	3.42:1 (2.56:1 with paddle-shift automatic)

were equipped with dry-sump oiling, a rear-mounted battery, and differential cooler, items best suited, of course, for the track.

All Grand Sports were powered by the LS3, with or without optional dual-mode exhausts, and all C6 paint choices carried over as well. Setting the GS apart was a unique body, widened at the corners, with "Grand Sport" badges integrated into the front fenders and Z06-style touches (front splitter, rear spoiler) at both ends. Functional brake cooling ducts also were standard, as were special painted wheels. Chromed wheels were optional.

Standard tires were 275/35ZR18 in front, 325/30ZR19 out back. Z06-size brakes and a track-ready suspension completed the package. A Grand Sport buyer also could've added the Heritage option, which featured two-tone seats and competition-style front fender hash marks.

As the Grand Sport arrived, the Z51 performance handling package departed. Grand Sport pricing was $55,720 for the coupe, $59,530 for the convertible. Production was 3,707 coupes, 2,335 convertibles.

"For track use, the Z06 Carbon is the best balanced Corvette yet," explained Tadge Juechter.

2011

2011

Specifications	2011
Model availability	coupe (with removable roof panel) and convertible; Grand Sport coupe (with removable roof panel) and convertible; Z06 and ZR1 coupes (with fixed magnesium roof)
Construction	composite body on hydroformed steel frame with aluminum and magnesium structural components (aluminum frame and unique carbon-fiber body panels for Z06/ZR1)
Wheelbase	105.7 inches
Length	174.6 inches (176.2 inches, Z06/ZR1/Grand Sport)
Width	72.6 inches (75.9 inches, Z06/ZR1/Grand Sport)
Height	49 inches (48.7 inches, Grand Sport)
Track (front/rear, in inches)	62.1/60.7 (coupe and convertible); 63.5/62.5 (Z06)
Curb weight (in pounds)	3,217 pounds (coupe), 3,246 pounds (convertible), 3,210 pounds (Z06), 3,350 pounds (ZR1), 3,311 (Grand Sport coupe), 3,289 (Grand Sport convertible)
Wheels (coupe and convertible)	18 x 8.5 inches, front; 19 x10 inches, rear
Wheels (Z06/Grand Sport, in inches)	18 x 9.5 inches, front; 19 x 12 inches, rear
Wheels (ZR1, in inches)	19 x 10 inches, front; 20 x 12 inches, rear
Tires (coupe and convertible)	Goodyear Eagle F1 Supercar Extended Mobility (EMT); P245/40ZR18 front, P285/35ZR19 rear
Tires (Z06)	Goodyear Eagle F1 Supercar EMT; P275/35ZR18 front, P325/30ZR19 rear
Tires (ZR1)	Michelin Pilot Sport PS2 ZP; P285/30ZR-19 front, P335/25ZR-20 rear
Tires (Grand Sport)	P285/35ZR18 front, P325/30ZR19 rear
Brakes	power-assisted four-wheel discs with ABS and electronic traction control
Brakes (ZR1)	power-assisted four-wheel drilled ceramic discs with ABS and electronic traction control; six-piston calipers front, four-piston calipers rear
Brake dimensions	12.8x1.26 inches, front; 12x1 inches, rear
Brake dimensions (Z06/Grand Sport)	14 x 1.3 inches, front; 13.4 x 1 inches, rear; cross-drilled rotors
Brake dimensions (ZR1)	15.5 inches, front; 15.0 inches, rear
Fuel tank	18 gallons
Suspension	short- and long-arm (SLA) double wishbone cast-aluminum control arms, transverse composite leaf springs, and stabilizer bars front and rear, monotube shock absorbers, Active Handling electronics (Magnetic Selective Ride control with ZR1)
Steering	speed-sensitive, magnetic power-assisted rack and pinion (16.1:1 ratio)
Engine (LS3)	6.2L (376 cubic inches) sequential fuel injected (SFI) V8 with overhead valves and cast-aluminum cylinder block and heads, 10.7:1 compression
LS3 bore and stroke	4.06x3.62 inches
LS3 output	430 horsepower at 5,900 rpm, 424 lb-ft of torque at 4,600 rpm
Engine (LS7)	7.0L (427 cubic inches) SFI V8 with overhead valves and cast-aluminum cylinder block and heads, 11:1 compression, dry-sump oiling
LS7 bore and stroke	4.125x4.00 inches
LS7 output	505 horsepower at 6,300 rpm, 470 ft-lbs of torque at 4,800 rpm
Standard transmission	six-speed manual with 2.66:1 low
Optional transmission	six-speed automatic w/Paddle Shift
Axle ratio	3.42:1 (2.56:1 with automatic)

2011

The 2010 lineup rolled on unchanged into 2011, with the 430-horse LS3 coupe and convertible again forging the way, followed a second time around by the Grand Sport coupe and convertible. The two manual-trans-only fixed-roof coupes, Z06 and ZR1, carried on too, still with 505 and 638 horsepower, respectively.

Mixing and matching model features in 2010 to produce the Grand Sport proved so much fun for product planners that they tried the trick again. And again. RPO Z07, the Ultimate Performance package, made the ZR1's adaptive suspension, carbon-ceramic brakes, and wheel/tire combo available to Z06 customers. Available as well for the 505-horse Corvette was a new Carbon Fiber package (CFZ) that added most of the ZR1's lightweight body parts. Grand Sport buyers, in turn, could've opted for Magnetic Ride Control.

Further in-breeding resulted in Chevrolet's latest special C6, the Z06 Carbon Limited Edition, a hybrid that not only served to commemorate the 50th anniversary of the Corvette's first appearance at Le Mans but also could've perhaps made competition history itself. "For track use, the Z06 Carbon is the best balanced Corvette yet," explained Tadge Juechter. "It combines the lightweight and naturally-aspirated Z06 engine with the road-holding and braking of the ZR1."

Indeed, the ZR1's Magnetic Selective Ride Control and big Brembo carbon-ceramic brakes (fitted with specific dark gray metallic calipers) were standard for the Carbon Limited Edition, as were black 20-spoke wheels measuring 19 inches wide in front, 20 in back. Included too were the CFZ body parts, a special leather/suede interior, various specific logs, and black-accented headlamps. Only two exterior finishes were offered: Inferno Orange and Supersonic Blue. Production ended at 252.

How many more times the C6 can be repackaged remains to be seen as these words go to press in the summer of 2011. Early announcements of upcoming changes for 2012 included the addition of Michelin PS Cup tires for optional Z06 and ZR1 performance packages, new "personalization" options (Carlisle Blue Metallic paint and specially colored brake calipers), a new steering wheel, and revised seats. In April 2011, Chevrolet also announced the 2012 availability of its Centennial Edition Corvette, created to help mark the parent company's 100th

birthday. Along with its "sinister" (Chevy's own words) Carbon Flash Metallic finish, the Centennial model (RPO ZLC) will feature unique Satin Black wheels accented by red brake calipers and Magnetic Selective Ride Control. Red-stitched black leather will go inside, and Louis Chevrolet's image will appear on the car's B-pillars and wheel hubs. The ZLC option will be offered for all members of the Corvette fraternity: base, Grand Sport, Z06, and ZR1.

In keeping with tradition, Chevy's latest next-generation Corvette is late again for various reasons, not the least of which were the financial difficulties GM stumbled into in 2009. But no worries, mate. In May 2011, corporate officials announced they would invest $131 million to refurbish the Bowling Green plant, with the goal being to have it ready to start building the C7, hopefully soon.

Stay tuned.

Appendix
Options

1953 Options

CODE	DESCRIPTION	QTY	RETAIL $
2934	Base Corvette Roadster	300	$3,498.00
101A	Heater	300	91.40
102B	AM Radio, signal seeking	300	145.15

1954 Options

CODE	DESCRIPTION	QTY	RETAIL $
2934	Base Corvette Roadster	3,640	$2,774.00
100	Directional Signal	3,640	16.75
101A	Heater	3,640	91.40
102A	AM Radio, signal seeking	3,640	145.15
290B	Whitewall Tires, 6.70x15	3,640	26.90
313M	Powerglide Automatic Transmission	3,640	178.35
420A	Parking Brake Alarm	3,640	5.65
421A	Courtesy Lights	3,640	4.05
422A	Windshield Washer	3,640	11.85

1955 Options

CODE	DESCRIPTION	QTY	RETAIL $
2934-6	Base Corvette Roadster, six-cylinder	7	$2,774.00
2934-8	Base Corvette Roadster, V8	693	2,909.00
100	Directional Signal	700	16.75
101	Heater	700	91.40
102A	AM Radio, signal seeking	700	145.15
290B	Whitewall Tires, 6.70x15	–	26.90
313	Powerglide Automatic Transmission	–	178.35
420A	Parking Brake Alarm	700	5.65
421A	Courtesy Lights	700	4.05
422A	Windshield Washers	700	11.85

1956 Options

CODE	DESCRIPTION	QTY	RETAIL $
2934	Base Corvette Convertible	3,467	$3,120.00
101	Heater	–	123.65
102	AM Radio, signal seeking	2,717	198.90
107	Parking Brake Alarm	2,685	5.40
108	Courtesy Lights	2,775	8.65
109	Windshield Washers	2,815	11.85
290	Whitewall Tires, 6.70x15	–	32.30
313	Powerglide Automatic Transmission	–	188.50
419	Auxiliary Hardtop	2,076	215.20
426	Power Windows	547	64.60
440	Two-Tone Paint Combination	1,259	48.45
684	Heavy Duty Racing Suspension	51	780.10
685	4-Speed Manual Transmission	664	188.30

1957 Options

CODE	DESCRIPTION	QTY	RETAIL $
2934	Base Corvette Convertible	6,339	$3,176.32
101	Heater	5,373	118.40
102	AM Radio, signal seeking	3,635	199.10
107	Parking Brake Alarm	1,873	5.40
108	Courtesy Lights	2,849	8.65
109	Windshield Washers	2,555	11.85
276	Wheels, 15x5.5 (5)	51	15.10
290	Whitewall Tires, 6.70x15	5,019	31.60
303	3-Speed Manual Transmission, close ratio	4,282	0.00
313	Powerglide Automatic Transmission	1,393	188.30
419	Auxiliary Hardtop	4,055	215.20
426	Power Windows	379	59.20
440	Two-Tone Paint Combination	2,794	19.40
469A	283ci, 245hp Engine (2x4 carburetors)	2,045	150.65
469C	283ci, 270hp Engine (2x4 carburetors)	1,621	182.95
473	Power Operated Folding Top	1,336	139.90
579A	283ci, 250hp Engine (fuel injection)	182	484.20
579B	283ci, 283hp Engine (fuel injection)	713	484.20
579C	283ci, 250hp Engine (fuel injection)	102	484.20
579E	283ci, 283hp Engine (fuel injection)	43	726.30
677	Positraction Rear Axle, 3.70:1	327	48.45
678	Positraction Rear Axle, 4.11:1	1,772	48.45
679	Positraction Rear Axle, 4.56:1	–	48.45
684	Heavy Duty Racing Suspension	51	780.10
685	4-Speed Manual Transmission	664	188.30

1958 Options

CODE	DESCRIPTION	QTY	RETAIL $
867	Base Corvette Convertible	9,168	$3,591.00
101	Heater	8,014	96.85
102	AM Radio, signal seeking	6,142	144.45
107	Parking Brake Alarm	2,883	5.40
108	Courtesy Light	4,600	6.50
109	Windshield Washers	3,834	16.15
276	Wheels, 15x5.5 (5)	404	0.00
290	Whitewall Tires, 6.70x15	7,428	31.55
313	Powerglide Automatic Transmission	2,057	188.30
419	Auxiliary Hardtop	5,607	215.20
426	Power Windows	649	59.20
440	Two-Tone Exterior Paint	3,422	16.15
469	283ci, 245hp Engine (2x4 carburetors)	2,436	150.65
469C	283ci, 270hp Engine (2x4 carburetors)	978	182.95
473	Power Operated Folding Top	1,090	139.90
579	283ci, 290hp Engine (fuel injection)	504	484.20
579D	283ci, 290hp Engine (fuel injection)	1,007	484.20
677	Positraction Rear Axle, 3.70:1	1,123	48.45
678	Positraction Rear Axle, 4.11:1	2,518	48.45
679	Positraction Rear Axle, 4.56:1	370	48.45
684	Heavy Duty Brakes and Suspension	144	780.10
685	4-Speed Manual Transmission	3,764	215.20

Printed with permission from *Corvette Black Book 1953–2006*, MBI Publishing Company 0-7603-2446-8

1959 Options

CODE	DESCRIPTION	QTY	RETAIL $
867	Base Corvette Convertible	9,670	$3,875.00
101	Heater	8,909	102.25
102	AM Radio, signal seeking	7,001	149.80
107	Parking Brake Alarm	3,601	5.40
108	Courtesy Light	3,601	6.50
109	Windshield Washers	7,929	16.15
121	Radiator Fan Clutch	67	21.55
261	Sunshades	3,722	10.80
276	Wheels, 15x5.5 (5)	214	0.00
290	Whitewall Tires, 6.70x15	8,173	31.55
313	Powerglide Automatic Transmission	1,878	199.10
419	Auxiliary Hardtop	5,481	236.75
426	Power Windows	587	59.20
440	Two-Tone Exterior Paint	2,931	16.15
469	283ci, 245hp Engine (2x4 carburetors)	1,417	150.65
469C	283ci, 270hp Engine (2x4 carburetors)	1,846	182.95
473	Power Operated Folding Top	661	139.90
579	283ci, 250hp Engine (fuel injection)	175	484.20
579D	283ci, 290hp Engine (fuel injection)	745	484.20
675	Positraction Rear Axle	4,170	48.45
684	Heavy Duty Brakes and Suspension	142	425.05
685	4-Speed Manual Transmission	4,175	188.30
686	Metallic Brakes	333	26.90
1408	Blackwall Tires, 6.70x15 nylon	–	–
1625	24 Gallon Fuel Tank	–	–

1960 Options

CODE	DESCRIPTION	QTY	RETAIL $
867	Base Corvette Convertible	10,261	$3,872.00
101	Heater	9,808	102.25
102	AM Radio, signal seeking	8,166	137.75
107	Parking Brake Alarm	4,051	5.40
108	Courtesy Light	6,774	6.50
109	Windshield Washers	7,205	16.15
121	Temperature Controlled Radiator Fan	2,711	21.55
261	Sunshades	5,276	10.80
276	Wheels, 15x5.5 (5)	246	0.00
290	Whitewall Tires, 6.70x15	9,104	31.55
313	Powerglide Automatic Transmission	1,766	199.10
419	Auxiliary Hardtop	5,147	236.75
426	Power Windows	544	59.20
440	Two-Tone Exterior Paint	3,312	16.15
469	283ci, 245hp Engine (2x4 carburetors)	1,211	150.65
469C	283ci, 270hp Engine (2x4 carburetors)	2,364	182.95
473	Power Operated Folding Top	512	139.90
579	283ci, 250hp Engine (fuel injection)	100	484.20
579D	283ci, 290hp Engine (fuel injection)	759	484.20
675	Positraction Rear Axle	5,231	43.05
685	4-Speed Manual Transmission	5,328	188.30
686	Metallic Brakes	920	26.90
687	Heavy Duty Brakes and Suspension	119	333.60
1408	Blackwall Tires, 6.70x15 nylon	–	15.75
1625A	24 Gallon Fuel Tank	–	161.40

1961 Options

CODE	DESCRIPTION	QTY	RETAIL $
867	Base Corvette Convertible	10,939	$3,934.00
101	Heater	10,671	102.25
102	AM Radio, signal seeking	9,316	137.75
242	Positive Crankcase Ventilation	–	5.40
276	Wheels, 15x5.5 (5)	337	0.00
290	Whitewall Tires, 6.70x15	9,780	31.55
313	Powerglide Automatic Transmission	1,458	199.10
353	283ci, 275hp Engine (fuel injection)	118	484.20
354	283ci, 315hp Engine (fuel injection)	1,462	484.20
419	Auxiliary Hardtop	5,680	236.75
426	Power Windows	698	59.20
440	Two-Tone Exterior Paint	3,351	16.15
468	283ci, 270hp Engine (2x4 carburetor)	2,827	182.95
469	283ci, 245hp Engine (2x4 carburetor)	1,175	150.65
473	Power Operated Folding Top	442	161.40
675	Positraction Rear Axle	6,915	43.05
685	4-Speed Manual Transmission	7,013	188.30
686	Metallic Brakes	1,402	37.70
687	Heavy Duty Brakes and Suspension	233	333.60
1408	Blackwall Tires, 6.70x15 nylon	–	15.75
1625	24 Gallon Fuel Tank	–	161.40

1962 Options

CODE	DESCRIPTION	QTY	RETAIL $
867	Base Corvette Convertible	14,531	$4,038.00
102	AM Radio, signal seeking	13,076	137.75
203	Rear Axle, 3.08:1 ratio	–	0.00
242	Positive Crankcase Ventilation	–	5.40
276	Wheels, 15x5.5 (5)	561	0.00
313	Powerglide Automatic Transmission	1,532	199.10
396	327ci, 340hp Engine	4,412	107.60
419	Auxiliary Hardtop	8,074	236.75
426	Power Windows	995	59.20
441	Direct Flow Exhaust System	2,934	0.00
473	Power Operate Folding Top	350	139.90
488	24 Gallon Fuel Tank	65	118.40
582	327ci, 360hp Engine (fuel injection)	1,918	484.20
583	327ci, 300hp Engine	3,294	53.80
675	Positraction Rear Axle	14,232	43.05
685	4-Speed Manual Transmission	11,318	188.30
686	Metallic Brakes	2,799	37.70
687	Heavy Duty Brakes and Steering	246	333.60
1832	Whitewall Tires, 6.70x15	–	31.55
1833	Blackwall Tires, 6.70x15 nylon	–	15.70

1963 Options

RPO #	DESCRIPTION	QTY	RETAIL $
837	Base Corvette Sport Coupe	10,594	$4,252.00
867	Base Corvette Convertible	10,919	4,037.00
898	Genuine Leather Seats	1,114	80.70
941	Sebring Silver Exterior Paint	3,516	80.70

1963 Options (continued)

RPO #	DESCRIPTION	QTY	RETAIL $
A01	Soft Ray Tinted Glass, all windows	629	16.15
A02	Soft Ray Tinted Glass, windshield	470	10.80
A31	Power Windows	3,742	59.20
C07	Auxiliary Hardtop (for convertible)	5,739	236.75
C48	Heater and Defroster Deletion (credit)	124	-100.00
C60	Air Conditioning	278	421.80
G81	Positraction Rear Axle, all ratios	17,554	43.05
G91	Special Highway Axle, 3.08:1 ratio	211	2.20
J50	Power Brakes	3,336	43.05
J65	Sintered Metallic Brakes	5,310	37.70
L75	327ci, 300hp Engine	8,033	53.80
L76	327ci, 340hp Engine	6,978	107.60
L84	327ci, 360hp Engine (fuel injection)	2,610	430.40
M20	4-Speed Manual Transmission	17,973	188.30
M35	Powerglide Automatic Transmission	2,621	199.10
N03	36 Gallon Fuel Tank (for coupe)	63	202.30
N11	Off Road Exhaust System	–	37.70
N34	Woodgrained Plastic Steering Wheel	130	16.15
N40	Power Steering	3,063	75.35
P48	Cast Aluminum Knock-Off Wheels (5)	–	322.80
P91	Blackwall Tires, 6.70x15, (nylon cord)	412	15.70
P92	Whitewall Tires, 6.70x15 (rayon cord)	19,383	31.55
T86	Back-up Lamps	318	10.80
U65	Signal Seeking AM Radio	11,368	137.75
U69	AM-FM Radio	9,178	174.35
Z06	Special Performance Equipment	199	1,818.45

1964 Options

RPO #	DESCRIPTION	QTY	RETAIL $
837	Base Corvette Sport Coupe	8,304	$4,252.00
867	Base Corvette Convertible	13,925	4,037.00
–	Genuine Leather Seats	1,334	80.70
A01	Soft Ray Tinted Glass, all windows	6,031	16.15
A02	Soft Ray Tinted Glass, windshield	6,387	10.80
A31	Power Windows	3,706	59.20
C07	Auxiliary Hardtop (for convertible)	7,023	236.75
C48	Heater and Defroster Deletion (credit)	60	-100.00
C60	Air Conditioning	1,988	421.80
F40	Special Front and Rear Suspension	82	37.70
G81	Positraction Rear Axle, all ratios	18,279	43.05
G91	Special Highway Axle, 3.08:1 ratio	2,310	2.20
J50	Power Brakes	2,270	43.05
J56	Special Sintered Metallic Brake Package	29	629.50
J65	Sintered Metallic Brakes, power	4,780	53.80
K66	Transistor Ignition System	552	75.35
L75	327ci, 300hp Engine	10,471	53.80
L76	327ci, 365hp Engine	7,171	107.60
L84	327ci, 375hp Engine (fuel injection)	1,325	538.00
M20	4-Speed Manual Transmission	19,034	188.30
M35	Powerglide Automatic Transmission	2,480	199.10
N03	36 Gallon Fuel Tank (for coupe)	38	202.30
N11	Off Road Exhaust System	1,953	37.70

1964 Options (continued)

RPO #	DESCRIPTION	QTY	RETAIL $
N40	Power Steering	3,126	75.35
P48	Cast Aluminum Knock-Off Wheels (5)	806	322.80
P91	Blackwall Tires, 6.70x15 (nylon cord)	372	15.70
P92	Whitewall Tires, 6.70x15 (rayon cord)	19,977	31.85
T86	Back-up Lamps	11,085	10.80
U69	AM-FM Radio	20,934	176.50

1965 Options

RPO #	DESCRIPTION	QTY	RETAIL $
19437	Base Corvette Sport Coupe	8,186	$4,321.00
19467	Base Corvette Convertible	15,378	4,106.00
–	Genuine Leather Seats	2,128	80.70
A01	Soft Ray Tinted Glass, all windows	8,752	16.15
A02	Soft Ray Tinted Glass, windshield	7,624	10.80
A31	Power Windows	3,809	59.20
C07	Auxiliary Hardtop (for convertible)	7,787	236.75
C48	Heater and Defroster Deletion (credit)	39	-100.00
C60	Air Conditioning	2,423	421.80
F40	Special Front and Rear Suspension	975	37.70
G81	Positraction Rear Axle, all ratios	19,965	43.05
G91	Special Highway Axle, 3.08:1 ratio	1,886	2.20
J50	Power Brakes	4,044	43.05
J61	Drum Brakes (substitution credit)	316	-64.50
K66	Transistor Ignition System	3,686	75.35
L75	327ci, 300hp Engine	8,358	53.80
L76	327ci, 365hp Engine	5,011	129.15
L78	396ci, 425hp Engine	2,157	292.70
L79	327ci, 350hp Engine	4,716	107.60
L84	327ci, 375hp Engine (fuel injection)	771	538.00
M20	4-Speed Manual Transmission	21,107	188.30
M35	Powerglide Automatic Transmission	2,021	199.10
N03	36 Gallon Fuel Tank (for coupe)	41	202.30
N11	Off Road Exhaust System	2,468	37.70
N14	Side Mount Exhaust System	759	134.50
N32	Teakwood Steering Wheel	2,259	48.45
N36	Telescopic Steering Column	3,917	43.05
N40	Power Steering	3,236	96.85
P48	Cast Aluminum Knock-Off Wheels (5)	1,116	322.80
P91	Blackwall Tires, 7.75x15 (nylon cord)	168	15.70
P92	Whitewall Tires, 7.75x15 (rayon cord)	19,300	31.85
T01	Goldwall Tires, 7.75x15 (nylon cord)	989	50.05
U69	AM-FM Radio	22,113	203.40
Z01	Comfort and Convenience Group	15,397	16.15

1966 Options

RPO #	DESCRIPTION	QTY	RETAIL $
19437	Base Corvette Sport Coupe	9,958	$4,295.00
19467	Base Corvette Convertible	17,762	4,084.00
–	Genuine Leather Seats	2,002	79.00
A01	Soft Ray Tinted Glass, all windows	11,859	15.80
A02	Soft Ray Tinted Glass, windshield	9,270	10.55
A31	Power Windows	4,562	57.95
A82	Headrests	1,033	42.15
A85	Shoulder Belts	37	26.35
C07	Auxiliary Hardtop (for convertible)	8,463	231.75
C48	Heater and Defroster Deletion (credit)	54	-97.85
C60	Air Conditioning	3,520	412.90
F41	Special Front and Rear Suspension	2,705	36.90
G81	Positraction Rear Axle, all ratios	24,056	42.15
J50	Power Brakes	5,464	42.15
J56	Special Heavy Duty Brakes	382	342.30
K19	Air Injection Reactor	2,380	44.75
K66	Transistor Ignition System	7,146	73.75
L36	427ci, 390hp Engine	5,116	181.20
L72	427ci, 425hp Engine	5,258	312.85
L79	327ci, 350hp Engine	7,591	105.35
M20	4-Speed Manual Transmission	10,837	184.35
M21	4-Speed Man Trans, close ratio	13,903	184.35
M22	4-Speed Man Trans, close ratio, heavy duty	15	237.00
M35	Powerglide Automatic Transmission	2,401	194.85
N03	36 Gallon Fuel Tank (for coupe)	66	198.05
N11	Off Road Exhaust System	2,795	36.90
N14	Side Mount Exhaust System	3,617	131.65
N32	Teakwood Steering Wheel	3,941	47.40
N36	Telescopic Steering Column	3,670	42.15
N40	Power Steering	5,611	94.80
P48	Cast Aluminum Knock-Off Wheels (5)	1,194	316.00
P92	Whitewall Tires, 7.75x15, (rayon cord)	17,969	31.30
T01	Goldwall Tires, 7.75x15 (nylon cord)	5,557	46.55
U69	AM-FM Radio	26,363	199.10
V74	Traffic Hazard Lamp Switch	5,764	11.60

1967 Options

RPO #	DESCRIPTION	QTY	RETAIL $
19437	Base Corvette Sport Coupe	8,504	$4,388.75
19467	Base Corvette Convertible	14,436	4,240.75
–	Genuine Leather Seats	1,601	79.00
A01	Soft Ray Tinted Glass, all windows	11,331	15.80
A02	Soft Ray Tinted Glass, windshield	6,558	10.55
A31	Power Windows	4,036	57.95
A82	Headrests	1,762	42.15
A85	Shoulder Belts	4,426	26.35
C07	Auxiliary Hardtop (for convertible)	6,880	231.75
C08	Vinyl Covering (for auxiliary hardtop)	1,966	52.70
C48	Heater and Defroster Deletion (credit)	35	-97.85
C60	Air Conditioning	3,788	412.90
F41	Special Front and Rear Suspension	2,198	36.90
G81	Positraction Rear Axle, all ratios	20,308	42.15
J50	Power Brakes	4,766	42.15

1967 Options (continued)

RPO #	DESCRIPTION	QTY	RETAIL $
J56	Special Heavy Duty Brakes	267	342.30
K19	Air Injection Reactor	2,573	44.75
K66	Transistor Ignition System	5,759	73.75
L36	427ci, 390hp Engine	3,832	200.15
L68	427ci, 400hp Engine	2,101	305.50
L71	427ci, 435hp Engine	3,754	437.10
L79	327ci, 350hp Engine	6,375	105.35
L88	427ci, 430hp Engine	20	947.90
L89	Aluminum Cylinder Heads for L71	16	368.65
M20	4-Speed Manual Transmission	9,157	184.35
M21	4-Speed Man Trans, close ratio	11,015	184.35
M22	4-Speed Man Trans, close ratio, heavy duty	20	237.00
M35	Powerglide Automatic Transmission	2,324	194.35
N03	36 Gallon Fuel Tank (for coupe)	2	198.05
N11	Off Road Exhaust System	2,326	36.90
N14	Side Mount Exhaust System	4,209	131.65
N36	Telescopic Steering Column	2,415	42.15
N40	Power Steering	5,747	94.80
N89	Cast Aluminum Bolt-On Wheels (5)	720	263.30
P92	Whitewall Tires, 7.75x15	13,445	31.35
QB1	Redline Tires, 7.75x15	4,230	46.65
U15	Speed Warning Indicator	2,108	10.55
U69	AM-FM Radio	22,193	172.75

1968 Options

RPO #	DESCRIPTION	QTY	RETAIL $
19437	Base Corvette Sport Coupe	9,936	$4,663.00
19467	Base Corvette Convertible	18,630	4,320.00
–	Genuine Leather Seats	2,429	79.00
A01	Soft Ray Tinted Glass, all windows	17,635	15.80
A02	Soft Ray Tinted Glass, windshield	5,509	10.55
A31	Power Windows	7,065	57.95
A82	Headrests	3,197	42.15
A85	Custom Shoulder Belts (std with coupe)	350	26.35
C07	Auxiliary Hardtop (for convertible)	8,735	231.75
C08	Vinyl Covering (for auxiliary hardtop)	3,050	52.70
C50	Rear Window Defroster	693	31.60
C60	Air Conditioning	5,664	412.90
F41	Special Front and Rear Suspension	1,758	36.90
G81	Positraction Rear Axle, all ratios	27,008	46.35
J50	Power Brakes	9,559	42.15
J56	Special Heavy Duty Brakes	81	384.45
K66	Transistor Ignition System	5,457	73.75
L36	427ci, 390hp Engine	7,717	200.15
L68	427ci, 400hp Engine	1,932	305.50
L71	427ci, 435hp Engine	2,898	437.10
L79	327ci, 350hp Engine	9,440	105.35
L88	427ci, 430hp Engine	80	947.90
L89	Aluminum Cylinder Heads with L71	624	805.75
M20	4-Speed Manual Transmission	10,760	184.35
M21	4-Speed Man Trans, close ratio	12,337	184.35
M22	4-Speed Man Trans, close ratio, heavy duty	80	263.30

1968 Options (continued)

RPO #	DESCRIPTION	QTY	RETAIL $
M40	Turbo Hydra-Matic Automatic Transmission	5,063	226.45
N11	Off Road Exhaust System	4,695	36.90
N36	Telescopic Steering Column	6,477	42.15
N40	Power Steering	12,364	94.80
P01	Bright Metal Wheel Cover	8,971	57.95
PT6	Red Stripe Tires, F70x15, nylon	11,686	31.30
PT7	White Stripe Tires, F70x15, nylon	9,692	31.30
UA6	Alarm System	388	26.35
U15	Speed Warning Indicator	3,453	10.55
U69	AM-FM Radio	24,609	172.75
U79	AM-FM Radio, stereo	3,311	278.10

1969 Options

RPO #	DESCRIPTION	QTY	RETAIL $
19437	Base Corvette Sport Coupe	22,129	$4,781.00
19467	Base Corvette Convertible	16,633	4,438.00
–	Genuine Leather Seats	3,729	79.00
A01	Soft Ray Tinted Glass, all windows	31,270	16.90
A31	Power Windows	9,816	63.20
A82	Headrests	38,762	17.95
A 85	Custom Shoulder Belts (std with coupe)	600	42.15
C07	Auxiliary Hardtop (for convertible)	7,878	252.80
C08	Vinyl Covering (for auxiliary hardtop)	3,266	57.95
C50	Rear Window Defroster	2,485	32.65
C60	Air Conditioning	11,859	428.70
F41	Special Front and Rear Suspension	1,661	36.90
G81	Positraction Rear Axle, all ratios	36,965	46.35
J50	Power Brakes	16,876	42.15
J56	Special Heavy Duty Brakes	115	384.45
K05	Engine Block Heater	824	10.55
K66	Transistor Ignition System	5,702	81.10
L36	427ci, 390hp Engine	10,531	221.20
L46	350ci, 350hp Engine	12,846	131.65
L68	427ci, 400hp Engine	2,072	326.55
L71	427ci, 435hp Engine	2,722	437.10
L88	427ci, 430hp Engine	116	1,032.15
L89	Aluminum Cylinder Heads with L71	390	832.05
MA6	Heavy Duty Clutch	102	79.00
M20	4-Speed Manual Transmission	16,507	184.80
M21	4-Speed Man Trans, close ratio	13,741	184.80
M22	4-Speed Man Trans, close ratio, heavy duty	101	290.40
M40	Turbo Hydra-Matic Automatic Transmission	8,161	221.80
N14	Side Mount Exhaust System	4,355	147.45
N37	Tilt-Telescopic Steering Column	10,325	84.30
N40	Power Steering	22,866	105.35
P02	Deluxe Wheel Covers	8,073	57.95
PT6	Red Stripe Tires, F70x15, nylon	5,210	31.30
PT7	White Stripe Tires, F70x15, nylon	21,379	31.30
PU9	White Letter Tires, F70x15, nylon	2,398	33.15
TJ2	Front Fender Louver Trim	11,962	21.10
UA6	Alarm System	12,436	26.35
U15	Speed Warning Indicator	3,561	11.60
U69	AM-FM Radio	33,871	172.75
U79	AM-FM Radio, stereo	4,114	278.10
ZL1	Special L88 (aluminum block)	2	4,718.35

1970 Options

RPO #	DESCRIPTION	QTY	RETAIL $
19437	Base Corvette Sport Coupe	10,668	$5,192.00
19467	Base Corvette Convertible	6,648	4,849.00
–	Custom Interior Trim	3,191	158.00
A31	Power Windows	4,813	63.20
A85	Custom Shoulder Belts (std with coupe)	475	42.15
C07	Auxiliary Hardtop (for convertible)	2,556	273.85
C08	Vinyl Covering (for auxiliary hardtop)	832	63.20
C50	Rear Window Defroster	1,281	36.90
C60	Air Conditioning	6,659	447.65
G81	Optional Rear Axle Ratio	2,862	12.65
J50	Power Brakes	8,984	47.40
L46	350ci, 350hp Engine	4,910	158.00
LS5	454ci, 390hp Engine	4,473	289.65
LT1	350ci, 370hp Engine	1,287	447.60
M21	4-Speed Man Trans, close ratio	4,383	0.00
M22	4-Speed Man Trans, close ratio, heavy duty	25	95.00
M40	Turbo Hydra-Matic Automatic Transmission	5,102	0.00
NA9	California Emissions	1,758	36.90
N37	Tilt-Telescopic Steering Column	5,803	84.30
N40	Power Steering	11,907	105.35
P02	Deluxe Wheel Covers	3,467	57.95
PT7	White Stripe Tires, F70x15, nylon	6,589	31.30
PU9	White Letter Tires, F70x15, nylon	7,985	33.15
T60	Heavy Duty Battery (std with LS5)	165	15.80
UA6	Alarm System	6,727	31.60
U69	AM-FM Radio	14,529	172.75
Y79	AM-FM Radio, stereo	2,462	278.10
ZR1	Special Purpose Engine Package	25	968.95

1971 Options

RPO #	DESCRIPTION	QTY	RETAIL $
19437	Base Corvette Sport Coupe	14,680	$5,496.00
19467	Base Corvette Convertible	7,121	5,259.00
–	Custom Interior Trim	2,602	158.00
A31	Power Windows	6,192	79.00
A85	Custom Shoulder Belts (std with coupe)	677	42.00
C07	Auxiliary Hardtop (for convertible)	2,619	274.00
C08	Vinyl Covering (for auxiliary hardtop)	832	63.00
C50	Rear Window Defroster	1,598	42.00
C60	Air Conditioning	11,481	459.00
ZQ1	Optional Rear Axle Ratio	2,395	13.00
J50	Power Brakes	13,558	47.00
LS5	454ci, 365hp Engine	5,097	295.00
LS6	454ci, 425hp Engine	188	1,221.00
LT1	350ci, 330hp Engine	1,949	483.00
M21	4-Speed Man Trans, close ratio	2,387	0.00
M22	4-Speed Man Trans, close ratio, heavy duty	130	100.00
M40	Turbo Hydra-Matic Automatic Transmission	10,060	0.00
N37	Tilt-Telescopic Steering Column	8,130	84.30
N40	Power Steering	17,904	115.90
P02	Deluxe Wheel Covers	3,007	63.00
PT7	White Stripe Tires, F70x15, nylon	6,711	28.00
PU9	White Letter Tires, F70x15, nylon	12,449	42.00
T60	Heavy Duty Battery (std with LS5, LS6)	1,455	15.80
UA6	Alarm System	8,501	31.60

1971 Options (continued)

RPO #	DESCRIPTION	QTY	RETAIL $
U69	AM-FM Radio	18,078	178.00
U79	AM-FM Radio, stereo	3,431	283.00
ZR1	Special Purpose LT1 Engine Package	8	1,010.00
ZR2	Special Purpose LS6 Engine Package	12	1,747.00

1972 Options

RPO #	DESCRIPTION	QTY	RETAIL $
19437	Base Corvette Sport Coupe	20,496	$5,533.00
19467	Base Corvette Convertible	6,508	5,296.00
–	Custom Interior Trim	8,709	158.00
AV3	Three Point Seat Belts	17,693	–
A31	Power Windows	9,495	85.35
A85	Custom Shoulder Belts (std with coupe)	749	42.15
C07	Auxiliary Hardtop (for convertible)	2,646	273.85
C08	Vinyl Covering (for auxiliary hardtop)	811	158.00
C50	Rear Window Defroster	2,221	42.15
C60	Air Conditioning	17,011	464.50
ZQ1	Optional Rear Axle Ratio	1,986	12.65
J50	Power Brakes	18,770	47.40
K19	Air Injection Reactor	3,912	–
LS5	454ci, 270hp Engine (n/a California)	3,913	294.90
LT1	350ci, 255hp Engine	1,741	483.45
M21	4-Speed Manual Trans, close ratio	1,638	0.00
M40	Turbo Hydra-Matic Automatic Transmission	14,543	0.00
N37	Tilt-Telescopic Steering Column	12,992	84.30
N40	Power Steering	23,794	115.90
P02	Deluxe Wheel Covers	3,593	63.20
PT7	White Stripe Tires, F70x15, nylon	6,666	30.35
PU9	White Letter Tires, F70x15, nylon	16,623	43.65
T60	Heavy Duty Battery (std with LS5)	2,969	15.80
U69	AM-FM Radio	19,480	178.00
U79	AM-FM Radio, stereo	7,189	283.35
YF5	California Emission Test	1,967	15.80
ZR1	Special Purpose LT1 Engine Package	20	1,010.05

1973 Options

RPO #	DESCRIPTION	QTY	RETAIL $
1YZ37	Base Corvette Sport Coupe	25,521	$5,561.50
1YZ67	Base Corvette Convertible	4,943	5,398.50
–	Custom Interior Trim	13,434	154.00
A31	Power Windows	14,024	83.00
A85	Custom Shoulder Belts (std with coupe)	788	41.00
C07	Auxiliary Hardtop (for convertible)	1,328	267.00
C08	Vinyl Covering (for auxiliary hardtop)	323	62.00
C50	Rear Window Defroster	4,412	41.00
C60	Air Conditioning	21,578	452.00
–	Optional Rear Axle Ratio	1,791	12.00
J50	Power Brakes	24,168	46.00
LS4	454ci, 275hp Engine	4,412	250.00
L82	350ci, 250hp Engine	5,710	299.00
M21	4-Speed Manual Trans, close ratio	3,704	0.00
M40	Turbo Hydra-Matic Automatic Transmission	17,927	0.00
N37	Tilt-Telescopic Steering Column	17,949	82.00

1973 Options (continued)

RPO #	DESCRIPTION	QTY	RETAIL $
1YZ37	Base Corvette Sport Coupe	25,521	$5,561.50
1YZ67	Base Corvette Convertible	4,943	5,398.50
–	Custom Interior Trim	13,434	154.00
A31	Power Windows	14,024	83.00
A85	Custom Shoulder Belts (std with coupe)	788	41.00
C07	Auxiliary Hardtop (for convertible)	1,328	267.00
C08	Vinyl Covering (for auxiliary hardtop)	323	62.00
C50	Rear Window Defroster	4,412	41.00
C60	Air Conditioning	21,578	452.00
–	Optional Rear Axle Ratio	1,791	12.00
J50	Power Brakes	24,168	46.00
LS4	454ci, 275hp Engine	4,412	250.00
L82	350ci, 250hp Engine	5,710	299.00
M21	4-Speed Manual Trans, close ratio	3,704	0.00
M40	Turbo Hydra-Matic Automatic Transmission	17,927	0.00
N37	Tilt-Telescopic Steering Column	17,949	82.00
N40	Power Steering	27,872	113.00
P02	Deluxe Wheel Covers	1,739	62.00
QRM	White Stripe Steel Belted Tires, GR70x15	19,903	32.00
QRZ	White Letter Steel Belted Tires, GR70x15	4,541	45.00
T60	Heavy Duty Battery (standard with LS4)	4,912	15.00
U58	AM-FM Radio, stereo	12,482	276.00
U69	AM-FM Radio	17,598	173.00
UF1	Map Light (on rearview mirror)	8,186	5.00
YF5	California Emission Test	3,008	15.00
YJ8	Cast Aluminum Wheels (5)	4	175.00
Z07	Off Road Suspension and Brake Package	45	369.00

1974 Options

RPO #	DESCRIPTION	QTY	RETAIL $
1YZ37	Base Corvette Sport Coupe	32,028	$6,001.50
1YZ67	Base Corvette Convertible	5,474	5,765.50
–	Custom Interior Trim	19,959	154.00
A31	Power Windows	23,940	86.00
A85	Custom Shoulder Belts (std with coupe)	618	41.00
C07	Auxiliary Hardtop (for convertible)	2,612	267.00
C08	Vinyl-Covered Auxiliary Hardtop	367	329.00
C50	Rear Window Defroster	9,322	43.00
C60	Air Conditioning	29,397	467.00
FE7	Gymkhana Suspension	1,905	7.00
–	Optional Rear Axle Ratios	1,219	12.00
J50	Power Brakes	33,306	49.00
LS4	454ci, 270hp Engine	3,494	250.00
L82	350ci, 250hp Engine	6,690	299.00
M21	4-Speed Manual Trans, close ratio	3,494	0.00
M40	Turbo Hydra-Matic Automatic Transmission	25,146	0.00
N37	Tilt-Telescopic Steering Column	27,700	82.00
N41	Power Steering	35,944	117.00
QRM	White Stripe Steel Belted Tires, GR70x15	9,140	32.00
QRZ	White Letter Steel Belted Tires, GR70x15	24,102	45.00
U05	Dual Horns	5,258	4.00
U58	AM-FM Radio, stereo	19,581	276.00

1974 Options (continued)

RPO #	DESCRIPTION	QTY	RETAIL $
U69	AM-FM Radio	17,374	173.00
UA1	Heavy Duty Battery (std with LS4)	9,169	15.00
UF1	Map Light (on rearview mirror)	16,101	5.00
YF5	California Emission Test	–	20.00
Z07	Off Road Suspension and Brake Package	47	400.00

1975 Options

RPO#	DESCRIPTION	QTY	RETAIL $
1YZ37	Base Corvette Sport Coupe	33,836	$6,810.10
1YZ67	Base Corvette Convertible	4,629	6,550.10
–	Custom Interior Trim	–	154.00
A31	Power Windows	28,745	93.00
A85	Custom Shoulder Belts (std with coupe)	646	41.00
C07	Auxiliary Hardtop (for convertible)	2,407	267.00
C08	Vinyl Covered Auxiliary Hardtop (conv)	279	350.00
C50	Rear Window Defroster	13,760	46.00
C60	Air Conditioning	31,914	490.00
FE7	Gymkhana Suspension	3,194	7.00
–	Optional Rear Axle Ratios	1,969	12.00
J50	Power Brakes	35,842	50.00
L82	350ci, 205hp Engine	2,372	336.00
M21	4-Speed Manual Trans, close ratio	1,057	0.00
M40	Turbo Hydra-Matic Automatic Transmission	28,473	0.00
N37	Tilt-Telescopic Steering Column	31,830	82.00
N41	Power Steering	37,591	129.00
QRM	White Stripe Steel Belted Tires, GR70x15	5,233	35.00
Qrz	White Letter Steel Belted Tires, GR70x15	30,407	48.00
U05	Dual Horns	22,011	4.00
U58	AM-FM Radio, stereo	24,701	284.00
U69	AM-FM Radio	12,902	178.00
UA1	Heavy Duty Battery	16,778	15.00
UF1	Map Light (on rearview mirror)	21,676	5.00
YF5	California Emission Test	3,037	20.00
Z07	Off Road Suspension and Brake Package	144	400.00

1976 Options

RPO #	DESCRIPTION	QTY	RETAIL $
1YZ37	Base Corvette Sport Coupe	46,558	$7,604.85
–	Custom Interior Trim	36,762	164.00
A31	Power Windows	38,700	107.00
C49	Rear Window Defogger	24,960	78.00
C60	Air Conditioning	40,787	523.00
FE7	Gymkhana Suspension	5,368	35.00
–	Optional Rear Axle Ratios	1,371	13.00
J50	Power Brakes	46,558	59.00
L82	350ci, 210hp Engine	5,720	481.00
M21	4-Speed Manual Trans, close ratio	2,088	0.00
M40	Turbo Hydra-Matic Automatic Transmission	36,625	0.00
N37	Tilt-Telescopic Steering Column	41,797	95.00
N41	Power Steering	46,385	151.00
QRM	White Stripe Steel Belted Tires, GR70x15	3,992	37.00
QRZ	White Letter Steel Belted Tires, GR70x15	39,923	51.00

1976 Options (continued)

RPO #	DESCRIPTION	QTY	RETAIL $
U58	AM-FM Radio, stereo	34,272	281.00
U69	AM-FM Radio	11,083	187.00
UA1	Heavy Duty Battery	25,909	16.00
UF1	Map Light (on rearview mirror)	35,361	10.00
YF5	California Emission Test	3,527	50.00
YJ8	Aluminum Wheels (4)	6,253	299.00

1977 Options

RPO #	DESCRIPTION	QTY	RETAIL $
1YZ37	Base Corvette Sport Coupe	49,213	$8,647.65
A31	Power Windows	44,341	116.00
B32	Color Keyed Floor Mats	36,763	22.00
C49	Rear Window Defogger	30,411	84.00
C60	Air Conditioning	45,249	553.00
D35	Sport Mirrors	20,206	36.00
FE7	Gymkhana Suspension	7,269	38.00
G95	Optional Rear Axle Ratios	972	14.00
K30	Speed Control	29,161	88.00
L82	350ci, 210hp Engine	6,148	495.00
M21	4-Speed Manual Trans, close ratio	2,060	0.00
M40	Turbo Hydra-Matic Automatic Transmission	41,231	0.00
NA6	High Altitude Emission Equipment	854	22.00
N37	Tilt-Telescopic Steering Column	46,487	165.00
QRZ	White Letter Steel Belted Tires, GR70x15	46,227	57.00
UA1	Heavy Duty Battery	32,882	17.00
U58	AM-FM Radio, stereo	18,483	281.00
U69	AM-FM Radio	4,700	187.00
UM2	AM-FM Radio, stereo with 8-track tape	24,603	414.00
V54	Luggage and Roof Panel Rack	16,860	73.00
YF5	California Emission Certification	4,084	70.00
YJ8	Aluminum Wheels (4)	12,646	321.00
ZN1	Trailer Package	289	83.00
ZX2	Convenience Group	40,872	22.00

1978 Options

RPO #	DESCRIPTION	QTY	RETAIL $
1YZ87	Base Corvette Sport Coupe	40,274	$9,351.89
1YZ87/78	Limited Edition Corvette (pace car)	6,502	13,653.21
A31	Power Windows	36,931	130.00
AU3	Power Door Locks	12,187	120.00
B2Z	Silver Anniversary Paint	15,283	399.00
CC1	Removable Glass Roof Panels	972	349.00
C49	Rear Window Defogger	30,912	95.00
C60	Air Conditioning	37,638	605.00
D35	Sport Mirrors	38,405	40.00
FE7	Gymkhana Suspension	12,590	41.00
G95	Optional Rear Axle Ratio	382	15.00
K30	Cruise Control	31,608	99.00
L82	350ci, 220hp Engine	12,739	525.00
M21	4-Speed Manual Trans, close ratio	3,385	0.00
MX1	Automatic Transmission	38,614	0.00

1978 Options (continued)

RPO #	DESCRIPTION	QTY	RETAIL $
NA6	High Altitude Emission Equipment	260	33.00
N37	Tilt-Telescopic Steering Column	37,858	175.00
QBS	White Letter SBR Tires, P255/60R15	18,296	216.32
QGR	White Letter SBR Tires, P225/70R15	26,203	51.00
UA1	Heavy Duty Battery	28,243	18.00
UM2	AM-FM Radio, stereo with 8-track tape	20,899	419.00
UP6	AM-FM Radio, stereo with CB	7,138	638.00
U58	AM-FM Radio, stereo	10,189	286.00
U69	AM-FM Radio	2,057	199.00
U75	Power Antenna	23,069	49.00
U81	Dual Rear Speakers	12,340	49.00
YF5	California Emission Certification	3,405	75.00
YJ8	Aluminum Wheels (4)	28,008	340.00
ZN1	Trailer Package	972	89.00
ZX2	Convenience Group	37,222	84.00

1979 Options

RPO #	DESCRIPTION	QTY	RETAIL $
1YZ87	Base Corvette Sport Coupe	53,807	$10,220.23
A31	Power Windows	20,631	141.00
AU3	Power Door Locks	9,054	131.00
CC1	Removable Glass Roof Panels	14,480	365.00
C49	Rear Window Defogger	41,587	102.00
C60	Air Conditioning	47,136	635.00
D35	Sport Mirrors	48,211	45.00
D80	Spoilers, front and rear	6,853	265.00
FE7	Gymkhana Suspension	12,321	49.00
F51	Heavy Duty Shock Absorbers	2,164	33.00
G95	Optional Rear Axle Ratio	428	19.00
K30	Cruise Control	34,445	113.00
L82	350ci, 225hp Engine	14,516	965.00
M21	4-Speed Manual Trans, close ratio	4,062	0.00
MX1	Automatic Transmission	41,454	0.00
NA6	High Altitude Emission Equipment	56	35.00
N37	Tilt-Telescopic Steering Column	47,463	190.00
N90	Aluminum Wheels (4)	33,741	380.00
QBS	White Letter SBR Tires, P255/60R15	17,920	226.20
QGR	White Letter SBR Tires, P225/70R15	29,603	54.00
U58	AM-FM Radio, stereo	9,256	90.00
UM2	AM-FM Radio, stereo with 8-track	21,435	228.00
UN3	AM-FM Radio, stereo with cassette	12,110	234.00
UP6	AM-FM Radio, stereo with CB	4,483	439.00
U75	Power Antenna	35,730	52.00
U81	Dual Rear Speakers	37,754	52.00
UA1	Heavy Duty Battery	3,405	21.00
YF5	California Emission Certification	3,798	83.00
ZN1	Trailer Package	1,001	98.00
ZQ2	Power Windows and Door Locks	28,465	272.00
ZX2	Convenience Group	41,530	94.00

1980 Options

RPO #	DESCRIPTION	QTY	RETAIL $
1YZ87	Base Corvette Sport Coupe	40,614	$13,140.24
AU3	Power Door Locks	32,692	140.00
CC1	Removable Glass Roof Panels	19,695	391.00
C49	Rear Window Defogger	36,589	109.00
FE7	Gymkhana Suspension	9,907	55.00
F51	Heavy Duty Shock Absorbers	1,695	35.00
K30	Cruise Control	30,821	123.00
LG4	305ci, 180hp Engine (required in California)	3,221	-50.00
L82	350ci, 230hp Engine	5,069	595.00
MM4	4-Speed Manual Transmission	5,726	0.00
MX1	Automatic Transmission	34,838	0.00
N90	Aluminum Wheels (4)	34,128	407.00
QGB	White Letter SBR Tires, P225/70R15	26,208	62.00
QXH	White Letter SBR Tires, P255/60R15	13,140	426.16
UA1	Heavy Duty Battery	1,337	22.00
U58	AM-FM Radio, stereo	6,138	46.00
UM2	AM-FM Radio, stereo with 8-track	15,708	155.00
UN3	AM-FM Radio, stereo with cassette	15,148	168.00
UP6	AM-FM Radio, stereo with CB	2,434	391.00
U75	Power Antenna	32,863	56.00
UL5	Radio Delete	201	-126.00
U81	Dual Rear Speakers	36,650	52.00
V54	Roof Panel Carrier	3,755	125.00
YF5	California Emission Certification	3,221	250.00
ZN1	Trailer Package	796	105.00

1981 Options

RPO #	DESCRIPTION	QTY	RETAIL $
1YY87	Base Corvette Sport Coupe	40,606	$16,258.52
AU3	Power Door Locks	36,322	145.00
A42	Power Driver Seat	29,200	183.00
CC1	Removable Glass Roof Panels	29,095	414.00
C49	Rear Window Defogger	36,893	119.00
DG7	Electric Sport Mirrors	13,567	117.00
D84	Two-Tone Paint	5,352	399.00
FE7	Gymkhana Suspension	7,803	57.00
F51	Heavy Duty Shock Absorbers	1,128	37.00
G92	Performance Axle Ratio	2,400	20.00
K35	Cruise Control	32,522	155.00
MM4	4-Speed Manual Transmission	5,757	0.00
N90	Aluminum Wheels (4)	36,485	428.00
QGR	White Letter SBR Tires, P225/70R15	21,939	72.00
QXH	White Letter SBR Tires, P255/60R15	18,004	491.92
UL5	Radio Delete	315	-118.00
UM4	AM-FM Radio, etr stereo with 8-track	8,262	386.00
UM5	AM-FM Radio, etr stereo with 8-track/CB	792	712.00
UM6	AM-FM Radio, etr stereo with cassette	22,892	423.00
UN5	AM-FM Radio, etr stereo with cassette/CB	2,349	750.00
U58	AM-FM Radio, stereo	5,145	95.00
U75	Power Antenna	32,903	55.00
V54	Roof Panel Carrier	3,303	135.00
YF5	California Emission Certification	4,951	46.00
ZN1	Trailer Package	916	110.00

1982 Options

RPO #	DESCRIPTION	QTY	RETAIL $
1YY87	Base Corvette Sport Coupe	18,648	$18,290.07
1YY07	Corvette Collector Edition Hatchback	6,759	22,537.59
AG9	Power Driver Seat	22,585	197.00
AU3	Power Door Locks	23,936	155.00
CC1	Removable Glass Roof Panels	14,763	443.00
C49	Rear Window Defogger	16,886	129.00
DG7	Electric Sport Mirrors	20,301	125.00
D84	Two-Tone Paint	4,871	428.00
FE7	Gymkhana Suspension	5,457	61.00
K35	Cruise Control	24,313	165.00
N90	Aluminum Wheels	16,844	458.00
QGR	White Letter SBR Tires, P225/70R15	5,932	80.00
QXH	White Letter SBR Tires, P255/60R15	19,070	542.52
UL5	Radio Delete	150	-124.00
UM4	AM-FM Radio, etr stereo with 8-track	923	386.00
UM6	AM-FM Radio, etr stereo with cassette	20,355	423.00
UN5	AM-FM Radio, etr stereo with cassette/CB	1,987	755.00
U58	AM-FM Radio, stereo	1,533	101.00
U75	Power Antenna	15,557	60.00
V08	Heavy Duty Cooling	6,006	57.00
V54	Roof Panel Carrier	1,992	144.00
YF5	California Emission Certification	4,951	46.00

1984 Options

RPO #	DESCRIPTION	QTY	RETAIL $
1YY07	Base Corvette Sport Coupe	51,547	$21,800.00
AG9	Power Driver Seat	48,702	210.00
AQ9	Sport Seats, cloth	4,003	625.00
AR9	Base Seats, leather	40,568	400.00
AU3	Power Door Locks	49,545	165.00
CC3	Removable Transparent Roof Panel	15,767	595.00
D84	Two-Tone Paint	8,755	428.00
FG3	Delco-Bilstein Shock Absorbers	3,729	189.00
G92	Performance Axle Ratio	410	22.00
KC4	Engine Oil Cooler	4,295	158.00
K34	Cruise Control	49,832	185.00
MM4	4-Speed Manual Transmission	6,443	0.00
QZD	P255/50VR16 Tires/16" Wheels	51,547	561.20
UL5	Radio Delete	104	-331.00
UM6	AM-FM Stereo Cassette	6,689	153.00
UN8	AM-FM Stereo, Citizens Band	178	215.00
UU8	Stereo System, Delco-Bose	43,607	895.00
V01	Heavy-Duty Radiator	12,008	57.00
YF5	California Emission Requirements	6,833	75.00
Z51	Performance Handling Package	25,995	600.20
Z6A	Rear Window+Side Mirror Defoggers	47,680	160.00

1985 Options

RPO #	DESCRIPTION	QTY	RETAIL $
1YY07	Base Corvette Sport Coupe	39,729	$24,403.00
AG9	Power Driver Seat	37,856	215.00
AQ9	Sport Seats, leather	–	1,025.00
AR9	Base Seats, leather	–	400.00
–	Sport Seats, cloth	5,661	625.00
AU3	Power Door Locks	38,294	170.00
CC3	Removable Transparent Roof Panel	28,143	595.00
D84	Two-Tone Paint	6,033	428.00
FG3	Delco-Bilstein Shock Absorbers	9,333	189.00
G92	Performance Axle Ratio	5,447	22.00
K34	Cruise Control	38,369	185.00
MM4	4-Speed Manual Transmission	9,576	0.00
NN5	California Emission Requirements	6,583	99.00
UL5	Radio Delete	172	-256.00
UM6	AM-FM Stereo Cassette	2,958	122.00
UN8	AM-FM Stereo, Citizens Band	16	215.00
UU8	Stereo System, Delco-Bose	35,998	895.00
V08	Heavy-Duty Cooling	17,539	225.00
Z51	Performance Handling Package	14,802	470.00
Z6A	Rear Window+Side Mirror Defoggers	37,720	160.00

1986 Options

RPO #	DESCRIPTION	QTY	RETAIL $
1YY07	Base Corvette Sport Coupe	27,794	$27,027.00
1YY67	Base Corvette Convertible	7,315	32,032.00
AG9	Power Driver Seat	33,983	225.00
AQ9	Sport Seats, leather	13,372	1,025.00
AR9	Base Seats, leather	–	400.00
AU3	Power Door Locks	34,215	175.00
B4P	Radiator Boost Fan	8,216	75.00
B4Z	Custom Feature Package	4,832	195.00
C2L	Dual Removable Roof Panels (coupe)	6,242	895.00
24S	Removable Roof Panel, blue tint (coupe)	12,021	595.00
64S	Removable Roof Panel, bronze tint (coupe)	7,819	595.00
C68	Electronic Air Conditioning Control	16,646	150.00
D84	Two-Tone Paint (coupe)	3,897	428.00
FG3	Delco-Bilstein Shock Absorbers	5,521	189.00
G92	Performance Axle Ratio, 3.07:1	4,879	22.00
KC4	Engine Oil Cooler	7,394	110.00
K34	Cruise Control	34,197	185.00
MM4	4-Speed Manual Transmission	6,835	0.00
NN5	California Emission Requirements	5,697	99.00
UL5	Radio Delete	166	-256.00
UM6	AM-FM Stereo Cassette	2,039	122.00
UU8	Stereo System, Delco-Bose	32,478	895.00
V01	Heavy-Duty Radiator	10,423	40.00
Z51	Performance Handling Package (coupe)	12,821	470.00
Z6A	Rear Window+Side Mirror Defog (coupe)	21,837	165.00
4001ZA	Malcolm Konner Special Edition (coupe)	50	500.00

1987 Options

RPO #	DESCRIPTION	QTY	RETAIL $
1YY07	Base Corvette Sport Coupe	20,007	$27,999.00
1YY67	Base Corvette Convertible	10,625	33,172.00
AC1	Power Passenger Seat	17,123	240.00
AC3	Power Driver Seat	29,561	240.00
AQ9	Sport Seats, leather	14,119	1,025.00
AR9	Base Seats, leather	14,561	400.00
AU3	Power Door Locks	29,748	190.00
B2K	Callaway Twin Turbo (not GM installed)	188	19,995.00
B4P	Radiator Boost Fan	7,291	75.00
C2L	Dual Removable Roof Panels (coupe)	5,017	915.00
24S	Removable Roof Panel, blue tint (coupe)	8,883	615.00
64S	Removable Roof Panel, bronze tint (coupe)	5,766	615.00
C68	Electronic Air Conditioning Control	20,875	150.00
DL8	Twin Remote Heated Mirrors (convertible)	6,840	35.00
D74	Illuminated Driver Vanity Mirror	14,992	58.00
D84	Two-Tone Paint (coupe)	1,361	428.00
FG3	Delco-Bilstein Shock Absorbers	1,957	189.00
G92	Performance Axle Ratio, 3.07:1	7,286	22.00
KC4	Engine Oil Cooler	6,679	110.00
K34	Cruise Control	29,594	185.00
MM4	4-Speed Manual Transmission	4,298	0.00
NN5	California Emission Requirements	5,423	99.00
UL5	Radio Delete	247	-256.00
UM6	AM-FM Stereo Cassette	2,236	132.00
UU8	Stereo System, Delco-Bose	27,721	905.00
V01	Heavy-Duty Radiator	7,871	40.00
Z51	Performance Handling Package (coupe)	1,596	795.00
Z52	Sport Handling Package	12,662	470.00
Z6A	Rear Window+Side Mirror Defog (coupe)	19,043	165.00

1988 Options

RPO #	DESCRIPTION	QTY	RETAIL $
1YY07	Base Corvette Sport Coupe	15,382	$29,489.00
1YY67	Base Corvette Convertible	7,407	34,820.00
AC1	Power Passenger Seat	18,779	240.00
AC3	Power Driver Seat	22,084	240.00
AQ9	Sport Seats, leather	12,724	1,025.00
AR9	Base Seats, leather	9,043	400.00
B2K	Callaway Twin Turbo (not GM installed)	125	25,895.00
B4P	Radiator Boost Fan	19,035	75.00
C2L	Dual Removable Roof Panels (coupe)	5,091	915.00
24S	Removable Roof Panel, blue tint (coupe)	8,332	615.00
64S	Removable Roof Panel, bronze tint (coupe)	3,337	615.00
C68	Electronic Air Conditioning Control	19,372	150.00
DL8	Twin Remote Heated Mirrors (convertible)	6,582	35.00
D74	Illuminated Driver Vanity Mirror	14,249	58.00
FG3	Delco-Bilstein Shock Absorbers	18,437	189.00
G92	Performance Axle Ratio, 3.07:1	4,497	22.00
KC4	Engine Oil Cooler	18,877	110.00
MM4	4-Speed Manual Transmission	4,282	0.00
NN5	California Emission Requirements	3,882	99.00
UL5	Radio Delete	179	-297.00
UU8	Stereo System, Delco-Bose	20,304	773.00

1988 Options (continued)

RPO #	DESCRIPTION	QTY	RETAIL $
V01	Heavy-Duty Radiator	19,271	40.00
Z01	35th Special Edition Package (coupe)	2,050	4,795.00
Z51	Performance Handling Package (coupe)	1,309	1,295.00
Z52	Sport Handling Package	16,017	970.00
Z6A	Rear Window+Side Mirror Defog (coupe)	14,648	165.00

1989 Options

RPO #	DESCRIPTION	QTY	RETAIL $
1YY07	Base Corvette Sport Coupe	16,663	$31,545.00
1YY67	Base Corvette Convertible	9,749	36,785.00
AC1	Power Passenger Seat	20,578	240.00
AC3	Power Driver Seat	25,606	240.00
AQ9	Sport Seats, leather	1,777	1,025.00
AR9	Base Seats, leather	23,364	400.00
B2K	Callaway Twin-Turbo (not GM installed)	67	25,895.00
B4P	Radiator Boost Fan	20,281	75.00
CC2	Auxiliary Hardtop (convertible)	1,573	1,995.00
C2L	Dual Removable Roof Panels (coupe)	5,274	915.00
24S	Removable Roof Panel, blue tint (coupe)	8,748	615.00
64S	Removable Roof Panel, bronze tint (coupe)	4,042	615.00
C68	Electronic Air Conditioning Control	24,675	150.00
D74	Illuminated Driver Vanity Mirror	17,414	58.00
FX3	Selective Ride and Handling, electronic	1,573	1,695.00
G92	Performance Axle Ratio	10,211	22.00
K05	Engine Block Heater	2,182	20.00
KC4	Engine Oil Cooler	20,162	110.00
MN6	6-Speed Manual Transmission	4,113	0.00
MN5	California Emission Requirements	4,501	100.00
UJ6	Low Tire Pressure Warning Indicator	6,976	325.00
UU8	Stereo System, Delco-Bose	24,145	773.00
V01	Heavy-Duty Radiator	20,888	40.00
V56	Luggage Rack (convertible)	616	140.00
Z51	Performance Handling Package (coupe)	2,224	575.00

1990 Options

RPO #	DESCRIPTION	QTY	RETAIL $
1YY07	Base Corvette Sport Coupe	16,016	$31,979.00
1YY67	Base Corvette Convertible	7,630	37,264.00
AC1	Power Passenger Seat	20,419	270.00
AC3	Power Driver Seat	23,109	270.00
AQ9	Sport Seats, leather	11,457	1,050.00
AR9	Base Seats, leather	11,649	425.00
B2K	Callaway Twin-Turbo (not GM installed)	58	26,895.00
CC2	Auxiliary Hardtop (convertible)	2,371	1,995.00
C2L	Dual Removable Roof Panels (coupe)	6,422	915.00
24S	Removable Roof Panel, blue tint (coupe)	7,852	615.00
64S	Removable Roof Panel, bronze tint (coupe)	4,340	615.00
C68	Electronic Air Conditioning Control	22,497	180.00
FX3	Selective Ride and Handling, electronic	7,576	1,695.00
G92	Performance Axle Ratio	9,362	22.00

1990 Options (continued)

RPO #	DESCRIPTION	QTY	RETAIL $
K05	Engine Block Heater	1,585	20.00
KC4	Engine Oil Cooler	16,221	110.00
MN6	6-Speed Manual Transmission	8,101	0.00
MN5	California Emission Requirements	4,035	100.00
UJ6	Low Tire Pressure Warning Indicator	8,432	325.00
UU8	Stereo System, Delco-Bose	6,701	823.00
U1F	Stereo System with CD, Delco-Bose	15,716	1,219.00
V56	Luggage Rack (convertible)	1,284	140.00
Z51	Performance Handling Package (coupe)	5,446	460.00
ZR1	Special Performance Package (coupe)	3,049	27,016.00

1991 Options

RPO #	DESCRIPTION	QTY	RETAIL $
1YY07	Base Corvette Sport Coupe	14,967	$32,455.00
1YY67	Base Corvette Convertible	5,672	38,770.00
AR9	Base Seats, leather	9,505	425.00
AQ9	Sport Seats, leather	10,650	1,050.00
AC1	Power Passenger Seat	17,267	290.00
AC3	Power Driver Seat	19,937	290.00
B2K	Callaway Twin-Turbo (not GM installed)	71	33,000.00
CC2	Auxiliary Hardtop (convertible)	1,230	1,995.00
C2L	Dual Removable Roof Panels (coupe)	5,031	915.00
24S	Removable Roof Panel, blue tint (coupe)	6,991	615.00
64S	Removable Roof Panel, bronze tint (coupe)	3,036	615.00
C68	Electronic Air Conditioning Control	19,233	180.00
FX3	Selective Ride and Handling, electronic	6,894	1,695.00
G92	Performance Axle Ratio	3,453	22.00
KC4	Engine Oil Cooler	7,525	110.00
MN6	6-Speed Manual Transmission	5,875	0.00
MN5	California Emission Requirements	3,050	100.00
UJ6	Low Tire Pressure Warning Indicator	5,175	325.00
UU8	Stereo System, Delco-Bose	3,786	823.00
U1F	Stereo System with CD, Delco-Bose	15,345	1,219.00
V56	Luggage Rack (convertible)	886	140.00
Z07	Adjustable Suspension Package (coupe)	733	2,155.00
ZR1	Special Performance Package (coupe)	2,044	31,683.00

1992 Options

RPO #	DESCRIPTION	QTY	RETAIL $
1YY07	Base Corvette Sport Coupe	14,604	$33,635.00
1YY67	Base Corvette Convertible	5,875	40,145.00
AR9	Base Seats, leather	10,565	475.00
AR9	Base Seats, white leather	752	555.00
AQ9	Sport Seats, leather	7,973	1,100.00
AQ9	Sport Seats, white leather	709	1,180.00
AC1	Power Passenger Seat	16,179	305.00
AC3	Power Driver Seat	19,378	305.00
CC2	Auxiliary Hardtop (convertible)	915	1,995.00
C2L	Dual Removable Roof Panels (coupe)	3,739	950.00
24S	Removable Roof Panel, blue tint (coupe)	6,424	650.00
64S	Removable Roof Panel, bronze tint (coupe)	3,005	650.00
C68	Electronic Air Conditioning Control	18,460	205.00
FX3	Selective Ride and Handling, electronic	5,840	1,695.00
G92	Performance Axle Ratio	2,283	50.00
MN6	6-Speed Manual Transmission	5,487	0.00
NN5	California Emission Requirements	3,092	100.00
UJ6	Low Tire Pressure Warning Indicator	3,416	325.00
UU8	Stereo System, Delco-Bose	3,241	823.00
U1F	Stereo System with CD, Delco-Bose	15,199	1,219.00
V56	Luggage Rack (for convertible)	845	140.00
Z07	Adjustable Suspension Package (coupe)	738	2,045.00
ZR1	Special Performance Package (coupe)	502	31,683.00

1993 Options

RPO #	DESCRIPTION	QTY	RETAIL $
1YY07	Base Corvette Sport Coupe	15,898	$34,595.00
1YY67	Base Corvette Convertible	5,692	41,195.00
AR9	Base Seats, leather	8,509	475.00
AR9	Base Seats, white leather	766	555.00
AQ9	Sport Seats, leather	11,267	1,100.00
AQ9	Sport Seats, white leather	622	1,180.00
AC1	Power Passenger Seat	18,067	305.00
AC3	Power Driver Seat	20,626	305.00
CC2	Auxiliary Hardtop (convertible)	976	1,995.00
C2L	Dual Removable Roof Panels (coupe)	4,204	950.00
24S	Removable Roof Panel, blue tint (coupe)	6,203	650.00
64S	Removable Roof Panel, bronze tint (coupe)	4,288	650.00
C68	Electronic Air Conditioning Control	19,550	205.00
FX3	Selective Ride and Handling, electronic	5,740	1,695.00
G92	Performance Axle Ratio	2,630	50.00
MN6	6-Speed Manual Transmission	5,330	0.00
NN5	California Emission Requirements	2,101	100.00
UJ6	Low Tire Pressure Warning Indicator	3,353	325.00
UU8	Stereo System, Delco-Bose	2,685	823.00
U1F	Stereo System with CD, Delco-Bose	16,794	1,219.00
V56	Luggage Rack (for convertible)	765	140.00
Z07	Adjustable Suspension Package (coupe)	824	2,045.00
Z25	40th Anniversary Package	6,749	1,455.00
ZR1	Special Performance Package (coupe)	448	31,683.00

1994 Options

RPO #	DESCRIPTION	QTY	RETAIL $
1YY07	Base Corvette Sport Coupe	17,984	$36,185.00
1YY67	Base Corvette Convertible	5,346	42,960.00
AC1	Power Passenger Seat	17,863	305.00
AC3	Power Driver Seat	21,592	305.00
AQ9	Sport Seats	9,023	625.00
CC2	Auxiliary Hardtop (convertible)	682	1,995.00
C2L	Dual Removable Roof Panels (coupe)	3,875	950.00
24S	Removable Roof Panel, blue tint (coupe)	7,064	650.00
64S	Removable Roof Panel, bronze tint (coupe)	3,979	650.00
FX3	Selective Ride and Handling, electronic	4,570	1,695.00
G92	Performance Axle Ratio	9,019	50.00
MN6	6-Speed Manual Transmission	6,012	0.00
NG1	New York Emission Requirements	1,363	100.00
UJ6	Low Tire Pressure Warning Indicator	5,097	325.00
U1F	Stereo System with CD, Delco-Bose	17,579	396.00
WY5	Tires, Extended Mobility	2,781	70.00
YF5	California Emission Requirements	2,372	100.00
Z07	Adjustable Suspension Package (coupe)	887	2,045.00
ZR1	Special Performance Package (coupe)	448	31,258.00

1995 Options

RPO #	DESCRIPTION	QTY	RETAIL $
1YY07	Base Corvette Sport Coupe	15,771	$36,785.00
1YY67	Base Corvette Convertible	4,971	43,665.00
AG1	Power Driver Seat	19,012	305.00
AG2	Power Passenger Seat	15,323	305.00
AQ9	Sport Seats	7,90	625.00
CC2	Auxiliary Hardtop (convertible)	459	1,995.00
C2L	Dual Removable Roof Panels (coupe)	2,979	950.00
24S	Removable Roof Panel, blue tint (coupe)	4,688	650.00
64S	Removable Roof Panel, bronze tint (coupe)	2,871	650.00
FX3	Selective Ride and Handling, electronic	3,421	1,695.00
G92	Performance Axle Ratio	10,056	50.00
MN6	6-Speed Manual Transmission	4,784	0.00
NG1	New York Emission Requirements	268	100.00
N84	Spare Tire Delete	418	-100.00
UJ6	Low Tire Pressure Warning Indicator	5,300	325.00
U1F	Stereo System with CD, Delco-Bose	15,528	396.00
WY5	Tires, Extended Mobility	3,783	70.00
YF5	California Emission Requirements	2,026	100.00
Z07	Adjustable Suspension Package (coupe)	753	2,045.00
Z4Z	Indy 500 Pace Car Replica (convertible)	527	2,816.00
ZR1	Special Performance Package (coupe)	448	31,258.00

1996 Options

RPO #	DESCRIPTION	QTY	RETAIL $
1YY07	Base Corvette Sport Coupe	17,167	$37,225.00
1YY67	Base Corvette Convertible	4,369	45,060.00
AG1	Power Driver Seat	19,798	305.00
AG2	Power Passenger Seat	17,060	305.00
AQ9	Sport Seats	12,016	625.00
CC2	Auxiliary Hardtop (convertible)	429	1,995.00
C2L	Dual Removable Roof Panels (coupe)	3,983	950.00
24S	Removable Roof Panel, blue tint (coupe)	6,626	650.00
64S	Removable Roof Panel, bronze tint (coupe)	2,492	650.00
F45	Selective Real Time Damping, electronic	2,896	1,695.00
G92	Performance Axle Ratio	9,801	50.00
LT4	350 cubic-inch, 330 horsepower Engine	6,359	1,450.00
MN6	6-Speed Manual Transmission	6,359	0.00
N84	Spare Tire Delete	986	-100.00
UJ6	Low Tire Pressure Warning Indicator	6,865	325.00
U1F	Compact Disc Delco-Bose (reqs PEG 1)	17,037	396.00
WY5	Tires, Extended Mobility	4,945	70.00
Z15	Collector Edition	5,412	1,250.00
Z16	Grand Sport Package ($2,880 w/convertible)	1,000	3,250.00
Z51	Performance Handling Package	1,869	350.00

1997 Options

RPO #	DESCRIPTION	QTY	RETAIL $
1YY07	Base Corvette Sport Coupe	9,752	$37,495.00
AAB	Memory Package	6,186	150.00
AG2	Power Passenger Seat	8,951	305.00
AQ9	Sport Seats	6,711	625.00
B34	Floor Mats	9,371	25.00
B84	Body Side Moldings	4,366	75.00
CC3	Removable Roof Panel, blue tint (coupe)	7,213	650.00
C2L	Dual Removable Roof Panels	416	950.00
CJ2	Electronic Dual Zone Air Conditioning	7,999	365.00
D42	Luggage Shade and Parcel Net	8,315	50.00
F45	Selective Real Time Damping, electronic	3,094	1,695.00
G92	Performance Axle Ratio (Automatic only)	2,739	100.00
MN6	6-Speed Manual Transmission	2,809	815.00
NG1	Massachusetts/New York Emissions	677	170.00
T96	Fog Lamps	8,829	69.00
UN0	Delco Stereo System with CD	6,282	100.00
U1S	Remote Compact 12-Disc Changer	4,496	600.00
V49	Front License Plate Frame	2,258	15.00
YF5	California Emissions	885	170.00
Z51	Performance Handling Package	1,077	350.00

1998 Options

RPO #	DESCRIPTION	QTY	RETAIL $
1YY07	Base Corvette Sport Coupe	19,235	$37,495.00
1YY67	Base Corvette Convertible	11,849	44,425.00
AAB	Memory Package	24,234	150.00
AG2	Power Passenger Seat	28,575	305.00
AQ9	Sport Seats	22,675	625.00
B34	Floor Mats	30,592	25.00
B84	Body Side Moldings	17,070	75.00
C2L	Dual Removable Roof Panels (coupe)	5,640	950.00
CC3	Removable Roof Panel, blue tint (coupe)	6,957	650.00
CJ2	Dual Zone Air Conditioning	26,572	365.00
D42	Luggage Shade and Parcel Net (coupe)	16,549	50.00
F45	Selective Real Time Damping, electronic	8,374	1,695.00
G92	Performance Axle (3.15 ratio for automatic)	13,331	100.00
JL4	Active Handling System	5,356	500.00
MN6	6-Speed Manual Transmission	7,106	815.00
NG1	Massachusetts/New York Emissions	2,701	170.00
N73	Magnesium Wheels	1,425	3,000.00
T96	Fog Lamps	29,310	69.00
UN0	Delco Stereo System with CD	18,213	100.00
U1S	Remote Compact 12-Disc Changer	16,513	600.00
V49	Front License Plate Frame	16,087	15.00
YF5	California Emissions	3,111	170.00
Z4Z	Indy Pace Car Replica ($5,804 w/manual)	1,163	5,039.00
Z51	Performance Handling Package	4,249	350.00

1999 Options

RPO #	DESCRIPTION	QTY	RETAIL $
1YY07	Base Corvette Sport Coupe	18,078	$39,171.00
1YY37	Base Corvette Hardtop	4,031	38,777.00
1YY67	Base Corvette Convertible	11,161	45,579.00
AAB	Memory Package (coupe & conv)	23,829	150.00
AG1	Power Driver Seat (hardtop)	3,716	305.00
AG2	Power Passenger Seat (coupe & conv)	27,089	305.00
AQ9	Sport Seats (coupe & conv)	24,573	625.00
AP9	Parcel Net (hardtop)	2,738	15.00
B34	Floor Mats	32,706	25.00
B84	Body Side Moldings	19,348	75.00
C2L	Dual Removable Roof Panels (coupe)	6,307	950.00
CC3	Removable Roof Panel, blue tint (coupe)	5,235	650.00
CJ2	Dual Zone Air Conditioning	25,672	365.00
D42	Luggage Shade and Parcel Net (coupe)	18,058	50.00

1999 Options (continued)

RPO #	DESCRIPTION	QTY	RETAIL $
F45	Selective Real Time Damping (coupe & conv)	7,515	1,695.00
G92	Performance Axle (3.15 ratio for automatic)	14,525	100.00
JL4	Active Handling System	20,174	500.00
MN6	6-Speed Manual Trans (coupe & conv)	13,729	825.00
N37	Telescopic Steering, Power (coupe & conv)	16,847	350.00
N73	Magnesium Wheels	2,029	3,000.00
T82	Twilight Sentinel (coupe & conv)	18,895	60.00
T96	Fog Lamps	28,546	69.00
TR9	Lighting Package (hardtop only)	3,037	95.00
UN0	Delco Stereo System with CD	20,442	100.00
UV6	Head Up Instrument Display	19,034	375.00
UZ6	Bose Speaker Package (hardtop)	3,348	820.00
U1S	Remote Compact 12-Disc Changer	16,997	600.00
V49	Front License Plate Frame	17,742	15.00
YF5	California Emissions	3,336	170.00
Z51	Performance Handling Pkg (coupe & conv)	10,244	350.00
86U	Magnetic Red Metallic Paint (coupe & conv)	2,733	500.00

2000 Options

RPO #	DESCRIPTION	QTY	RETAIL $
1YY07	Base Corvette Sport Coupe	18,113	$39,475.00
1YY37	Base Corvette Hardtop	2,090	38,900.00
1YY67	Base Corvette Convertible	13,479	45,900.00
AAB	Memory Package (coupe & conv)	26,595	150.00
AG1	Power Driver Seat (hardtop)	1,841	305.00
AG2	Power Passenger Seat (coupe & conv)	29,462	305.00
AQ9	Sport Seats (coupe & conv)	27,103	700.00
AP9	Parcel Net (hardtop)	938	15.00
B34	Floor Mats	33,188	25.00
B84	Body Side Moldings	18,773	75.00
C2L	Dual Removable Roof Panels (coupe)	6,280	1,100.00
CC3	Removable Roof Panel, blue tint (coupe)	5,605	650.00
CJ2	Dual Zone Air Conditioning	29,428	365.00
D42	Luggage Shade and Parcel Net (coupe)	15,689	50.00
F45	Selective Real Time Damping (cpe & conv)	6,724	1,695.00
G92	Performance Axle (3.15 ratio for automatic)	14,090	100.00
JL4	Active Handling System	22,668	500.00
MN6	6-Speed Manual Trans (cpe & conv)	13,320	815.00
N37	Telescopic Steering, Power (cpe & conv)	22,182	350.00
N73	Magnesium Wheels	2,652	2,000.00
QF5	Polished Aluminum Wheels	15,204	895.00
T82	Twilight Sentinel (coupe & conv)	23,508	60.00
T96	Fog Lamps	31,992	69.00
TR9	Lighting Package (hardtop)	1,527	95.00
UN0	Delco Stereo System with CD	24,696	100.00
UV6	Head Up Instrument Display	26,482	375.00
UZ6	Bose Speaker Package (hardtop)	1,766	820.00
U1S	Remote Compact 12-Disc Changer	15,809	600.00
V49	Front License Plate Frame	17,380	15.00
YF5	California Emissions	3,628	0.00
Z51	Performance Handling (std w/hardtop)	7,775	350.00
79U	Millennium Yellow (coupe & conv)	3,578	500.00
86U	Magnetic Red Metallic Paint (cpe & conv)	2,941	500.00

2001 Options

RPO #	DESCRIPTION	QTY	RETAIL $
1YY07	Base Corvette Sport Coupe	15,681	$40,475.00
1YY37	Base Corvette Z06 Hardtop	5,773	47,500.00
1YY67	Base Corvette Convertible	14,173	47,000.00
1SB	Preferred Equipment Group-Sport Coupe	2,514	1,639.00
1SB	Preferred Equipment Group-Convertible	1,710	1,769.00
1SC	Preferred Equipment Group-Sport Coupe	11,558	2,544.00
1SC	Preferred Equipment Group-Convertible	11,881	2,494.00
AAB	Memory Package (Z06 hardtop)	4,780	150.00
B34	Floor Mats	34,907	25.00
B84	Body Side Moldings	20,457	75.00
C2L	Dual Removable Roof Panels (coupe)	5,099	1,100.00
CC3	Removable Roof Panel, blue tint (coupe)	4,769	650.00
DD0	Electrochromic Mirrors (Z06 hardtop)	4,576	120.00
F45	Selective Real Time Damping (cpe & conv)	5,620	1,695.00
G92	Performance 3.15 Axle (automatic, cpe & conv)	12,882	300.00
MN6	6-Speed Manual Trans (cpe & conv)	16,019	815.00
N73	Magnesium Wheels (cpe & conv)	1,022	2,000.00
QF5	Polished Aluminum Wheels (cpe & conv)	22,980	895.00
R8C	Corvette Museum Delivery	457	490.00
UL0	Delco Stereo Cassette (replaces std radio)	6,844	-100.00
UN0	Delco Stereo System with CD	28,783	100.00
U1S	Remote 12-Disc Changer (cpe & conv)	14,198	600.00
V49	Front License Plate Frame	18,935	15.00
Z51	Performing Handling Pkg (cpe & conv)	7,817	350.00
79U	Millennium Yellow w/tint coat	3,887	600.00
86U	Magnetic Red Metallic Paint (cpe & conv)	3,322	600.00

2002 Options

RPO #	DESCRIPTION	QTY	RETAIL $
1YY07	Base Corvette Sport Coupe	14,760	$41,450.00
1YY37	Base Corvette Z06 Hardtop	8,297	50,150.00
1YY67	Base Corvette Convertible	12,710	47,975.00
1SB	Preferred Equipment Group-Sport Coupe	1,359	1,700.00
1SB	Preferred Equipment Group-Convertible	1,379	1,800.00
1SC	Preferred Equipment Group-Sport Coupe	11,136	2,700.00
1SC	Preferred Equipment Group-Convertible	10,964	2,600.00
AAB	Memory Package (Z06 hardtop)	7,794	150.00
B84	Body Side Moldings	21,422	75.00
C2L	Dual Removable Roof Panels (coupe)	5,079	1,200.00
CC3	Removable Roof Panel, blue tint (coupe)	4,208	750.00
DD0	Electrochromic Mirrors (Z06 hardtop)	7,394	120.00
F45	Selective Real Time Damping (cpe & conv)	4,773	1,695.00
G92	Performance 3.15 Axle (automatic, cpe & conv)	9,646	300.00
MN6	6-Speed Manual Transmission (cpe & conv)	8,553	815.00
N73	Magnesium Wheels (cpe & conv)	114	1,500.00
QF5	Polished Aluminum Wheels (cpe & conv)	22,597	1,200.00
R8C	Corvette Museum Delivery	371	490.00
UL0	Delco Stereo Cassette (cpe & conv)	4,210	-100.00
U1S	Remote 12-Disc Changer (cpe & conv)	13,725	600.00
V49	Front License Plate Frame	19,948	15.00
Z51	Performance Handling Pkg (cpe & conv)	6,106	350.00
79U	Millennium Yellow w/tint coat	4,040	600.00
86U	Magnetic Red Metallic Paint (cpe & conv)	3,298	600.00

2003 Options

RPO #	DESCRIPTION	QTY	RETAIL $
1YY07	Base Corvette Sport Coupe	12,812	$43,895.00
1YY37	Base Corvette Z06 Hardtop	8,635	51,155.00
1YY67	Base Corvette Convertible	14,022	50,370.00
1SB	Preferred Equipment Group-Sport Group	7,310	1,200.00
1SB	Preferred Equipment Group-Convertible	6,643	1,200.00
1SC	50th Anniversary Edition-Sport Coupe	4,085	5,000.00
1SC	50th Anniversary Edition-Convertible	7,547	5,000.00
AAB	Memory Package (Z06 hardtop)	8,241	175.00
B84	Body Side Moldings	22,243	150.00
C2L	Dual Removable Roof Panels (coupe)	5,184	1,200.00
CC3	Removable Roof Panel, blue tint (coupe)	3,150	750.00
DD0	Electrochromic Mirrors (Z06 hardtop)	8,227	120.00
F55	Magnetic Selective Ride Control (cpe & conv)	14,992	1,695.00
G92	Performance 3.15 Axle (auto, cpe & conv)	9,785	395.00
MN6	6-Speed Manual Transmission (cpe & conv)	8,590	915.00
N73	Magnesium Wheels (cpe & conv)	293	1,500.00
QF5	Polished Aluminum Wheels (cpe & conv)	10,290	1,295.00
R8C	Corvette Museum Delivery	787	490.00
UL0	Delco Stereo Cassette (cpe & conv)	4,664	0.00
U1S	Remote 12-Disc Changer (cpe & conv)	14,979	600.00
V49	Front License Plate Frame	20,605	15.00
Z51	Performance Handling Package (cpe & conv)	2,592	395.00
79U	Millennium Yellow w/tint coat	3,900	750.00

2004 Options

RPO #	DESCRIPTION	QTY	RETAIL $
1YY07	Base Corvette Sport Coupe	16,165	$44,535.00
1YY37	Base Corvette Z06 Hardtop	5,683	52,385.00
1YY67	Base Corvette Convertible	12,216	51,535.00
1SB	Preferred Equipment Group-Sport Coupe	11,446	1,200.00
1SB	Preferred Equipment Group-Convertible	9,334	1,200.00
1SB	Commemorative Edition-Z06	2,025	4,335.00
1SC	Commemorative Edition-Sport Coupe	2,215	3,700.00
1SC	Commemorative Edition-Convertible	2,659	3,700.00
AAB	Memory Package (Z06 hardtop)	5,446	175.00
B84	Body Side Moldings	20,626	150.00
C2L	Dual Removable Roof Panels (coupe)	5,079	1,400.00
CC3	Removable Roof Panel, blue tint (coupe)	4,356	750.00
DD0	Auto-dimming Mirrors (Z06 hardtop)	5,446	160.00
F55	Magnetic Selective Ride Control (cpe & conv)	5,843	1,695.00
G92	Performance 3.15 Axle (auto, cpe & conv)	10,367	395.00
MN6	6-Speed Manual Transmission (cpe & conv)	6,928	915.00
N73	Magnesium Wheels (cpe & conv)	1,110	995.00
QF5	Polished Aluminum Wheels (cpe & conv)	22,487	1,295.00
R8C	Corvette Museum Delivery	142	490.00
UL0	Delco Stereo Cassette (cpe & conv)	3,860	0.00
U1S	Remote 12-Disc Changer (cpe & conv)	14,668	600.00
V49	Front License Plate Frame	19,520	15.00
Z51	Performance Handling Package (cpe & conv)	3,672	395.00
79U	Millennium Yellow w/tint coat	2,641	750.00
86U	Magnetic Red II	3,596	750.00

2005 Options

RPO #	DESCRIPTION	QTY	RETAIL $
1YY07	Base Corvette Coupe	26,728	$44,245.00
1YY67	Base Corvette Convertible	10,644	52,245.00
1SA	Preferred Equipment Group-Coupe	3,763	1,405.00
1SB	Preferred Equipment Group-Coupe	22,319	4,360.00
1SB	Preferred Equipment Group-Convertible	10,306	2,955.00
C2L	Dual Removable Roof Panels (coupe)	2,585	1,400.00
CC3	Removable Roof Panel, transparent (coupe)	8,469	750.00
CM7	Power Convertible Top	7,541	1,995.00
F55	Magnetic Selective Ride Control	9,041	1,695.00
G90	Performance 3.15 Axle (w/automatic transmission)	15,112	395.00
MX0	4-Speed Automatic Transmission	22,380	0.00
QG7	Polished Aluminum Wheels	27,080	1,295.00
R8C	Corvette Museum Delivery	831	490.00
UE1	OnStar System	19,634	695.00
U2K	XM Satellite Radio	21,896	325.00
U3U	AM/FM CD w/DVD Navigation, Bose Prem System	4,676	1,400.00
Z51	Performance Package	15,345	1,495.00
45U	Velocity Yellow exterior Paint (late)	760	750.00
19U	LeMans Blue exterior paint	3,759	300.00
79U	Millennium Yellow exterior paint	2,002	750.00
80U	Monterey Red exterior paint (late)	717	750.00
86U	Magnetic Red exterior paint	3,409	750.00

2006 Options

RPO #	DESCRIPTION	QTY	RETAIL $
1YY07	Base Corvette Coupe	16,598	$44,600.00
1YY67	Base Corvette Convertible	11,151	52,335.00
1YY87	Z06 Corvette	6,272	65,800.00
2LT	Equipment Group-Coupe	1,904	1,495.00
2LZ	Preferred Equipment Group-Z06	4,854	2,900.00
3LT	Preferred Equipment Group-Coupe	10,953	4,795.00
3LT	Preferred Equipment Group-Convertible	9,972	3,395.00
C2L	Dual Removable Roof Panels (coupe)	3,726	1,400.00
CC3	Removable Roof Panel, transparent (coupe)	3,561	750.00
CM7	Power Convertible Top	8,537	1,995.00
F55	Magnetic Selective Ride Control (cpe/conv)	5,709	1,695.00
MX0	6-Speed Paddle Shift Automatic Trans (cpe/conv)	19,094	1,250.00
QG7	Polished Aluminum Wheels (cpe/conv)	16,133	1,295.00
QL9	Polished Z06 Aluminum Wheels	3,449	1,295.00
QX1	Competition Gray Aluminum Wheels (cpe/conv)	279	295.00
QX3	Chrome Aluminum Wheels (cpe/conv)	2,803	1,995.00
R8C	Corvette Museum Delivery	1,172	490.00
UE1	OnStar System	12,869	695.00
U3U	AM/FM CD w/DVD Nav ($1,600 w/2LZ)	17,474	3,340.00
US9	AM/FM 6-CD, Bose Speakers, XM Radio	10,690	1,740.00
Z51	Performance Package (cpe/conv)	10,338	1,895.00
19U	LeMans Blue exterior paint	3,459	300.00
45U	Velocity Yellow exterior paint	4,122	750.00
80U	Monterey Red exterior paint	5,052	750.00

2007 Options

RPO #	DESCRIPTION	QTY	RETAIL $
1YY07	Base Corvette Coupe	21,484	$44,995.00
1YY67	Base Corvette Convertible	10,418	52,910.00
1YY67	Indy 500 Pace Convertible (Z4Z)	500	66,995.00
1YY87	Z06 Corvette (increased to $70,000 7-26-06)	7,760	66,465.00
1YY87	Ron Fellows Z06 Special Edition (Z33)	399	77,500.00
2LT	Equipment Group-Coupe	2,606	1,495.00
2LZ	Equipment Group-Z06	6,487	3,485.00
3LT	Equipment Group-Coupe	11,934	4,945.00
3LT	Equipment Group-Convertible	9,533	5,540.00
C2L	Dual Removable Roof Panels (coupe)	3,558	1,400.00
CC3	Removable Roof Panel, transparent (coupe)	4,370	750.00
D30	Non-recommended color/trim/top combo	126	590.00
F55	Magnetic Selective Ride Control (cpe/conv)	5,619	1,995.00
MX0	6-Speed Paddle Shift Auto Trans (cpe/conv)	24,422	1,250.00
Q44	Competition Gray Aluminum Wheels (Z06)	545	395.00
QG7	Polished Aluminum Wheels (cpe/conv)	3,461	1,295.00
QL9	Polished Aluminum Wheels (Z06)	3,459	1,495.00
QX1	Competition Gray Aluminum Wheels (cpe/conv)	1,091	395.00
QX3	Chrome Aluminum Wheels (cpe/conv)	19,850	1,850.00
R8C	Corvette Museum Delivery	1,104	490.00
UE1	OnStar System (3LT or 2LZ req'd)	18,074	695.00
U3U	AM/FM, CD Nav, XM, Bose ($3,640 1LZ)	20,653	1,750.00
US9	AM/FM 6-CD, XM, Bose (w/ 1LZ)	9,970	1,890.00
Z51	Performance Package (coupe/conv)	13,696	1,695.00
19U	LeMans Blue exterior paint	3,854	300.00
45U	Velocity Yellow exterior paint	3,755	750.00
80U	Monterey Red exterior paint	5,023	750.00
83U	Atomic Orange exterior paint	3,790	750.00
**6	Two-Tone Seats with Embroidery (cpe/conv)	------	695.00

2008 Options

RPO #	DESCRIPTION	QTY	RETAIL $
1YY07	Base Corvette Coupe	19,796	$45,995.00
1YY67	Base Corvette Convertible	7,283	54,335.00
1YY07	Indy 500 Pace Coupe (Z4Z)	234	59,090.00
1YY67	Indy 500 Pace Convertible (Z4Z)	266	68,160.00
1YY87	Z06 Corvette	7,226	71,000.00
1YY87	427 Limited Edition Z06 (Z44)	505	84,195.00
2LT	Equipment Group-Coupe	3,086	1,495.00
2LZ	Equipment Group-Z06	4,929	3,045.00
3LT	Equipment Group-Coupe	9,201	4,505.00
3LT	Equipment Group-Convertible	5,879	5,100.00
3LZ	Equipment Group-Z06	1,460	6,545.00
4LT	Equipment Group-Convertible	528	8,600.00
4LT	Equipment Group-Coupe	834	8,005.00
C2L	Dual Removable Roof Panels (coupe)	2,773	1,400.00
CC3	Removable Roof Panel, transparent (cpe)	3,251	750.00
D30	Non-recommended color/trim/top combo	189	590.00
F55	Magnetic Selective Ride Control (cpe/conv)	4,666	1,995.00
GU2	Rear Axle 2.73 Ratio (w/ auto trans)	8,839	395.00
MX0	6-Speed Paddle Shift Auto Trans (cpe/conv)	19,136	1,250.00
NPP	Dual Mode Exhaust System (cpe/conv)	13,454	1,195.00
Q44	Competition Gray Aluminum Wheels (Z06)	395	395.00
Q76	Chrome Aluminum Wheels (Z06)	5,101	1,995.00
Q9V	Chrome Forged Aluminum Wheels (cpe/conv)	2,932	1,850.00
QL9	Polished Forged Aluminum Wheels (cpe/conv)	5,412	1,295.00
QX1	Competition Gray Aluminum Wheels (cpe/conv)	1,781	395.00
QX3	Original Design Chrome Wheels (cpe/conv)	9,626	1,850.00
R8C	Corvette Museum Delivery	954	490.00
U3U	AM/FM, CD, Navigation, Bose	16,807	1,750.00
Z51	Performance Package (coupe/conv)	10,706	1,695.00
U3U	AM/FM, CD, Navigation, Bose	16,807	1,750.00
Z51	Performance Package (coupe/conv)	10,706	1,695.00
45U	Velocity Yellow exterior paint	3,264	750.00
83U	Atomic Orange exterior paint	2,246	300.00
89U	Crystal Red exterior paint	5,420	750.00
**6	Modified Two-Tone Seats (2LT & 3LT)	5,807	695.00

2009 Options

RPO #	DESCRIPTION	QTY	RETAIL $
1YY07	Base Corvette Coupe	8,632	$47,895.00
1YY67	Base Corvette Convertible	3,326	52,550.00
1YY07	Competition Sport Special Edition	52	55,765.00
1YY07	GT1 Championship Edition Coupe	53	65,410.00
1YY67	GT1 Championship Edition Convertible	17	71,915.00
1YY87	Z06 Corvette	3,386	73,255.00
1YY87	Competition Sport Special Edition Z06	20	77,600.00
1YY87	GT1 Championship Special Edition Z06	55	86,486.00
1YY87	ZR1 Corvette	1,415	103,300.00
2LT	Equipment Group-Coupe	1,193	1,545.00
2LT	Equipment Group-Convertible	686	3,540.00
2LZ	Equipment Group-Z06	1,654	3,015.00
3LT	Equipment Group-Coupe	3,256	4,555.00
3LT	Equipment Group-Convertible	1,974	6,550.00
3LZ	Equipment Group-Z06	1,163	6,515.00
3ZR	Equipment Group-ZR1	1,202	10,000.00
4LT	Equipment Group-Convertible	449	10,050.00
4LT	Equipment Group-Coupe	307	8,055.00
C2L	Dual Removable Roof Panels (coupe)	1,051	1,400.00
CC3	Removable Roof Panel, transparent (coupe)	1,417	750.00
D30	Non-recommended color/trim/top combo	71	590.00
F55	Magnetic Selective Ride Control (cpe/conv)	2,105	1,995.00
GU2	Rear Axle 2.73 Ratio (w/ auto trans)	3,971	395.00
MX0	6-Speed Paddle Shift Auto Trans (coupe/conv)	8,560	1,250.00
NPP	Dual Mode Exhaust System (coupe/conv)	6,238	1,195.00
Q44	Competition Gray Aluminum Wheels (Z06)	372	395.00
Q6B	Chrome 20-spoke Aluminum Wheels (ZR1)	1,132	2,000.00
Q76	Chrome Aluminum Wheels (Z06)	795	1,995.00
Q8A	Spider Chrome Aluminum Wheels (Z06)	1,903	1,995.00
Q9V	Forged Chrome Aluminum Wheels (cpe/conv)	5,649	1,850.00
QG7	Forged Polished Aluminum Wheels (cpe/conv)	1,989	1,295.00
QL9	Polished Aluminum Wheels (Z06)	13	1,495.00
QX1	Competition Gray Aluminum Wheels (cpe/conv)	1,028	395.00
R8C	Corvette Museum Delivery	392	490.00
R8E	Gas Guzzler Tax (ZR1)	1,415	1,700.00
U3U	AM/FM, CD, Navigation, Bose	7,903	1,750.00
VPK	Exterior Appearance Package	67	2,095.00
VPL	Exterior Appearance Package w/ wheels	433	5,475.00
Z51	Performance Package (coupe/conv)	4,515	1,695.00
45U	Velocity Yellow exterior paint	1,370	750.00
83U	Atomic Orange exterior paint	726	300.00
85U	Jetstream Blue exterior paint	1,367	750.00
89U	Crystal Red exterior paint	1,987	750.00
**6	Modified Two-Tone Seats w/ embroidery	1,543	695.00

2010 Options

RPO #	DESCRIPTION	QTY	RETAIL $
1YY07	Base Corvette Coupe	3,054	$49,880.00
1YY67	Base Corvette Convertible	1,003	54,530.00
1YG07	Grand Sport Corvette Coupe	3,707	55,720.00
1YG67	Grand Sport Corvette Convertible	2,335	59,530.00
1YY87	Z06 Corvette	518	75,235.00
1YY87	ZR1 Corvette	1,577	107,830.00
2LT	Equipment Group-Coupe	831	1,195.00
2LT	Equipment Group-Convertible	214	3,190.00
2LZ	Equipment Group-Z06	193	2,665.00
3LT	Equipment Group-Coupe	3,458	4,205.00
3LT	Equipment Group-Convertible	2,304	6,200.00
3LZ	Equipment Group-Z06	193	7,170.00
3ZR	Equipment Group-ZR1	1,426	10,000.00
4LT	Equipment Group Coupe	431	7,705.00
4LT	Equipment Group-Convertible	541	9,700.00
C2L	Dual Removable Roof Panels (coupe)	1,050	1,400.00
CC3	Removable Roof Panel, transparent (cpe)	1,336	750.00
D30	Non-recommended color/trim/top combo	86	590.00
F55	Magnetic Selective Ride Control (cpe/conv)	2,334	1,995.00
MX0	6-Speed Paddle Shift Auto Trans (cpe/conv)	6,913	1,250.00
NPP	Dual Mode Exhaust System (cpe/conv)	6,268	1,195.00
OB1	Crossed Flag Headrest Embroidery	1,679	300.00
PYD	Competition Gray Alum Wheels (Grand Sport)	534	395.00
PYE	Chrome Aluminum Wheels (Grand Sport)	4,693	1,995.00
Q44	Competition Gray Aluminum Wheels (Z06)	84	395.00
Q6B	Chrome 20-spoke Aluminum Wheels (ZR1)	1,347	2,000.00
Q6J	Competition Gray Aluminum Wheels (ZR1)	123	395.00
Q76	Chrome Aluminum Wheels (Z06)	82	1,995.00
Q8A	Spider Chrome Aluminum Wheels (Z06)	286	1,995.00
Q9V	Forged Chrome Aluminum Wheels (cpe/conv)	2,617	1,850.00
QX1	Competition Gray Aluminum (cpe/conv)	183	395.00
R8C	Corvette Museum Delivery	307	490.00
R8E	Gas Guzzler Tax (ZR1)	1,557	1,300.00
U3U	AM/FM, CD, Navigation, Bose	6,626	1,750.00
US9	AM/FM 6-CD	1,905	395.00
VK3	Front License Plate Bracket	7,952	15.00
VPK	Exterior Appearance Package	10	2,110.00
VPL	Exterior Appearance Package w/ wheels	11	1,195.00
Z15	Grand Sport Heritage Package	1,531	1,195.00
45U	Velocity Yellow exterior paint	694	850.00
85U	Jetstream Blue exterior paint	969	850.00
89U	Crystal Red exterior paint	1,714	850.00
**6	Modified Two-Tone Seats w/ embroidery	-----	695.00

2011 Options

RPO #	DESCRIPTION	RETAIL $
1YY07	Base Corvette Coupe	$49,900.00
1YY67	Base Corvette Convertible	54,550.00
1YG07	Grand Sport Corvette Coupe	55,740.00
1YG67	Grand Sport Corvette Convertible	59,950.00
1YY87	Z06 Corvette	75,255.00
1YY87	Z06 Carbon Limited Edition 1LZ ($98,130 w/ 3LZ)	90,960.00
1YY87	ZRI Corvette	110,750.00
2LT	Equipment Group-Coupe	1,195.00
2LT	Equipment Group-Convertible	3,190.00
2LZ	Equipment Group-Z06	2,665.00
3LT	Equipment Group-Coupe	4,205.00
3LT	Equipment Group-Convertible	6,200.00
3LZ	Equipment Group-Z06	7,170.00
3ZR	Equipment Group-ZR1	10,000.00
4LT	Equipment Group-Coupe	7,705.00
4LT	Equipment Group-Convertible	9,700.00
C2L	Dual Removable Roof Panels (coupe)	1,400.00
CC3	Removable Roof Panel, transparent (coupe)	750.00
CFZ	Carbon Fiber Package (Z06)	3,995.00
D30	Non-recommended color/trim/top combo	590.00
ER1	Battery Protection Package	100.00
F55	Magnetic Selective Ride Control ($1,695 w/ GS)	1,995.00
H33	Headlamp Color, Gray (H34=Silver, H35=Black)	590.00
J55	Cross Drilled Brake Rotors (coupe/conv)	500.00
MX0	6-Speed Paddle Shift Auto Trans (coupe/conv)	1,250.00
NPP	Dual Mode Exhaust System (coupe/conv)	1,195.00
OB1	Crossed Flag Headrest Embroidery	300.00
PBC	Engine Plant Build Experience (Z06, ZR1)	5,800.00
PYD	Competition Gray Aluminum Wheels (Grand Sport)	395.00
PYE	Chrome Aluminum Wheels (Grand Sport)	1,995.00
Q44	Competition Gray Aluminum Wheels (Z06)	395.00
Q6B	Chrome 20-spoke Aluminum Wheels (ZR1)	2,000.00
Q6J	Competition Gray Aluminum Wheels (ZR1)	395.00
Q8A	Spider Chrome Aluminum Wheels (Z06)	1,995.00
QX1	Competition Gray Aluminum Wheels (cpe/conv)	395.00
QX3	Chrome Aluminum Wheels (cpe/conv)	1,850.00
RQ1	Machine Faced Aluminum Wheels (cpe/conv)	895.00
R8C	Corvette Museum Delivery	490.00
R8E	Gas Guzzler Tax (ZR1)	1,300.00
U3U	AM/FM, CD, Navigation, Bose	1,795.00
US9	AM/FM 6-CD	395.00
VK3	Front License Plate Bracket	15.00
Z07	Z06 Ultimate Performance Package	9,495.00
Z15	Grand Sport Heritage Package	1,195.00
36S	Custom Stitch, Yellow (37S=Blue, 38S=Red)	395.00
28U	Inferno Orange exterior paint	300.00
45U	Velocity Yellow exterior paint	850.00
85U	Jetstream blue exterior paint	850.00
89U	Crystal Red exterior paint	850.00
GLB	Supersonic Blue exterior paint	300.00
**6	Modified Two-Tone Seats w/ embroidery	695.00

Index